RIGHT
TURNS

RIGHT TURNS

Unconventional
Lessons from a
Controversial Life

MICHAEL MEDVED

CROWN
FORUM
NEW YORK

While all of the incidents in this book are true, some of the names and personal characteristics of the individuals involved have been changed in order to protect their privacy. Any resulting resemblance to persons living or dead is entirely coincidental and unintentional.

Grateful acknowledgment is made to Random House, Inc., for permission to reprint an excerpt from the poem "September 1, 1939," copyright © 1940 and renewed 1968 by W. H. Auden, from *Collected Poems* by W. H. Auden. Reprinted by permission of Random House, Inc.

Published by Crown Forum, an imprint of the Crown Publishing Group, a division of Random House, Inc.
www.crownpublishing.com

CROWN FORUM and the Crown Forum colophon are trademarks of Random House, Inc.

Printed in the United States of America

DESIGN BY BARBARA STURMAN

Library of Congress Cataloging-in-Publication Data is available upon request.

ISBN 1-4000-5187-8

2 4 6 8 10 9 7 5 3 1

First Edition

For

David Bernard Medved,

My Mentor, My Hero, My Protector, My Dad

and for

Diane,

My Partner—in Everything

CONTENTS

I believe that we are lost here in America, but I believe we shall be found. And this belief, which mounts now to the catharsis of knowledge and conviction, is for me—and I think for all of us—not only our own hope, but America's everlasting, living dream.

—Thomas Wolfe, *You Can't Go Home Again*

May it be Your will, Lord our God and the God of our forefathers, that you inaugurate this month upon us for goodness and blessing. May You give us long life—a life of peace, a life of goodness, a life of blessing, a life of sustenance, a life of physical health, a life in which there is fear of heaven and fear of sin, a life in which there is no shame nor humiliation, a life of wealth and honor, a life in which we will have love of Torah and fear of heaven, a life in which our heartfelt requests will be fulfilled for the good. Amen, Selah.

—Blessing of the New Month, traditional Jewish prayer book

RIGHT TURNS

A Cornucopia of Contradictions

An enraged caller to my talk radio show recently denounced me as the rankest hypocrite in the country.

"You're the biggest phony in the whole United States!" he bellowed. "You're always attacking Hollywood for turning out such crap, but you get rich telling people about movies. You brag about how you don't own a TV, and you tell everybody else to turn off the tube, but you had your own show for years and you show up on television all the time. You're a coward and a right-wing blowhard who wants to go to war all over the place, but when you had a real chance to serve your country in Vietnam, you figured out a way to get out of the draft."

If the caller had paused in his explosion of invective I could have provided him with additional examples of contradictions in my life:

— I'm proud to identify as an observant Jew and served for fifteen years as president of an Orthodox congregation, but grew up spending the Sabbath on the beach or at movie matinees, and used to pursue a passionate search for Chinese restaurant buffets that offered the tastiest possible sweet-and-sour pork.

➤ I'm an unapologetic Jewish nationalist with close family members (my father and brother) who have chosen to make their lives in Israel, but for twenty years I've worked most closely in my career and political endeavors with fervent evangelical Christians and traditionalist Catholics.

➤ I wrote my first best-seller about growing up in the '60s and earned press designation (in my twenties) as "Bard of the Baby Boom Generation," but more recently I've expressed impassioned contempt for that generation and all its works.

➤ I have spoken for years about the importance of traditional approaches to the institution of marriage, emphasizing common values over fleeting chemistry, judging potential relationships with your head as well as your heart; but then at age thirty-four, I went to the beach one weekday afternoon in Santa Monica, California, met a gorgeous blonde in a bikini while body-surfing—and married her sixteen months later.

➤ The blonde turned out to be a clinical psychologist, and later the author of controversial, conservative books like *The Case Against Divorce*. Like her, I rail against the Divorce Industrial Complex and denounce the myth (yes, it is a myth) of a 50 percent divorce rate, but my wife and I both went through divorces before our marriage, and my own parents divorced after twenty-eight years together.

➤ I'm an outspoken conservative on both political and cultural issues, and I could broadcast my radio show from anywhere, but in my forties I made a conscious choice to make my life and raise my kids in Seattle—one of America's most notoriously liberal and flamboyantly freewheeling metropolitan areas.

➤ I despise smoking of all kinds, I've never owned a gun, I hate the idea of hunting, and I've been a tender-hearted vegetarian for many years— and yet I resent the self-righteous fanaticism of antismoking fanatics, oppose new gun control initiatives, enthusiastically support the idea of widespread fire arms ownership, and think that the modern animal rights movement is both insane and dangerous.

➤ Like many other worried parents in the throes of middle age, I want our three children to honor consistently conservative and sensible approaches to politics and personal life, despite the fact that both Diane and I indulged in our own youthful adventures with messianic leftism.

In a sense, the contradictions in my life might count as common, reflecting the tortured progress and belated maturation of an entire generation. Even George W. Bush, another currently conservative son of the wild and woolly '60s (and my erstwhile college classmate), admits that "when I was young and stupid, I was young and stupid." Unlike Mr. Bush, however, I'm eager to talk about the young and stupid part—because I'm convinced that these recollections help make the case for the worldview I advance today. My experience suggests that there's a core of integrity, even of inevitability, to my right turns.

After all, I'm not the only one in the country to make the journey from skeptically secular to intently religious, from adventurous single status to devoted and doting daddy, from a gloomy critic of "our sick society" to an optimistic and impassioned promoter of American patriotism, from idealistic and instinctive save-the-world liberalism to hard-headed and experience-based do-it-yourself conservatism.

I get the chance to clarify my ideas on pop culture and politics for three hours on the radio every day, with more than two million people a week (in more than 140 markets, coast to coast) participating in the conversation. My listeners know about my convictions and conclusions, but they don't know the story of how I reached them. The most common question I get in e-mails, letters, on-air phone calls, or from audiences at lectures I've delivered in forty-eight states involves the story of my personal transition to "Cultural Crusader." The answer doesn't fit into convenient sound bites; it requires this juicy book, teeming with contradictions and challenges, more than conclusions.

Beyond the frequently representative contradictions of my experience, I've accumulated acquaintances, connections, and confrontations that can only count as eccentric, or even bizarre:

➤ As a youthful, full-time campaign volunteer, I was present at Bobby Kennedy's final victory party in Los Angeles—and close enough to the assassination that the FBI questioned me repeatedly.

➤ At two key turning points (separated by more than two decades), I received crucial and substantive advice from my friends Hillary Clinton . . . and Rush Limbaugh.

➤ As a student of Americana, I hitchhiked twice from coast to coast across the United States, and on another occasion crossed Canada; by age twenty-three, I'd carefully recorded some 82,000 miles as a hitchhiker.

➤ During a brief but blazingly intense period, I assisted Barbra Streisand on movie projects and politics, while personally organizing (and leading) her son's Bar Mitzvah; shortly thereafter, I received a media award from President Reagan.

➤ In front of Rupert Murdoch (and then–secretary of defense Dick Cheney), I played the dominant role in a media forum that was famously disrupted by a male stripper—leading to the on-the-spot firing of the head of the Fox network.

➤ I've conducted long, intimate, confessional interviews with Peter Fonda, Dan Quayle, Bob Haldeman, Dennis Hopper, and Dick Cheney.

➤ In college and law school at Yale my friendly acquaintances included Garry Trudeau, John Kerry, Joe Lieberman, George Pataki, Bill Clinton, and Hillary Rodham. My closest personal friends included Lanny Davis (former White House counsel to President Clinton), who comes on my radio show from time to time for bickering and banter. George W. Bush, Howard Dean, and Clarence Thomas also crossed paths with me in New Haven, but somehow I avoided getting to know them at the time.

➤ I wrote an embarrassing, badly received, but lavishly performed "choral ballet" at age fifteen under the supervision of classical composer Roy Harris; at age twenty-one, I addressed fifty-thousand people as a highly publicized leader of the Vietnam Moratorium.

➤ I've hosted my own popular movie show on British television, appeared for twelve years across the United States on PBS, and cohosted a wildly popular New York City stage show with my kid brother and the *Penthouse* Pet of the Year.

Looking back in my mid-fifties on this assortment of oddities and epiphanies, I find it easy to connect the dots and identify the themes; there is, amazingly enough, a strange consistency in all the eventful excess.

I'm still the same guy, with the same obsessions, as the kid voted "Most Radical" in his high school class poll. My story doesn't involve some smug, melodramatic conversion—from new lefty to neocon, or from hippie to Chassid. My affiliations and philosophy clearly evolved, but without the benefit of a straight-line pilgrimage from immaturity to wisdom, or from error to truth. Instead, I've applied the same passions that always animated my enthusiasm, but with drastically different results. In other words, changing ideas never caused the startling events of my experience, but the startling events did result in changing ideas. I didn't shape my biography to fit my conclusions, but I have shaped my conclusions in response to my biography.

The fact that I learned these lessons from personal experience doesn't mean that the lessons apply only to me. This book isn't about "my truth"; it's about The Truth, to the extent that I can apprehend and explain it.

My approach, in other words, runs counter to all trendy notions of moral relativism, which suggest that someone with different life experiences will inevitably reach different conclusions, and that these conclusions deserve no less respect than mine. According to this line of nonreasoning, no ideas, no philosophies, and no cultures qualify as uniquely correct or effective, and the ultimate sin involves a "judgmental" attitude toward people and their values. As a film critic, however, I must make judgments about movies and their effectiveness as entertainment, and I would argue that it's appropriate—essential, in fact—to evaluate the ideas that animate any piece of popular culture. The refusal to draw bright-line distinctions between nourishing and dysfunctional principles contributes immeasurably to the confusion and paralysis in both pop culture and politics. The unthinking commitment to relativism makes it impossible, or at least uncomfortable, to highlight even the most obvious contrasts between insight and insanity. For instance, at this point in history, sane human beings should be able to agree that indulgence in recreational use of cocaine or promiscuous sex with strangers count as bad ideas, while the disciplined habits associated with regular exercise, consuming healthy foods, or nourishing long-term marital stability qualify as good ideas.

Anecdotal exceptions don't invalidate these rules: a neohippie computer geek may make himself a billionaire despite a nasty drug dependency, but his progress would prove difficult to replicate. On the other hand, the middle-class virtues which I extol—hard work, saving money, loyalty to family and friends, planning for the future—may not produce reliable rewards for every individual, but they will work in the overwhelming majority of cases.

Principles earn our commitment only if they can prove their usefulness in application to the wider world. Some notions work better and last longer than others because they are truer and more timeless than others. My incident-based conclusions make sense not because the events of my life are so broadly representative (in many cases they are, in fact, fairly bizarre), but because the lessons I've drawn from these circumstances hold up in broader terms when measured by logic and history. The evaluation is ultimately more important than the experience.

Ralph Waldo Emerson arrogantly but appropriately declared, "To believe that what is true for you in your private heart is true for all men—that is genius." I do not claim such genius for myself, but I do insist on relevance. Hundreds of thousands, perhaps millions of Americans have migrated as I have from the political left to the center and the right. For most of us, the hackneyed label "neoconservative" fails to do this journey justice. The dominant model of youthful Trotskyites (Norman Podhoretz, Irving Kristol) who opened their eyes to Communist corruption and enlisted in America's cause at the height of the Cold War applies to an older (no doubt nobler) generation more than it does to my Boomer battalions and those who followed. The Soviet Union collapsed some fifteen years ago, but citizens in significant numbers continue to move in conservative directions, creating for the first time in the seventy-five years since the Roosevelt revolution an almost perfect statistical balance between self-described Republicans and Democrats.

While the courageous refugees from the left in an earlier era focused almost entirely on issues of foreign policy and global conflict, more recent transformations involve a belated awakening to economic realities, the embrace of the traditional family, and America's ongoing and underreported religious revival. Many of the newly minted conservatives who play a crucial role in the Republican coalition might be more accurately designated as theocons rather than neocons. We have shifted our political and cultural affiliations based not only on the imperatives of protection and patriotism, but through our experience with paychecks, parenthood, and prayer. These elements all played essential roles in my personal transformation.

In that context, I make the case that the turns I have taken aren't just right, they are Right. Yes, I will describe what happened to me and enumerate the personal lessons and public principles I've learned from those events. But that doesn't amount to the end of an argument. It is, in fact, only the beginning.

LESSON

1

America Isn't Normal

Before she came to this country, my grandmother watched five of her six children die.

They were all girls, lost between the ages of three weeks and fourteen years, doomed by malnutrition, disease, persecution, and war.

There was nothing extraordinary, nothing exceptional about this series of tragedies; Eastern European parents commonly buried their children in the early decades of this century and learned to accept and expect a dismal pattern of suffering.

It was America, on the other hand, that proved radically different, utterly abnormal—a land bizarrely blessed in defiance of all laws of history. My grandmother understood American exceptionalism before she ever set eyes on the USA—in fact, she staked her life on it.

She was born in 1881 in the ramshackle village of Machnovka in the Ukraine, the blue-eyed, vivacious daughter of a slaughterer, a *shochet*, deemed respectable and comfortable by the standards of that time and place. At twenty-one, she married a barrel maker, Hershel Medved—hardworking, quiet, and reliable—who relocated to her town from Chmelnik, some twenty miles away, an even more remote and dreary corner of the Pale of Settlement. They bore children nearly every year that they lived together, before my grandfather made the journey to America in 1906. He traveled with his older brother and found work and lodgings in Philadelphia, living miserably but sending home money every month, saving his remaining pennies to pay for the steamship tickets that would bring his wife and children to the New World. After two years, he returned to Russia for a springtime visit that ended up lasting for nearly twelve months, long enough to produce another pregnancy. My grandfather returned to Philadelphia and never met the resulting twin girls, who barely clung to life—one of them lasting only three weeks and the other losing her fight for survival after several months. While my grandmother busied herself with the funeral arrangements for the second twin, she left her three-year-old in the care of a nearby relative. With the mourning period concluded, she reunited with her surviving children—immediately recognizing the deathly pallor of the youngest, Chansi, who had contracted one of the fevers ravaging the region. She died within days, enveloping my grandmother in overlapping cycles of grief.

In Philadelphia, through fanatical labor and self-denial, my grandfather sent money every month to Russia so that the blue-eyed wife he adored could accumulate enough to pay her way to America. She needed to save the cost of ship's passage across the Atlantic, train fare for herself and the children all the way to the Baltic port city of Riga, and bribe money to deal with the corrupt and sadistic Czarist bureaucrats who supervised the complicated border crossings. My grandmother painstakingly packed her nine-year-old son, Moshe (known affectionately as Moish), and her remaining two daughters, along with her elderly father, who refused to remain behind at home. They sold most of their meager belongings and tearfully departed their Ukrainian village in the summer of 1914.

They rode crowded trains, stifling with heat and sweat, herded together with other would-be emigrants. The swaggering immigration agents, demanding daily bribes to keep their unauthorized charges moving west, forced the mothers to tape shut the mouths of their children so they couldn't cry. When they arrived at Ostrolenka, on the border between Austria and Poland, the officials led the crowds to a row of huts where they could spend the night before crossing the frontier the next morning. According to my grandmother's vivid recollection it was a balmy, beautiful mid-summer evening with an orange-tinted half moon, a dazzling canopy of stars, and the fresh smell of pine forest drifting into the shack where the frightened refugees tried to sleep. That lovely night also happened to mark the beginning of World War I, with the weary Jews awakened before dawn and told to run for their lives (*"Yiddin, loif!"*) and to find their way back to their home villages. With Russia and Austria-Hungary suddenly at war the border had been sealed and the police had begun rounding up or robbing all immigrant bands without the proper papers.

With three wailing children and her frail and ailing father, my grandmother straggled back to the Ukraine, dodging both police and bandits. By the time she arrived, the aborted journey had drained every kopek of the money her husband had sent her from America, as well as the funds she had assembled by selling her possessions. The war that began on that August night lasted for more than three bloody years, followed by revolution, civil war, starvation, persecution, and chaos. My grandmother watched her father die a slow, wasting death she could do nothing to stop, and then her two surviving daughters perished with merciful speed in the same grim and hungry year. Her son, Moshe, the only remaining member of the immediate family, became desperately ill and survived only through the ministrations and prayers of a mysterious, ragged, elderly stranger who had been passing through the village. Till the end of her life, my grandmother identified the visitor as Elijah the Prophet, eternal protector of his suffering people, come to earth in a wretched Ukrainian shtetl to spare her the final, crushing stroke of pain.

More than nine years passed from the time of her first attempt to leave Russia, fourteen years since she had last set eyes on her husband. For months, even years at a time, he lost contact with his grieving wife and only surviving child but when he could reach them reliably he continued to send them money from America, their only hope of survival. Finally, late in 1923, with Lenin consolidating the grip of his Communist dictatorship on a broken and bleeding Russia, her eighteen-year-old son led my terrified grandmother out of the only world she had ever known and they successfully boarded a ship to America.

Once again, their timing proved almost inconceivably poor: by the time their squalid ship made its way to New York Harbor, the year was

1924 and the United States had adopted a strict new immigration law, abruptly and harshly enforcing an act of Congress designed to stop the "invading" hordes, particularly from eastern and southern Europe. After forty years of mass immigration, native-born Americans worried that any sense of national identity and cohesion might be lost; after all, the percentage of U.S. residents born in another nation was even higher then (14 percent) than it is today (11 percent).

In any event, the new legislation took effect during the time my grandmother and her son had been at sea, so the American officials informed them that they had arrived just a few days too late: no immigrant ships could disgorge their human cargo in the United States. This declaration caused hysteria and near riot from the passengers, some of whom threatened to jump overboard and risk drowning rather than give up their goal so close to the promised land. My grandmother could see my grandfather on the deck, dressed in the only suit he owned, waving at her with both arms, but remaining painfully, perhaps permanently, out of reach. For two days, the matter remained unresolved, especially regarding the newcomers who had left Europe before immigration restrictions had taken force and who traveled to America for the purpose of family reunion (theoretically permitted, even under the new law).

Given the circumstances of her arrival, I cannot imagine my grandmother's emotions when she finally descended the gangplank, searching for her husband among the waiting crowds. My grandfather had said goodbye to a vital and reportedly beautiful bride of twenty-nine, with six tiny children. He now welcomed a forty-three-year-old survivor of uncounted horrors, accompanied by one wary, adult son. They would have been virtual strangers to him and to the life he'd built over all those years of toil in the crowded city of Philadelphia. The fact that they managed to renew their marriage, to sustain their love, without hesitation or complaint must in itself count as a miracle.

But the miraculous aspects of the family history don't end there. In 1925, my grandmother fell ill, gaining weight at the same time she lost appetite. The neighbor ladies who she had befriended in their Yiddish-speaking enclave of South Philadelphia made an instant diagnosis: she undoubtedly suffered with a tumor and must immediately visit the doctor. She hesitated, keeping the problem from her hardworking husband, unwilling to allow more bad news to enter a life that had already accumulated its full share. When she could delay the examination no longer she dragged herself to the neighborhood physician, who determined that against all logic, against any expectation, she was pregnant. My father, David Bernard Medved, arrived in February 1926. Because of the widespread local assumption that it had been a tumor, not a baby, growing in my grandmother's body, my father drew the ironic nickname *Tumerel*—or "Little Tumor"—during his childhood. In an era when most people—especially poor people—aged far more rapidly than today's time-defying Boomers, his mother was forty-five and his father was fifty in the year of his startling birth.

No wonder that my own earliest memories feature a sense of wonder, of gratitude, or providential intervention, of anything-possible optimism regarding our family's place in America, this Land of New Life. Leaving behind the years of mourning and loss in the Continent of Death, my grandparents could come together and in every way begin again.

They read an obvious significance in my grandmother's name—she was Sarah, following the example of her ancestor, the matriarch of Israel. The Bible reports that Abraham's wife conceived at age ninety, after "the manner of women had ceased to be with Sarah" (Genesis 18:11). Her husband had reached the ripe age of one hundred, making them each exactly twice the age of my grandparents at the time or the arrival of their own wondrous, American-born child.

Rabbinic scholars through the ages have pondered the purpose of the Torah text in going out of its way to emphasize the child-bearing difficulties in each generation among the mothers of Israel. Following Sarah, her daughter-in-law Rebecca is described as "barren" before God intervenes to mandate conception of twin sons (Genesis 25:21). The beloved wife of one of those twins, Rachel, also "remained barren" until God "opened her womb" (Genesis 29:31 and 30:22) and facilitated the birth of Joseph. What was it with these early Jews and their inheritance of fertility problems?

The sages suggest that the Torah hopes to make a crucial point about the unnatural—indeed supernatural—existence and persistence of the Jewish people. From its very inception, this nation struggled for existence, requiring divine assistance even in the earliest generations. Nothing can be taken for granted, or viewed as automatic or inevitable, in our unlikely and illogical history.

In the same sense, America arose from abnormal origins. The nation didn't grow organically or gradually from indigenous tribes—like, say, the French or the Poles—but emerged out of courageous, conscious acts of will by Pilgrims and Patriots. Many peoples boast national holidays (Cinco de Mayo, Bastille Day, St. Patrick's Day, and so forth), but the United States alone celebrates a clear-cut birthday (July 4, of course) marking the incontestable, openly declared commencement of our historical enterprise.

As a boy, I knew far more about the distinctive and fateful aspects of America's origins than I did about Biblical references to the forefathers and foremothers of Israel. We weren't notably religious in those days, but my dad, as the utterly unexpected American-born gift that blessed his immigrant parents' old age, passed on to me a sense of the freakish fortune and favor associated with this new nation. Even before I reached my twenties and consciously embraced belief in God, I felt an instinctive, irresistible sense of some higher power potently, undeniably entangled with the strange course of the American adventure.

Consider, for example, the outrageously improbable coincidence that bound together the two individuals most responsible for the Declaration of Independence, John Adams and Thomas Jefferson. Though they later became political rivals, opposing each other for the presidency in both 1796 and 1800, they eventually reestablished their friendship. The two men each lived into unusually old age for their era (Adams to nearly ninety-one and Jefferson, eighty-three) before they died—on precisely the same day. And that day was none other than the Fourth of July—in fact, the fiftieth anniversary of the great Declaration that Adams and Jefferson had made possible. The citizens of the young Republic—including President John Quincy Adams—marveled at the timing and universally saw the hand of Providence at work.

This historical fluke fascinated me from the age of ten, when I first discovered it in a children's biography of Thomas Jefferson. How would you compute the odds that the two great men would die on the same day? And how much more unlikely would it be for that day to fall on the Fourth of July? And how could you rationally expect that the dramatic Independence Day on which they both expired would occur on no ordinary anniversary, but in the festive fiftieth year of an experiment in self-government that practical people might reasonably expect to have failed?

The more you dig into this stuff about the origins of the Republic, the more peculiar and far-fetched some of it becomes, with some of the same compelling but creepy elements often imputed to contemporary paranormal phenomena, but vastly better documented than UFOs or crop circles.

There is, for instance, the bizarre matter of George Washington's battlefield invulnerability, more appropriate to a comic book superhero than to a historical figure. As a commander, he may have failed frequently, but he enjoyed ludicrous and illogical good fortune when it came to his personal safety. On innumerable occasions in two major wars he exposed his huge form (at 6'3" he easily towered over his contemporaries) to enemy fire but to the amazement of his colleagues no bullet ever touched his body. At the Battle of Monongahela in the French and Indian War, for example, the twenty-three-year-old colonel played a conspicuously gallant role in a military disaster in which more than two-thirds of his fellow officers and 60 percent of all enlisted men were killed or wounded. The next day the young soldier wrote to his brother, "By the all-powerful dispensations of Providence, I have been protected beyond all human probability or expectation; for I had four bullets through my coat, and two horses shot under me, yet escaped unhurt, although death was leveling my companions on every side of me."As commander in chief during the Revolution, he often rode to the front of battle as shots whizzed harmlessly past his head.

It might seem illogical, even outrageous, to juxtapose stirring stories about George Washington with my grandparents' adventures in making their way to a new continent and welcoming their amazing, unexpected, American-born boy. How can I connive to construct a kinship between powdered, periwigged Colonial aristocrats and my own Yiddish-speaking, inelegant, impoverished ancestors? Actually, one more aspect of Washington's biography permits and even encourages such affiliation.

The Father of Our Country never became a father of children, a personal sorrow that constituted the greatest disappointment of his life. Martha, a wealthy widow when she married George, brought with her two offspring from her previous marriage, and the general lovingly adopted them as his stepchildren. But in their tragically brief lives, Jackie and Patsy

Custis never took Washington's name or fulfilled his dynastic dreams. This means that no one today can claim descent from the First President. I can claim America's father as my ancestor, my own forefather, just as much as any Virginia blue blood. Washington's letters late in life suggest that he regretted his lack of biological progeny, but as the progenitor of a nation that endlessly adopts orphans from everywhere, his status makes perfect sense.

As a youngster, I couldn't get enough of such stories and pointedly collected tales of freakish occurrences pointing to some supernatural destiny for America. This focus never provided a path to religious faith, but for many years served me as a substitute for it. I might be unsure of the existence of God, but I never doubted the idea of a special Providence for my country—a notion that seemed to flow as naturally from my own family's past as it did from my reading of history.

Even Oscar Wilde, one of the most charmingly cynical of nineteenth-century European visitors to these shores, famously concluded, "The Almighty bestows his indulgent protection on infants, imbeciles, drunkards, and the United States of America."

During the 1960s, most of my friends in college and colleagues in the antiwar movement impatiently scoffed at such notions. In place of John Adams's vision of a national future providing "rays of ravishing light and glory," they saw a future of Spenglerian gloom. To emphasize the nation's allegedly Nazi nature, they spelled "Amerika" in the Germanic manner, with a "k" (also a reference to Kafka's nightmarish novel, *Amerika*, no doubt). After the assassination of Bobby Kennedy in 1968, novelist John Updike (whom I immoderately admired) pronounced that "God has now withdrawn his special blessing from America." During that era when conventional wisdom tirelessly indicted our "sick society," the experts and sophisticates pointed knowingly to the work of historian Arnold Toynbee, who emphasized the immutable, cyclical nature of human history. According to this pessimistic view, every nation, every empire, inevitably rose and fell, and America in the second half of the twentieth century would experience an unstoppable and accelerating decline.

No matter how persuasive these arguments might seem, and despite the fact that they were all but universally accepted in the "enlightened" and highly educated circles in which I traveled, I never bought them for a moment. Even in my days of most fervent leftist activism, I felt unshakably out of step with the common contempt for nationalism and its symbols; the specter of spoiled, angry kids abusing the flag and blaming the United States for all the world's ills, offended me just as intensely at age twenty as it does today. This reflected instinct, temperament, and family ties more than ideology or coherent conviction, but those grateful patriotic instincts never failed me. The grim rules of history might apply to ordinary nations, but America, I knew, wasn't normal. The experience of my father and his parents made that lesson unshakably clear.

The American Dream Promises Improvement, Not Paradise

In the 110 years between 1815 and 1925 (the year after my grandmother's arrival), more than 35 million individuals left their homes in Europe and crossed the ocean to America—taking part in the greatest mass migration in human history. Despite the nostalgia and sentimentality we inevitably associate with this sweeping population transfer, not all immigrant stories came equipped with preordained happy endings.

My own family provides a tragic example of a voyager who felt cheated and embittered by his American adventure and who, like more than 10 percent of one-time arrivals in this country (according to estimates by immigrant historians), ultimately returned to his nation of origin. At the time of his first arrival in the New World in 1906, my grandfather shared a tenement apartment with his stoic, taciturn older brother, Aaron Medved. Aaron spent a total of two decades working at dreary jobs in Philadelphia and New York, but then made a fateful decision to go back to the ravaged Ukraine in the early years of Stalinism. He may have felt encouraged by optimist Soviet propaganda about New Economic Policies and Five-Year Plans—after all, he lived within an immigrant community in which many of his neighbors maintained stubborn and surprising sympathy to Communist and Socialist dreams of building a "Workers' Paradise." According to family lore, however, he abandoned America more out of a desire to flee from his nasty and insufferable wife than to escape his disappointing progress in the United States. In any event, he sailed back to the old country with a few dollars in his pocket, captured the affection of a new young wife (who may not have known about the family which had been abandoned in America), and proceeded to father six children. During World War II, my grandfather lost touch with his big brother for six years, before discovering that Aaron and his wife and small children had all perished in the Holocaust. My grandfather and the rest of the family in Philadelphia went through the seven days of prescribed, if belated, mourning.

This experience no doubt reassured my grandfather about his own commitment to the new land, even if his life remained humble and harsh. Some of my father's earliest memories center on greeting his elderly father as he returned from work, after grueling ten- and twelve-hour days making barrels for Publicker's, a surviving nineteenth-century distillery on the gritty Delaware River waterfront. The child would painstakingly remove the long wood splinters from the old man's swollen, sometimes bloody hands.

This work must have seemed particularly dispiriting because it followed a few years of short-lived prosperity for my grandparents, in the late 1920s, when my father became the envy of the neighborhood with his shiny new bicyclye. It wasn't the stock market crash or the Great Depression that put an end to that period of middle-class splendor; in fact, it was the end of Prohibition in 1933 that ruined by grandfather's professional success. For a brief time my grandfather had a flourishing career as a bootlegger. His younger and more flamboyant brother Abe (universally known as "Uncle Abe the Bootlegger" until his death in 1962) initially got into the business of making and selling illegal whiskey and then got my grandfather involved in distilling the stuff in the upstairs bathtub of his rented row house and on a basement contraption known to my father as "the bubble machine."

When alcoholic beverages became legal and plentiful after Franklin Roosevelt's election, my grandfather disentangled himself from the suddenly struggling booze operation and went back to shaping barrels. My grandparents never lived up to the famous old dreams of easy money or sudden wealth in a Golden Land; they discovered that the crowded streets of South Philadelphia had been paved only with rough cobblestones, not precious metals. Despite a brief flirtation with bourgeois comfort (and adventurous illegality) during the Prohibition era, my grandfather went through nearly fifty years of punishing, ceaseless labor without ever leaving the lowest rung of the U.S. working class. The only home he ever owned, a rundown row house with a sinking foundation and horribly tilting floors, was bought for him after he reached the age of seventy, purchased by my father, his upwardly mobile son.

Nonetheless, neither my grandfather nor other members of his extended family felt cheated or abused by their American experience. Whatever their hardships and heartbreak, they never lost sight of the incomparably more dire suffering of their kin and compatriots across the ocean. America might not make you rich, but at the very least it let you live.

In the twenty-first century it's become fashionable to emphasize the difficulties and disappointments encountered by newcomers to this country, particularly the more recent immigrants to the United States. It is definitely in vogue to trash "The American Dream," and to deride the naive expectation that in the United States, even one of life's losers can toil himself to triumph. Social critics now sneer at the old confidence in upward mobility, belaboring the obvious point that most welfare moms never will become millionaires—as if a truly just society required such miraculous transformations as a matter of course. In the long, brutal sweep of mankind's history, the most common outcome of an impoverished upbringing has always been a hopeless lifetime of poverty, followed by progeny who feel helpless to avoid the same fate. In abnormal America, on the other hand, most families of European or Asian origin pass through penury in two generations or less, on their way to middle-class choices—or more. Even the African-American descendants of slaves have experienced stunning mobility in the past half-century, with black homeowners vastly more numerous today than black welfare recipients.

Ironically, the left and the right now unite to deny the astonishing mobility that continues to characterize the American experience. From the liberal perspective, activists cite those families that remain mired in hopelessness and dysfunction in order to justify ambitious new programs to restructure the social and economic order. Conservative critics point to a culture of dependence passed on in an unbroken succession for generations to prove the ineffective and indeed corrosive nature of government welfare programs—or to inveigh against the dangers of a society overwhelmed by waves of slovenly, unmotivated immigrant hordes.

People at both ends of the political spectrum ignore the fact that striking economic progress remains the rule rather than exception for both native- and foreign-born Americans. Over time, very few Americans remain at the lowest rung of the income ladder. In June 1992, for instance, the *Wall Street Journal* used official government tax data to measure upward mobility. An astonishing 86 percent who had qualified as part of the poorest 20 percent in 1979 had moved out of that bottom quintile within ten years. A breathtaking 14.7 percent had worked themselves all the way from the lowest quintile into the top 20 percent in just a decade.

Most importantly, the American people continue to confound the purported experts of both right and left with their incurable (and appropriate) belief in better tomorrows. In April 2003, the *Wall Street Journal* reported on a survey of one thousand adults in which only 2 percent described themselves currently as "rich," but a whopping 31 percent expected that they would "become rich someday." Among those eighteen to twenty-nine, an absolute majority—51 percent—believed that they would eventually earn their way to notable wealth.

In the context of the class-bound, calcified, immobile societies that limit opportunity in the rest of the world, it's remarkable enough when even a few individuals can beat the odds for inspiring examples of extraordinary advancement, let alone that ordinary people—in fact, most of our fellow citizens—enjoy options that their ancestors could scarcely imagine. Nevertheless, America stands indicted because she fails to guarantee redemption for each and every downtrodden soul.

The members of my grandfather's generation maintained a more healthy understanding of the possibilities of their new country: for them, the American dream didn't promise paradise, just improvement. And improvement, for the majority of dedicated dreamers, has always been enough.

The Gift of America Isn't Just the Absence of Oppression but the Presence of Generosity

Viewed from a distance, my father's journey seems not only improbable but preposterous. Born to a home with no material resources whatever, as the child of elderly immigrants who never went to school and never spoke English, he became a Shakespeare-loving classical music nut, a world-class woodsman, hiker, and camper, a scientist astronaut, and an internationally recognized physicist with three Ivy League degrees. Moreover, he made the transition from poverty to prominence in less than three decades, despite spending most of his youth in a Depression era noted for its economic hardship and limited opportunities. Such transitions and accomplishments proved common among what we now know as the "Greatest Generation," though history suggests that their epic achievements reflected extraordinary aspects of society itself as much as the individuals' exceptional abilities.

At age fourteen, in December of 1940, my father wrote a brief autobiography as a ninth-grade English project. He emphasized a series of grim childhood illnesses and near-fatal accidents that undoubtedly convinced his terrified parents that this child of their old age might follow his five older sisters to an early grave. His attendance at public school brought additional problems. "When I entered fifth grade my troubles began," he wrote. "The teacher singled me out as the disruptive element in the class. Even though I did excellent work in subjects such as arithmetic, history, etc., I talked, got into fights and was a general trouble-maker."

Part of my father's problem undoubtedly stemmed from his difficulties in fitting in with the rest of the extended family. He floated above this crowded tangle of cousins and co-conspirators like some privileged exchange student—only tangentially connected to their world. American-born, athletic, taller by several inches than everyone else, he came naturally to the coddling and indulgence he received. After all, his father had already reached the age of sixty-three at the time of my dad's Bar Mitzvah, a lavish affair funded entirely by his proud big brother, Moish. The neighborhood still viewed him as something of a miracle child, the golden consolation prize for his unlucky old-country parents and their long lives of loss.

According to my father's teenaged autobiography, the Bar Mitzvah represented a turning point when "by accident I entered upon my life work. I had received a chemistry set for a present and was suddenly inspired to keep notes. Every book on science that happened to fall into my hands was read thoroughly. In the space of a year and a half I have learned more chemistry than a graduated high school student." The turnaround continued when "I entered Furness Jr. High School. Here was my supreme triumph. For four consecutive report periods with the exception of a 'G' in Music once I have had a perfect record."

Could my father, at age fourteen, solemnly announcing his "supreme triumph," count as a snotty adolescent who was insufferably full of himself? Or did the leap from the grimy realities of a slum neighborhood to a place among the nation's academic elite require precisely that sort of preening self-confidence?

Helping my father make this transition was Moish, twenty-one years his senior and by this time the dominant influence in his life. Making good money as a self-taught electrician, with a big blue truck proclaiming the Biblical slogan of his electrical service ("Let There Be Light!"), Moish spent his free time eagerly exploring all the concerts, lectures, libraries, and art museums that the proudly cultured city of Philadelphia had to offer. This culture vulture, who possessed no formal education but spoke a half-dozen languages and read philosophy for recreation, dragged Davey along with him to make the boy civilized. At the monumental art museum overlooking the Schuylkill River, the two brothers—a bespectacled electrician in a grimy jumpsuit and a gangly kid—could marvel at limitless splendors reserved in prior generations for the highest nobility. In the movies, Rocky Balboa prepared for his big fight by running up the broad steps of this same magnificent art museum; my uncle prepared my father better by taking him inside.

But the key bridge to success for my father was Central High School, one of the most celebrated institutions of public secondary education anywhere in the United States. Established in 1838 with the help of an unprecedented contribution of federal funds to the Commonwealth of Pennsylvania, Central became the first American high school of its kind, emphasizing scientific excellence and proudly providing opportunities for the brightest young men of impoverished as well as elite backgrounds. In 1845, two English visitors traveled through the United States to investigate the emerging public school system and reported in particularly glowing terms on the new Central High School. "We see in it four hundred boys selected from all classes of society," they wrote, "without respect to rank or patronage, whose only certificate of admission is superiority of talent and capacity for learning. . . . Here are seen, side by side, the child of the judge and the child of the laborer, the children of the physician . . . with those of the bricklayer, . . . studying without distinction under masters and professors of the same attainments in halls and classrooms equaling those of many of our colleges."

Much the same was true nearly a century later, when Central welcomed my father just months before the attack on Pearl Harbor. His school yearbook shows that by this time the student body featured a striking preponderance of Jewish boys from South Philadelphia, along with a mix of other ethnics (Italians, Ukrainians), a smattering of brilliant African-Americans, and a substantial representation of the centuries-old Philadelphia elite, with three and four Anglo-Saxon names strung together and often followed by roman numerals.

The astonishing aspect in all of this involves the obvious willingness, even eagerness of the ancient establishment to welcome raw, unpolished newcomers like my father. Though my dad also worked a full forty hours a week as a chemist at Publicker's—the same distillery where his father built barrels, and which was willing to hire a smart, cocky sixteen-year-old kid for a scientific job while most high school and college graduates were away at the war—he excelled at his studies. In 1944, at the time of his graduation, he applied for the Mayor's Scholarship, a competitive honor that provided an all-expenses-paid education at the University of Pennsylvania—the prestigious institution established by Benjamin Franklin in 1749 as the first colonial college to focus on preparation for business and public service rather than training future members of the clergy. After taking several days of grueling exams and then facing an interview with the Mayor's Scholarship Committee—a collection of stuffy and deeply distinguished members of Philadelphia high society—my father learned that he had been ranked first out of all scholarship contestants in a city of two million people. When his parents read the news in the *Evening Bulletin,* they openly wept, considering that afternoon the happiest moment of their lives, the ultimate validation of their American adventure. Their miracle boy would attend Penn, and at the university's expense.

He managed to complete three weeks of class work that autumn before reporting to the Navy at age eighteen for his wartime service, joining some sixteen million of his fellow citizens. Had Truman not brought the war to an abrupt end by dropping the bomb, my father would have played a role in the inevitably bloody invasion of the home islands of Japan that the high command had planned. After my father's discharge in April 1946, the GI Bill supplemented his Mayor's Scholarship, financing his education at Penn all the way through a Ph.D.

In short, my father served his country, worked hard at jobs and school, and made the most of each of his opportunities. But what opportunities they were! My father benefited from nearly all these initiatives of kindness and conscience, many of which combined the resources of private business and, yes, government. In fact, his trajectory clearly contradicts the comfortable conservative clichés about the self-reliant Man of Destiny, making his way to glory and achievement so long as government and bureaucrats stayed out of his way. The GI Bill—a vastly generous federal program—made possible his graduate degrees. He attended decent, caring public schools as a child, and his distinguished high school had been founded with proceeds from a most unusual federal grant. The Social Security payments to my grandfather helped the elderly barrel maker to live out his life in modest dignity, reducing the burdens on his two sons who were struggling to advance in the middle class.

It makes sense, in other words, that my entire family should identify with the left side of the political spectrum in the '30s, '40s, '50s, and '60s. (I can still remember the charcoal sketch of FDR, clipped from a magazine and placed in a cracked glass frame, that occupied a place of honor on my grandparents' parlor wall.) Many of my relatives who remained impassioned liberals (including my mother, one of my three brothers, and assorted cousins) have made precisely this point to me. The society in which my father made his way provided not only opportunity but also assistance, they argue, so how can the descendants of successful strivers now refuse to provide such assistance for others simply because our position on the social ladder has changed?

Of course, the conservative response insists that it's the nature of the proffered aid that's changed. The GI Bill, for instance, was a reward for military service, not an entitlement for merely breathing. The compassionate cohorts of earlier generations focused their efforts on the "deserving poor"—concentrating consciously on the most promising, not the most troubled, among the disadvantaged. The Mayor's Scholarship program in my father's day amounted to the sort of mechanistic, race-blind meritocracy that today's liberals deride, with a selection process based almost entirely on test scores. The current mania for ethnic engineering would never tolerate the obvious domination of an elite public institution like Central High School by so many Feigenbaums, Cohens, and Chomskys (yes, the notorious leftist gadfly Noam Chomsky was one of my dad's Central—and Penn—classmates). Even the Social Security System operated very differently—until 1951, my father and his employers paid a combined total of less than 3 percent of his paycheck into Old-Age, Survivors, and Disability Insurance (OASDI), less than a fourth of the bite now taken from the income of working people. This meant that my parents could afford to provide a few dollars to buy a house for my grandfather, and to make his life more dignified. It was the old man's hardworking son, relatively unencumbered by punishing taxation, rather than government bureaucrats in the Housing and Urban Development Department (which didn't even exist), who made that progress possible.

Moreover, the institutions which enriched my father's life and promoted his progress represented the sort of private, community-based initiatives (sometimes with government cooperation, it's true) that conservatives always applauded. The University of Pennsylvania remains a private, Ivy League institution with minimal connection to the state government in Harrisburg, distributing Mayor's Scholarships as part of a deal with the city of Philadelphia in return for the land grant for the school's expansion. The orchestras, libraries, science institutes, parks, and art museums that still swing open their gilded doors to the masses didn't emerge out of the agitation of politicians or social workers, but through the generosity of wealthy philanthropists and business leaders—the class of intrepid, creative, and heroic operators so frequently denied the grateful recognition they deserve.

The opportunities which opened to my father counted as normal for his time and place—so normal as to obscure their truly miraculous nature and to lead most Americans to take such transformations for granted. Everyone in my family on both sides started off in this country poor, but none of them—neither the doctors nor the bootleggers—stayed poor. When people talk of the good fortune their ancestors encountered in America, they generally cite the absence of persecution and oppression in this favored nation; they note the contrast with the dysfunction and injustice that the new arrivals left behind in their blighted homelands. For my family, however, the most important lesson isn't the cruelty that America lacked, but the kindness she possessed. It's not just that they avoided holocausts and pogroms by coming here, but that they availed themselves of a startling array of gifts and assistance designed to help struggling greenhorns exactly like them.

Business Isn't Exploitative—
It's Heroic

One of the oddest quirks of the contemporary Jewish community is the widespread, unshakeable tendency to romanticize the labor movement as the source of our American success. A few years ago I delivered a lecture to a Jewish student group at a major university and made some passing negative reference to teachers unions and their destructive role in blocking education reform. During the question period, an impassioned student denounced my disrespect toward the sacred purity of organized labor as the rankest ingratitude. "If it weren't for the unions," she shrilled, "we'd all still be working in sweatshops!"

In responding to her peculiar view of the past, I first asked a simple question: had any one in her family, past or present, spent a significant amount of time in labor activism? As it turned out, both her father and grandfather had been successful businessmen, not labor activists. But she insisted that their experience represented the exception, not the rule.

She was precisely wrong, of course. The engine of advancement for all immigrant groups in the United States, and especially for American Jews, has always been the small businessman—the neighborhood shopkeeper, the proprietor of a laundry or pizzeria, the operator of a gardening service, the builder or repairman, the peddler with his pushcart. Yes, Jews played a prominent role in the leadership of the American labor movement—including cigar worker Samuel Gompers, who helped found the American Federation of Labor. But among our ancestors, far more earned their way into the middle class by selling goods on the street or opening a storefront than through union activism and organizing.

In part, the disproportionate emphasis on unions stems from the labor connections of popular historians, like socialist intellectual Irving Howe, author of the influential best-seller *World of Our Fathers*. The refusal to acknowledge our debt to the entrepreneurial spirit and the free-market system also arises from the dismissive attitude toward business and its values that characterizes the elite universities that young Jews disproportionately attend. It took me a full ten years after my graduation from Yale, for instance, before it suddenly dawned on me that my family on all sides was populated by independent businessmen. I had preferred to designate them in more respectable, less nakedly capitalistic terms, like "electrician," "deli owner," "food chemist," "physicist," "chicken farmer," "bootlegger," "family practice doctor," "paper goods manufacturer," "tailor," and so forth. But all these people—my parents, grandparents, uncles, aunts, and cousins—were in some sense, or at one time, in business for themselves. Gradually recognizing the constructive, daring, even heroic nature of their enterprises played a significant role in liberating me from my adolescent sense of smug, snotty superiority to a more mature and accurate perspective on the risk takers and enterprise builders who make all of America go.

Given the entrepreneurial background on both sides of the family, it's ironic that my parents actually met each other at Commie camp—a rustic retreat on the banks of the Severn River in Maryland run by the most militantly Marxist wing of the Zionist movement.

My father had never been a particularly ideological member of *HaShomer HaTzayir* ("The Young Guard" in Hebrew), but he felt attracted to its outdoorsy emphasis on camping, hiking, and singing around campfires—and to its reputation for the wildest, most uninhibited women anywhere in the Jewish world.

My mother didn't fit the bill for a typical, liberated nonconformist in this "Young Guard" movement: she was too bourgeois, too proper, far too cautious. She came along to the Maryland camp as the guest of a couple she knew, looking for a stimulating summer vacation experience, not an absorbing Marxist commitment. She had lived in the United States for only twelve years, having emigrated from Germany with her family at the age of nine. Her father, a wounded and decorated (Iron Cross, no less) noncommissioned officer who served four years in the Kaiser's army in the First World War, owned a prosperous candy company in the quaint, woodsy resort town of Bad Homburg in the hills outside Frankfurt. In April of 1934, however, the labor union at my grandfather's factory demanded that he fly the swastika flag to honor the birthday of the new "National Socialist" chancellor, Adolf Hitler—or else they threatened to close down his business. He temporarily surrendered to the union thugs (what choice did he have?), saw the hated banner raised over the production facility adjacent to his home, and immediately began making plans to move his wife and two children to the United States.

Of course, his brother, his sister, his in-laws, and other assorted relatives felt that the one-time warrior was overreacting to an unpleasant provocation: surely, the recently begun Nazi nonsense would soon dissipate, and if anyone should feel safe from persecution or abuse it would be a decorated veteran like my grandfather. During the next five years, as the Nazis assumed totalitarian power and their anti-Semitic agitation intensified, some forty of these relatives eventually made their way to the United States or Switzerland—nearly all of them sponsored or assisted by my grandfather.

When he left Germany in 1934, his resources remained behind with his family (and were quickly tied up with government restrictions) so that my mother, only nine years old when they arrived, watched her father's fall in status from a war hero industrialist commanding chauffeurs and butlers to an immigrant hourly worker with only broken English who toiled at somebody else's assembly line. These circumstances only temporarily deterred him, as he studied chemistry, English, and American civics at night school and quickly set up his own small business in the food industry that he knew so well from Germany. His new company, Serv-Agen, produced puddings and other desserts, and enjoyed modest success, creating two dozen jobs (many of them going to relatives as they arrived from Germany). My grandfather had just begun saving money and feeling comfortable again at precisely the moment the doctors diagnosed his stomach cancer. He died within six months, at age fifty-eight, leaving behind a respectable if not imposing estate (valued at $8,000—the equivalent of nearly $100,000 today) and a will so eloquent that it actually received attention in a feature article in the leading local newspaper.

Even in the midst of a World War (May 1944), the *Philadelphia Inquirer* found space for a headline proclaiming "HIRSCH WILL TELLS PHILOSO-PHY OF LIFE." The piece quoted extensively from the "Last Will and Testament" of my grandfather, Saly Hirsch. This document, translated by friends from his original German, seems to capture this industrious, sober-minded, no-nonsense capitalist whom I never met. "Death is something that must come sometimes, and it is also natural. Neither my wife nor my children shall mourn for me," he ordered. "They shall honor my memory rather by endeavoring to be decent upright people and to help other people."

He made careful arrangements to ensure that the family would continue to control and operate his company, and also expressed special concern for his wife's sister, the kind-hearted spinster of the family who traveled with them from Germany and always shared their home, mentioning her even before he writes of his own children. "My sister-in-law Irene Idstein has in all these difficult years since our emigration, in an unselfish manner helped to establish our existence. Therefore she should also share in our success." He also specified that "in the event that my wife marries again, to which I have no objection, my estate automatically shall go to my children" but only if those children "behave the way they should towards their mother, as well-reared, decent people."

Finally, he declared, "All my life I strove to be a true, caring father, and to help the members of my family first, and also by deed and word to assist other people; I wish that my survivors continue the family life in this spirit. . . . If by reason of sudden death I do not have the opportunity to say farewell to my next of kin and fellowmen, then in this way I ask for forgiveness from those whom in my lifetime I may have done any harm. It was not my intention. I was much more striving to do the right thing and to fill out my place in the world and amongst my fellowmen."

Holding this sixty-year-old document in my hands, trying to come to terms with my long-departed grandfather's personality and legacy, I find it bizarre that my mother—his daughter—should have leaned left in her political orientation for her entire adult life. No, she never developed an interest in the Communist Party, but her youthful fascination with various "advanced" radical and Marxist groups represented a decisive break from the solid, even stern, bourgeois respectability of a powerful father—an entrepreneur and military man—she always purported to worship.

Considering his concern for family members behaving like "well-reared, decent people," the proper, Germanic proprietor of Serv-Agen Puddings might have had difficulty welcoming my bohemian, free-spirited, bushy-haired, rail-skinny father, especially given the militantly leftist *HaShomer HaTzayir* setting in which he and my mother met. In fact, relatives on both sides questioned the match. When my father brought my mother to South Philly for the first time, my grandmother refused to believe that she was Jewish—after all, she spoke English and German but no Yiddish, and with her white gloves and new shoes she looked uncomfortable confronting the shabby East European atmosphere of their row house with the tilting floor. Finally, my father coaxed my mother into reciting a few lines of Hebrew prayer, after which my worried grandmother delivered a line that has lived forever in our family lore: *"Oy! A shikza vos kent di Shema!"* ("Oy! A non-Jewish girl who knows the Shema prayer!").

They married anyway, in a rented hotel meeting room with only a few dozen of the closest family members, serving the cheapest kosher meal they could find. My mother was twenty-two, my father just twenty-one—barely old enough to buy liquor legally, let alone make a lifetime commitment to each other. They made out so passionately in the taxi cab on the way to the hotel room for their first night of marriage that they left behind the traditional Hebrew wedding contract the rabbi had just signed, and never recovered it. My mother later cited this bit of postadolescent carelessness as a malevolent omen, foretelling if not preordaining the difficult course of their marriage.

I arrived eleven months later—"an accident," as both parents endlessly reminded me. "We wanted to do great things in science, great things in Zionism, before we had kids," my father recalled, "but then Michael came along." That didn't stop them from taking me to Israel when I was six months old, drawn by the intoxicating afterglow of the Jewish state's recent victory in the War of Independence, and by peer pressure from their friends and colleagues in the Zionist movement to live up to the socialist ideals that had originally brought them together at camp. Like many members of their generation, they took for granted the free enterprise opportunities that their business-based reality had provided them in the United States. They lasted in Israel all of six months, frustrated by the fumbling bureaucracy, the absence of privacy, the outrageous demands on all new arrivals, and the refusal to make adequate provisions for a young couple with a baby. Moreover, they began to realize that my father might never live up to his scientific potential if he failed to finish his graduate study at Penn. My mother had already completed her master's degree in chemistry at Rutgers in New Jersey, and that credential went to waste during our brief sojourn in Israel. As soon as we flew back to the states, however, she got a job as a biochemist at a cardiac unit at Philadelphia General Hospital.

Her work provided our family's chief support (as she never tired of recalling in later years) while my father returned to his studies, eventually shifting his focus from chemistry to physics. We lived in a tiny basement unit at Lindley Court Apartments—a gray collection of squat, massive, Stalinist-style, concrete structures in a grim corner of North Philadelphia adjacent to the Logan Subway Station. Just below the ceiling we had the only windows in our apartment—little slots that looked out at pavement level so you could watch the feet of occasional passersby. Despite their discomforts, my parents maintained confidence about the future. Everyone knew that my dad would get his Ph.D. and go on to glory in the burgeoning aerospace industry on his way to winning the Nobel Prize. I was five years old on the morning that my father tried on his graduation robes as my mother straightened his mortarboard, so proud that now people would call him "Doctor Medved." His own mother felt confused enough by the new title that she never fully mastered the ability to explain to her South Philadelphia friends that a "Doctor of Physics" (or, more properly, a "Doctor of Philosophy in Physics") could do nothing to help them with their sore elbows or upset stomachs.

Meanwhile, my other grandmother, my mother's mother, overcame adversity by reaffirming the unacknowledged business traditions of our family—not that anyone noticed at the time.

Despite the clear intentions of her late husband's famous will, she had lost her controlling share of his company, and after several years the new managers ran it into the ground. Left with no regular source of income (beyond minimal payments from Social Security), my grandmother did what came naturally at that point: she opened a little shop in order to support herself and pay her bills. Together with her younger sister, my maiden aunt, Irene, she sold the big house on Camac Street and purchased a new, smaller row house with a tiny store in front of the living area. There, the two gray-haired sisters opened a "variety store," selling a mind-numbing array of junk—school supplies, greeting cards, bubble gum, baseball cards, candy, little toys marked "Made in Japan," lipstick, batteries, and much more. In the store, "Irene's," they displayed the merchandise literally from floor to ceiling, since the retail area was impossibly cramped and narrow. Carefully stocking the shelves and regularly replenishing the supply, they managed to eke out their living—aided by their Sunday afternoon traffic: Pennsylvania's strict blue laws prohibited most businesses from opening their doors on the Lord's Day, but my grandmother earned an exception as a Jewish Sabbath observer who always closed her store on Saturday.

This impeccably organized, tightly wound, but incomparably kind old lady quickly became the most important figure in my early childhood—my adored and adoring, proud and protective, inescapably German "Oma." My parents both worked late—my mom at her hospital job, my father at his grad school lab—so I spent most of my time with my grandmother and aunt. I so preposterously cherished Oma's company that I learned to speak English with a slight German accent for the first few years of my life.

I showed up at Oma's house every day in the early afternoon, after the school bus dropped me off from nursery school. The moment I went through that door I felt happier, more secure—and, yes, more spoiled—than anywhere else. Oma ran her little store in her stone-faced row house on Chelten Avenue in West Oak Lane (North Philadelphia), on a block of tidy little retail establishments—Fox's Grocery on the corner (with an old-fashioned pickle barrel near the front door), Cohen's Drug Store (with its soda fountain) on the other corner, Dash's Fish Store (with the fresh catch of the day displayed on top of a big box of ice on the sidewalk) right next door. I was treated like family by all of my grandmother's neighbors, who, like her, lived above and behind their commercial facilities. Across the street, the former Morris Mansion had been transformed into a verdant city park with a playground and a corral with three horses who used to eat lump sugar out of my hand when my grandmother or my aunt took me up to the chain-link fence.

Some forty years later, during a lecture appearance in Philadelphia in 1993, I had a few free hours in the late afternoon to pay a return visit to the old neighborhood. The cab driver urged me not to get out of the car, but I wanted to see if any of the shops I remembered so fondly had survived in any form. They hadn't, of course—a few boarded-up windows reflected the once commercial nature of the block, but the other stores had been haphazardly converted into substandard housing. The entire area reflected the despair and palpable menace of the nation's most blighted districts—covered with graffiti and trash and broken glass, with several gutted buildings abandoned altogether. The once lovely park no longer offered trees or lawns or horses—only cracked pavement, broken benches, and a selection of stupefied transients and apparent drug dealers.

This brief visit to my grandmother's home (a decade after her death, twenty-five years after she left the place) made me appreciate her hard work. In a sense, the wretched state of the neighborhood when I saw it represented nature, or human nature, taking its course: entropy and chaos will overwhelm everything in the absence of enterprise and effort. The fanatically focused energy needed to keep alive those modest little businesses—the fish stores and druggists and variety stores—made possible the pleasant, wholesome atmosphere I so vividly recalled. The surly indolence that now prevailed, whatever its roots in recent or ancient wrongs, swept away the relics of that era of effort. My grandmother exemplified a German word which she always considered especially honorable: *fleissig,* meaning industrious, busy, and hardworking.

She lived and died with the conviction that tidy habits and a crowded schedule could keep misery and insecurity at bay—even for an immigrant widow and her spinster sister. To a ridiculous extent, they filled every moment with work—managing their little store, scrubbing and dusting every speck of the two stories of their house, toiling at all hours over "netzas," or hair nets, which they produced on a piecework basis, in between customers at the store or while watching their favorite TV programs. At night, after closing time, Oma retreated to her "office"—a little room with a desk under one naked bulb in their ancient stone cellar where she meticulously recorded every penny of their marginal operation, registering each trivial sale of candy bars or deodorant so they could reorder and restock appropriately. Trained in bookkeeping in the old country, where her late husband once ran his far more substantial enterprise, she took pride in her perfectly maintained multiple account books and neatly arranged file cabinets, organizing every detail of her life with Teutonic precision.

No one should underestimate the significance or power of such brazenly bourgeois virtues. For many Americans, they exert their irresistible but unappreciated influence down through the generations. How many intellectuals and yuppies and environmental activists and aspiring film directors owe their privileged positions, their multiplicity of choices and opportunities, to a grandparent somewhere sitting in a cellar, toiling over account books to ensure that earnings exceed expenditures? Oma grasped, and passed along, one of the greatest truths of life: it doesn't matter how much you earn, so long as you spend less than you bring in—and thereby put aside savings, even pennies, day by day. Prosperity doesn't come from winning the lottery or overnight fame, but from selling a few ballpoint pens, marbles, and Slinkies each afternoon. Even the most "enlightened" contemporary thinkers, the most advanced postmodernist elitists, can probably recall some tirelessly plugging relative like my grandmother, but if they've been ruined by the pseudo-sophistication of prestige universities, they will fail to recognize the essential nobility, even heroism, in the businessman's daily grind.

If social workers, teachers, media executives, psychologists, journalists, and unionized workers could spend just a month running, say, a neighborhood variety store, they might reconnect with some of the deepest sources of the nation's strength. The independent businessman can only succeed by serving other people—giving his customers, his neighbors, something that they want in either goods or services. The pursuit of profit will attune an individual more reliably to the real needs and desires of others than any sociological analysis or ideological agenda. Napoleon, that grand and celebrated misleader of men, might sniff at his English adversaries as "a nation of shopkeepers," but he never acknowledged that those same shopkeepers ultimately whipped his Imperial, Frenchified rear end. You may sneer all you want at the shopkeepers' values, but you will do so only at your mortal peril.

Of course, most of our present-day business bashers insist that they have nothing against small, localized enterprises like my grandmother's store, and they reserve their contempt for grasping, multinational corporate exploiters. During my own era of anti-entrepreneurial invective—in college, law school, and a half-dozen years beyond—it never occurred to me to associate the grandmother I worshipped with the capitalist values I ridiculed. Only when I left academia and politics and made my first serious personal forays into competitive commerce did I finally realize that far more Americans run struggling little operations like Oma's variety store than administer major corporations. By 1990, the number of our working fellow citizens who described themselves as "independent businessmen" (15 percent) had surpassed the number who affiliated with organized labor (13 percent). Small businesses (like Microsoft once was) produce more new jobs, fresh ideas, and enterprising energy than the most lavish corporate start-ups. Among immigrants, especially, it's the mom-and-pop operations—gardening services, motels, convenience stores—that continue to provide a reliable path to middle-class respectability and family advancement. Such personalized enterprises reflect the restless, creative spirit of America—from Washington's obsession with frontier land speculation (and turning a profit on the complex operations of his Mount Vernon farm), to Lincoln's impassioned concern with building his personal wealth and investments as a railroad lawyer, to Edison's ingenious if untutored tinkering, to the flamboyant fantasies of today's more audacious Internet entrepreneurs. To keep in touch with that life force, we should remember how we reached this point—both in terms of our family chronicles and our national history. The free-market system still relies on individual commitment and imagination—it's intimate, not impersonal, as much about "Irene's" as it is about Enron.

Never Feel Embarrassed

Most children begin feeling embarrassed by their parents when they become teenagers, but my burning humiliation commenced long before the ravages of puberty.

A month before my sixth birthday, my parents loaded up their newly acquired '53 Plymouth for a transcontinental drive to San Diego, where my father had secured his first big job after his Ph.D., at the defense contractor Convair. After a few weeks in a tacky apartment, they bought their first house—a newly constructed two-bedroom box with a tiny yard of raw, yellow dirt. Despite its ambiguous location in a freshly developed, down-market section of the generally pleasant Point Loma neighborhood, it felt like a palace in comparison to our basement apartment in Philly, but somehow the bland, barely finished home, which only slowly filled up with furniture, emphasized the loneliness of our situation. Instead of the constantly *kibbitzing* collection of aunts and uncles and cousins and grandparents on both sides, we now lived in a sleepy, charming Navy town (as San Diego was in those days) in which we knew absolutely no one. The Jewish community had not yet developed and represented an estimated three thousand souls of the city's half-million residents, so when my parents sought out an appropriate synagogue (there were only three in town), it required more than a half hour's drive to get there.

My father worked late hours at Convair, I felt consumed by the excitement of school (first grade!), and my mother bore the burden of our odd-ball status and the sudden lack of family and friends. My parents argued all the time, even after my mom secured another hospital job and even after the birth of my brother Jonathan (when I was seven). The atmosphere at home wasn't cruel or cold; it was, rather, incurably chaotic, relentlessly intense, emotional, even melodramatic. It wouldn't have occurred to me that we were an unhappy family except that my mother, who lovingly tucked me in each night, frequently told me so. She worried over her weight gain, making her feel unloved and unattractive, which of course only encouraged more compulsive eating.

I hated my mother's determined impersonation of a poverty-stricken bag lady. Especially after the arrival of my youngest brothers (Ben, the third child, came when I was nine, then Harry—a rude surprise to my bickering parents—when I was twelve), she felt terrible about her body and clothed it in shabby tents acquired from thrift stores and bargain racks. Whenever we went shopping, we bought only cut-rate merchandise—including baked goods, meats, and vegetables at the very edge of spoilage. By this time my dad earned a decent living, but my mother actually took perverse pride in what she regularly described as her "Depression mentality." For open house at Loma Portal Elementary School I always tried to avoid acknowledging my mother, who looked so disreputable and sounded so brittle and edgy with her Philadelphia accent in comparison to the pert WASPy matrons in Capris or flouncy skirts who escorted the other kids.

My father contributed additional moments of acute embarrassment nearly every weekend. On Saturdays he hauled the four boys off to a selection of San Diego's famous beaches. We not only schlepped armloads of float toys and blankets and snack food from the car to the water, but my dad invariably brought along a big garden shovel for constructing elaborate sand castles with my brothers. I tried to hide beneath a collection of towels, reading some snooty, way-above-grade-level book (Dickens and Dumas were special favorites), praying that no one I knew from school would recognize me with these three little brats who claimed to be my brothers or with the broad-shouldered, curly-haired dad who acted like the youngest, most frenetic of us all.

If we didn't go to the beach we went to swimming pools in some of San Diego's snazziest resort hotels. My father simply parked in the parking lots, then led his boys out to the pools, diving boards, chaise lounges, and outdoor showers reserved for registered guests. On occasion, we even waltzed through the busy hotel lobbies, without challenge. "Try to look like you belong here," my father told us. "Why should we feel ashamed? What law are we breaking?"

My mother mostly chuckled over these raids on ritzy tourist establishments and tried to cure me of my exaggerated embarrassment. "Okay, so it's not completely kosher, but what are you so worried about?" she reasoned. "The people who see you are strangers. They don't know who you are. They'll never see you again. They'll never hurt you, they have no power over you. Why should you be afraid of them? Only stupid people waste their time worrying about what strangers are going to think. What difference does it make if they give you a funny look? It's some sort of crime to buy stuff at a bargain bin? You should look around and try to hide because somebody doesn't like your clothes? You're going to try to crawl under your desk at school because somebody thinks you're weird, or doesn't like your glasses, or some dummy wants to tease you? The important thing is to remember who you are, to get better grades than the rest of them, and then dirty looks don't matter."

My parents, in other words, provided me with an intense education in shamelessness. At times, however, their admirable (and arrogant) instruction went too far. During my senior year of high school, full of willful defiance, I applied to only two universities (Harvard and Yale). I was therefore unspeakably nervous the night that the Harvard alumni representative—a local lawyer with horn-rim glasses and a skinny tie—came over to our house to interview me. The conversation seemed to be going well, and I felt pleased that my mother had exiled the rest of the family to the other side of the house, not just to reduce the noise level but also to preserve the (false) impression that I lived under civilized circumstances. That image collapsed beyond repair when suddenly my father appeared dressed solely in his underwear—briefs and T-shirt. Without a hint of discomfort, he strode over, extended a hand to the embarrassed Harvard man, and introduced himself as "Professor Dave Medved" (he was, indeed, part of the UCLA faculty at the time). I, meanwhile, recited lines from *Hamlet*, Act I, Scene II, in my mind as I suffered in silence: "O, that this too too solid flesh would melt, / Thaw, and resolve itself into a dew." I wanted to disappear—but only after I murdered my father.

Harvard turned me down, by the way. I'm not sure if the underwear assault played a role.

I am certain, however, that my parents' refusal to feel embarrassed, their insistence on defying all bland, conformist standards of respectability and decorum, provided me with some essential preparation for a career in the public eye. In the Medved household, no one considered it a crime to qualify as "a character"; that designation amounted to a certification of vitality, authenticity, even integrity. By the time I left home in mid-adolescence, I had overcome the normal pubescent urge to make myself invisible or at least bland and anonymous, and had learned to relish the fact that my parents, my brothers, and many of our assorted friends and relatives counted as colorful originals.

As a media professional, I've managed to withstand innumerable well-intentioned attempts to remake me along more conventional or stylish lines. During my television career as cohost of *Sneak Previews*, frustrated producers on three occasions hired image consultants in a desperate attempt to upgrade my onscreen image. Fortunately, their often ludicrous recommendations (one year, they mandated sweater vests and bow ties) received respectable attention for only a week or two before I managed to slink back into my customarily curmudgeonly and inelegant ways. In dealing with scathing book reviews, or hostile callers and angry guests as a radio host, I continue to hear my mother's advice: If you maintain an unblushing ability to be yourself, embarrassment becomes not only unnecessary but irrelevant.

LESSON

6

Liberals Love Losing Because It Makes Them Feel Virtuous

"Weird" may have been okay during my upbringing, but "stupid" most emphatically was not. And Republican affiliation seemed to my parents to represent the most glaring and appalling example of stupidity.

In this, they once more flaunted their nonconformity: in a staunchly conservative town (the Navy presence and the numerous defense contractors helped make San Diego the most Republican big city in California) they proudly stood out as die-hard Democrats. The first election campaign that I remember took place in 1956, with my mother patiently explaining that Adlai Stevenson deserved to be president because he was an intellectual and Ike was a dummy. My mother tried to put it in terms I could understand: "Think about it. Who would you choose to be president of your school, Michael? Would you want a 'C' student who's nice and popular, or an 'A' student who's really smart?" This question actually confused me, because I noticed that in all classroom elections the popular students—the pretty girls with neat clothes and the athletic guys who were chosen first in all team sports—always got more votes than the smart, geeky kids. I logically concluded that our man Stevenson didn't stand a chance.

In any event, my father took me to a big Stevenson rally in October of 1956, shortly after my eighth birthday, building it up as a historic opportunity. But the rally (at Starlight Bowl in Balboa Park) proved disappointing, even depressing. The sparse attendance allowed us to sit right in front, so I got a good look at the candidate and his running mate, Senator Estes Kefauver of Tennessee. To my eight-year-old ears, Kefauver (who waved his arms and pounded the podium in an old-fashioned, stem-winding, southern senator sort of way) sounded much more impressive than the professorial Mr. Stevenson, with the spotlight gleaming over his sweaty, bald head. Nevertheless, we applauded dutifully, and even waved an ADLAI AND ESTES sign they had handed us as we entered the rally.

Walking back to the car on the fragrant fall night, I held my father's hand and tried to sound appropriately excited. "They kept saying that Adlai is the next president of the United States," I noted. "That means he wins for sure. Right, Dad?"

"Naw," he laughed. "He'll lose in a landslide. Everybody's going to vote for Eisenhower. But that doesn't mean that Ike is a better man."

This youthful training conditioned me for the next twenty years of liberal losers. Except for John F. Kennedy (who won by a whisker) and Lyndon Johnson (in that freakish, post-assassination election against the scary Goldwater), all the candidates that we most actively supported went down to ignominious defeat; in some cases, they got utterly crushed (like Pat Brown running for governor against that silly actor Ronald Reagan in 1966, or George McGovern carrying only Massachusetts in the 1972 presidential election). My parents conditioned me to believe that our candidates were better not in spite of but *because* of the fact that they lost. Mom and Dad spoke proudly and nostalgically about their first involvement in a presidential campaign, as youthful organizers for the Progressive Party in 1948 and its unabashedly left-wing candidate, former vice president Henry Wallace. It didn't matter that he made a pathetic showing against Truman and Dewey (he drew a paltry 2.4 percent of the total vote); they felt proud that they had worked for Wallace because he represented "peace" (actually, he advocated appeasement of Joe Stalin, but that's another story). It didn't matter if more than 97 percent of the country rejected the best man for the office, or if voters spurned Adlai the Egghead on two different occasions. After all, many of those same voters actually backed the mean and despicable Joe McCarthy (whose snarling, grubby face on our tiny TV screen riveted my parents' attention during the Army-McCarthy hearings when I was a very small boy). I learned at an early age that we should feel proud to stand aside from the "slob-ocracy"—all the dumb, uneducated, comformist, easily manipulated people out there—and go our own way.

Actually, I received conflicting messages about "the common people." On the one hand, we loved and admired the working man, the ordinary guy, the poor-but-honest bus driver or janitor or barrel maker, like my grandfather. My dad loved the old Frank Capra movies (*You Can't Take It with You, Mr. Smith Goes to Washington,* and so on), which showed how simple, decent people always knew better than the swells and the stuffed shirts. At the same time, when the common man made ridiculous mistakes (like voting Republican at any time or at any level), we shook our heads and remembered the amazing fact that at any given moment half of all Americans are, by definition, below average in intelligence. That meant that the Republicans could concentrate on all the fools and slow thinkers and if they supplemented that base with just a few normal or above-average people, they would have their majority.

Why did my parents feel such unquestioning loyalty in those days to the pervasive proposition that the Democrats amounted to the party of superior intelligence and virtue? I asked my mother (who remained a fervent Democrat all her life) that question shortly after I had made the switch to the GOP and scandalized the family by working for Reagan in 1980. "I guess we never thought about it," she said with a shrug. "We were Democrats because that's just who we were. It was like being Jewish. You didn't have to find a reason, and it didn't matter if the rest of the world hated you. It's just who you were, and it was natural. But now, for so many young Jewish people, there's assimilation. Or there's intermarriage. Or they become Moonies. You can't take anything for granted. And for people like you . . . all of a sudden, you turn conservative."

For my mother, abandoning the Democratic Party compared to leaving your faith—never mind that my political shift corresponded to a religious intensification, and a disproportionate number of Orthodox Jews identify as Republicans. For many Jewish Democrats—comfortable and proud in their underappreciated minority status in both politics and religion—the two identities connect instinctively with each other.

This bittersweet pride in simultaneous superiority and rejection comes across in a cherished anecdote about Adlai Stevenson himself. During his first race for the presidency in 1952, an enthusiastic matron came up to him and predicted inevitable victory. "Governor Stevenson, I am so proud to meet you!" she declared. "I'm just sure that every single intelligent person in the country will vote for you for president."

"Unfortunately, Madam," the wry candidate replied, "I need a majority."

LESSON

7

Young Idealists Must Beware
the Scarlet Plague

At age eleven, through no fault of my own and completely against my will, I endured the single most unforgettable conversation of my childhood.

It occurred during one of the sweet, sticky summers I spent with Oma and Aunt Irene at their variety store in Philadelphia. I may have been the only child in the history of the human race strange and obstinate enough to insist on leaving San Diego in July and August, when the balmy ocean breezes make the weather there nearly ideal, for a tiny upstairs bedroom in the sweltering City of Brotherly Love. But I actually took pride in my ability to survive the hot, wet nights, since they strengthened my self-image as a gritty Philadelphia kid. It seemed to me an accident, perhaps even a mistake, that I lived during the school year in San Diego. Part of this sense of alienation stemmed for my mad passion for the Philadelphia Phillies—mad, because year after year the Phutile Phils racked up a dismal record. Nevertheless, I embraced them as my team (San Diego didn't have a major league franchise at the time), and during the summers, my older cousin Sandy took me to some of the sparsely attended and gloriously dispiriting games at Connie Mack Stadium.

I also liked spending time with Sandy's dad—my father's older brother—Moish. During these Philly summers my grandmother introduced me to a favorite feature of *Reader's Digest* magazine called "The Most Unforgettable Person I Ever Met," and I thought even at the time that my Uncle Moish might qualify as my candidate. With his wild hair, horsy teeth, watery brown eyes behind thick glasses, brilliant mind, infectious laugh, and coiled-spring ferocity, he easily dominated any room he entered. Born in Ukraine in 1905, he had no formal education but he read everything (from Greek tragedians to existential philosophers), knew everything (with more than a smattering of mathematics, classical music, ancient and modern history, political theory, Zionism and Talmudic study), easily handled himself in a half-dozen languages, and advanced his opinions with uncompromising passion and a sneering contempt for any hint of disagreement. He also worked fanatically at his business as an electrician, played a robust role in the local Jewish community, and raised three children on his own (his wife had died suddenly when their youngest was only ten).

He took special interest in me from the beginning because, he claimed, he saw a chance with me to redeem past mistakes and to do a better job in shaping a finished product than he had done in "raising" his kid brother, my father. I appreciated my uncle's solicitous attention—especially since both my parents assured me (during our emotional long-distance phone conversations) that I could learn a great deal from Moish and should make the most of the opportunity. Nevertheless, I was only eleven and found it difficult to ignore my other pressing priorities: most notably, my obsession with tacky science fiction movies. I began to pester Uncle Moish to take me to see a heavily advertised shocker called *The Brain from Planet Arous.*

To my surprise, Moish at least kept the door open to the idea that he would escort me to *The Brain from Planet Arous.* But first he insisted on taking me out to dinner at a "fancy restaurant" for a very important and very serious conversation.

I dressed up in my one suit for this solemn occasion and remember the discomfort of a too-tight tie and the too-snug shoulders during our steak dinner. Moish allowed me to order absolutely anything I wanted from the menu—in contrast to my unfailingly cost-conscious mother on those rare occasions when I went out to eat with my parents. Looking around that shiny, busy dining room, with all the well-dressed and prosperous adults, I remember feeling conscious of my status as the only kid in the place. After dinner, feeling very important and grown up, I ordered dessert before my uncle leaned his long, serious face conspiratorially across the table.

"Now is the time, Mike, for the talk we need to have. Maybe your parents think you're too young, or they don't want you to hear. But I think you're ready. I think you need it. I think you are going to remember."

I do indeed remember, and can recapture with uncanny vividness the queasy feeling that came over me along with my fear that he was about to disclose some disgusting, gross-out secrets about "the birds and the bees"—nasty information that I hadn't yet received from anyone and wanted with all my heart to avoid as long as possible. Fortunately, Uncle Moish meant to talk politics, not sex.

"First of all, let me ask you. Have you ever heard of the Scarlet Plague?"

"I know about the Black Death, Uncle Moish. That was the disease that killed all those people in the Middle Ages."

"That's very good, but no, the Scarlet Plague is even worse. It's not about the Middle Ages. It's about right now, and fifty years ago. It kills more people, ruins more lives, than any other disease. And the worst part about it is the people who are most likely to get sick, and who are going to suffer the most, are the brightest minds, the biggest idealists, the natural leaders of this world. They are people just like you."

I warmed to his compliment, and tried to smile away my fear and discomfort.

"But I don't want you to get sick. That's why we need this talk. Maybe you've already been exposed to the Scarlet Plague, and maybe you haven't. But if you haven't, I know that you will be exposed, and probably soon. When you go to high school, when you go to college, this sickness will be all around you. You'll see some of your best friends get sick, and lose their ability to think or to work or to enjoy life. Do you know what I'm talking about? Do you know about this disease?"

I was totally confused. Seeing my worried face, my uncle got to the point.

"The Scarlet Plague is Communism. It's Scarlet because they call themselves Reds, and also that is the color of blood. And there's blood everywhere with the Communists, of the people they kill, that they torture and they cripple. I know because I saw it myself—I saw it starting in Russia before we got out in 1924. But it's not only Russia, you know. It's everywhere. It's in America. It's in Israel. Especially with intellectuals! If you're not ready for it, you may get infected—so you have to understand."

And he went on to lay out the most gripping, convincing, and altogether persuasive case against the Communists and their lies and their cruelty and their insatiable lust for power and destruction. More than a decade later, when I first read Solzhenitsyn's epochal (and then brand new) *Gulag Archipelago,* I thought of my Uncle Moish making the same sort of case, with equal passion, in that ritzy restaurant in Philadelphia. I tried to remember all the names and dates and stories he told me, but the underlying message emerged more clearly than any details. I knew something about "The Cold War" and the threat from the Soviet Union, but Moish made the danger feel far more immediate, insidious, almost supernatural.

"And when you tell your father that we had this talk—and you should tell him—he'll just laugh and make fun of me. He'll tell you not to worry. He thinks because the Reds never infected him that there's nothing to worry about. He's too relaxed about everything! Because he doesn't know the way they're going to go after you—I know they will!—and they're going to go after millions and millions of other people in your generation. Your father doesn't take it seriously but I need you to take it seriously. I need you to be prepared. You're in the Boy Scouts, right? 'Be prepared' is the motto! Be ready to fight back against the Scarlet Plague!"

It all seemed impossibly heavy and melodramatic, as if Moish worried that my mostly Republican, middle-class San Diego world had already been infested with active cells of preteen Commie agents. Nevertheless, I promised to heed his lecture and to keep his pleas in mind in the years ahead.

And amazingly enough, I did. Less than six years after the diatribe, I was surrounded in college by honest-to-goodness leftist lunatics, and in trying to deal with the psychos from the SDS (Students for a Democratic Society), I thought repeatedly of my uncle's warnings about the Scarlet Plague. On the fringes of the antiwar movement in which I became active,

I easily perceived a disease—a spreading infection of anti-Americanism, a morbid infatuation with nihilistic violence. I'd like to believe that I would have rejected extremist temptations even without my uncle's warnings, but as I made progress in my political journey, his unforgettable harangue seemed more and more prescient, even profound.

We never did make it to the movie theater to see *The Brain from Planet Arous*. My uncle had already filled my head with a more frightening science fiction scenario, based on genocidal reality.

LESSON

8

The Establishment Is Not Only
Assailable—It's Accessible

In order to qualify for the fashionable status of wounded victim, most celebrities need to recall (or imagine) some long-ago incident of devastating child abuse. Such revelations inspire not only pity but an odd sort of respect, as if personal eccentricities now fit into an appropriately dramatic, even tragic context. Since both my parents conducted themselves with consistent decency, kindness, and generosity to all four of their children, I couldn't provide appropriately shocking details if Oprah Winfrey or Jerry Springer (heaven forbid!) ever asked me for a confessional concerning my painful childhood.

But one parental decision at the time did seem perversely cruel, selfish, and ultimately unforgivable: their determination to disrupt my high school career by moving our entire family to Los Angeles. Looking back on that calamity, I realize that the fateful shift bears all the marks of blameless inevitability: my dad, after all, had lost his job. Convair/General Dynamics had begun phasing out his entire division and in the San Diego cutbacks of the early '60s, literally thousands of scientists and engineers had to leave town. My father secured a position teaching physics at UCLA along with a job as a research scientist for a promising company called Electro Optical Systems. Suddenly I found myself in an intimidating new world of spoiled rich kids and Hollywood tinsel, and I dreaded the prospect of entering another high school as a junior, playing the role of anonymous new kid and trying to penetrate one of the well-established social groupings.

We moved to a house in Crestwood Hills above Sunset Boulevard—a place my parents rented for $350 a month (an absolute steal, even then) from another UCLA professor away on sabbatical. This arrangement placed my middle-class family in the midst of a neighborhood of privileged people whose income and sophistication placed them vastly out of our league. On the first day of school, I rode the school bus from our rented hillside home, surrounded by the children of doctors (especially psychiatrists), movie writers, TV actors, lawyers, and prominent politicians. The school in which I enrolled—Palisades High—had been built just two years before as a favored enclave within the LA city schools, providing the best physical resources (and a splendid view of mountains and ocean) for the pampered offspring of the well-to-do residents of Brentwood, Crestwood Hills, Mandeville Canyon, and Pacific Palisades.

I felt conspicuously less wealthy and less worldly than the nearly three thousand other students, none of whom even knew my name. For the first few weeks, I daydreamed about devising some scheme that would enable me to return to my secure, familiar environment in San Diego—just as I'd yearned to return to Philadelphia during our initial move to California nine years before.

My desperation led to a ruthless strategy that quickly ended my painful invisibility at Palisades High School and taught me profound, lasting lessons about the value of publicity. Like any other high school in the United States, Pali nursed a giddy, fall semester obsession with football— despite the fact that the miserably mediocre team (the Mighty Dolphins) stood no chance of winning significant victories, and played its home games on the marshy, poorly drained turf of the freshly constructed football field in a canyon just below the newly opened campus. Arguing with seatmates on the school bus every morning, I began making the case that the football field could serve the school more effectively as a rice paddy than as the setting for desultory gridiron warfare. In 1963, with conflict in

Vietnam notably intensifying, the rice paddy reference achieved a rich topical resonance. Some people (particular faculty and administration) assumed I was serious (and seriously weird), but most kids felt that the entire plan sounded goofy enough to provide outrageous amusement. I had recently joined the debate club, which gamely agreed to sponsor "The Great Rice Paddy Debate," in which representatives of the feckless football team would be called upon to defend their very existence.

Every day for at least two weeks we coordinated demonstrations during lunch hour—eventually drawing hundreds of students, linking arms and chanting our favored slogans: "Rice is Nice!" or "Equal Rice for All!" As the Great Rice Father and indefatigable mouthpiece of a movement, I became an instant celebrity, despised by the cheerleaders and athletes, of course, but identifiable to everyone in my new school.

In fact, this outrageous grab for attention did its work so well that a few months later, despite my status as a new kid in school, I won election to student body office (beating a cheerleader, no less) by reassembling the same coalition of outsiders and disenfranchised tenth graders who had fueled the rice paddy crusade in the first place.

Despite all my fears at my parents' relocation, in other words, Palisades High turned out to be a much better fit for my personality and interests than my old school in San Diego. The heavily Jewish makeup of the student body (nearly a third of my classmates, by most estimates) and the abundance of kids from self-consciously intellectual or entertainment industry homes allowed me to thrive in a noisy, hyperactive way that the cozy provincialism of Point Loma would have discouraged. One of the music teachers at Pali, impressed with my immoderate passion for symphonic fare (which I had picked up directly from my Brahms-and-Vivaldi-loving parents), urged me to apply for a scholarship studying composition and creating a musical theater piece with American master Roy Harris—the distinguished symphonist whose work had been performed around the world and who had been compared with Aaron Copland and Virgil Thompson. I won the place, along with four other teenagers from a far-flung collection of Southern California high schools, and spent the first six months of 1964 working with the others under the supervision of Dr. Harris in writing a stage work incorporating spoken word (I wrote the libretto), ballet, choral singing, soloists, and full symphony orchestra. The

Hollywood Theater Arts Workshop would perform our creation (pretentiously titled *Liberty?*, complete with that obnoxious question mark) as a special summer project for gifted young people throughout the LA Unified School District.

The composition of *Liberty?* involved real excitement, and the rehearsals leading up to its performance (at the end of a summer session at Hollywood High) delivered even more electricity. It didn't matter that the work we patched together sounded overblown and tacky and, particularly in my libretto, full of insufferable, incoherent adolescent whining ("I am a man—my own living, thinking entity / If I do not have myself, what do I have?"). We still got to work with a famous American composer and to see our ideas realized by flesh-and-blood musicians and singers and dancers who performed it with respect and enthusiasm.

Shortly after this international debut of a work that never will (and never should) receive a second performance, I traveled to the East Coast to connect with some of the political excitement of that election year and to take a look at the college campuses that most seriously interested me. The Democratic National Convention took place in Atlantic City, New Jersey, that year, and I had been invited to join a festive national gathering of thousands of Young Democrats, which allowed me to tell my parents and friends back in California that President Johnson's reelection might ultimately depend on my participation. Though only fifteen, I considered myself something of a political veteran: back in San Diego, I'd stuffed envelopes and handed out leaflets at street corners for Democratic candidates for governor and for the Kennedy-Johnson national ticket. Also, to support San Diego Democrat Frank Curran's mayoral campaign, I'd served as the tireless chair of "Students for Curran"—an unstoppable mass movement that boasted, at its peak, eight members. Unfortunately, the charming Curran proved so flagrantly corrupt that he ended up indicted on bribery charges and left office in disgrace (raising serious questions, I suppose, about my teenaged qualifications as a judge of character).

Perhaps my prior association with Frank Curran helped me look past the sleazy aspects of Lyndon Johnson's career and personality (stolen elections, shady business deals, grotesque egotism, ruthless arm-twisting) and to join other partisan enthusiasts in viewing the new president as a candidate for Rushmore. The tall Texan had taken over for the murdered

Kennedy less than a year before the convention and in that brief period had displayed the sort of liberal activism and mastery of Congress that reassured even doubters from the "enlightened," progressive, Stevensonian wing of the party. Despite my admiration for the president, however, I felt somewhat put off by the convention: with the huge photographs of LBJ everywhere you turned, and the gushing, endless stream of worshipful words toward the Leader of the Free World, the event bore a distinctly Stalinist stamp—more like a coronation than a nomination. The only hint of dissent came from a huge billboard which the feisty Republicans had installed at the Atlantic City Boardwalk so that the Democratic delegates couldn't miss it. It featured an image of their jut-jawed nominee, Senator Barry Goldwater of Arizona, with the incendiary message: "IN YOUR HEART YOU KNOW HE'S RIGHT." The Young Democrats snickered at the menacing image overlooking our proceedings and constructed our own responses to the GOP provocation. "Yeah, he's right," we said. "*Far* right!" or else we laughingly intoned, "In your guts you know he's nuts!"

The widespread conviction that Goldwater represented some dangerous departure from the American mainstream helped to shape my political consciousness for the next several years. In place of my childhood identification with a sensitive, superior, but powerless liberal clique (based on my parents' enthusiasm for doomed candidates like Henry Wallace and Adlai Stevenson), I now felt part of an overwhelming majority behind our visionary leader, Lyndon Johnson, who had already inspired the nation with the announcement of his messianic "War on Poverty." The election unfolded without the slightest doubt as to its outcome, and LBJ crushed the snarling and menacing Republican with 61 percent of the popular vote (an all-time record) and 90.34 percent of the electoral votes. In a sense, the victory seemed so effortless and automatic that elections looked less interesting to me; in the same way that the end of the Cold War led some celebrated observers to proclaim "The End of History," LBJ's landslide in 1964 marked for me "The End of Politics." The good guys had won decisively and I naturally assumed that the United States would live happily ever after.

With that sort of warming confidence in the electoral outcome, I left the Democratic Convention in the midst of the celebratory excitement and proceeded on my brief East Coast campus tour. Though I visited Princeton and relished its historic associations with Woodrow Wilson, F. Scott Fitzgerald, and Adlai Stevenson, I had already set my heart on New England. I'd never before journeyed north of New York City, but a wealth of literary and historical enthusiasms led me to fantasize about the home base of Paul Revere, Robert Frost, Henry David Thoreau, Winslow Homer, and Jack Kennedy. As a young boy I became obsessed with nostalgic *Life* magazine or calendar images of picturesque small towns in Vermont or New Hampshire. At times, I clipped these photos and posted them around my desk at home. "You're a Jewish boy," my worried mother said. "What do you want with all these pictures of churches?"

"Mom, it's not the churches. They're New England towns, and the steeples are just part of it."

In this frame of mind, I naturally went nuts over Harvard and the earthy, bustling big city across the Charles. I took the trolley into Cambridge and marveled at Harvard Yard, Widener Library, the Fogg Art Museum. A summer thunderstorm came up that afternoon and I sought shelter in the Longfellow House, a historic shrine off campus that the great poet Henry Wadsworth Longfellow had inhabited for almost half a century until his death in 1882. Here he wrote his celebrated love song to joyous family life:

> *Between the dark and the daylight,*
> *When the night is beginning to lower,*
> *Comes a pause in the day's occupations,*
> *That is known as the Children's Hour.*
>
> *I hear in the chamber above me*
> *The patter of little feet,*
> *The sound of a door that is opened*
> *And voices soft and sweet.*

When I emerged from the quiet home onto the glistening Cambridge street, I began weeping, for reasons that still feel mysterious nearly forty years later, and couldn't stop myself. Wracked by sobs, struggling to catch my breath, worried about alarming any passersby, I grabbed hold of the thick trunk of an ancient maple, trying simultaneously to steady myself and to hide.

Why the tears? In part because Longfellow's loving, gracious family life so far exceeded the chaotic, raw relationships that awaited me at home in Los Angeles? Because this old house, so redolent of the noble New England past, spoke to me of a world I could never recapture? Or did I somehow assume that all this honorable excellence surrounding Harvard and Boston and New England would never, in fact, open up to me—a perennial outsider trying to connect with inhospitable ghosts?

Walking back to catch the trolley as the rain let up and the afternoon faded, I convinced myself I had been crying tears of joy. At age fifteen, with unlimited possibilities, perhaps I wept at the sense of careening for the first time in my own direction, outside the orbit of my parents.

Much to my dismay I never won admission to Harvard. Instead I shocked myself and my parents by getting into Yale—the only other school to which I applied and a campus I'd never bothered to visit. My father hated the idea of Yale in part because of the extra financial burden it placed upon the family (even with the modest grant I received as a National Merit Scholar). He couldn't understand why I wanted to freeze through Connecticut winters instead of continuing at UCLA (or even Berkeley) since I'd already won admission and begun taking classes (during my senior year of high school) at the then tuition-free University of California system. For one thing, my father pointed out the abundance of beautiful (and adventurous) women at the California schools, whereas Yale remained at that time an all-male environment. My mother, on the other hand, supported my adolescent infatuation with New England, and months in advance, she began helping me pack for the thrilling but intimidating journey to New Haven.

LESSON 9

The Highway Provides a Better Education Than the Ivy League

The day I boarded the plane to the East Coast, my mom got up before dawn to finish cramming my oversized suitcases full of clothes, books, toothbrushes, and photos of the family, with favorite candies and other snacks wedged into hidden compartments. She began weeping as the sun came up, and by the time I left for the airport, all three of my kid brothers, who ranged in age from three to nine, had joined in the wrenching sobs. I was sixteen years old (I'd skipped a grade in San Diego)—absurdly young to be leaving home so definitively and utterly unprepared to confront a snooty, self-enclosed Ivy League world that threatened to overwhelm me.

In anticipation of my start at Yale, I read every book I could find about the school and its traditions so that by the time I arrived on campus I expected to discover the genteel wit of Cole Porter and the robust idealism of Dink Stover permeating all the hallowed halls. I showed up several days earlier than everyone else, camping out in my Durfee Hall dorm room (with special permission and a sleeping bag) and wandered around New Haven in the September rain, trying to familiarize myself with my new home of the next four years. In this context, I experienced Yale at its best—

the magnificent imitation-gothic buildings, redolent of power and history and serious intentions, the foliage just beginning its autumnal transition, the drenching downpours making even the grubbier streets glisten with vitality. All this grandeur, all these impressive ghosts, laid out before me, and they were mine, mine! I joyously explored the material Yale (having never even visited the place before I arrived as a freshman), but felt almost instantly cheated by the flesh-and-blood reality that began functioning within that noble shell as soon as students arrived and classes began.

In September of 1965, the university faced jolting transitions—most notably between an unabashedly WASPy fortress of privilege, dominated by alumni families and prep school products (like upperclassmen George W. Bush and John Kerry, or Howard Dean, who would enroll two years later), and the "New Yale"—a fiercely competitive meritocracy in which brash, brainy, often Jewish graduates of public high schools (like Joe Lieberman, who graduated just before my arrival) suddenly predominated. Public school graduates represented more than 60 percent of my Class of '69, an unprecedented figure for my all-male cohort—the last class in more than 250 years of Yale College history to graduate before the fateful and earthshaking arrival of co-education.

I honestly expected to like and admire the preppies of the ancient elite, since they theoretically enjoyed a head start in their exposure to the timeless New England virtues of aristocratic excellence, self-discipline, sacrificial service, and so forth, but I ended up rooming with two real-life preppies from Exeter who instinctively disliked me, while the fourth occupant of our suite was a foul-mouthed, frantically funny, beer-guzzling doctor's son from Omaha who seemed similarly indifferent to the grand traditions I romanticized. Across the hall lived one of the celebrities of our class: the preternaturally preppy son of Pennsylvania's Governor William Scranton, the country club Republican who had battled Barry Goldwater for the most recent GOP presidential nomination. The younger Scranton eventually became Pennsylvania's lieutenant governor himself and an important conservative politician in the Keystone State, but during freshman year, in his loafers, chinos, and immaculate powder blue or maize-colored shirts, with the loud, drunken parties every weekend in his room, he represented the sort of suave self-assurance that I simultaneously envied and resented.

Despite my underlying sense of myself as a misfit and outcast, the *Yale Alumni Magazine* featured an interview with me for its cover story "Who Is the Yale Freshman?"

"I must admit I'm somewhat disappointed in my classmates," I told the eager reporter. "My hopes were too high. The physical plant and the faculty at Yale are so much better than anything I had imagined, but I find the students to be cynical—their cynicism is pervasive. Most of these people are too sophisticated to be alive. They worry so much about being 'in'—the social conventions they follow are suffocating. For instance, I was reading the *Iliad* for ancient history and I was getting all steamed up about it. My roommates thought I was a clod. You don't get excited about things like the *Iliad* if you want to be 'in.' These guys are so super-sophisticated they aren't young anymore. This is the only thing that bothers me. There's no idealism for idealism's sake. I want to remain unsophisticated enough to stay alive. . . . I'm not anxious to have the standard social life here. I refused to pay the $20 social fee because I didn't think I'd have time to partake of the type of activity it paid for. I wasn't looking forward to mixers because the girl you meet at a mixer is too difficult to get to know. Too many girls come up here just aching to latch on to a Yalie. Besides I don't like the prevailing attitude toward females and I don't like the widespread and indiscriminate drinking that goes on around here. This just isn't my idea of a pleasant way to spend an evening."

Instead, the insufferably earnest twit who expressed such sentiments preferred shivering in a sleeping bag beside a lonely highway as a far more "pleasant way to spend an evening." I didn't tell the interviewer about it, but I'd already constructed my own alternative to the normal pattern of undergraduate partying—breaking loose for random, spontaneous, and frenetic escapes from New Haven in order to travel anywhere or nowhere. My father had told me exciting tales about hitchhiking around California during shore leave from the Navy, and he had thumbed his way through the Rocky Mountains with my dubious mom when she was six months pregnant with me. Jack Kerouac never counted as one of my favorite authors (I felt repelled by the emphasis on drugs and drinking), but the open highway formlessness of *On the Road* irresistibly appealed to me. I naturally associated these stories with the passage to manhood and independence—especially since my problems with winning a motor vehicle license (I flunked the driving test three times) made it impossible to consider road trips in my own car. I was a middle-class teenager with thick glasses and good grades, longing to remake myself in a more daring, virile, and adventurous mode, so the idea of traveling great distances by bumming rides with strangers satisfied some of my deepest needs.

My first experiment with this mode of transportation took place the day of my high school graduation rehearsal. Rather than showing up for this boring and meaningless formality (staged at the very football field that I'd failed to transform into a rice paddy), I persuaded my best friend, Laurence Cooper, to spend the entire day with me in a hitchhiking escapade we kept secret from our parents, seeing how far north we could go and still make it back in time for the next day's graduation ceremony. We got a friend to drop us off not far from our school at the western end of Sunset Boulevard where that notoriously winding thoroughfare intersects with the Coast Highway and the Pacific Ocean. With great fanfare and soaring excitement we put out our thumbs, got a first lift from a Malibu surfer, and were on our way.

By late afternoon of that balmy, luminous June day we had arrived at the dusty farming community of Salinas—John Steinbeck country, as I duly noted at the time—more than three hundred miles away from home. We could have turned around and headed back exactly the way we came, but instead we cut over to the coast and tried our luck with legendary Highway 1, the spectacular two-lane road that hugs the lonely cliffs of the rugged Big Sur country in the most desolate, inaccessible corner of the California shore.

Standing in the thickening twilight on an absolutely deserted stretch of poorly maintained highway, edged by towering redwoods on both sides, we listened to the Pacific Ocean crashing and surging far below. Long minutes passed with no cars at all, so each time some motorist ignored us we felt more threatened and desperate. We didn't know much about hitchhiking, but we understood it would be much harder to persuade someone to pick us up in the dark, so we decided to block the highway to force the next car to stop. Fortunately, the guy driving that Ford Falcon elected not to run us down, and in fact he took us all the way to San Luis Obispo, where the road connected with the much busier Highway 101. From there, a single ride took us all the way home by 11 P.M.—the two guys in their VW van even dropped us off at a pre-graduation party in Pacific Palisades that was just breaking up. We managed a dramatic entrance, telling our suitably amazed classmates about our glorious, dangerous, wonderfully pointless adventure—even some of the most glamorous (and generally inaccessible) girls of the Class of '65 listened with eager attention to our feverish narrative. After we got rides home with friends, our parents asked about the rehearsal and the party, never suspecting that we'd covered nearly seven hundred miles that day.

With this singular experience making me a self-appointed expert on hitchhiking, I tried to persuade my acquaintances at Yale to join me on various expeditions but most often found myself traveling alone. Every weekend, I explored a different destination: Manhattan was only 70 miles away, while Boston beckoned only 130 miles to the North. With a sleeping bag and a backpack I could spend the night anywhere—even camping under a tree and behind a rock in Central Park after one Saturday night drinking espresso (for the first time) and listening to folk singers at a Greenwich Village café.

On another occasion, I impulsively hitchhiked to western Pennsylvania with a lovesick fellow freshman who wanted to visit his girlfriend near Pittsburgh; along the way, we slept on the battlefield at Gettysburg. A farmer from the vicinity had dropped us off on a dark, lonely road (Highway 15) after eleven at night. We walked more than two miles across fields and pastures to the border of the Gettysburg National Military Park, looking for a place to camp for the night. Only briefly discouraged by the elaborate fencing and numerous signs that ordered "No Trespassing" and "No Camping," we clambered through the wooden rail and barbed-wire barriers that protected the federal land and what Lincoln had called "this hallowed ground." On a chill, hushed, moonless November night, we marched over the famous battlefield, climbing up behind the key Federal position at Little Round Top where so many determined Confederates lost their lives. In fact, more than fifteen thousand young Americans on both sides were reported killed or missing, with nearly fifty thousand total casualties in the three-day battle—a fact I foolishly recalled to my already queasy pal as we tramped along Cemetery Ridge. We began to sense shadowy, larger-than-life military figures looming out of the misty night on all sides of us—part of the statuary on the monuments to the various regiments and states who participated in the great struggle in 1863. "This is creepy. It's horrible," my friend said with a shiver. "We shouldn't be here at all."

He was right, of course, but I argued that at this point we had no choice but to throw down our sleeping bags and try to pass the time till dawn. We tramped over damp, frosty grass to within sight of the Pennsylvania Memorial—a huge, four-story Victorian monstrosity with cannon and sentry statues, multiple columns, soaring arches, and a dome, all of which seemed to offer some sense of protection or reassurance. Nevertheless, sleep remained completely out of the question as we exchanged hushed, frightened words with the sleeping bags drawn up to our eyes. The noises we heard all night could connect to rational explanations—birds, owls, foxes, raccoons, deer, or other creatures that might normally wander through open country. The visual shocks made far less sense, however: about 4 A.M., shivering and shuddering and trying to catch some sleep, we both suddenly sensed moving figures not more than thirty yards away. "Do you hear that?" I hissed, grabbing his arm. My friend pulled his head deep into the sleeping bag and tried to cover his ears, but I propped myself up on my elbows, peering through the darkness and felt my blood race when I saw a small squadron of uniformed figures—perhaps eight of them, not more than a dozen—carrying weapons and running at full tilt along the ridge. They looked gray and shadowy, but notably lighter (almost illuminated, in fact) than the gloomy mist behind them, before they careened out of view in about six seconds.

Of course, Civil War reenactors love the battlefield at Gettysburg, and their costumes and equipment often look chillingly authentic. But why would a group of modern-day history buffs and weekend warriors suddenly turn up at four in the morning, running away from the Pennsylvania Memorial and disappearing into the silence within seconds? We remained too terrified to talk and waited through the excruciating minutes until the dawn—which was announced ahead of time by the mournful lowing of some cows that must have been let out of their barn by a farmer behind the ridge. At first light we jumped up, threw together our packs, and ran in panic from the haunted battlefield.

Though I never shivered through any further ghostly visitations, I continued to spend the great majority of my free time on sporadic, largely unplanned voyages of discovery and exploration. During the week, I made occasional "lightning strikes"—quick trips to nearby cities or nature preserves that allowed me to get back without cutting too many classes. On the weekends, even in the depths of the Connecticut winter, I followed more ambitious itineraries, getting as far as the mountains of Vermont and Virginia, or the fishing villages of Maine and Maryland. I had little interest in staying on campus to attend the "mixers" that brought busloads of fresh-scrubbed girls from "sister" campuses (Vassar, Smith, Mount Holyoke, Connecticut College for Women) to all-male Yale—in large part because the girl who dominated my imagination and commanded my affection was at the other end of the continent.

I had nursed a killer crush on Lynn, now a student at UCLA, during my senior year at Palisades High School. She was a tall (5'9"), elegant, serious, buxom, superbly self-possessed overachiever I knew from drama class, where she starred in every one of our school plays. She had seemed altogether unapproachable, but by the time of our final semester, we had begun the oddest sort of secret romance—the first moments of real intimacy I ever enjoyed with a woman. She drove a battered, sputtering VW Beetle and started making it a practice to pick me up on school days before dawn. We drove together up lonely roads into the wild, undeveloped, brush-covered reaches of the Santa Monica Mountains, and there, with the classical music station KFAC playing on the glowing dial of her car radio, we watched the sun come up, eventually chugging down the hillside and making our way to school.

I never tried to kiss her or to otherwise "take advantage" of the situation, but on one unforgettable morning about a week before graduation we put on the radio and the host announced a special favorite—Aaron Copland's sweetly seductive, supremely sentimental "Appalachian Spring." This had become an artistic icon to me and I'd already infected Lynn with my enthusiasm, so its appearance on a random predawn broadcast seemed like an overwhelming omen. For the first time we held hands as we listened and waited for the sun, squeezing with such force that it almost hurt. In that dark car, I saw tears running down her cheeks and felt vaulting joy at the thought that I had become important to her.

Once firmly ensconced at Yale, I began writing her regularly and we started exchanging three or four letters every week. Lynn seemed particularly thrilled with detailed accounts of my hitchhiking adventures, and her awed reaction greatly encouraged my wandering ways. During Christmas vacation my freshman year, my parents paid for a plane ticket home, but I spent most of that ten days trying to see Lynn whenever possible and beginning to believe that I loved her. I tried to explain the situation to my mother, who very sensibly replied that it was probably a good thing that we lived so far apart, since I was in no sense ready for such over-the-top intensity.

I flew back to New Haven on New Year's Day, returning to slushy gray snow, dreary dorm life with a drunken roommate, and looming finals. I didn't want to think about ancient history or German verbs or Renaissance poetry; I only wanted to talk to Lynn, to embrace her, to declare my ferocious feelings (we'd kissed for the first time the night after Christmas). I dug dangerously deep into my savings (accumulated from a successful summer job selling encyclopedias) to pay for expensive long-distance calls, sometimes twice a day. Instead of studying, I began writing a cycle of nineteen sonnets—pretentious drivel for the most part—to honor her upcoming nineteenth birthday.

In the midst of this puerile literary labor, I hit upon the scheme of delivering the sonnets personally by hitchhiking home to California. Yale provided her stressed-out students with a "reading period" after Christmas break: a ten-day gap with no scheduled classes to enable undergraduates to prepare for finals and complete papers just before the end of the semester. I became obsessed with the notion that I could use the reading period for the great transcontinental trek: if I traveled day and night, I could make it across the country in four days, spend twenty-four hours with Lynn in Los Angeles, then turn around and arrive back at Yale just in time for my first final.

No one could get me to recognize the absurdly arrogant overconfidence of this plan, or to consider the dire consequences if it went wrong. I even managed to recruit a classmate to accompany me: a sunny, athletic free spirit from Orange County, California, named Steve, who had a real girlfriend to visit back home. He grew intrigued with the risky, irrational splendor of my plans, and refused to feel cowed by the academic pressures of Yale (in fact, he dropped out a few months later). At the Commons, the freshman dining hall, we spread maps across the dinner table as I outlined our route with a yellow highlighter. Our colleagues participated in the planning process with a combination of bemusement and horror, reminding us that the invariably icy conditions of mid-January represented the worst possible time for a cross-country "lightning strike."

We left on a Thursday night after stuffing ourselves at dinner, with a half-dozen classmates walking us through snow flurries to the on-ramp for the interstate. We carried knapsacks filled with sleeping bags, changes of socks and underwear, and a dozen boxes of dried apricots, our main nourishment for the journey. We also carried a large sketch pad with magic markers for producing situational signs: the first one announced "YALIES HEADING WEST," and we knew it would be easy to get our first ride out of New Haven.

In fact, the first twenty-four hours of our Great Migration unfolded as a resounding success. Whenever we got a ride, we asked our benefactors to drop us off at the last rest stop before their exit. This allowed us to avoid lonely roadsides or on-ramps; at rest stops, we could connect with new rides in well-lit, twenty-four-hour islands of gas stations, rest rooms, and cafés that always welcomed travelers. This circumstance made possible a direct and respectful verbal approach: "Excuse me, but we're students at Yale and we're trying to get home to California to visit our families." (We decided that a family visit sounded more wholesome and reassuring than a trip to see girlfriends.) "If you happen to be heading west, we'd very much appreciate a ride."

In less than a day we had covered more than nine hundred miles; by sunset we were at a massive truck stop just outside Chicago. In the punishing cold we sought our next ride, but our first success posed a difficult dilemma: a heavy-set, pipe-smoking guy in a bulky overcoat told us he'd be willing to take us all the way to Omaha. We were thrilled at the prospect of being taken nearly five hundred miles, but we also knew that this trip would require a major and risky change of course. We had hoped to take the classic highway Route 66—through St. Louis, Oklahoma, New Mexico, and Arizona—in part to avoid the cold and snow of the northern route. If we rode with our prospective benefactor to Omaha, that meant making an irrevocable commitment to Interstate 80—through the howling winds of the Great Plains and on past the high, lonely, blizzard-battered prairie of Wyoming. After the briefest glance at the maps and only a few moments of hesitation we decided to accept the trip to Nebraska, allowing fate and naive confidence to overcome reason and caution.

Rather than dropping us in Omaha itself, our ride took us out of his way a few miles beyond town where he suggested we'd have an easier time getting a ride. Unfortunately, he couldn't find a rest area or gas station so instead he left us at an on-ramp several miles from anything. Nonetheless, he assured us that all cars going west would come right past us and that we'd get a good ride with no worries.

Waving goodbye as he pulled away, we became fully conscious for the first time of the intensity of the cold. Snow had fallen throughout the night, and the morning wind howled across the prairie. We fought to hold the pages of our sketch pad down as we held it up with its new message, COLLEGE KIDS HEADING WEST (we figured that the term "Yalies" didn't count for anything in Nebraska and might even alienate passing motorists).

After only half an hour of waiting, the desperation and pain grew acute. Having planned a southwestern route, we wore only high-top tennis shoes and sweat socks. Worse, I had left my gloves at some Howard Johnson's on the Pennsylvania Turnpike. My hands and feet quickly froze. With nothing, not even a farmhouse, within walking distance, we briefly considered curling up in our sleeping bags for a few moments by the side of the road, but I entertained visions of the members of Napoleon's Grand Armee freezing to death in their bedrolls during the disastrous retreat from Russia.

Eventually, a car pulled over and offered to take us fifty miles up the road to Lincoln and we joyously welcomed our deliverance. In the warmth of the vehicle, however, my thawing hands began to ache in earnest and I almost cried out from the pain. The news broadcast on the radio identified the outside temperature as an unthinkable twenty below zero—a level of cold which the driver characterized as normal for January in Nebraska. My tennis shoes felt so comically stiff with frost that I made jokes about it to hide the mounting sense of dread and panic: even if we wanted to call off our insane trip, how could we possibly do it now?

At least this last ride let us off at a busy service area with a long, narrow restaurant that was actually suspended over the interstate so that diners could watch the speeding cars below. Still aching from the cold, we dutifully approached the hungry travelers who sat near us at the restaurant's counter, pleading for a ride to the sunny west.

We succeeded with a wary stranger named Tony, a weathered, muscular, fiftyish tough guy wearing a torn leather jacket and dirty gray sweatshirt. He described himself as a former Marine, and with his close-cropped hair both his pink scalp and his jutting jaw seemed to sparkle with silvery stubble. He drove a lumbering, aging, black '59 Lincoln which he proudly described as "the greatest car the world has ever seen." Most drivers felt content to head down the highway in silent contemplation, but Tony felt a powerful need to talk—chain-smoking and cursing and laughing for no particular reason while describing his achievements in the Korean War, his three failed marriages, and the many bosses who had cheated him in his construction work. He had just finished a framing job in Des Moines and now wanted to drive to Rock Springs, Wyoming, to collect an overdue debt from a former pal who tried to screw him.

The good news we gleaned from his chatter involved another ten hours in a warm car, crossing all of Nebraska and two thirds of Wyoming. But once we arrived in Rock Springs (an appallingly obscure, middle-of-nowhere location), what then? We had already suffered with the cold outside of Omaha, but the snow only grew deeper and more crushing as we drove west. In place of my prior visions of Napoleon on the frozen steppes, I now began to worry over the dire fate of the Donner Party.

To our amazement and delight, however, our driver Tony began to melt. When he asked us about our trip and heard about the plan to cross the country for just twenty-four hours with our girlfriends, he roared with laughter and appreciation over the stupidity and impulsiveness and audacity of the gesture. He also peppered us with questions about Los Angeles, hoping we could verify the fabled beauty of the women and the beaches, and asking how much money we were carrying with us for our trip. He said he had traveled most of the world but somehow had never made it to California. He could do construction jobs anywhere, so he figured why not work in sunshine instead of snow? He would be willing to keep on going and drive us all the way home, and all he expected was money for gas, if we had enough to help him make it to the coast. Pooling our resources, including a few loose coins, we came up with just over forty-four bucks.

Though Tony had filled his tank in Cheyenne, by the time we approached Rock Springs he personally began to run out of gas. He suggested that we spend a few hours sleeping in town; he knew a woman at a hotel who would give us a room for free. Then we could get a fresh start at daybreak, shoot down to Salt Lake City, and make a clear shot to LA.

Tony's "hotel" looked more like a flophouse—a shabby nineteenth-century brick building across from the railroad station, with a rickety fire escape its only notable feature. We arrived after midnight, with neon lights from three downtown bars offering the only sign of life in the sleeping cowboy town. Tony asked us to stay in the car while he went in and spoke to the "management"; we watched through the front window as he argued and joked for a few minutes with an obese woman with dyed red hair, and then he came out and led us to our room. Clutching our knapsacks, we walked through the tiny lobby filled with badly stained, mismatched, overstuffed 1920s furniture, and decorated by a single mournful elk's head on the wall.

Once we had gotten established in the room, Tony announced his intention to go out for a little while to try to collect the money from the bastard who owed him. It was late, and he promised to be back in plenty of time to load us all into the car for a 5 A.M. departure. Lying in bed, we talked for a few moments and munched dried apricots. We expected Tony's imminent return, but gradually drifted into profound sleep.

I woke up abruptly the next morning, with abundant sunshine pouring in through the unshaded window. My watch said 8:30, nearly three hours after our scheduled departure. Without even putting on my glasses, I saw Tony's empty and undisturbed bed, made up exactly as it had been the night before. With our money in his pocket, he had simply disappeared. I staggered to the window to look down on the snowy street for his car, but no Lincoln had been parked in front of the hotel. I saw only a single tumbleweed blowing ominously across the nearby railroad tracks while the wind rattling the window made the walls seem pathetically frail. I woke up Steve and we sat at the edge of the beds assessing our situation. He rightly observed that if Tony had indeed ditched us, he probably left us with responsibility to pay the hotel, too. We had exactly five bucks between us, and a daunting total of more than twelve hundred miles to get us home. What could we do? Make a humiliated call to our parents and ask them to wire us money, somehow, in Rock Springs, Wyoming? If we then took a Greyhound back to New Haven, could we even arrive in time for finals?

After some hesitation, we pulled on our clothes and walked down to the lobby to figure out to confront the complexity of looming catastrophe. Halfway down the final flight of creaky stairs we spotted Tony, seated on an ancient couch under the elk head, sound asleep. Laughing with relief and gratitude, we came up and shook him awake. "What's wrong with you fellas?" he coughed and laughed. "You way overslept. I was sitting here waiting, but then I conked out myself. Get your stuff and let's get outta here—the Lady Lincoln is parked in the alley in back. Maybe we should get a cuppa coffee once we hit the road."

He kept his promise the rest of the way and drove us all the way to my parents' doorstep in the hills above Sunset Boulevard. He alluded to a long night of boozing and battling before he met us, and his face looked slightly cut and bruised, but he remained in good spirits—even though he said he never did collect his money. We invited him to come in with us when we arrived at 5:30 A.M. but he refused. "Your folks will be shocked enough to see you. They sure don't want to see some beat-up old bum."

He drove off, saying he'd look up some buddies from the Marine Corps, with his muffler-challenged Lincoln threatening to wake up the neighborhood. We, meanwhile, knocked repeatedly and decisively until my bleary-eyed mother, her bathrobe clutched at her throat, warily opened the door. She was stunned to see me, gasping with open mouth and bug eyes, but then expressed relief to hear I hadn't been expelled. She'd never met Steve, but she began making breakfast of corned beef and eggs while my dad and my startled brothers got out of bed, one by one. Rather than feeling indignant or reproachful over the fact that we had hitchhiked all the way home, they felt amused and proud to listen to our adventures. Steve's parents got his phone call and drove from Orange County to pick him up later that day. Both families insisted on scraping together the money for one-way plane fare back to the East Coast, rather than allowing us to try a hitchhiking return trip.

I realized my fondest desire by spending most of a full day with Lynn, presenting her with the sonnet cycle, rolled into a scroll and tied with a royal blue ribbon. She expressed all the appropriate amazement and gratitude at the gesture I'd made in crossing North America to see her, but her reaction still seemed somehow anticlimactic after the nature of our trip.

In fact, my hitchhiking mania made everything else seem anticlimactic, two dimensional, predictable, and drab. Over the next five years I continued to hit the road at every opportunity, keeping detailed records of every trip and logging the astonishing total of 82,000 miles. I crossed the continent on two other occasions, ventured deep into mountains and rain forests of the Pacific Northwest, and camped in two dozen national parks. Along the way I met a stunning assemblage of kind and vital people who, on several occasions, took me into their homes, caught up with the energy of my adolescent wanderlust. On my way to Acadia National Park, where the achingly blue Atlantic crashes against the desolate rocks and pine trees of the Maine coast, I got a ride to the picturesque town of Camden from a city councilman, whose wife and daughters fed and cared for me for three days. In the course of thousands of miles of travel I met a handful of lunatics and oddballs but never felt seriously threatened or abused. Unlike the doomed heroine of *A Streetcar Named Desire,* I found I could successfully rely on "the kindness of strangers."

This experience also protected me from the contemptuous and dismissive attitude of so many coastal elitists to what is famously known as "flyover country." I learned to love the South and the Midwest as much for the human landscape as the lyrical and natural beauty of the countryside. On one of my final hitchhiking trips before I gave up the adventures in my mid-twenties, I made it all the way to the rugged Porcupine Mountains of the ridiculously remote and sparsely inhabited Upper Peninsula of Michigan; until making that trip, I knew nothing of the robust Finnish-American culture that thrives in that rich, green North Woods outpost surrounded by the sparkling opulence of three Great Lakes. On the way back to Connecticut, I managed to get a rare ride with a burly, tattooed truck driver at a rest stop on the Ohio Turnpike. As we drove along, he popped a tape in his tape deck and to my utter amazement began to play the Schubert *Symphony in C Major.* I recognized the music and we began a two-hour conversation about the comparative virtues of Schubert and Beethoven. This guy had never finished high school, but he proudly owned his own home, sent his two kids to parochial school, and saved his money to buy tickets for the Cleveland Orchestra. The Ivy League snobs who loved to look down on "Middle America" loved music less meaningfully, and lived their lives less honorably, than this simultaneously ordinary and extraordinary blue-collar citizen.

The hitchhiking exploration not only separated me from the increasingly decadent and drug-soaked social life at Yale but also gave me a perspective that most classmates pointedly lacked. On a Saturday night in the fall of 1969, during my first semester of law school, I went out with a half-dozen fellow students to see the new movie sensation *Easy Rider*. I hated almost everything about the movie, and we argued about it over burgers and fries. I specifically remember that my classmate Hillary Rodham felt especially enthusiastic about what she understood to be the message of the film: when the violent rednecks, in their pick-up truck with its prominent gun rack, senselessly murder the two hippie bikers (Peter Fonda and Dennis Hopper), she thought the movie made a powerful statement about intolerance and conformity and repressed rage among the exploited yahoos of the American underclass. I insisted that the cruelty and viciousness depicted in the film bore no connection to the heartland or southern communities I knew, and suggested that the local townsfolk would be more likely to feed and welcome even long-haired visitors than to shoot them. The argument continued into the night with most of my friends defending the movie and attacking our "sick society," but I stubbornly held my ground. Despite their intelligence and sophistication and political enlightenment, I felt that they knew nothing about the back roads and rest stops and farm towns of the real America; but thanks to my education as a hitchhiker, I could say that I had been there.

Don't Turn Out Like John Kerry!

Yale of the mid-'60s expected every undergraduate to participate in one or more campus organizations. If you failed to involve yourself in some way in extracurricular life and concentrated solely on your course work, your faculty advisers as well as your fellow students would write you off as a hopeless grind and a lonely, one-dimensional loser. At the beginning of my Yale career, I considered getting involved with the *Yale Daily News,* which produced imposing campus figures (as the paper's all-powerful chairmen) like Joe Lieberman, who had graduated just before my arrival and was now a star at Yale Law School, and his pal and protégé Lanny Davis, who later became one of my best friends in politics and, twenty-five years after that, served our classmate Bill Clinton as White House counsel. But the prospect of grinding out dull stories about changing course requirements, faculty hiring disputes in the sociology department, or Bulldog odds to top the Ivy League in lacrosse looked singularly uninspiring and threatened to interfere with my hitchhiking priorities.

I was drawn instead to the Yale Political Union, the university debating society. The Political Union brought prominent speakers to campus nearly every week, including senators, governors, cabinet members, and journalistic stars. It also hosted in-house debates on political controversies of the day, asking members of the organization to cast solemn, on-the-record votes—as if the whole world waited breathlessly to see whether the august deliberative body known as the Yale Political Union would lend its all-important endorsement to the new Voting Rights Act or support President Johnson's Great Society spending.

These votes involved complex and Byzantine parliamentary maneuvering and shifting coalitions among the five formal parties in the PU—the relatively radical Party of the Left; the mainstream, earnest, Kennedyesque Liberal Party (my own political home at the time); the mushy moderates known as the Progressive Party; the fun-loving, party-hearty Conservatives (the largest single grouping in the union during my freshman year); and the effete, eccentric, bow-tied, neomonarchist, unapologetically anglophilic Party of the Right, whose chairman appeared at all meetings wearing a gold medallion on a red ribbon showing the "martyred" King Charles I. The master manipulator of the Political Union during my tenure was the affable, articulate, very tall, and unfailingly popular chairman of the Conservatives, a scholarship kid (at one point he worked a part-time job serving meals in his dining hall) from upstate New York named George Pataki. Among his most anonymous and least reliable backbenchers in the Conservative Party was another George, just one class ahead of me—George W. Bush. The future president paid his dues to the organization but made no significant impression on its members, due to his spotty attendance at PU meetings and his vastly more passionate commitment to his fraternity. The president of the union (selected after elaborate horse-trading among the various parties and their chairmen) was another nice-guy Conservative, J. Harvie Wilkinson of Virginia, with a moonlight-and-magnolias accent so thick that it inevitably sounded courtly and nostalgic. Wilkinson today serves as the distinguished chief judge of the United States Court of Appeals for the Fourth Circuit; he was reportedly near the top of the list for a potential Supreme Court appointment by his former classmate, George W. Bush.

The Yale Political Union represented a bizarre hot-house world of dueling egos and raw ambition, but one figure stood out above all others as the most revered and reviled puerile politico of them all: John Forbes

Kerry of Massachusetts. He had served as chairman of the Liberal Party, leading our faction to challenge traditional Conservative and POR (Party of the Right) dominance of the union, and had eventually negotiated his way into the presidency of the overall organization. His attempts to imitate the recently assassinated President Kennedy generated nearly universal ridicule—Kerry not only sported "JFK" cufflinks (they were, after all, his initials too), but spoke at this time with the jabbing forefinger of his idol, and with his left-hand inserted in the side pocket of his blazer or suit jacket, just like the late president. He also arranged his perfectly groomed hair in the precise style of the male members of the Bay State's leading family, as if he might be ready at any moment to join Senators Teddy and Bobby as a long-lost brother.

The one Kennedy characteristic that Kerry couldn't come close to replicating involved their sparkling wit and the twinkle in their *authentically* Irish eyes (Kerry himself bears no ancestral connection with the Auld Sod, despite his pretensions). With his towering height, long face, deep voice, and preposterously ponderous manner, he always seemed like one of those joyless, ceaselessly striving "future leaders of America" who calculated every friendship, every seating arrangement in the dining hall, for maximum advantage. Everyone knew that he would one day run for president of the United States, and he seemed to strain against the cruel constitutional requirement that would force him to wait till age thirty for his first race for the Senate from Massachusetts.

After a few months of enthusiastic participation in Political Union debates, I discovered that the Liberal Party's leaders had selected me as one of the three most promising freshmen to be accorded the ultimate honor: a private audience with the Great Kerry. In his senior year, he had formally retired from the union to concentrate on the mysterious, prestigious secret society Skull and Bones (which drew only fifteen members each year), but he still cared enough about the Liberals and their future to try to encourage their most committed new recruits. I vividly remember every detail of our meeting: with JFK seated behind a desk in his dorm room like a putative president, wearing a powder blue shirt with immaculate white collar and cuffs, a royal blue tie with white polka dots, and his hands crossed authoritatively on the desk in front of him. He droned on in portentous tones and at appalling length about the way the Liberal Party and the PU would enrich our lives and the possibility—nay, the virtual certainty—that if we worked with single-minded intensity we might one day rise to the unspeakably glorious heights of party chairmanship and union-wide office that he, the Great Kerry, had achieved. During the course of the one-way conversation he made no attempt to learn anything at all about the three of us—where we called home, what we planned to study, nothing. We were, after all, lowly freshmen and JFK represented the dizziest heights of senior class achievement. The entire nature of the encounter seemed designed to make a lasting impression (it most certainly did that) and to underline Kerry's present and future greatness.

Meeting him again after thirty-five years at the 2000 Democratic Convention in Los Angeles, I was struck by how little his arrogant attitude had changed. Most politicians manage to project at least some suggestion of superficial conviviality and warmth, but John Kerry remains uniquely frosty, haughty, and full of himself. Many biographical sources try to suggest that his preternatural seriousness stems from his service in Vietnam, which put an abrupt end to his carefree youth and produced his gloomy, haunted, sepulchral personality. Of course, I encountered the future politico as a Yale undergraduate, months before he'd even enlisted in the Navy, and I can attest to the fact that his dour, pompous mien had already reached full flower. I give no credence to the notion that the war in Southeast Asia destroyed his youthful joy and innocence because it's hard to imagine that the John F. Kerry I met through the Political Union had ever been joyous, innocent, or youthful.

And that weighty, arrogant attitude on the part of so many of the posturing princes and potentates of the PU led to my ultimate disillusionment with the organization. I worked hard to advance my own stock in the Liberal Party—spending countless hours stuffing envelopes, folding leaflets, and writing articles and drawing political cartoons for the party newsletter (incongruously called *The Libertarian*). I also served as an official party "whip," calling our members from a master list to coax them into attending union debates, and eventually was elected chief whip, just two notches below party chairman. I wanted to lead our faction in a more innovative, less conventional and predictable direction and ruffled many feathers with my battle to get the Liberal Party to endorse William F. Buckley for mayor of New York City in his 1965 campaign. I wish I could claim that this gesture represented some early precursor of conservative consciousness, but it essentially was an attempt at attention grabbing. I argued that despite his right-wing positions (as candidate of the splinter Conservative Party in New York), Buckley provided the only chance to shake up the city's corrupt political machine. To my astonishment and delight, we came within a handful of votes of orchestrating an official endorsement by the Yale Liberal Party of Yale's most celebrated conservative son—a caper which Mr. Buckley, who closely followed all developments at his alma mater, reportedly found highly amusing.

By the end of freshman year, however, my career in sandbox politics had ceased to amuse *me*. The heavy time commitments required by my PU responsibilities not only detracted from my course work but, far more importantly, limited my hitchhiking possibilities. Shortly after assuming my post as chief whip of the Liberals, I participated in a soul-searching, all-night conversation with my counterpart in the Progressive Party, and by the time we went down to breakfast we had decided we would both resign. To strengthen our resolve, we paced around the lovely gothic courtyard of Branford College repeating the same determined mantra: "We can't turn out like John Kerry! We can't turn out like John Kerry!" It wasn't that he came across as a bad guy, exactly, but rather that he perfectly and painfully exemplified a Political Union hack that seemed dry, bloodless, pretentious, old, and stuffy before his time. Never mind the fact that he had gotten "tapped" for Skull and Bones and graduated as one of the biggest of big men on the Yale campus. In our ardently adolescent eyes, the defiant chant "We can't turn out like John Kerry!" represented an undergraduate equivalent of Peter Pan's declaration "I won't grow up!"—expressing our refusal to walk the respectable and materially rewarding pathways of the establishment.

I not only resigned my party office but quit the union altogether. As a sophomore, I decided to devote part of the time I saved to a volunteer program for inner-city kids called the U.S. Grant Foundation. Three afternoons a week I tutored a class of a half-dozen boys of middle school age, nearly all of them impoverished and African-American. While I had been too young for "Freedom Rides" or voter registration projects in the South at the height of the civil rights movement, U.S. Grant gave me a sense of belated participation in the nationwide drive for social justice given eloquent expression by Dr. Martin Luther King. I connected instantly and instinctively with the kids assigned to me—some of them the same ages as my little brothers at home—and discovered the exhilaration and satisfaction of teaching. This work appealed to me so powerfully that I remained engaged as a volunteer tutor for the next three years and also devoted two full summers to intensive, immersion programs designed to help needy students prepare for college.

In retrospect, these efforts encouraged a distinctly patronizing, missionary attitude—with all-knowing Yalies making themselves available to inspire and ennoble the less fortunate through their enlightened example. Despite our privileged academic status, we never had all the answers we thought we had, nor were our underprivileged charges nearly as helpless or hopeless as we believed. In terms of common sense, street smarts, and authentic energy, the students had much to teach their teachers. Nevertheless, no one could deny the enhanced confidence and improved skills which these programs fostered, or the sense of gratitude which the children expressed to us on many occasions. Instead of spending my time making unwelcome phone calls to get members of the Liberal Party to attend a totally meaningless debate on the recognition of Red China, I could take pride in the achievements of my prize pupil Jacob Elder with his round, sweet, beaming face, as he vastly improved his report card in the eighth grade. In a sense, we may have inspired each other, since my own grades also shot up and continued an inexorable rise the further I moved away from the stifling, rejected world of John Kerry and preening, self-important politics.

The 1960s Counterculture Promoted
Stupidity and Self-Destruction

The drug culture arrived at Yale with such abrupt, instantaneous impact that the campus transformation amounted to an earthquake rather than a revolution. Within a few weeks near the end of 1966, the corrupt, all-conquering "new consciousness" swept aside all pockets of resistance. At the opening of that academic season (my sophomore year), I knew no one—literally no one—who smoked marijuana (or at least admitted to it); by the end of the spring semester, only a few stubborn holdouts rejected the allure of pot and self-exploration. Of course, definitive statistics would be impossible to compile, but my observations at the time suggest that in the course of a single school year between '66 and '67, at least 90 percent of the student body experienced illegal drugs for the first time—and the majority of those experimenters became regular users.

Overnight, beer kegs and fraternity mixers became passé, while preppy partygoers morphed themselves into dazed dopers, complete with the appropriate switch in wardrobe and hairstyles. The startlingly swift transformation recalled one of those movies where black-and-white film stock suddenly gives way to Technicolor—as in *The Wizard of Oz* or, more to the point, *Pleasantville*—except for the fact that the new weed-infested, psychedelic Yale actually proved more monochromatic and conformist than the old place. Those who most eagerly embraced the new lust for mind-bending recreation also learned to speak the same oddly inflected language, to listen to the same music, to parrot the same pseudo-philosophical conclusions, and to post the same splashy, hallucinatory posters on their dorm room walls.

In retrospect, the mystifying speed of this conquest probably had less to do with news from Vietnam or revolutionary trends in rock 'n' roll than with mundane questions of marketing and distribution. Eager entrepreneurs managed to set up for the first time a reliable network for the importation, dissemination, and sale of major quantities of grass and psychedelics (particularly LSD) in New Haven: the supply (at surprisingly modest prices) helped to create the demand, rather than the other way around. The druggie demimonde developed its foothold at Yale thanks in large part to guerilla marketing by a handful of enthusiasts who pursued their goals with evangelical fervor, convening the Ivy League, psychedelic equivalent of Tupperware parties to quickly expand their market base.

Many '60s survivors from other campuses and neighborhoods across the country have recalled similar experiences with the seemingly instant introduction of the pot pestilence and its attendant inanities. Of course, most such first-person participants look back on their drug-induced detours with altogether inappropriate nostalgia, nursing their retroactive self-image as intrepid voyagers on uncharted seas of discovery. The now-aging adventurers of the Age of Aquarius might more productively consider the possibility that they were consumer dupes of an exploitative scheme, the stoned, stupefied pawns of some distinctly unsavory forces that almost certainly included organized crime at the highest levels.

At the time, however, most of the best minds I knew embraced their experiments with marijuana, LSD, and other mind-altering substances as an expression of intellectual curiosity and personal courage. Fortunately, I remained an incurable coward: I didn't even drink and heartily disliked the taste of beer, so that I felt no attraction at all to the new forms of intoxication that involved the added excitement of illegality. To me, even the language of the new culture sounded damaging and distinctly unattractive: "getting stoned" implied brain damage, as did "getting wasted," while "blowing your mind" suggested induced and irretrievable retardation. What ever happened to the sturdy old slogan, "A mind is a terrible thing to waste"?

My cohorts' indulgence led to every sort of outrage and abuse. On one occasion, a dormmate dropped acid with three friends on a cold winter night and registered such a negative reaction that he ran outside in a bare-foot, delusional state. I joined more than a half-dozen others in a desperate search for the poor guy, hoping to locate him before he encountered the police or else wound up as a frozen casualty in some grimy New Haven snow drift. Eventually we found him in a fetal position on a squash court, quivering, weeping, and begging for his parents' forgiveness. It took three of us to carry him to the Student Health Service, which had begun to develop considerable expertise in treating the frequent casualties from the battlefield of recreational drugs. The next day, at dinner in the dining hall, inhaling double and triple portions of the cafeteria food, he spoke enthu-siastically about the gorgeous, soaring, blue-orange visions of his LSD adventure and treated his briefly terrifying "bad trip" as a momentary inconvenience during an otherwise worthwhile experience.

The manic effusions of dopester dementia ultimately swept through every corner of the country, spreading far beyond the insulated confines of elite university campuses. In June of '67, when I went home to LA for a brief visit, I reconnected with one of my former high school debate part-ners. This particular clean-cut friend still favored neatly pressed pants, skinny belts, conservative short-sleeved shirts, and impeccably combed hair; he was one of the last people on earth I would have associated with marijuana mischief. Nevertheless, after he, with exaggerated reverence, sat me down to listen to the new Beatles album *Sgt. Pepper's Lonely Hearts Club Band*, he took a little wooden box out of his dresser, held up a pinch of what looked like oregano, and wordlessly offered me some grass. Six months later, I learned that he had been arrested by undercover narcotics agents on the campus of the University of California at Berkeley for selling tabs of LSD to literally hundreds of eager customers out of his bulging but neatly arranged attaché case. This unfortunate run-in with the law ruined his university career and cost his parents' many thousands in legal fees but bore the unexpected benefit (as we saw it at the time) of providing a crim-inal record that exempted him from the draft.

I saw many friends go through similar evolutions. Unable to share or fathom the general enthusiasm for pot, acid, mescaline, psilocybin, uppers, downers, 'shrooms, peyote, or cocaine (or for the drugged-out popular music that inevitably accompanied such indulgence), I retreated into my own fortress of defensive superiority, alienated from those classmates I liked best and admired most. My contrarian position produced an inevitable sense of isolation and loneliness. I made up my own version of the nostalgic old Sammy Fain song "Wedding Bells Are Breaking Up That Old Gang of Mine":

> *Now and then we meet again*
> *But they don't seem the same.*
> *Gee, I get a lonesome feeling*
> *When they get stoned all the time.*
> *Smoking dope is breaking up that old gang of mine.*

The pervasive drug culture did at least bring me one invaluable gift: provoking my first ever self-consciously conservative impulses. I applied this attitude to aesthetics rather than politics, but nonetheless reveled in my own notoriously reactionary posture. My friends and classmates listened to Jefferson Airplane and Cream, while I obsessed more than ever on the classical eighteenth- and nineteenth-century repertoire, even spending my afternoons working at minimum wage as a sales clerk at Cutler's Record Shop so I could acquire my first several hundred vinyl discs. The sophisticates who surrounded me eagerly championed experimental fiction by Barthelme and Pynchon, while I insisted on the immeasurable superiority of Tolstoy and Dickens. In the residential college suite that I shared with assorted druggies, I posted a sign in ornate gothic lettering above the door to my bedroom declaring, "You Are Now Entering the Nineteenth Century." In my wallet, I carried little pictures of Brahms, Tolstoy, and Prokofiev. "Because they are my real family," I pretentiously explained to anyone who cared to inquire about those forbidding faces. When I tried this line on my mother, she felt understandably hurt.

In addition to the reinforcement I received from music and books I also felt vastly strengthened by my relationship with Lynn, which had only grown more intense. The fact that we studied at opposite ends of the continent (she continued her work at UCLA) gave rise to an absurdly intense correspondence—we wrote to each other at least once a day—and marathon long-distance phone calls. I shared nothing about this relationship with my roommates or friends, feeling that their jaded and bawdy comments could only soil my pristine and perfect infatuation. I actually went to great lengths to hide the countless letters I wrote and received, and the elaborate packages of Mozart and Bach records I sent to California in order to share—or, more accurately, impose—my aesthetic passions on the woman I loved. She responded eagerly, and she actively encouraged my contempt for the countercultural crap that surrounded us both. In mutually supportive snobbishness, we shared and amplified our respective sense of exile from our surroundings.

During my senior year, I made my one fateful (though not fatal) compromise with the continually encroaching drug culture. Though I majored in American history, I had pursued my literary ambitions by taking every available creative writing class at Yale College and earned the right to get independent study credit for completing a novel in my final year. I simultaneously qualified for the writing seminar conducted by the legendary Robert Penn Warren (known as "Red" to his friends and favorite students), the acclaimed author of *All the King's Men* and later poet laureate of the United States. My own novelistic output—a gelatinous, unplotted outpouring of undergraduate angst called *This Time Around*—hardly merited my own time and energy, let alone serious consideration by the great Red Warren. Nevertheless, he encouraged me (and eventually recommended me to his New York agent) but was especially critical of the central sequence of my project, which described a disastrous pot party in which the protagonist goes through a melodramatic breakdown. In his slightly hoarse Old South growl, Professor Warren commented that the rest of my book had a sense of immediacy and authenticity but when it came to describing drugs, I didn't seem to know what I was talking about. My independent study adviser strongly agreed, arguing that the entire, elaborately choreographed pot party chapter (which I had labored for months to create) was so feeble that it deserved ruthless elimination.

Unwilling to admit defeat in my attempt at writing about the doper indulgence that I hated, I resolved to gain the experience that I lacked and to make one more try at more convincing description. My adviser explicitly endorsed that idea (as most faculty members either approved of or were indifferent to drug use) and I announced my intention to my friends to smoke pot on one occasion only for the sake of literary immortality. They celebrated this news, all but certain that after a single experience getting high I would surrender forever to the clutches of demon weed. The great occasion brought out a half-dozen classmates, who eagerly provided the illegal herb, the background sitar music, and a wealth of helpful hints to maximize the impact of the experiment. For two hours, under intense tutelage, I made a determined effort to get high but to my intense embarrassment experienced not the slightest change in consciousness. My many mentors insisted that I had failed to retain the smoke in my lungs in the requisite manner; as a nonsmoker, I erupted in coughing fits with every attempt to swallow the pungent fumes.

As it turned out, I didn't meet Bill Clinton till a year and a half later, but this experience gave me a distinctive insight into the future president. Despite the Hollywood images that suggested that just a few puffs on a marijuana joint would send any imbiber into ecstasy, I learned from my one personal experience with the stuff that it is indeed possible to make an attempt—even a concerted attempt—to use it and remain untouched. In other words, despite all of my strenuously expressed contempt for President Clinton's prominent public prevarications, I felt uniquely sympathetic to one of them: when it came to marijuana, I knew what it meant to have smoked but not inhaled.

You Cannot Escape History

In a sense I grew up with the Vietnam War. Even as a junior in high school, I had been aware of the conflict as a minor, distant struggle involving a few American advisers and an Asian ally of the United States. In the presidential election of 1964, part of my passionate preference for Lyndon Johnson involved his solemn declaration that "I seek no wider war" and his promise to bring American boys home. By the time I arrived at Yale in September of '65, of course, LBJ had greatly expanded the U.S. role. But with campus life mostly isolated from the increasingly brutal realities of the war—the college deferment provided protection from the draft for all those who maintained satisfactory grades at a recognized university—student body support for the administration's Vietnam policy remained high. In February 1966, more than two-thirds of Yale students polled (including myself) favored a continuation of LBJ's war policy; only 10 percent preferred American withdrawal. The largest demonstration that academic year took place on Beinecke Plaza—to condemn the excesses of the fledgling antiwar movement. At the time John Kerry graduated, in June of '66, he was hardly alone in committing himself to military service. As *News-*

week reported some thirty-eight years later, "his closest friends in Skull and Bones, the Yale senior society for the best and the brightest, were signing up."

During my first two years, I tried my best to avoid thinking about the war or its political ramifications, preoccupied with my love letters to Lynn, my afternoon job at the record shop, my inner-city tutoring, my continued hitchhiking adventures (including a four-thousand-mile trek on the Trans-Canada Highway), and even occasional class work. Having abandoned the Political Union, I paid no attention whatever to the elections of 1966, in which Republicans exploited disillusionment with LBJ to gain forty-seven seats in the House of Representatives and a mediocre movie actor named Reagan won a landslide gubernatorial victory back home in California.

During my sophomore year, the mood of the campus changed radically and permanently. In part, the sudden invasion by the drug culture encouraged a more rebellious attitude, which quickly produced significant changes in day-to-day campus life. In response to sudden student pressure, the university abruptly dropped its time-honored coat-and-tie rule—which had mandated that in order to receive dining hall service anywhere at Yale for any meal (including breakfast), students must wear jacket and tie. Within days, the guys who stubbornly favored the timeless preppie look, with their blazers, striped ties, and loafers, became a distinct minority on campus—almost an endangered species—engulfed by a muddy tide of soiled sweatshirts, scruffy leather jackets, or neohippie foppery.

Meanwhile, the university chaplain, Reverend William Sloane Coffin, made national headlines when the Justice Department decided to prosecute him (along with four other individuals, including the celebrated baby doctor Benjamin Spock) for conspiracy in counseling resistance to the Vietnam draft. Immediately, Coffin achieved greater influence and prominence than ever before and even students who might otherwise never attend Sunday morning services at grand, high-Victorian Battell Chapel now came out to hear his fiery antiwar sermons. At the time, I had developed neither passion nor curiosity for religious life and never participated in Jewish services, but along with other disaffiliated or agnostic kids I woke up on Sunday mornings to hear Coffin's spellbinding leftist rants.

I also sought out the beefy Presbyterian clergyman for private conversation on political and theological issues. The warm, gruff, good-humored, and unfailingly accessible Coffin made no effort whatever to lead me toward Christianity but presented his dire, Manichean vision of contemporary America in the most persuasive, even seductive terms. Pointing to the urban riots that had scarred so many American inner cities and to the rising tide of antiwar activism on campuses, he warned of the likelihood of full-scale revolution—complete with violent pitched battles in the streets. In this coming conflict, the forces of racial justice, rebellion, and enlightenment might stand little chance of success, but with bloodshed on the barricades, people of conscience and faith could hardly remain disengaged.

The sense of approaching apocalypse intensified enormously with the Selective Service System's announcement that students would no longer receive draft deferments for graduate and professional school. This changed everything for the students of the era, forcing us to confront the war more personally, more painfully than before. The traditional student deferment policy had protected the ivory tower atmosphere of the university, keeping us far removed from the raging conflict in Southeast Asia and other unpleasant aspects of the "real world." The new rules meant that we could not blithely move on to one graduate program or another after graduation to keep the military at a distance. Only medical students and divinity students would remain exempt from their armed forces obligations. Naturally, tens of thousands of applicants discovered new enthusiasm for healing or holy careers. (Most historians of religion in America trace the sharp leftward tilt in most denominations to the draft-avoidance strategies that soon filled seminaries and divinity schools beyond capacity.)

The looming draft pushed nearly all university campuses in an impassioned antiwar direction. Contrary to self-serving Baby Boomer mythology, our opposition to the war didn't arise out of idealism, independent thinking, or admirable compassion for Vietnamese peasants. Naked self-interest unmistakably drove the peace movement, as it has energized all powerful political initiatives since the dawn of history. For college students of the late 1960s, our strident opposition to the war didn't inspire our overriding determination to shun military service; rather, our overriding determination to shun military service inspired our strident opposition to the war. Those who question this analysis should consider the fact that the mass peace movement abruptly died at the very moment Richard Nixon stopped drafting people into combat in December 1971. In Southeast Asia the war raged on for four more years (and included the devastating Christmas bombing of December '72), but on the suddenly draft-free college campuses, the organized protest all but evaporated.

As my thoughts turned more and more to the war, I found myself listening to, and discomfited by, one particularly melodramatic piece by my old favorite, Aaron Copland. "The Lincoln Portrait," written in 1942 in a spirit of earnest wartime patriotism, grabs instant attention with the composer's stentorian, heroic style, followed by a bit of folksy and nostalgic Americana, and then—over a gripping orchestral background—the stirring words of the sixteenth president:

> My fellow citizens, we cannot escape history. We of this Congress and this administration will be remembered in spite of ourselves. No personal significance or insignificance can spare one or another of us. The fiery trial through which we pass will light us down, in honor or dishonor, to the latest generation. We—even we here—hold the power and bear the responsibility.

I played this music and recitation again and again on my little Zenith portable stereo. I realized that the stresses and bitterness of the Vietnam era—however horrifying they seemed to me—couldn't compare to the epochal struggle and sacrifice of the War Between the States. Nevertheless, the themes of Copland's piece and Lincoln's words spoke to me directly, with their sense of ordinary people trapped by extraordinary events, pursued by huge forces beyond their control, despite any "personal significance or insignificance."

In the spring of 1967, I occasionally joined the dozen or so true believers who attended one-hour silent vigils for peace on the New Haven Green sponsored by the local Quaker community. The vigils brought together university students plus a few middle-aged (and even elderly) "townies," spread out in a single line, holding signs condemning the administration war policy as we stared straight ahead with determined, silent faces at the midday crowds hurrying past. I knew this smug, gentle gesture accomplished nothing in the way of influencing opinion or applying political pressure, but the "witness for peace" at least delivered a sense of fellowship and engagement.

I became more engaged by an early meeting for the "Dump Johnson" movement at the Law School Auditorium in the fall of 1967. Allard Lowenstein, a bespectacled Yale Law graduate, former head of the National Students Association, and famous civil rights organizer in Mississippi, stood before the spotty crowd with his ill-fitting jacket, unkempt, thinning hair, and loose tie askew to deliver a speech of soaring power and inspirational impact. He argued against despair, nihilism, or violent radicalism, suggesting instead that our conventional involvement in the political process could deny Lyndon Johnson the Democratic nomination and bring the war to an end. I joined with about a dozen other members of the energized audience to surround Lowenstein after his talk like eager groupies demanding a piece of a singularly unglamorous but undeniably fascinating rock star. We went out to a local greasy spoon and listened with rapt attention as the visiting guru outlined his far-fetched but exhilarating scheme to unseat a president. Over the next four years I heard Al Lowenstein speak on scores of occasions (particularly when I worked on his congressional campaign) and to this day he remains the most spectacularly gifted, most consistently electrifying orator I have ever heard, despite his sloppy appearance.

The Dump Johnson cause appealed to me because it offered a unique fusion of the gestural antiwar protests that had become trendy at Yale, with the Democratic Party political mechanics that had always fascinated me. Lowenstein's hard-headed prescription for persuading voters within the system made far more sense than Reverend Coffin's end-of-the-world visions of race war and revolution. The "New Politics" offered by Dump Johnson generated new energy in November, when Senator Eugene McCarthy of Minnesota announced that he would challenge the president who had been elected in a landslide just three years before. Volunteering whenever possible for menial tasks in the McCarthy campaign, I felt delighted to find a middle course between the antiwar radicals who advocated draft resistance along with system-shattering civil disobedience and the apathetic campus crowds that worried only about partying or getting high.

At first, no one expected any success for the silver-haired, professorial McCarthy in his quixotic quest—not in New Hampshire, not anywhere else. But distant events changed everything in the late winter of '68. In

February, our North Vietnamese adversaries launched a massive, well-coordinated offensive on their lunar new year, Tet, and the resulting television images destroyed public faith in the Johnson administration's happy-talk pronouncements about progress on the battlefield. Historians now conclude that the Tet Offensive actually represented a military disaster for the Communist forces—the North Vietnamese gains were short-lived, and their losses were devastating—but the televised images of the offensive demoralized public opinion at home.

While most Americans watched the carnage and the determined enemy assaults with horror, some antiwar radicals on campus celebrated every U.S. setback. I remember a small group of smug, scruffy, shaggy-haired, leftist dopers who gathered every evening around the TV set in the Branford College Common Room and laughed, clapped, and cheered over the news of heavy American casualties and North Vietnamese advances. One night I got into a nasty, pushing-and-shoving argument (broken up by more reasonable bystanders), as I condemned their callous and snotty stupidity. They insisted that every dead GI, every wrecked plane or helicopter, would bring a quicker end to the war and a defeat for American imperialism.

A few days later (February 27), a big crowd gathered around that same TV set to watch a much-hyped special report from the universally admired CBS anchor man, Walter Cronkite. The title, "Who, What, When, Where, Why: Report from Vietnam by Walter Cronkite," promised an authoritative take on the mystifying events in Southeast Asia. The show opened with the beloved correspondent standing in front of a devastated location halfway around the world. "These ruins are in Saigon," he began, "capital and largest city of South Vietnam." After a series of depressing interviews and tours of the ravaged countryside, Cronkite concluded the show back behind his anchor desk in New York, offering conclusions that he described as "speculative, personal, and subjective"—but that nonetheless proved powerfully persuasive, coming from the Most Trusted Man in America. In what amounted to a direct assault on the Johnson administration, Cronkite solemnly intoned, "We have been too often disappointed by the optimism of the American leaders, both in Vietnam and Washington, to have faith any longer in the silver linings they find in the darkest clouds." He concluded, "It is increasingly clear to this reporter that the only rational way out will be to negotiate, not as victors, but as an honorable people who lived up to their pledge to defend democracy, and did the best they could."

To me, this famous broadcast signaled the semiofficial acknowledgment that we had already lost the war. That conviction, and the overwhelmingly negative media coverage of hardships for our troops, did more to energize the McCarthy campaign than the thousands of college students who flocked to New Hampshire. Though the conventional wisdom holds that the student volunteers turned the tide of the primary, many of us who trekked to the frosty north spent most of our time hanging around headquarters, flirting with members of the opposite sex, and talking almost exclusively to one another rather than pounding the pavement and persuading voters. Even with the invasion of eager but unfocused collegiate campaigners, McCarthy failed to win a majority of votes in the Granite State—drawing a mere 23,280, or 42 percent, compared to 50 percent for President Johnson, who never campaigned in the state.

Nevertheless, the unexpected closeness of the New Hampshire vote amounted to a humiliating debacle for LBJ and the ultimate validation of the Dump Johnson movement—especially when Robert Kennedy, the late president's brother and the senator from New York, jumped into the race just four days after the New Hampshire primary. Thrilled by RFK's announcement, I saw no reason whatever to delay in switching my allegiance from McCarthy to Kennedy, a candidate who could actually beat Lyndon Johnson and win the White House. Yet most other McCarthy backers on Yale's campus greeted Bobby-Come-Lately's entrance into the race with disgust rather than celebration, attacking Kennedy as a ruthless, selfish leader of an old-fashioned political machine, unworthy of support from those who wanted to create a revolutionary "New Politics." These tender souls remained incurably immune to the application of electoral logic: by splitting the antiwar, anti-administration vote, McCarthy die-hards would succeed only in handing victory to the figure they despised, Lyndon Johnson. At a moment of moral crisis and political confrontation, they turned their fire on a leader who agreed with them on all major issues.

These maddening disputes in March of '68 represented my first-ever exposure to a deeply rooted division that appears in every corner of American politics: the fault line between purists and pragmatists. As both a youthful liberal and grown-up conservative, I've felt ferociously frustrated at arrogant ideologues who prefer gestures and poses to practical progress. Insisting on "voting their conscience," some throw away the sacred franchise on one irrelevant third (or fourth) party or another. During the breathlessly close presidential contest of 2000, for instance, 98,004 presumably sane conservatives voted for Howard Phillips of the Constitution Party (known on my radio show as the Constipation Party). What difference would it have made to the history of the Republic had the portly Mr. Phillips received, say, 68,004 votes or, for that matter, 128,004? Meanwhile, a few hundred ballots in Florida (or in desperately close New Mexico, Iowa, Oregon, New Hampshire, and Wisconsin) decided the outcome in the Electoral College. Stubborn, holier-than-thou ideologues love to cite the famous sound bite by Henry Clay ("I would rather be right than be president") without recognizing that this trimming politician (known, after all, as "The Great Compromiser") offered these words as the ultimate sour grapes long after he'd lost his third presidential contest. Anyone with even a nodding acquaintance with history or common sense understands that you advance your political cause by winning, rather than losing, elections. This simple proposition remained obvious to me in the face of smirking McCarthyite recalcitrance in 1968—and continues to trump the illogic of puffed-up purists among the Naderites, Buchananites, and Losertarians of our own day.

Keeping in mind the Lincolnian exhortation that "we cannot escape history," I tried to volunteer for Robert Kennedy. But before I could get through to the hectic, late-starting campaign, President Johnson made a dramatic announcement in a nationally televised Sunday night address. First he declared a partial bombing halt in Vietnam and promised to pursue peace negotiations with our enemies—the same course advocated by Kennedy and McCarthy (and Walter Cronkite). Then the president dramatically paused, looked out to the nation, and made a declaration that shocked even his closest associates. "Fifty-two months and ten days ago," he drawled, "in a moment of tragedy and trauma, the duties of this office fell upon me. I have concluded that I should not permit the presidency to become involved in the partisan divisions that are developing in this political year. Accordingly, I shall not seek, and I will not accept, the nomination of my party for another term as your president."

I was watching the speech in the crowded Branford Common Room, and after a few seconds of shocked silence, my fellow students and I exploded in cheers. Yalies hugged one another, rushed out onto campus quads to dance and yell, then spontaneously flowed together from a dozen directions onto the New Haven Green. Someone thought to bring along a big American flag, waving it triumphantly, and townie kids lit random firecrackers in celebration. Patriotic songs filled the damp spring air, as we repeated "Glory, Glory Hallelujah!" over and over again to the point of painful hoarseness.

Four days later, on Thursday night, April 4, hundreds of us returned to the same spot for a very different demonstration: this time holding lit candles in the drizzle, softly singing "We Shall Overcome," and reacting to the awful news of the assassination of Dr. Martin Luther King. Later that night, New Haven's black neighborhoods (like inner-city districts in three dozen other cities) exploded in riots. We heard police sirens and climbed one of the towers in our residential college, watching the flames less than two miles away. If anything, the King assassination and the national agony that followed it only intensified my commitment to Kennedy's candidacy: in contrast to the lily white, suburban cast of the McCarthy campaign, the senator from New York generated passionate support from the black community and from Mexican Americans (who thrilled to RFK's early support for farm workers leader Cesar Chavez). After three years of urban unrest and rising violence (and a national Riot Commission that blamed the destruction on white racism), Bobby's presidential crusade promised the sort of messianic, multiracial brotherhood that appealed to me in the tutoring programs for which I volunteered.

With decisive and dramatic primary battles unfolding far to the west, I found it difficult to stay focused on my life in New Haven. In a sense, romance collided with political priorities, since the decisive confrontation of the nomination fight had been scheduled for June 4 in California—where Lynn was fretting under the pressure of our long-distance relationship. I devised a plan to escape from New Haven a month early and to return to LA for the simultaneous purpose of nurturing my love life and campaigning for Robert Kennedy in the California primary. Naturally, I told my professors and my deans only of my determination to volunteer in the presidential campaign, and even though they nearly all supported McCarthy (along with the rest of the academic intelligentsia), they maintained enough respect for the other "peace candidate" to facilitate my scheme. In just two weeks, I completed my course work to the satisfaction of university authorities.

I flew home to Los Angeles at the end of April, and when I first saw Lynn, we drove to a park near my parents' home in her battered VW bug. When I tried to embrace her, she insisted we needed to talk. I then listened in stunned silence as she unceremoniously dumped me, declaring her immediate, unilateral, and irrevocable termination of the absurdly sentimental relationship we had sustained for nearly three years. She felt that at age nineteen, I hardly counted as a candidate for marriage (especially since my parents so obviously frowned on any match with a non-Jewish girl) while she, at age twenty-one, wanted to get on with her life. And she did. A few months after our breakup, she reconnected with a much-older gentleman she had previously met in Europe—a West German diplomat with a Heidelberg degree, an aristocratic pedigree, financial resources, and a dueling scar. They married just weeks after her college graduation, and she went on to the stylish, globe-trotting, sophisticated "vagabond" life that I never could have provided.

The night that we parted, she seemed so incomparably desirable that I felt with sickening certainty that some such glamorous fate awaited her, while I predicted a life of loneliness and desolation for myself. Exhausted and humiliated, I spent the next two days on a sofa in the den of my parents' home with the blankets pulled up over my head. My father rested alongside me in a hospital bed—immobilized with a back injury after a serious traffic accident, hoping that traction would allow him to avoid surgery to his spinal column. Very obviously, he had suffered the more serious injury, yet he managed to offer comfort to my shattered pride. He persuaded me to get up off the couch, borrow his car (since I had recently—and finally—secured a driver's license), and make my way to Kennedy headquarters to get involved in the campaign, which was, after all, my official excuse for leaving school early.

I spent the next month working eighteen-hour days for the Kennedy cause. I compared myself to a volunteer for the French Foreign Legion—impelled by the proverbial broken heart to dashing service in a remote corner of the Empire (LA felt appropriately remote from New Haven). In fact, the "Students for Kennedy" operation offered prompt and potent salve for my wounded ego. I immediately took responsibility for supervising and recruiting other volunteers as we spent day and night laboring over phone banks to make the calls which, we believed, might determine the outcome of the California primary. Using thick lists of all the registered Democrats in West Los Angeles, we were trying to identify likely Kennedy voters or at least those leaning toward RFK—people our get-out-the-vote volunteers could target on primary day.

Though I was working for a Kennedy, I felt the odd exhilaration of fighting for an underdog, since the conventional wisdom held that even if RFK swept every primary, Vice President Hubert Humphrey might still win the nomination because the party bosses who controlled the delegates strongly favored the establishment candidate. More pressingly, McCarthy won a startling upset victory in the Oregon primary, just one week before the California showdown. Many of my fellow campaign loyalists wept openly at the Oregon returns and spoke in melodramatic terms of the "death of the dream." When Kennedy promised he would quit the race if McCarthy won another victory in California, we knew that our primary would decide the fate of the entire campaign.

Undistracted by school or personal entanglements, I could devote all my time to the campaign. I rose quickly in the ranks and soon was dividing my time between our "Students for Kennedy" office in Westwood and the big statewide headquarters downtown. In that bustling nerve center of the campaign high command (which officials of the national campaign regularly blew through), I got word that after the primary the campaign brass would find a place for me on the permanent staff, helping set up our on-the-ground logistics for the upcoming Democratic National Convention in Chicago. I felt intoxicated with the all-consuming process of making history.

When I came home each night in the small hours of the morning, I spent some time talking to my father—still in traction on his hospital bed in the den—sharing details, letting him live my campaign adventure vicariously. He had recently gone through his own setbacks—not just the back injury, but the single biggest defeat of his otherwise triumphal scientific career. He had worked for NASA in the mid-'60s as chief designer of a celebrated ion wake experiment on the Gemini Spacecraft, and when NASA launched a new Scientist Astronaut program, he made it through several cuts to a final group of twenty candidates out of more than five thousand original applicants (all of them Ph.D.'s and MD's). My own irrepressible dad, the barrel maker's son from South Philly, believed he might become the first Jewish astronaut. Unfortunately, his mouth did him in: an extensive dental exam revealed minor gum recession, and NASA officials worried that he might lose teeth if he went into space. In October of '67, my father got the word personally from Alan Shepard—America's first man in space—that he had been dropped from the program. Seven months later, he hadn't fully recovered from his disappointment, and the whole family understood that his time in traction represented a period of emotional as well as physical healing. Our late-night talks about the Kennedy campaign seemed to play a part in that process: for the first time, my dad seemed to look at elements of my young life as at least comparably exciting to the endeavors in his own.

His attention and my rising stock at headquarters meant that the self-pity and crippled confidence that my erstwhile girlfriend had imposed on me now dissolved almost entirely—especially as I began to capture adoring attention from two of my fellow volunteers. Debbie and Iris were best friends, a few years older than I was, and vastly more experienced when it came to social and sexual relationships. We started hanging out together, the three of us, and then at the end of long, exhausting campaign days I went out with each of them separately. Debbie was prettier—a pert, athletic blonde—more idealistic and emotional, and more interesting to me in the long run. Iris was smarter, sassier, and sexually more aggressive—in fact, she was the naughtiest, most free-spirited woman I had met to that time, often making jokes about the advantages of her thick, luxuriant, carefully painted lips. They each encouraged me in this odd simultaneous pursuit, and both determined to coddle and cuddle me to soothe the hurts left over from my breakup with Lynn (hurts which I lavishly described, of course). Powerfully attracted to both of them, I felt absolutely thrilled when Iris proposed that they would both be my dates at the party after the California primary—a grand celebration (so we intently hoped) at the shabby, sprawling, but storied Ambassador Hotel, home of the legendary Coconut Grove and locus of old Hollywood glamour going back to the 1930s. Both women teasingly promised that after the big public celebration we could go back to Iris's apartment for a private celebration, just the three of us—a night, they both hinted, I would never forget.

Of course, I pushed through primary day (beginning with a pep rally for volunteers at six in the morning) on a jet-stream of wild, feverish, libidinous expectation. The sexual revolution that everybody talked about had generally left me to one side—in part because I self-consciously looked down on all this reckless physical experimentation and instead concentrated on desperate, over-the-top, emotionally fraught romances. But now in the midst of this political warfare, feeling like a bone-weary soldier whose cause could collapse at any moment, I decided I might be entitled to the comfort of camp followers.

The activity on primary Tuesday proved frenetic to the point of hysteria, as I tried to instruct scores of volunteers (including new faces who showed up for the first time that day) on what they had to do. Trying to get the committed Kennedy voters we had identified in our previous phone calls out to the polls, I drove all over the Los Angeles basin, from East LA to Santa Monica to Crenshaw to Fairfax, shouting and hectoring, pleading and cajoling, doing my best to troubleshoot a vastly complicated deployment of preparations and personnel. We would do anything to make sure our supporters cast their votes; at one point late in the afternoon I deployed my limited Yiddish language skills to persuade elderly Jewish voters in Venice that they should interrupt their conversations, place their trust in a stranger, get into my car, and drive with me to the polling place to cast their votes for the next president of the United States.

As the sun sank toward the Pacific on that perfect June day, I finally made my way to the Ambassador Hotel. The crowds streaming toward the rambling old hotel were exhilarated, and it felt electrifying, joyous, to see the cross section of California—Mexican-Americans in brightly colored party dresses; blacks dressed in somber dark suits of dashikis; hippies with flowing hair, peasant shirts, and beads; elderly volunteers with canes and button-up sweaters, carrying "Kennedy" signs.

I met Debbie and Iris at a preappointed time and they both looked sensational, wearing sandals and bare legs and nearly matching, snug-fitting, thigh-high dresses—Debbie in dark blue, Iris in white. With a laughing girl on each arm, I felt my heart race. I also consumed several drinks (yeah, I was underage, but no one paid much attention on this gala, historic occasion) and began to feel pleasantly dizzy as the returns came in on the TV screens displayed everywhere around the Ambassador ballroom, which was jammed with more than fifteen hundred people. When various functionaries and campaign celebrities came to the podium, I lifted my dates one by one up on my shoulder so they could see the proceedings. Just feeling their thighs against my cheek amplified my sense of exhilaration and anticipation.

In the crowded room, we sweated and fretted as we monitored the vote count. According to the TV reports, early returns indicated a Kennedy victory in a close race, but the journalistic experts remained cautious and indecisive, and we anxiously awaited a definitive announcement. In that milling, swirling mass of humanity, I kept crossing paths with various friends and colleagues from the campaign, one of whom invited me—and my two dates—to a private party at the Factory, a very hot nightclub at the time. Senator Kennedy himself would be there, he said. Debbie and Iris hugged me tighter.

Shortly after 11 P.M., word spread that the senator was on his way to give his victory speech. We had beaten McCarthy, the television reported, 46 percent to 42 percent—an uncomfortably close margin—with 11 percent for an "uncommitted" pro-Humphrey slate. More people seemed to press into the ballroom, which rocked with chants of "We want Bobby! We want Bobby!" and then "R-F-K! R-F-K!" You could barely move with the density in that space. With Debbie and Iris in tow, I began to press and slither forward, trying to get closer to the podium so as to see Kennedy clearly when he came to speak.

Then he arrived, to explosive cheers and applause, looking small in the midst of a burly group of supporters and bodyguards, including the giant pro football player Roosevelt Grier. We stood no more than twenty feet from the podium. I lifted Iris to my shoulder to see more clearly. During one burst of applause, I shouted, "We love you, Bobby!" (you can hear my voice on the tapes of the occasion). I remember noting how pink and sunburned Kennedy looked—he had spent much of the day at the beach with his children. He began by congratulating Dodger pitcher Don Drysdale on setting a record with his sixth consecutive shutout. But baseball scores seemed like a distraction within our political bubble.

He spoke briefly, magnanimously, thanking all of us who had made victory possible, clearly relieved at a win—however narrow—that kept his campaign alive. He made a specific pitch for the McCarthy troops to join him in the days ahead, "not for myself, but for the cause and the ideas which moved you to begin this great popular movement." He concluded with a call for unity that transcended party or faction. "I think we can end the divisions in the United States," he said. "What I think is quite clear is that we can work together in the last analysis. . . . We are a great country, an unselfish country, and a compassionate country. And I intend to make that my basis for running over the period of the next few months." The crowd erupted in confident cheers. "So my thanks to all of you, and now it's on to Chicago and let's win there!"

He flashed a V-for-victory sign (which also counted as a peace sign in 1968) and walked away behind the podium, taking a short cut through the kitchen to go upstairs for a TV press conference before joining the private parties later on that night.

With that destination in mind, I echoed the candidate, flashing a V-for-victory sign to my companions. "Now it's on to the Factory," I said, "and let's win there!" We began pushing through the jammed ballroom to get to the parking lot so we could reach the nightclub ahead of the crowds. But then I heard some balloons popping behind the podium—several quick pops, right in a row—and then there was a woman's piercing scream and other voices crying, "Oh, no, no, no!" and "Not again! Not again!" Suddenly, everyone in the ballroom was moaning or screaming or gasping, with the sound joining into a single, frightening, animalistic roar—a wail that spread in a rising wave from the front of the crowd to the back, then echoing back again. Everyone knew, without being told. JFK had died less than five years before. An aura of danger and destiny, of risk and edge, had attached itself to Bobby's campaign from the beginning, simultaneously firing and frightening his crowds.

Now people wanted to flee the ballroom, instinctively recoiling from a place of horror, but hotel and law enforcement officials sealed the building—no one was allowed to go. With word spreading of multiple victims (four others had been wounded by the eight shots), rumors circulated about multiple shooters: no one wanted to make it easy for guilty conspirators to get away. The stunned campaign workers who had been celebrating only moments before now wandered through hallways, or collapsed on the floor, or straggled back into the ballroom to watch the latest bulletins on TV. A lady in a light blue dress came to the podium and spoke through a microphone, telling the crowd, "Senator Kennedy has been shot"—which everyone already knew—"but he's all right. He's wounded but it isn't serious. They've taken him to the hospital and they will be performing surgery." This produced applause, and an attempt at a cheer, but a mood of disbelief and doom clung to the shattered gathering like a foul odor. The television sets displayed around the room offered less comforting news. Kennedy had been shot in the head. The hospital offered no definitive word on his condition.

In that stifling atmosphere, we all looked for support—seeking out chairs or the overstuffed banquettes in the hallway, or sprawling on the musty carpeting, or leaning against the walls or one another. Weeping strangers hugged one another without exchanging words. Debbie cried openly, her makeup running down her cheeks. Iris hugged my arm tightly enough to cause pain.

We stayed in the Ambassador the entire night, less capable of understanding the situation than ordinary Americans who watched TV at home. The assassin with the odd double name—Sirhan Sirhan—remained a mystery. Some sources claimed that authorities wanted to question an unidentified stocky woman in "a polka dot dress," suspected as an accomplice of the killer. Through the power of suggestion, almost everyone vaguely remembered that they had seen such a figure in the course of the evening but no one knew where she had gone. Finally, with the clock showing five in the morning, they allowed us to stagger out of the building, with police taking names and addresses, checking IDs, of everyone who had been there. The latest reports indicated that the doctors had just operated on Senator Kennedy's brain, removing bullet fragments. Some broadcasters made it sound likely that he would survive, but none of the exhausted survivors from the hotel could bring themselves to believe it.

I parted from Debbie and Iris in the predawn chill; they drove home separately while I steered my parents' battered Mercury station wagon down deserted Wilshire Boulevard. It felt more appropriate, somehow, to creep along the shadowy surface streets, with the city still asleep on all sides, rather than injecting myself into the already quickening pulse of some fast-moving freeway. The sky faded from black to gray, with painterly touches of pink at the eastern horizon line behind me, hauntingly visible in the rearview mirror. With the stoplights looking unnaturally vivid in their explosions of red and green, I wearied of the repetitive news stories on the radio and switched to Top 40 music. That strange and obscenely popular Merrilee Rush song "Angel of the Morning" sounded oddly pertinent on my way home.

By the time I pulled into my parents' driveway, the sun had come up and kids were congregating to wait for their school buses. My mother, hysterically worried over my safety, embraced me fiercely when I walked through the door, then made a big breakfast that I didn't touch. I watched television in silence with my dad. No change in Kennedy's condition, but the grim faces of his spokesmen conveyed the ultimate outcome. My mother pleaded with me to sleep, but I couldn't.

My former girlfriend, Lynn, called before noon, assuming that I had been there at the hotel because she knew of my commitment to the campaign. She begged to see me, so I went over to her parents' house. Speaking in hushed, hoarse tones, I described everything that had happened to me in the weeks since we broke up. No one was home except us, with both her parents at work, and she insisted on embracing me. She took me into her bedroom, and when we hugged on the bed, she responded with sudden and startling heat and passion. To this day I don't understand why. She had expelled me from her life, she would soon marry someone else, and here I was, broken and exhausted and hopeless and confused. We did nothing, beyond holding each other and exchanging kisses on the cheek.

I went home and surrendered to my mother's food—other than the drinks at the Ambassador, I'd consumed nothing in the past thirty hours. I tried to read newspapers and magazines, with the TV providing a nonstop accompaniment. We waited for announcements on the senator's condition. Assuming the worst, I had no idea what I would do—the next day or for the rest of the summer. I no longer nurtured the dream of going to Chicago as part of the Kennedy campaign. How could we continue a campaign with a candidate who had been shot in the head? Finally, at nine at night I fell into a deep sleep after nearly forty hours of feverish wakefulness, collapsing on the couch in the den beside my father's hospital bed, as he continued monitoring the television set on low volume.

I awoke to the sounds of my father sobbing in the darkened room. It was two in the morning. "He's gone," my father said, in a high, wavering voice. "Bobby's gone. Oh, my God, our poor country!" I stood up from the couch and came over to hug him. I grabbed him fiercely at first, then more gently so as not to hurt his suffering back. We cried together.

"Dad, you know what I'm going to do?" I said after a while. "When I have a son, my first son, I'm going to name him after Bobby. I'm going to name him Robert Kennedy. I'm making that promise now, but I know I'll remember forever."

My father didn't object. In fact, he hugged me closer and seemed to be comforted by the notion of an unborn grandson anointed with a noble name.

Of course, when my real son finally entered this world some twenty-four years later, we called him Daniel Joshua and never even considered the name Robert. Or Kennedy. At the bris—the circumcision ceremony—I asked my dad if he remembered my long-ago promise, and he shrugged and laughed at the very idea that I'd name one of my children after one of the Kennedys. By that time, I'd become active in Republican politics and developed decidedly mixed feelings about my one-time hero as political figure and as a human being. I doubted whether he—whether we—had even been right about the war, which loomed as the all-important issue at the time. For all our fervent intentions, we can't freeze loyalties, values, and judgments for the future, any more than we can erase or alter passions of the past. History moves on, no matter how much we yearn to stay put, and can force us against our will to go along for the ride.

LESSON
13

Publicity Is Power—
and TV Changes Everything

I never saw Iris again after that night at the Ambassador, and I met Debbie only once, for coffee. After the assassination, whatever chemistry had once existed between us had vanished just as definitively as the political crusade that nourished it.

For several weeks, I refused to accept the brutal but obvious fact that the political movement to which I'd committed myself had died along with its candidate. With some other "Students for Kennedy" operatives, I took the lead in putting together a new national group called "Kennedy Students for a New America"—trying to maintain a separate organizational identity without merging into one of the other campaigns, which inspired little enthusiasm. We never endorsed a Democratic candidate, but I traveled to Chicago two months before the party's national gathering for a planning meeting of the National Coalition for an Open Convention. By this point the Hubert Humphrey nomination had become unstoppable, so we talked about plans for platform fights and principled last stands, hoping for an opportunity to rally around an obscure South Dakota senator named George McGovern who was considering offering himself as a new antiwar candidate. The coalition's endless meetings, full of self-important strategizing and puffed-up posturing, left me depressed, bored, and cynical. I knew, too, as everyone knew, that there would be chaos in the Chicago streets when the Democrats ultimately gathered in late August, and I wanted no part of this pointless apocalypse.

Instead I accepted an invitation to come back to New Haven for the summer to fill a vacancy in the U.S. Grant Foundation's tutoring program. In early September, however, Yale friends convinced me to "honor Bobby's memory" by getting involved in the upstart congressional campaign of Al Lowenstein, the Pied Piper of the Dump Johnson movement. Lowenstein had won the Democratic nomination in a middle-class Long Island district that tilted Republican, and his only hope for victory involved importing hundreds of foot soldiers, many of us veterans of the McCarthy or Kennedy campaigns. Gary Hart, the slick, efficient future senator and presidential candidate, served as one of Lowenstein's most trusted assistants and apologized to me (and nearly everyone else) for the haphazard, seemingly improvised nature of the campaign. But against all logic and expectations, Lowenstein won his congressional seat in a November election squeaker (with a margin of 2,600 votes). By that time, though, I had already abandoned the field and returned to New Haven for the beginning of my senior year.

Shortly after classes began, I threw myself into a very different sort of campaign that offered selfish satisfaction more than service to a cause. From the age of ten I'd been fascinated and entertained by NBC's weekly quiz show *GE College Bowl*, in which teams of four top students from America's colleges and universities competed with one another. At Palisades High School, I had competed in the high school equivalent, *Scholarquiz*, broadcast on the local CBS affiliate, leading the Pali High team to the Southern California championship. Since the launch of *GE College Bowl* in 1959, Yale and Harvard had refused to participate in the show, with these two prestigious powerhouses believing they had everything to lose and nothing to gain by sending teams to a TV studio to compete with less celebrated institutions. But NBC producers finally devised a way to overcome the schools' reluctance: rather than featuring teams that officially represented the two mighty universities, the show would invite special squads made up of staff members from their student newspapers, the *Yale Daily*

News and the *Harvard Crimson,* in a one-time-only face-off to be aired the weekend of the famous Yale-Harvard football game.

Though my only contributions to the *Yalie Daily* had come in the form of a few letters to the editor, I made the team because the leaders of the paper understood that the upcoming battle was too important to limit our team to actual student journalists and so allowed "ringers" from the university at large (and, as it turned out, our team of four featured no actual *Daily News* staff members). We spent weeks ruthlessly preparing for the grudge match against our ancient archrival (whose team included James K. Glassman, today a well-known economist, columnist, and author who's been a frequent guest on my radio show). The day before we traveled to New York for the broadcast, the Yale football team—considered one of the best in university history, with three future NFL pros—took its perfect record into a famous confrontation with Harvard, only to see its formidable lead squandered in the final minutes through onsides kicks and questionable calls. The resulting tie remains a subject of heartbreak, even tears, for alumni old enough to remember, so as we went into our *College Bowl* showdown, we felt overwhelming pressure to avenge the honor of the old school. And that we did: we crushed our rivals by a final margin of 230 to 80.

Along the way we displayed enough obnoxious cheek to persuade NBC that they'd been fortunate to only feature one show with Yale. During the "halftime" interviews with the host, Robert Earle, my teammate David Mannis responded to a question about his future plans by declaring his intention to become "an enlightened slum lord." I shouldered a special burden: one of my classmates had dared me to mention the word "moose" on national TV, and offered to pay me ten dollars for each time I managed to invoke the ungainly beast. When Mr. Earle inquired about my college major, I explained "that I'm completing a special major on moose—a moose program concentrating on the role of the moose, the image of moose, the deeper significance of moose in all of American culture." This drew disbelieving laughter and applause from the studio audience and earned me a cool fifty dollars—a not inconsiderable sum in 1968. In subsequent weeks, an assortment of random television viewers from around the country also sent me an eccentric collection of moose memorabilia—including porcelain statues, hand-painted china, wildlife photographs, miniature antlers, and even a campaign ribbon from Teddy Roosevelt's ill-fated Bull Moose campaign of 1912.

After the victory over Harvard, I emerged for the first time as a significant senior in a university full of ambitious and overachieving stars—if not quite a conquering hero, at least a campus celebrity. Television, I learned, quickly changes everything.

For one thing, the exposure made me a political player on every campus issue in a contentious year. Shortly after his congressional victory, Al Lowenstein visited campus to plead with both old and new friends to stand up against the violent extremists who threatened to take control of the antiwar movement. He denounced radical factions like the SDS—Students for a Democratic Society—that sanctioned confrontations with police and destruction of property and discredited all those who tried to work for peace. With uncanny acuity, Lowenstein predicted that the new president, Richard Nixon, would attempt to use the antisocial excesses of a few fringe groups to portray all his opponents as anti-American and pro-Communist. Al instilled in many of us a sense that the leftist creeps who chanted "Ho! Ho! Ho Chi Minh! NLF is gonna win!" (NLF stood for the National Liberation Front, the Communist guerillas in Vietnam) represented a political enemy every bit as dangerous as any right-winger.

The first opportunity to follow through on Al's exhortations came on the occasion of our Senior Class Dinner. Through some appalling lapse in judgment, the committee planning this event had scheduled as our featured speaker McGeorge Bundy, the former national security adviser under both Kennedy and Johnson, and one of the most prominent architects of a war nearly all of us opposed. The SDS on campus—a group of nylon-jacketed, relentless, rodent-faced ideologues who endlessly churned out mimeographed Marxist manifestos with tiny, crowded lettering—threatened to disrupt the occasion with violence, if necessary. Another organization, the A.H.C.T.T.F.A.Mc.B., or Ad Hoc Committee to Throw Food at McGeorge Bundy, placed posters all over campus that promised a more direct response. I became involved as the most visible leader of a group that represented the middle road of campus opinion—guys who wanted to express disapproval of Bundy's selection but not to wreck the entire occasion. Fortunately, our well-publicized efforts managed to co-opt the more radical elements, who grudgingly supported the gesture we planned.

At the dinner, we waited till the moment Bundy got up to speak, at which point I walked to the front of the room and shouted out our prepared statement: "We leave this dinner not as a sign of disrespect or rudeness to Mr. Bundy, but as an expression of our deep opposition to a war that is tearing apart our beloved country." I then grabbed the American flag from its stand beside the podium and led more than a hundred classmates out of the hall, with all of us melodramatically singing "The Battle Hymn of the Republic." The befuddled, bespectacled Bundy actually praised us to the discomfited crowd that remained behind. According to newspaper accounts, he generously declared that "this protest, so sincerely felt, is entirely proper and an appropriate civil action." Television cameras captured the whole silly show (which, despite Bundy's endorsement, feels idiotically *inappropriate* in recollection) while newspapers fretted over the first ever "mass walkout" at a Yale senior dinner.

This episode cast me in the unaccustomed and increasingly uncomfortable role of an overpublicized leader of on-campus protest. I wanted to concentrate on *This Time Around*, my novel, but my prominence virtually commanded my involvement in every aspect of the agitation that roiled the university community. According to the national press, Yale stood as a shining example of moderation and sanity at a time of academic turmoil and destruction. Both Harvard and Columbia had experienced bloody riots, and at Cornell, black radicals armed with rifles and bandoliers had seized the student center, winning all their significant demands. In New Haven, the supple and ingeniously accommodating administration of university president Kingman Brewster had managed to keep the peace, altogether avoiding student strikes or building occupations, despite the sustained efforts of campus radicals to stage some showy explosion.

With the onset of spring, the leading leftists of the senior class faced the frightening prospect that they might graduate without ever having caused significant trouble at Yale. Nervously watching the calendar, they saw just one last chance to match their counterparts on other campuses: they would fight for a sweeping ban of the ROTC—the Reserve Officers Training Corps. This program allowed undergraduates to attend Yale largely at the expense of the Army or Navy in return for taking accredited classes in military science and serving as a commissioned officer at the time of graduation. With their university headquarters decorated with antique artillery, and their well-scrubbed uniforms complemented by neatly trimmed haircuts, the cadets (representing less than 4 percent of the student body) stood out at a time of general surliness and scruffiness. Kingman Brewster had already succumbed to protests and ruled that students could no longer receive academic credit for ROTC courses, but the SDS and other leftist activists wanted more, with the intention of striking a "hammer blow" against American imperialism.

I came to represent a group of students informally known as "the moderate coalition"—antiwar enthusiasts, to be sure, but deeply committed to avoiding some ugly disaster that could damage Yale and ruin our senior year. The determined SDS radicals represented a tiny minority of student opinion, but other campuses provided chilling examples of a handful of crazies polarizing and paralyzing an entire community. After torturous negotiations, we agreed with SDS to demand the right to debate the issues openly at a university-wide gathering, with a decisive vote of the entire campus community to force the administration's hand.

To our surprise, the powers-that-be clearly preferred working with "moderates" like me to facing the militants who chanted "Up against the wall, Mother Yale!" The university president even invited me to meet with him privately in his elegant, lavishly decorated home on Hillhouse Avenue. He received me while he posed for his formal university portrait, clad in flowing academic roles, talking with his hands while the gray-haired painter dabbed with painstaking precision at the half-completed canvas. Brewster was a strikingly handsome figure of suave, aristocratic charm— deftly caricatured (and ultimately immortalized) as "President King" in *Doonesbury* by Garry Trudeau, who, during my senior and his junior year, had already established himself as reigning cartoonist at the *Yale Daily News*. When Brewster asked me to describe my primary goal in an upcoming university meeting, I began the familiar recitation of platitudes about severing connections with ROTC to make a significant statement against the war and our government. He cut me off in midflight, explaining that he'd victimize the students who relied on the ROTC program for their tuition, and repeated his question, slightly rephrased: what was my main, *attainable* objective?

After a moment's hesitation I told him that I wanted to use a university-wide gathering for an open discussion that could defuse any chance of violent disruption. Brewster immediately brightened and welcomed me, with effusive gratitude, as a co-conspirator. He shook my hand warmly at parting and left me with the sense that however much we might represent warring forces in public, we actually shared a commitment to an overarching script—like professional wrestlers rigging their match and preparing their acrobatic moves in advance.

The big confrontation occurred on May Day—a sacred occasion to the leftists who'd been pushing for it—and drew more than four thousand people into the Yale hockey rink. The audience included students, faculty members, visiting celebrities (such as sportscaster Howard Cosell and syndicated columnist Stewart Alsop), and such Yale trustees as Mayor John Lindsay of New York, former governor (and presidential candidate) William Scranton of Pennsylvania, future secretary of state Cyrus Vance, and the aging plutocrat John Hay Whitney. The colorless university provost, Charles Taylor, called the meeting to order at 8:15 P.M. and, according to Brewster's biographer Geoffrey Kabaservice, "almost immediately lost control of it." While Taylor authoritatively announced the formal schedule of speakers—which allowed for no spontaneous discussion from the floor— I jumped out of my seat and jogged dramatically toward the podium. As Kabaservice described it in his book, *The Guardians*, "Michael Medved (then a leftist, later a conservative media critic) rushed up to the stage, shirttails flapping. He was one of the seniors who had organized the protest, and his proposal to get rid of Brewster's plan for a fixed slate of speakers and open the debate to speeches from the floor met with a great roar of approval."

We had painstakingly planned our insurgency in advance. With the provost still droning into the microphone, I struggled to make my voice heard in the cavernous arena. While the huge crowd fretted and gasped, Brewster waved off campus police who were about to grab me. For more than a minute our well-prepared plants in the bleachers shouted, "Let him talk! Let him talk!" and others chanted my name. Finally the provost stepped aside and allowed me to come to the microphone (to huge applause), where I demanded that the administration open up the meeting and treat the concerned students like equals, rather than powerless infants. My impassioned harangue drew deafening encouragement, and I felt giddy and electrified, as if I'd participated in some dangerous moment from the French Revolution. Eventually, the administration acceded to what was known that evening as "the Medved plan," turning the meeting over to a popular political science professor and facilitating raucous debate.

Only at the end of a long evening did President Brewster manage to turn the tide. In his speech, he emphasized that the university would not break its legally enforceable contracts with the military. "I happen to respect and even honor those who decide to serve their country in the military forces," he said to scattered boos and catcalls. "I also hope that we can make it possible for individual students to make individual choices as to whether and how they will serve." He also declared that the course of the evening had made him feel "profoundly depressed and at other times profoundly exhilarated" as he saluted the prevailing sense of community and those students "who hope there are better ways than confrontation."

After extensive and noisy discussion running long into the night, we voted on the nonbinding resolution I had pushed that demanded the immediate termination of ROTC. The painstaking counting of paper ballots revealed the improbable result—an exact tie of 1,286 to 1,286, a tally certified by a dozen students and faculty from all points of view who jointly oversaw the count. As bizarre as the deadlock was, it effectively dissolved all danger of some angry explosion. On that starry spring night, nearly everyone went home amazed, entertained, satisfied, and relieved. We had, as planned, seized control of the famous meeting, while neither side had lost the vote (which was, after all, purely symbolic). The university proceeded to the successful and uninterrupted conclusion of its academic year and I moved along, with considerable trepidation and thickening nostalgia, toward my graduation.

Fortunately, the thoughtless and childish crusade against ROTC did little immediate damage to the university, but I still look back on this episode with more shame and regret than any other aspect of my years of antiwar activism. The other demonstrations and campaigns focused on vague goals (negotiating a settlement with the Communists, bringing our boys home) that might in retrospect seem naive but not reprehensible. The push to eliminate the ROTC program, on the other hand, involved a specific aim that qualified as altogether arrogant, immature, and repugnant. For those of us who participated in this movement, it wasn't enough that we planned to avoid military service ourselves; we also insisted on taking away options from those few (only 174 enrolled in both Navy and Army ROTC in 1969) who chose to train for that service at Yale. Far from the appropriate attitude of respect and appreciation, we treated these cadets with contempt—to do otherwise might have placed our own priorities in question. The whole rancid endeavor resembled the contemporary movement to ban military recruiters from high school, college, and law school campuses at a time when the members of our armed forces risk their lives daily to try to protect those campuses (and the rest of the country) from terrorist murderers. Today, radicals cite the Defense Department's alleged discrimination against homosexuals as an excuse to keep representatives of the armed forces from telling students about their opportunities in serving their country; in our day, we railed against the ROTC to strike a blow against the American war effort in a conflict we opposed. In both cases, shallow young people reached the loathsome conclusion that they could best advance their own interests by weakening their nation's military might, wherever possible. Within two years of our ill-considered campaign, both the Army and the Navy finally succumbed to the seething student resentment and voluntarily abandoned the Yale campus; only after the surge of patriotism following the September 11 attacks did the university make the first tentative attempts to return an on-campus officer training option to one of the nation's leading educational institutions.

I knew American history, even then; how could I have possibly been so stupid and short-sighted? Part of it stemmed from the appalling isolation of major college campuses from what we derisively called "the real world." In the navel-gazing environment of a place like Yale, you might convince yourself that America at large cared deeply about the activities of its most competitive students and that our adolescent gestures (walking out of a Senior Class Dinner) inspired awe and analysis all across the continent.

The year after I graduated, student activists objected to murder charges brought against some Black Panther thugs (including their glamorous and corrupt national leader, Bobby Seale) who were indisputably guilty of the torture killing of a former member named Alex Rackley. In order to make sure that the accused got "justice" (in other words, that they escaped all responsibility for their crimes), earnest Yalies organized a student strike— as if a few thousand spoiled Ivy Leaguers staying away from classes and wasting their parents' substantial investment in tuition would force the entire criminal justice system to its knees and lead to the quick release of some stylishly scowling revolutionaries.

By the time of this insane eruption of activism (May 1970) I'd already traveled far enough away from undergraduate life to see all the solemn mass meetings, all the tedious manifestos, as symptoms of idiot indulgence. I was living off campus, teaching school, working in a senatorial campaign, and enjoying enough regular contact with some of our long-suffering, overtaxed, blue-collar neighbors (many of whom had sent sons to fight the war we disdained) to understand that they cared not one iota whether the spoiled brats at Yale attended class or not. Most ordinary citizens would have celebrated if the students had torn the entire university—and all other institutions like it—to the ground.

The Black Panther debacle may have been even less rational than our ROTC assault, but that doesn't excuse my own participation in the earlier insipidity. I had gotten caught up in the solemn self-importance and intoxicating energy of the moment. The only excuse for such folly—and the convenient rationalization for every asinine aspect of that era—concerned our obsessive, paralyzing, and poisonous fear of confronting our obligations under the military draft.

LESSON

14

Avoiding the Draft Didn't Mean
Escaping the War

During senior year, the draft became the all-consuming topic of conversation and concern, easily overshadowing more diverting subjects like women, sports, drugs, or politics, not to mention any consideration of personal plans for future education or careers.

The draft dominated every discussion in part because it connected to all those other interests. Women? We occasionally fantasized about using marriage as a means of avoiding service, but you needed more than a wife—you needed a wife *and* a kid before your draft board would make you a low priority for induction. Two former Yalies named Joe Lieberman and Dick Cheney both avoided the war on this basis, but exploiting the family option required more planning and commitment than most of us could muster. Sports and drugs also played a role in our draft dialogues because people speculated endlessly about athletic injuries or intensive psychedelic indulgence producing enough physical or mental damage to earn a coveted IV-F. Future presidential candidate Howard Dean (who was two years behind us at Yale) played intramural football and ultimately received his medical deferment due to a bad back. One of my friends from high school had discovered that at his height (5'8"), he'd be classified as too skinny for service if he managed to arrive at his physical weighing less than 107 pounds. He proceeded to starve himself for two months on a diet of vitamins and brewer's yeast and shed the 45 pounds he needed to lose. This heroic achievement earned him a I-Y classification and exactly three months of grace before the Selective Service System expected him to report for another medical exam.

With all the worry and all the scheming, no one I knew considered the most obvious and honorable option: serving the country in the Army, Navy, Air Force, or Marines. One acquaintance from my residential college, a lonely, outspoken supporter of the war and a Young Republican, had secured himself a place in the National Guard (and no, it wasn't George W. Bush—I didn't know him at Yale). Other than that, the determination to escape our military obligations looked all but universal. After all, the popular university chaplain, my friend Reverend Coffin, proudly endorsed draft resistance as an act of courage and nobility, so we could easily persuade ourselves that in pursuing our selfish interests we walked the path of righteousness and purity.

As a senior, I focused on the uncomfortable certainty that the Selective Service System would make plans for me if I didn't come up with an alternate strategy for myself. None of the options that I discussed with my friends looked even vaguely appealing. One of my marijuana-marinated acquaintances urged me to join him in applying to Hebrew Union College to study for the rabbinate in the liberal, easygoing Reform branch of Judaism, but at the time my skepticism toward God's existence made me an unlikely candidate for even the most undemanding clerical training. Another pal proudly showed off his collection of travel brochures of the most picturesque provinces of Canada, but in the end this outspoken advocate of an easy move across the border couldn't bring himself to leave the most significant nation on the planet for the quaint irrelevancy to the north. My mother, meanwhile, urged me to see a psychiatrist who might certify her long-standing suspicion that my looniness and emotionalism had crossed over into a diagnosable dementia that made me too crazy to kill for Uncle Sam. She prompted me to tell him all about the "rice paddy stuff," the years of reckless and obsessive hitchhiking, the embarrassing insistence on mentioning "moose" on *College Bowl*, and the oddball pictures of Tolstoy and Prokofiev I carried in my wallet. In my mom's opinion, if such disclosures didn't make me look weird enough to stay out of the Army, the shrink didn't know his business.

Reluctantly, I made my way to the Student Health Service for my one and only appointment with a staff psychiatrist, an unsmiling cipher with a bald head and wire-rim glasses. When I tried to alarm him with a long list of my peculiarities, he stopped me with an unexpected question. "It's obvious what you *don't* want to do next year—you don't want to get drafted and go into the Army," he properly observed. "But we really need to talk about the opposite side of the coin. What is it that you *do* want to do after you graduate?" I stammered and stalled, unable to produce with a coherent answer. I knew I wanted to stay in New Haven and, if possible, to continue some association with Yale—the only universe I'd known since leaving my parents' home at age sixteen. I planned to finish my novel and hoped to maintain a relationship with my new girlfriend, Faye, a cheerful, chirpy student at Connecticut College for Women in nearby New London. I had already applied to Yale Law School, not because I wanted to pursue a legal career but because it provided the most plausible means for keeping me around a familiar environment and providing me with a useful background for my general interest in politics. At the end of our hour the shrink announced his conclusion: I counted as confused (like most young men in my position) but not crazy—certainly not crazy enough to disqualify me for military service.

When Yale Law School admitted me—with a generous fellowship covering the full cost of tuition—my dilemma only intensified. I still didn't care about legal education, but having secured a place at so prestigious an institution, I didn't want to turn down the opportunity. The Selective Service System cut no slack to aspiring legal eagles, however, so I felt altogether stymied. Then one afternoon an old friend from California told me about a small Jewish school in New Haven that could arrange draft deferments in return for part-time teaching jobs. I loved teaching from my three years as a volunteer tutor and almost immediately set up an interview at the New Haven Hebrew Day School, headquartered (prior to its move to a new suburban location and its spectacular growth in recent years) in a dingy Victorian heap in a dicey part of town.

The school's rabbi, headmaster, and all-powerful founder intimidated me instantly, with his bristling gray Old Testament beard, burning eyes, booming voice, and long black coat. Before this visit, I hadn't realized the strictly Orthodox nature of the school. I had never heard of their fervent Chassidic sect known as Chabad-Lubavitch and had spent my four years of college almost totally removed from all aspects of Jewish life, but in my eagerness to get the job I dared not ask any questions about their religious or educational approach. Fortunately, the rabbi also found no need to question me too closely about my lack of Jewish commitment or my inappropriate personal relationships (including my Catholic girlfriend). Of course, they wanted me to teach secular, not spiritual subjects. I committed to giving them three hours every morning, after which I would be free to zip over to the law school for classes. The headmaster, pleading poverty, offered me only the most paltry of salaries, but more important than any payment, he promised he could secure a II-A occupational deferment from my draft board. I remember his odd comment about the arrangement, which initially struck me as quirky and endearing, delivered in his thick-as-chopped-liver New York accent: "You're gonna work hard when you teach for us, but it's better than shooting Chinamen in a rice barrel!"

After graduation, I rented a marvelously affordable apartment in a red-brick courtyard building between the law school campus and the Hebrew Day School and spent the summer finishing my rambling, unfocused novel—or at least managed to complete enough pages to pretend that I had finished. The William Morris agent Owen Laster (who has since gone on to great prominence and fame) had liked the first chunk of manuscript but now threw up his hands at the lack of a conclusion or, for that matter, plot structure of any kind in my hyperliterary meditations on the recently completed political campaigns of '68. He made incisive recommendations for rewriting my book, but I put them aside (forever, as it turned out) when my law school and teaching careers simultaneously commenced.

The resulting schedule proved both punishing and exhilarating as I divided my time between two alien cultures. At New Haven Hebrew Day School, I quickly learned that the black-coated rabbis who ran the place tolerated the secular teaching staff as a necessary but annoying distraction from the real business of the place: religious education. Two days before classes began I discovered that in addition to the seventh-grade English class I expected, I also had been assigned to teach eighth-grade science—despite my complete lack of interest or background in any of the sciences. The headmaster brushed off my complaints by suggesting that I only needed to stay one day ahead in the eighth-grade textbook.

Soon I faced a bigger problem. After a month of teaching I had not yet received my promised paycheck. When I went in to inquire about the money, the school brass told me to be patient: like many other religious institutions they depended on contributions to pay their bills so they experienced occasional cash flow challenges. A month later, still unpaid, I mustered my full store of righteous indignation and went back to confront the headmaster. He delivered bad news: their continuing financial difficulties made it impossible for them to pay me anything for the rest of the year. Under the circumstances, they could understand if I wanted to quit my job, but if I did they would naturally notify my draft board that I no longer worked in my occupationally deferred capacity. On the other hand, I might want to consider continuing with the students who liked me so much, and preventing any unpleasant surprises from Selective Service.

I walked out of that meeting numb with shock and self-disgust, but also full of grudging admiration for the exploitative ingenuity of the school's administration. They had imposed a rough justice on the situation: I had cheated the draft board out of a deferment, and now they cheated me out of my salary. I also understood some of the class dynamics that operated beneath the surface: they viewed me as a rich, irreligious Yalie with a prosperous papa. In their view, I deserved and needed the money much less than did the school itself.

If I felt increasingly alienated from the religious school I served every morning, I functioned as even more of a stranger at Yale Law School in the afternoons. My schedule made it impossible for me to participate in the major opportunities for socializing, since I ate meals on the fly and spent most evenings with my girlfriend rather than in the law school library with the other students. The only new friendships came from a handful of people I got to know through my first-year classes, with Hillary Rodham standing out as the warmest and most welcoming among them.

Even before she arrived in New Haven, she had earned a reputation as something of a star: as student body president at Wellesley, she'd been selected to deliver a tradition-breaking speech on commencement day expressing the widespread campus opposition to the war, and *Life* magazine had featured her photograph and extensive excerpts from the speech. Though most of our classmates declared their admiration for her famous remarks, judging them profound and significant (or "heavy" in the vernacular of the day), I remember feeling puzzled and frustrated by the impenetrable thicket of her words. "We're not interested in social reconstruction; it's human reconstruction," she portentously declared. "Words have a funny way of trapping our minds on the way to our tongues, but they are necessary means even in this multimedia age for attempting to come to grasps with some of the inarticulate, maybe even inarticulable, things that we're feeling. We are, all of us, exploring a world that none of us understands and attempting to create within that uncertainty. But there are some things we feel, feelings that our prevailing, acquisitive, and competitive corporate life, including, tragically, the universities, is not the way of life for us. We're searching for more immediate, ecstatic, and penetrating modes of living."

Reading through her incoherent ramblings, I found myself searching for more immediate, ecstatic, and penetrating modes of writing. Her talk, respectfully applauded by the national media, made her sound like one of my pot-saturated friends in full emotive flight. I therefore felt pleasantly surprised when this class celebrity arrived in person in New Haven and proceeded to charm everyone with her unpretentious warmth, accessibility, and kindness. Our first-year ranks of 165 students included fewer than 30 females, who could conveniently be divided into "princesses" or "pals," and Hillary definitely counted as a pal. She assumed this position in no small part because she so obviously eschewed traditional notions of glamour, with her thick glasses, mousy brown hair, heavy-set build, bulky sweatshirts, loose-fitting slacks, and sensible sandals. While she always possessed a winning, dimpled smile and a pleasant, friendly face, no one could describe the first-year law student I knew as a magnet for erotic male attention. Unlike most people, she unmistakably upgraded her appearance between her early twenties and her early fifties, making herself conspicuously thinner and blonder and vastly more fashionable.

In fact, I remember my shocked reaction when I watched an early speech by her husband, Governor Bill Clinton of Arkansas, near the beginning of his presidential campaign in 1992. I had traveled to Virginia for a lecture of my own and during a restless night in my hotel room, I idly flipped the dials of the television set until I settled on C-SPAN (usually a surefire cure for anyone's insomnia). The broadcast offered a taping of an Iowa rally in which local officials heaped lavish praise on my one-time classmate, Bill, and then proudly introduced his wife. "And now, here she is, the First Lady of Arkansas—Mrs. Clinton!" the master of ceremonies declared, at which point a slim, stylish, radiantly confident blonde babe strode across the platform and waved to the crowd. I reacted with horror, and said out loud to the TV screen, "Oh, my God—Bill dumped Hillary!" I'd lost touch with both of them for more than ten years and so had heard nothing of this newer, showier wife. Only after investigating the situation the next day did I learn that my confusion stemmed from personal transformation rather than remarriage.

In law school, Hillary's earthy and unprepossessing appearance equipped her perfectly for her primary social role: as unofficial den mother for all the boys in our class. She came across as more compassionate than competitive, demonstrating genuine concern for the well-being of all her friends and even acquaintances. One of our fellow classmates recalled running into Hillary on a Friday afternoon just before she departed for a trip to Vermont with a circle of friends. He expressed envy for her plans and suggested his own sense of dread at facing a full weekend of grinding toil to catch up on class work in which he'd fallen behind. The next night he got an unexpected phone call while buried in his books: Hillary took the trouble to ring him up long distance from Vermont simply to communicate her concern over his pressured state and to tell him she felt full confidence in his success.

In remembering any individual as world renowned as Hillary, retrospective exaggeration almost inevitably sets in—as with the fans who recall her (falsely) as the "most brilliant mind at the law school." Yale at the time was full of bright people and Hillary, while undeniably disciplined and capable, never stood out for her monster intellect. She did, however, achieve the status of a beloved figure on campus who earned nearly universal admiration; others have described her as the most popular member of our class, and that would hardly count as an exaggeration. We saw each other almost constantly because the academic schedule placed her in three of my four classes. She appreciated me as an established local leader of the anti-war movement and commented several times that my teaching job represented the most "honorable and constructive" possible means for dealing with the draft.

My other friends at law school also shared my commitment to antiwar activism and my background with Al Lowenstein, Dump Johnson, and the McCarthy campaign. The brilliant, acerbic, and eccentric Steve Cohen, for instance, had earned a national reputation as McCarthy's chief advance man during the historic New Hampshire primary, while the charismatic, dashing Greg Craig (later one of President Clinton's chief defense lawyers during his impeachment trial) had been elected student body president as a Harvard undergraduate and for more than four years served as one of the most significant leaders of the drive to use mainstream politics to end the war. Even before classes began, Greg and Steve took part in the early planning for a preposterously grandiose national "Moratorium" to force a conclusion to the war. The initial concept for this movement involved the adaptation of the classic European leftist tactic of a "general strike"—a sweeping work stoppage that would do major damage to the national economy until the nation's leaders bent to the will of the strikers. To introduce the American public to this daring idea, the new movement would begin with a one-day strike, or "Moratorium," scheduled for October 15, in which millions of people would leave work or school for a single day. A month later, on November 15, the Moratorium leaders hoped to recruit even more citizens willing to walk away from their jobs and to extend their time off to two days. December would see a three-day work stoppage, January a four-day stoppage, and so on, until the entire capitalist system began to unravel, or the Nixon administration agreed to stop the war—whichever came sooner.

To put this ambitious and apocalyptic plan into play, the Moratorium planners called for huge rallies to be locally organized in every major city in the country so that workers and students would feel motivated to abandon their normal schedules to come out and demonstrate. Greg and Steve asked me to become cochairman of the Moratorium and the local mouthpiece for the movement. I churned out daily press releases and frequently gave interviews to the local media, telling anyone who would listen that the upcoming Moratorium in New Haven represented the most exciting and revolutionary New England mass gathering since the Boston Tea Party.

At the same time, we struggled to maintain a consistently moderate tone and to distance ourselves from more radical antiwar elements; in fact, unlike other local leaders of this national mass movement, we refused to accept support or cooperation from SDS, the Black Panthers, or other left-ist factions. We wanted to make sure to say or do nothing to scare away suburban housewives, union members, military veterans, or congregants of black churches—we needed them all to venture out to the New Haven Green at midday on October 15. Everyone knew that college students op-posed the war, so a gathering of youthful dissidents would make little con-tribution to the cause; the Moratorium could succeed only if we deployed a much broader and deeper populist coalition.

To advertise the event and to raise funds, I personally designed a styl-ishly understated button that attempted to summarize the message of the movement: it featured the single word "enough." (with lower case "e" and the period at the end) in simple white letters on a dark blue background. These "enough." buttons became so improbably popular we could barely keep up with the demand for them, especially when the national Moratorium office asked for thousands of additional lapel pins to distribute around the coun-try. In general, our operation worked so smoothly (thanks largely to the logistical genius of Steve Cohen, and the incomparable coalition-building skills of the irresistibly likeable Greg Craig) that we began providing ad-vice to organizers in much larger cities, including New York, Washington, Chicago, and San Francisco.

Our lineup of speakers reflected our success in mainstreaming the antiwar message: it included not only prominent liberals such as our old friend Congressman Al Lowenstein (of course) and former secretary of the interior Stewart Udall but also conspicuously moderate establishment fig-ures like Richard Lee, mayor of New Haven; Vincent Sirabella, local head of the AFL-CIO; Connecticut secretary of state (and future governor) Ella Grasso; and Republican business leader Malcolm Baldridge (later com-merce secretary under President Reagan). Yale president Kingman Brewster also agreed to speak, in his first major public statement against the war.

With this impressive collection of reassuringly respectable dignitaries, we managed to raise the money for an intensive last-minute buy of radio ads and began advertising the Moratorium like a free rock concert. We boldly and publicly predicted that 10,000 participants would show up—an outrageously large crowd for a city of 150,000—but we secretly hoped we could draw twice as many.

As it turned out, the official estimates of attendance reached 50,000, and those of us who had summoned this mass of humanity on New Haven Green felt an almost indescribable surge of joy, power, and satisfaction. As the official voice of the Moratorium Committee, I was the first speaker to address the huge crowd. "The Moratorium to End the War, both locally and nationally, is firmly committed to an immediate and unconditional end to the American presence in Vietnam," I declared. "According to the Gallup poll last week, fifty-eight percent of the American people now think the war has been a mistake from the very beginning. We have already sacrificed forty-four thousand American lives to that mistake. And the sacrifice of a thousand—or a hundred—*or even one more American life*—will not make it any less a mistake. The war must end now!"

The sound of fifty thousand voices roaring back at me provided an almost physical thrill that seemed to lift me above the podium. I concluded my remarks by emphasizing that we occupied the middle ground in political discourse and delivering an unmistakable slap at the irresponsible campus rebels who had done so much to discredit the antiwar cause across the country. "Beyond this, there is another conviction that I believe we all share. And that conviction is that violence in the pursuit of peace is not only unwise—it is unjustifiable. This Moratorium is specifically committed to peaceful and constructive action, and we completely reject any violent or coercive tactics. It is time for responsible Americans to make their voices heard. Enough senseless killing in Vietnam. Enough irresponsible violence here at home." With this, I provided a not-so-subliminal plug for my "enough." buttons—how I wish I had been able to keep a percentage from their sale! I also couldn't resist the temptation, in front of that huge, enthusiastic assemblage, of invoking the name of my personal political hero. "We must turn from the work of destruction to the real job of building our country. That was the message that Robert Kennedy brought to the

American people—and were he alive, I am sure he would be with us on this day. For it is the ultimate purpose of this Moratorium that we may all become, in Robert Kennedy's own words, 'brothers and countrymen, once again.'"

The crowd went wild, of course, and the cheers echoed against the downtown buildings surrounding the green, making an amazing and unforgettable noise. As I sat down, Al Lowenstein said to me, "Now you know—a little bit—how Hitler felt."

The gathering on the Green amounted not only to the largest demonstration in New Haven history but also to one of the four or five biggest gatherings anywhere across the country on a day when more than two million Americans in more than 150 cities assembled to send their government a message. Just as important, the massive throng never erupted into violence and in fact remained cheerful and friendly throughout. Even outside observers felt impressed. "New Haven yesterday was a moving experience," wrote *New York Times* columnist Anthony Lewis. "I know it was not representative of the whole country, but no one who saw those 50,000 people on the Green could mistake the feelings there."

Despite the bright hopes of that balmy October afternoon, the grand ambitions of the national Moratorium movement soon collapsed in a welter of savage infighting and incompetence. The plans to stage a two-day mass observance just a month after the first demonstrations looked suddenly absurd, since the exhausted troops had no chance of replicating in a few short weeks the heroic effort it had taken to pull off the initial round of rallies. Instead, a very different and vastly more militant organization—the Mobilization to End the War—seized the initiative and moved ahead with their long-standing plan to call a huge march on Washington in place of the myriad of local events we favored. We hated "the Mobe," with its angry rhetoric and revolutionary ideas, and we particularly despised the notion of a single centralized march. Only students, hippie free spirits, or dedicated radicals would leave their hometowns and journey to the nation's capital, which would make it much easier for President Nixon to marginalize the Vietnam protestors by suggesting that "ordinary people" weren't involved. Sure enough, even before the Mobilization of November 15, the president delivered a brilliantly crafted address that introduced a potent new phrase to the national political lexicon. "And so tonight—to you, the great silent majority of my fellow Americans—I ask for your support," Nixon pleaded into the television cameras. "The more divided we are at home, the less likely the enemy is to negotiate at Paris. Let us be united for peace. Let us also be united against defeat. Because let us understand: North Vietnam cannot defeat or humiliate the United States. Only Americans can do that." Before the demonstrators even arrived in Washington, in other words, the president had definitively characterized the purpose of their gathering as to "defeat or humiliate the United States." It was a masterful preemptive maneuver.

I made the bus trip to Washington along with hundreds of other Yalies and shuffled along with the Mobe mobs around the Washington Monument on a bitter, freezing day. As I watched the 500,000 demonstrators—almost all of them young, with long hair and countercultural clothes—I knew that this march would only help the president turn public opinion in his direction. Flurries of violence by the malevolent crazies known as the Weathermen only made the situation worse. Sure enough, within days the Gallup poll showed Nixon's approval rating soaring to 68 percent, the highest since his inauguration; the "great silent majority" had spoken. Solid majorities (three hundred in the House and fifty-eight in the Senate) in the overwhelmingly Democratic Congress signed statements or cosponsored resolutions that supported the Republican president on the war.

I rode back on the bus that night in a sullen, disillusioned mood. I felt convinced beyond all reasonable doubt that the Mobilization had helped to alienate Americans from our cause, serving to prolong, not to shorten, the war. One of the most irritating myths left over from the '60s suggests that "peace marches" ended the war in Vietnam. It's nonsense, of course: the major demonstrations ended at least two years before American troops finally came home in 1973. It seemed obvious to me, then and now, that getting together with thousands of others and tramping around aimlessly in the freezing cold did nothing to persuade wavering voters to abandon their support of the war. By associating Vietnam critics with countercultural values (sex, drugs, rock 'n' roll, and rebellion) that Middle Americans loathed, most of the showy street theater—from the "Armies of the Night"

March on the Pentagon, to Chicago, to the Mobilization, to bloody Kent State—played directly into the hands of defenders of the war, with their visceral appeals to patriotism and decency.

Riding north through the November night on that crowded bus, I even questioned the effectiveness of my own Moratorium involvement, though such doubts felt too painful to explore for long. That ambitious movement had never developed into the focused general strike we had originally intended, and ultimately it left its participants with little more than pleasant memories of one exciting day communing with a big crowd. I understood at that point that the much-derided processes of conventional politics—the grubby business of trolling for votes and winning elections— offered a far more authentic hope for moving the country in a new direc-tion than any protest movement, and I began to make dramatic decisions to rearrange my personal life accordingly.

Sex—Not Money—Is the
Ultimate Fuel of Politics

On a hot night in June of 1970, I awoke with a start at three in the morning to the unexpected embraces of a nearly nude woman I didn't know. Underneath a tangle of sweaty sheets and blankets on the carpeted floor of a Hartford apartment, she wore only a loose-fitting T-shirt, so I vividly felt her big breasts pushing against my chest and her bare legs wrapping around my own. We had gone to sleep a few hours earlier after making the rounds of receptions and parties at the state Democratic convention, then coming back for additional consumption of a bottle of wine; three attractive, athletic, idealistic female volunteers from posh Mount Holyoke College shared this floor with me, while our host, a senior aide in our senatorial campaign, had retired to the bedroom with his girlfriend. I knew that the lady who had crawled across the floor to me had to be one of the three girls I had met earlier that same evening, but even as she nuzzled against my neck I couldn't be sure which one. In the stifling darkness, I summoned all available willpower and common sense to push her away, gently. "Be careful," I whispered into her ear. "We might wake up the others." She settled back, inserting a hand inside my pajama top to caress my chest, briefly, and then fell asleep while leaning against me. I took longer to return to slumber, thinking of the frantic demands that awaited me the next morning, trying to figure out which of the young women breathed softly beside me, and struggling to remember the names of all three of them.

The path to this unsettling predawn encounter began shortly after the Moratorium rally, when two of the leading political activists in Connecticut asked to meet with me. In 1968, Joe Duffey and Anne Wexler had led the state's insurgent McCarthy campaign, challenging the iron control of Connecticut's legendary Democratic boss John Bailey, who had also served eight years as chairman of the national party under Kennedy and Johnson. Duffey—a Congregationalist pastor, professor of urban ethics at Hartford Seminary, and president of the liberal pressure group Americans for Democratic Action (ADA)—planned to run for the U.S. Senate in 1970 against the scandal-plagued incumbent, Thomas J. Dodd (father of today's popular Connecticut senator Christopher Dodd). Having been impressed with my address at the Moratorium and with all my leaflets, manifestos, and press releases, he and Wexler, his campaign manager, invited me to draft Duffey's speech announcing his candidacy. Duffey delivered the speech I wrote with minor adjustments on November 10, 1969, almost a full year before the general election. The statement, in which he promised to force the first party primary in the history of the state, amounted to a declaration of war upon the party establishment and drew considerable attention in the press and in antiwar circles around the country.

I was thrilled when the candidate asked me to come on full time as a speechwriter, but I also knew that to join the campaign I would have to ask for a leave of absence from law school. When I briefly mentioned the idea on the phone to my mother, she expressed her enthusiasm by hanging up on me, then calling back and emotionally announcing her intention never to speak to me again if I walked away from my legal education and my generous Yale fellowship. I assumed that Duffey's underdog effort stood scant chance of success—which meant that after a few brief months of soaring rhetoric and surging adrenaline, I'd be free to return to Yale and resume my academic career. But why, I wondered, should I inconvenience myself at all to participate in a campaign without credibility or clout? Edgy with indecision, I consulted many friends and faculty. Most of them shrugged their shoulders and deepened my confusion, but Hillary Rodham stood out in offering solid and sensible advice. After intently listening to me talk about my conflicted emotions, she laughed and said, "Yale has been here forever. It'll still be here whenever you're ready for it. If you want to come back, you know they'll take you. But this campaign, this opportunity, this moment in history—it's like the train is leaving the station and it's going to pull away whether you get on or not. Thirty years from now, you could look back and say you missed out on something amazing and important." Within forty-eight hours I had requested a leave of absence from Yale.

The dean of the law school agreed without hesitation to grant the leave, proudly speaking of his friendly acquaintance with Joe Duffey. As pleased as I felt then, looking back now I find the entire arrangement impossibly partisan and unfair. It's hard to believe that a first-year law student asking for time off to work for President Nixon or Governor Reagan would have met with anything like the indulgence and encouragement that I received; academic officials, then as now, would have written off any Republican campaign as mere politics, while a liberal candidacy like Duffey's represented a higher cause. Part of the institutional advantage that the left enjoys in academia is the widespread assumption that liberal activism stems from idealism and generosity, while conservative activism expresses only ambition, or greed, or mental illness.

In order to protect my draft deferment I still showed up to teach my morning classes at the Hebrew Day School, which meant constantly shuttling the forty-five miles between New Haven and the Duffey headquarters in West Hartford. Despite the grueling schedule, I relished my work as a political wordsmith and developed an intense affection for Joe Duffey, who struck nearly everyone who met him as "too nice for politics." He had never before run for office and campaign manager Anne Wexler wanted to establish his connection with nitty-gritty local issues in every corner of the state. This meant that in addition to preparing ridiculously ambitious position papers on national and international affairs, I needed to familiarize myself with the concerns and controversies in every one of Connecticut's 169 cities and towns, and to develop a Duffey approach for each community.

Just as I had indulged my passion for hitchhiking vast distances, I developed a taste for motoring down wintry back roads in the blue Mustang convertible my dad had lent me for the campaign and familiarizing myself with every detail of every tiny community, from grim, faded factory towns like Winsted, to leafy, colonial country villages like Coventry, to glittery and sophisticated suburbs of New York City like New Canaan. But my focus on exploring the most obscure and arcane corners of southern New England actually made sense in the context of the campaign. The very survival of our cause depended on this localized approach, in fact, because of the quirky nature of Connecticut election law. Duffey had taken on an incumbent senator of his own party, and in order to force the first-ever statewide primary, the candidate needed to secure more than 20 percent of the delegate votes at the June convention in Hartford. The selection of the all-important delegates to the state convention occurred in meetings of local town committees or open caucuses. We placed all our hopes on infiltrating those tiny communities and packing their caucuses with the antiwar activists we needed to reach that magical threshold of 192 delegates to impose a primary. For that reason, the central headquarters campaign staff (including the head speechwriter) abandoned all normal tasks and flooded out into the field, directing the efforts of regional supporters.

We swept all the delegates of the caucuses I supervised, which provided me with a surge of excitement and made me feel like a political insider (though I was just twenty-one). That excitement, combined with the lyrical joy of cruising the scenic landscape in my Mustang convertible, propelled me through my twenty-hour days, but an even more elemental force—*the* most elemental force, in fact—kept me chugging without weariness or complaint. In contrast to my experience as an undergraduate at an all-male Yale, or in law school, where men outnumbered women more than five to one, the Duffey campaign boasted an energizing array of appealing females. Every day, I worked alongside flirtatious and voluptuous secretaries; sophisticated, expensively groomed, high-heeled, and miniskirted professionals from advertising and PR; countless fresh-faced volunteers of college and high school age; and any number of svelte, privileged, intensely dedicated suburban housewives.

It didn't take long before I struck up an especially chummy relationship with a volunteer named Annie, the uncomfortably sexy nineteen-year-old daughter of one of these earnest Peace Movement matrons who worked in our fund-raising department. Every time I found myself in the same room with this girl—who regularly wore boots, black tights, and ridiculously short plaid skirts—I felt a notable blast of head-clearing energy, like the first cup of black coffee in the morning. Eventually she began staying late at the lonely headquarters to keep me company as I toiled into the night before my long drive back to New Haven. One thing led to another on several occasions after I turned out the lights. I worried that she would come to demand more of my time and attention than I could possibly provide (since I maintained at least a pro-forma commitment to my schoolteacher girlfriend back in New Haven), but I soon learned that my fiery friend with the wild black hair provided simultaneous comfort to at least two other senior staff members in our campaign. She also cheerfully assumed that I would explore opportunities with the other young women who toiled at that headquarters; like so many true believers caught up in the excitement of some grand cause (including my former pals Debbie and Iris in the Bobby Kennedy campaign), she assumed that our epic-making effort amounted to an alternate, larger-than-life universe in which stuffy or ordinary rules never applied.

On the surface, the political operatives in our senatorial juggernaut worried over delegate counts, press coverage, cocktail parties with donors, rallies, and position papers, but underneath the work-a-day public façade we developed enough passion, betrayal, and ecstasy to inspire the raciest soap opera. The pressure-cooker atmosphere inevitably facilitated a sense of instant intimacy—like a co-educational commando unit deep in enemy territory. Even some of the grown-up, middle-aged members of the staff participated in the amatory escapades; age gaps didn't matter with impassioned people who shared so many commitments in common. The candidate himself—he held the title *Reverend* Duffey, after all—remained unsullied, almost saintly, in fact, and beloved (in the most innocent way) by all the mischievous children of all ages who toiled in his behalf. On the way home from a trip to Washington, D.C.—a city inundated, then as now, with lovely idealists who could (and often did) win the attention of members of Congress or other influential older men—Duffey said to me, "If we do win this thing, I don't know how we survive. How any marriage survives! I don't see how anybody manages to keep anything like a normal life in this place."

In May, the student unrest surrounding Nixon's Cambodia incursion, including the deadly riots at Kent State, gave a new urgency to our campaign and brought a surge of at least two hundred more volunteers from campuses throughout the East. That same month brought another important change to our operation: we learned that we would not be confronting the ardent Cold Warrior Senator Tom Dodd, the legendary opponent we had been targeting since the earliest days of our crusade. Less than a month before the climactic state convention, the senator suffered a minor heart attack and withdrew his candidacy for the Democratic nomination. In his place, state chairman John Bailey selected Alphonsus J. Donahue, a wealthy, genial titan of the zipper industry and father of twelve with no known enemies and no political experience. Suddenly, the main focus of the campaign (and its press coverage) shifted from the uphill effort to unseat the reigning Senator Dodd to the statewide organization's determination to stop the renegade Duffey at all costs.

We brought all our volunteers to Hartford for the convention, including the three winsome newcomers from Mount Holyoke who ended up sharing the floor with me at my friend's apartment. In the echoing Bushnell Auditorium, after all the demonstrations and denunciations, confetti and maneuvers, the convention duly nominated Al Donahue for the United States Senate, but Joe Duffey held on to more than enough delegates to force a primary. And we went on to shock the state and make national news by winning that primary, in part because a second "mainstream" candidate, state Senate Majority Leader Ed Marcus, divided the organization votes with Donahue (we took 43 percent, to Donahue's 37 percent). After that result, the Duffey forces resolved to punish Senator Marcus by blocking his renomination in his New Haven district and installing in his place one of our own: a recent Yale Law graduate and well-liked local boy named Joe Lieberman, who began his personal climb up the political ladder as part of our 1970 insurgency.

Though I had anticipated that we would lose the primary campaign, allowing my return to law school in the fall, I could not now walk away from the battle that many pundits described as "the most exciting Senate race in the country." Law school would have to wait a little longer. At least one of my problems was solved, however, when Richard Nixon ingeniously undermined the antiwar movement by instituting a lottery system that instantly exempted nearly half the draft-age population from the pressure of potential military service. The number I was awarded in the much-hyped random drawing meant that I would never be drafted. I no longer had to devote my mornings to the New Haven Hebrew Day School.

As I focused on getting Joe Duffey into the Senate, the candidate himself assured me that after our November victory I'd accompany him to Washington as one of his top aides. This prospect eased the sting of notably reduced status within our growing organization due to the arrival of the slick, out-of-state professionals imported to take over the campaign. Most of the Duffey veterans viewed these operatives as unwelcome interlopers; we derisively called them Hessians, after the German mercenaries who had been hired to fight for the British in the Revolution. Of the eight senior aides and department heads who began the campaign, Anne Wexler and I were the only two who survived in the same jobs for the full year from announcement day to Election Day.

The Hessians included such conspicuous operatives as the imperious Tony Podesta (who took the title campaign director), his younger brother John Podesta (who later served as President Clinton's last White House chief of staff), and the suave but overbearing Lawrence Kudlow (now known as a conservative economist and TV host on CNBC, but at that time a flaming antiwar liberal like the rest of us). One of the most controversial of the new arrivals passed only briefly through our Hartford headquarters before he made such a dazzling impression on the campaign brass that he instantly received the plum assignment of running our entire operation in the crucial Third Congressional District (greater New Haven). This brash operator, Bill Clinton, certainly won his share of admirers in the campaign (especially among the middle-aged suburban ladies, who went ga-ga for his earthy, unstoppably chatty charm), but many of us felt annoyed by the grandiose expectations he seemed to attach to himself. It became impossible to mention his name in even the most casual context without someone breathlessly declaring, "You know, he's going to be the senator from Arkansas one day!" In all my experience with budding politicians at Yale, both as an undergraduate and a law student, the only other individual who ever spoke as openly about personal plans of running for high office was John Kerry.

Those of us who looked skeptically at the new golden boy of the Duffey campaign dubbed him "The Arkansas Traveler," believing that he was only passing through and didn't share our deep loyalty to the candidate and his cause. I remember one discussion of Clinton's undeniable facility at conducting warm and jovial conversation anywhere, with anyone (black or white, WASP or ethnic), at any time. While his defenders marveled at this ability, I added the dismissive remark, "Sure, he's easy to talk to. All you have to do is keep your mouth closed and listen." He struck me, frankly, as a boisterous blowhard, utterly full of himself and palpably phony whenever he got all mushy and melty for the purpose of convincing you how much he cared. With my closest friends in the campaign, I compared him to the slimy Eddie Haskell on the old *Leave It to Beaver* show— whenever confronted by some authority figure in a position to help him, Clinton suddenly assumed a patently inauthentic mask of exaggerated courtesy, uncharacteristic deference, even obsequiousness. When I got to know him, he had just completed his studies at Oxford and prepared to start Yale Law School that autumn, though he knew he'd fall behind in his classes because of the campaign. While he worked for Duffey, he hadn't yet met my friend Hillary Rodham, and I remember feeling horrified a year later when I discovered their involvement.

I was walking across campus on my way home from an Ingmar Bergman movie at the Yale Film Society when I ran into Hillary, on Wall Street, just in front of the law school. She greeted me with a big hug and asked after my progress and plans. Bill Clinton stood just behind her, with a huge shock of reddish sandy hair and a short-sleeved yellow shirt with odd brown stripes on it. He looked like he'd swallowed a canary, utterly pleased with himself, and his smirk instantly announced that he and Hillary had formed an unlikely couple.

"You know Bill Clinton, don't you?" Hillary asked me, bringing him forward.

"Sure," I said. "From the Duffey campaign." We shook hands but he acted as if he didn't remember me, which I found infuriating in view of my prominent position in the campaign. She never asked my opinion of this new love in her life, but from the way she took his arm and turned an adoring gaze in his direction, her pride and delight in their relationship seemed obvious. They invited me to go out with them that night for pizza (a special passion of Bill's), but I felt uncomfortable at the prospect of sitting across the table and watching them make goo-goo eyes at each other. On every occasion that I saw them thereafter, they came across as an over-the-top lovey-dovey couple, physically affectionate to an almost embarrassing extent. I hated to see that because I couldn't shake my stubborn conviction that my pal Hillary—with her unpretentious kindness, innate class, and decency—deserved better than the slippery manipulations of the Arkansas Traveler.

Despite the application of his political skills to our Third District effort, despite all the organizational know-how of the dreaded Hessians, despite the party organization's nominal support, the Duffey campaign faced a tough time connecting with voters. To distinguish our campaign, I churned out speeches and ambitious, overly detailed "white papers" on virtually any issue: reforming the health care system (with greater government involvement, of course), radically reforming taxes (to make the rich and the corporations pay more, naturally), greatly expanding the scope of the national park system, increasing federal funding for the arts, enlarging the impact of urban renewal, offering a more generous commitment to welfare recipients, spending more for highway construction, helping the unemployed with a new federally funded public works program, cracking down on environmental polluters, and so forth. Duffey seemed to take bemused pride in the impressive output of his "issues shop," often telling reporters that "we have more positions than the Kama Sutra."

Some of the Hessians worried, however, that all the audacious and innovative proposals that I devised might come back to haunt the candidate, especially if he won the election and tried to deliver on his promises. Our new chief advance man Steve Robbins did a quick review of all the new programs we had endorsed in the course of the campaign and came to the conclusion that the cost of these activist initiatives would require at least a tripling of the federal budget—an analysis which may have exaggerated the truth only slightly. "What's the matter with you, Medved?" Robbins demanded over late-night drinks one evening. "Hasn't anybody ever told you that more government isn't the best answer to everything? Do you know what kind of taxes you would need to pay for all of this?"

"Better that people pay their money in taxes," I replied in all my twenty-one-year-old ignorance and arrogance, "than wasting it on a lot of consumer crap."

"You know, you're a dinosaur, Medved. A fossil and a fool. Sometimes

I think they put you in a time capsule in 1933 and only let you out just now. Hasn't anybody told you that it's now 1970 and the New Deal is over?"

Actually, I took any association with FDR as the highest imaginable compliment, and placed a portrait of that Democratic icon above my office desk, recalling the similar image in my grandmother's house in South Philly.

Unfortunately for us, a real New Dealer (who had worked for Roosevelt's National Youth Administration in the 1930s) soon reentered the race, making it all the more difficult for Joe Duffey to secure the Democratic base. Senator Tom Dodd declared his candidacy as an independent. Our polling showed Dodd drawing his heaviest support from the lunch-bucket Democrat, hard-hat voters we needed most to defeat Republican nominee Lowell Weicker.

Hoping to save our entire ticket, I began working closely with the speechwriter for Democratic gubernatorial nominee Emilio ("Mim") Daddario, Lanny Davis. Lanny had just finished at Yale Law and had already racked up considerable political experience, especially with Al Lowenstein. Since he also lived in New Haven and drove to Hartford every day to work at his campaign's headquarters, we began carpooling on that considerable commute. Those long drives early in the morning and late each night during a sparkling, invigorating Connecticut autumn helped to foster one of the warmest friendships in all my years in politics—and the only friendship with a former liberal associate that remains active to this day. Lanny, who later gained fame as White House counsel to Bill Clinton and the president's most ubiquitous defender on TV, assumed a role as the big brother I never had (he is four years older). He served as my seasoned romantic mentor, advising me on how to juggle social connections with four different nubile campaign staffers plus my increasingly resentful girlfriend back in New Haven. In the midst of swapping stories and insights, Lanny urged me to avoid guilt over my complicated, harried relationships since politics always came accompanied by emotional entanglements; he unblushingly emphasized its "aphrodisiac" impact on unattached females.

In the course of these confessional conversations with Lanny, I developed my own self-serving understanding for the behavior I witnessed and exemplified in a campaign context. The whole game of politics, obviously, is about seduction. Any effective candidate bears an unmistakable resemblance to a randy guy on the make; it's no coincidence that so many of the most effective candidates often turn out to be randy guys on the make. The best speeches or sound bites operate like well-crafted come-on lines designed to win the attention (or more) of desirable women at bars or cocktail parties. Both the politico and the lothario employ words to strike attractive poses and to overcome resistance so they can earn attention, affection, and, ultimately, surrender from strangers. After any electoral success, common parlance suggests that the new officeholder enjoys a "honeymoon" with the public—which reflects the essential similarity between a victory celebration and a wedding night. In both cases, there's a blast of climactic (or orgasmic) joy, made possible by the naive, romantic belief that a new commitment (to a candidate or a spouse) will allow all parties to live happily ever after. The language employed by political insiders tacitly acknowledges the sexual charge connected to all campaigns: if two pols decide to cooperate, for instance, observers will suggest that "they got into bed together."

Considering the overwhelming demands on anyone who intends to win and keep public office, the financial rewards remain absurdly modest. Almost anyone with the energy, ability, and personal appeal to win election to the House or the Senate (let alone the presidency) could earn vastly more money with a law firm or in the corporate world. Politics, however, provides perks unavailable elsewhere, in terms of an abundance of public-spirited young people, full of hope and trust and sweetness, looking at the candidate with adoring eyes as God's gift . . . to them. This form of worship provides potent satisfaction even to those politicos who don't play around. People who participate in the campaign seduction cycle become addicted to adoration. A certain amount of sexual hanky-panky is therefore expected, if not always accepted. This pattern emerged so clearly during that 1970 senatorial campaign that I felt less surprised than many others when, twenty-eight years later, our former Third District coordinator presided over the most notorious sex scandal in White House history.

While all political endeavors generate an inevitable byproduct of erotic energy, some campaigns definitely count as sexier than others—and the Duffey campaign boasted its fair share of mojo. During the final weeks of our two-front war against Weicker and Dodd, for instance, we arranged a Connecticut visit by one of the most admired politicians in America:

Senator Teddy Kennedy of Massachusetts. He gave us a full day on the road, going from town to town and generating huge, lusty crowds in every corner of the state. Given my emotional investment in his late brother Bobby, I expected to experience some sort of mystical connection with the youngest Kennedy brother, but during his day of frenetic campaigning he resembled a banal, bellowing, occasionally morose barroom braggart rather than the anointed surviving son of America's unofficial royal family. Only a year after his disastrous scandal at Chappaquiddick, Senator Kennedy displayed a shocking contrast between his hearty, roaring, stem-winding, wildly enthusiastic performances behind the podium and the dark, sullen, snappy, even vaguely self-pitying mood in evidence between speeches. Another disillusioned member of our staff described Teddy, aptly, as "a completely sincere phony."

I actually had a much better time campaigning with the other star we sent around the state: the irrepressible and irresistible Paul Newman, who came across as earthy, intelligent, sincerely impassioned, knowledgeable about the issues, and just slightly unhinged. The actor refused to use the stump speeches Anne Wexler had asked me to write for him, insisting on "speaking from the heart"—so that those of us who accompanied him lived in almost constant fear of some disastrous comment, or an inappropriately off-color joke (he loved to tell them both in public and private), or the sort of maudlin and meandering incoherence (as he spoke of the need for peace and racial justice and government that helps the little guy) that might attract nasty comments by the press. As it turned out, we needn't have worried: he was Paul Newman, and the youthful, mostly female, hysterically cheering throngs who flocked to his events—as well as the star-struck reporters who covered those events—longed to gaze upon his big-screen magnificence rather than to analyze his words. At one airport rally, he began as he usually did, declaring that he spoke not as a movie star but as a citizen, a taxpayer, a husband, and a father of five. When he mentioned the wife and children, a spectacularly buxom blonde in the front row released a disappointed "Awww!" Newman turned his laserlike, blue-eyed gaze directly upon her and promised, "Don't worry, honey! I've still got plenty of mustard left!"

The unexpected contrast between Newman and Kennedy (I found Newman more impressive and likeable in every way) left me unwilling to share later in the general hostility toward film celebrities "meddling" in politics. The fact that I learned to take Newman seriously for his commitment and decency made it easier for me to get behind another actor (with very different politics) exactly ten years later: Ronald Reagan.

In the end, however, the borrowed charisma of our celebrity campaigners wasn't nearly enough: the voters chose Republican Weicker by a decisive margin, 42 percent to our 34 percent. Senator Dodd drew just enough votes (24 percent) to deny Duffey any chance of victory. I had devoted a year of my life to this losing cause, but I never sacrificed as much as many others: of the eleven principal members of the staff who came to the effort as part of a married couple, eight got divorced or separated either during the course of the campaign or shortly after its conclusion. These broken relationships ultimately included both the candidate and his campaign manager: Joe and Anne shocked their associates by ending their marriages within a few years of their defeat and then, after a brief interval, wedding each other. For more than thirty years they've continued the partnership they began in politics, living as husband and wife and functioning as one of D.C.'s more prominent power couples.

The end of the campaign forced me to try to figure out what I planned to do next, personally and professionally. Having already missed a few months of the fall semester at Yale Law, I kept plugging at politics, taking on sporadic speechwriting jobs. At age twenty-two, I wanted to continue wearing my three-piece suit and impersonating a responsible adult while toiling away at Democratic politics; at the same time, I wanted to grow a beard, hit the road as a hitchhiker, and write another novel. I wanted to make up with my girlfriend, Faye, after all the preoccupations and flirtations of the campaign; I also wanted to dump her, for the sake of unattainable freedom and excitement, secure in the knowledge that I would still get a chance for stability and wholesomeness when I grew older.

The only personal values that informed these choices revolved around the goals of "the movement"—gauzy, conveniently elastic aims like ending the war, working for racial justice, closing the gap between rich and poor, and so on. If someone asked me to define my moral code at this time, I might have responded by handing over one of the laundry lists of pie-in-the-sky campaign proposals I had produced with such glib assurance. I had established no real home for myself, and gave very little to the people who were supposed to be closest to me; like so many others, it seemed enough for me to say, "I gave at the office." With an odd sort of pride, I acknowledged the fact that I had become a campaign junkie—one of those driven, single-minded political warriors (particularly common on the utopian left) for whom an overweening commitment to political morality obviates any need for personal morality. Waiting for the next great cause, I drifted like a military professional between wars, until an unexpected intergenerational jolt sent me along another path entirely.

LESSON

16

Sometimes Father Really Does Know Best

The late 1960s and early 1970s may have earned a dubious reputation as an era of free love and wild, adventurous sex, but among the women I actually encountered in the period the overwhelming majority seemed to crave exactly what their mothers had wanted: early marriage to some ambitious, high-achieving guy. There were exceptions, naturally—which made possible those odd, anonymous embraces on an apartment floor in Hartford—but even in the super-heated, Peyton Place environment of a political campaign, the assumption still prevailed that flirtation would lead to a relationship, and serious relationships in those days generally led to marriage. A few adventurous souls had begun challenging convention by living together out of wedlock (or "shacking up," according to the arcane terminology), but they kept such arrangements secret from parents and even landlords, who might feel uncomfortable at the idea of their property employed for immoral purposes. My children find it hard to believe it when I tell them about that lost world, but of my dozen closest friends in the Yale Class of '69, five got married to their girlfriends within a year or two of graduation.

My own girlfriend, Faye, clearly longed to don a traditional lacy, white gown of her own. We had met in the summer of '68 through the inner-city tutoring program that meant so much to me: she was participating as a teacher in a similar, sister program at Connecticut College in New London. Like me, she had been a Bobby Kennedy volunteer, but she felt more drawn to healing the world through teaching or social work than through politics. She laughed easily, took huge delight in little things (Chinese food, French movies, Impressionist art), and added cheerful energy to any social gathering. I loved the changing lights and colors in her sly, hazel eyes, appreciated her straight, lustrous chestnut hair, and got used to her tiny stature (she was barely 5'3").

The first Christmas of our connection she took me home to meet her parents in Marblehead, Massachusetts. I loved the town—an elegant, historic seaside suburb on Boston's windswept North Shore, with the original painting "The Spirit of '76" hanging in its colonial town hall—but I felt terrified by her family. Her prosperous doctor father—a growling, authoritarian Irishman with a thick Beantown accent—greeted me with unshakable suspicion, more than outright hostility, while her jittery, ceaselessly talkative mother made matters worse with her solicitous attention. At Christmas dinner she babbled to my embarrassment about a good friend whose daughter had just married a Jewish boy—such a smart boy!—who was just finishing medical school. "Very hardworking people, or so the saying goes," she offered. "And nowadays, it doesn't really matter what church you go to, does it?" Shortly thereafter, she dropped the turkey off its platter onto the floor, to the enormous discomfort of everyone present, and she kept apologizing during the rest of our visit for the accident.

On the night after Christmas, the parents went to a party at their yacht club; they didn't invite us to come along because, according to Faye, the restricted membership at the club excluded blacks and Jews. I found that hard to believe and assumed that her parents simply felt uncomfortable introducing me as their daughter's boyfriend.

Before this visit, the gap in our religious backgrounds had never occupied much of our attention since neither of us felt strongly committed to any particular faith. As a little girl, she had attended the local Catholic school, "Our Lady, Star of the Sea," which I jokingly and disrespectfully described as "Our Lady, Chicken of the Sea," but after going away at age thirteen to an exclusive prep school she spent no more time in church than I did in synagogue. Her parents felt painfully conscious of my Jewish ancestry, but they both repeatedly declared themselves free of "prejudice" and insisted (her father, through clenched teeth) that they wouldn't allow religious considerations to interfere with their daughter's happiness. Such conversations placed me under absurdly intense pressure to declare my serious marital intentions, but at age twenty, with college graduation and the draft and possibly law school all looming ahead of me, I refused to be pushed. I also resisted (and resented) her frequent hints about a reciprocal invitation to Los Angeles to meet my family. It wasn't that I worried that my parents wouldn't like her: I actually felt more concerned that they would. If they found her delightful, and embraced her as a prospective daughter-in-law, it could make my situation all the more untenable and undermine my visceral resistance to making a commitment. I therefore put off a visit as long as I could.

Eventually, after many months of resistance, I surrendered to the inevitable and scheduled our fateful trip to LA. For several years I'd missed out on my family's celebration of Passover, so I took it for granted that they'd feel delighted with my announcement that we'd join them for the festive holiday. The symmetry seemed initially appealing to me: Christmas with the Catholics in Marblehead, Passover with the Jews in Los Angeles. It never occurred to me in my impervious postadolescent arrogance that the most important home-centered festival of the year might not represent the ideal occasion for introducing my shiksa girlfriend to my family.

Thanks to the popular culture, I assumed I already knew the outcome of our visit: going back to the days of early vaudeville, nice Jewish boys always brought home their Irish sweethearts and after an amusing assortment of comical "*oy vay*"s, the haymish and the Hibernians united in group hugs. *Abie's Irish Rose*, about the refreshing romance of Abraham Levy and Rosemary Murphy, became a hit play on Broadway in 1922 and produced two successful movie versions (one of them produced by Bing Crosby). On television, just a few months after my own real-life version of *Guess Who's Coming to Seder*, the fictional Bernie Steinberg romanced the lovely Bridget Theresa Mary Colleen Fitzgerald in the CBS series *Bridget Loves Bernie*. Even in the unapologetically ethnic, award-winning series *Brooklyn Bridge* (1991–92), the barely pubescent hero Alan Silver discovered the attractions of the fair sex through the person of pretty little Katie Monahan from down the block. According to the Hollywood plot outline, the doctrinal differences between Irish Catholicism and any form of Judaism must never stand in the way of instinctual affinity or true love.

Unfortunately, my parents flatly rejected this script. I hadn't allowed them much chance to object to our relationship over the phone, but when they met Faye in person they decided to make a last stand. My mother picked us up at the airport and began weeping on the drive home. Faye sat in the backseat, smoldering with resentment and hurt as my mom stammered on about how hard it was for her even to think about a wedding in a church, or grandchildren "who'd want to talk to me all about Baby Jesus and the Christmas tree." We hadn't mentioned anything about plans for marriage, but then we didn't have to: I'd brought my own Irish rose across the country to present her at an elaborate festival meal where my parents always welcomed big crowds (often more than forty) of their closest friends.

The day of the big celebration, my father got home early from work to help with the frantic preparations. During the preceding three days of tension and melodrama, he'd managed to dodge any substantive conversation with me or with Faye, adding to her sense of rejection. But now, on the busiest afternoon of the year, I finally cornered him to demand that we talk. My position had become untenable: my wounded girlfriend insisted that we fly back to Connecticut as soon as possible. Sensing my desperation, my father ignored my mom's angry pleas that she needed help from both of us and agreed to take a drive down to the beach.

When we pulled up at Will Rogers Beach, I complained about the way that Mom's ludicrous, lachrymose reactions had made my girlfriend hate her. To my surprise, my father showed no inclination to temper the message of intolerance. After a deep sigh, he cleared his throat and declared that he would never attend a wedding for any of his four sons that included a non-Jewish bride. If I persisted in my current relationship, he'd still welcome occasional contact with his oldest boy but he never would associate in any way with the grandchildren who might result from a destructive, inappropriate union. If he accepted intermarriage on the part of his firstborn child, he explained, he never could make effective objection with the kids to come.

This uncompromising announcement, delivered in tones more wistful than stern, left me stunned, appalled, altogether outraged. Who ever asked him about grandchildren? The thought of offspring with Faye remained at least as foreign to me as it did to my parents, but I refused to give them the satisfaction of saying so. My father, a physicist and fun-lover, had given no prior hint—ever—of religious fanaticism. I knew him as an old-time lefty, a lover of humanity at large, rather than a defender of some atavistic sense of tribalism. Hadn't both parents always denounced bigotry, emphasizing solidarity with idealistic blacks in their struggle for dignity and brotherhood? They strenuously opposed segregation for others but made a point of enforcing it for themselves. How could they insist in good conscience on excluding my girlfriend from our imperfect, intensely emotional family circle simply because her ancestors had emigrated from the Emerald Isle? Given the lack of religious observance in our home, how could they claim that Faye failed to fit in? It's true that she followed no Jewish traditions or rituals, but then neither did I—and neither did my parents, for the most part. We all careened through our busy lives as decent, well-meaning, secular, liberal Americans, and any religious differences that separated us from our gentile neighbors involved a unique sense of nostalgia rather than any distinctions in daily behavior. My mom still lit candles on Friday night, but my father frequently worked late. They occasionally watched TV over Sabbath dinner, allowed my brothers to go out with friends, and followed no more restrictions on Saturday activities than did Faye's parents in Marblehead. Out of habit and inclination, my mother still kept pork products out of the house, but other than that (and her stubborn commitment to supermarket bargains of any sort) her shopping carts looked no different from those of her gentile neighbors. Intermarriage could cause some notable break in our family traditions only if the new daughter-in-law somehow insisted on affirming Christianity—an extremely unlikely eventuality in Faye's case, I assured them.

On the way back from the beach to our home in the Crestwood Hills, I told my dad that I had expected that Faye's liberal activism would matter more to him than any issues of ethnicity. Didn't he welcome the idea that I'd connected with a woman who shared our idealism, our general outlook on life? I challenged him with a disturbing hypothetical: what if I had brought home a girl who happened to be Jewish *but* was also—gasp!—a Republican? Wouldn't that have brought about even greater discomfort for my parents?

My dad effortlessly dispensed with that notion. "Come on, Michael," he laughed. "We know you'd never be interested in a Jewish *Republican!* And what's more, you probably couldn't find one." He then turned the question back on me, forcing me to face the essence of our argument. "See, that's the problem that you're not seeing. You're suggesting that Jewish identity is less important than politics—less significant than signing on with another campaign. But in politics, nothing stays the same. You win, you lose, the issues change. The whole idea of Jewish identity is that some things never change. We've been around a long time."

"Oh, come on, Dad, don't give me a Bar Mitzvah speech. Of course things change in Judaism! Just look at yourself. Your parents didn't speak English. They never ate a bite of nonkosher food as long as they lived, right? And now it's different for you and Mom. So why is it the end of the world if I go in a different direction, too?"

"It's not the end of the world," he shot back, "but it is the end of the line. If you end up without a Jewish wife, without Jewish kids, then you've cut yourself off. I know you want me to say that it's no big deal. But it is. You'd be separated from us, from the memory of your grandparents. From your history. From everybody who went before. You'd be disconnected. It's not a question of hurting us. In the long run, it's hurting you."

I slouched down in the seat of the car, sulking, taking note of the irritating fact that whenever parents adopted the most irrational and extreme positions they invariably insisted that they did so only for the sake of their poor, deluded kids. My father had made me feel pathetic, all right—surrounded by guilt on all sides. I felt guilt toward my girlfriend because she thought I wouldn't marry her; I felt guilt toward my parents because they thought I would.

We returned from the beach to a house full of chaotic activity, with every member of the family engaged in frenetic tasks connected to the big seder meal and the more than three dozen guests they expected within hours. My beloved Uncle Moish was there, having recently fled to my parents' home in California after the collapse of his electrician's business in Philadelphia and the emigration of his two daughters to Israel. His Orthodox boyhood in the Ukraine and his lifelong involvement in the Zionist movement made him far more knowledgeable of and committed to Jewish tradition than either of my parents, but he still managed to welcome Faye to our home with greater openness than they did. When I took him aside to thank him for his warmth and courtesy, he shrugged. "Why shouldn't I be nice to her?" he said. "She's a nice girl. She never did anything wrong. She's not the problem; you are. You're the one who's acting like a schmuck!"

Unbeknownst to Moish or my parents, I now prepared to take that schmuckiness to a whole new level. I went upstairs to the little guest room where Faye had locked herself away and found that she had packed her bags. She showed neither surprise nor disappointment when I told her that my heavy-duty conversation with my father had turned out to be a heavy-duty bust. It looked like we could fly standby on the ten o'clock flight to the East Coast, she said. But that meant leaving the seder long before its conclusion. If I refused to go along she swore that I would never see her again. If I did walk out in the midst of the most significant family gathering of the year, I would deliver an unforgettable, and perhaps unforgivable, blow to my mother. Frankly, I had begun to hate them all, wanting more than anything to escape from the middle of their vicious tug of war with me as the prize—especially since I didn't feel like much of a prize for anyone.

As the dusk thickened over the hills and the guests began ringing the bell at the front door, I finally reached a decision—choosing my girlfriend over my parents. If her committed Catholic family could come to terms with my alien origins, then surely my folks, with their eclectic and easygoing approach to all things Jewish, could get over their unfair insistence on judging her by her background rather than her character. I took my parents to one side as guests continued to arrive and told them that Faye and I would be catching the plane that night; we'd already scheduled a cab to pick us up in the middle of the proceedings. My mother began moaning and gasping, insisting that we would ruin her seder and embarrass the entire family, but my father waved her into silence. "If that's what he wants, then there's nothing we can do. If he has to go, he has to go. Leave it, Ronnie!" I felt almost disappointed with this understated response.

During the first part of the evening, I hid my face behind the Haggadah booklet, vaguely following the liturgical recitation that supposedly allowed each new generation of Jews to experience afresh the deliverance from Egyptian bondage. I listened to the Four Questions, the enumeration of the Ten Plagues (removing drops of wine from our otherwise full cups to take note of the suffering of the Egyptians), the raucous singing of *"Dayenu!"* (telling God that any single aspect of his kindness "would have been enough"). Faye fretted, listening for the arrival of the cab outside, but I struggled with the bittersweet sense that after tonight I'd never be able to come back, I'd never have the chance to listen to these familiar words and melodies again.

We heard the blaring car horn shortly after the formal meal began. Our abrupt departure in the midst of this very public meal reminded me uncomfortably of our much publicized walkout on McGeorge Bundy at the Senior Class Dinner, but I couldn't remember what I had meant to protest this time.

Just as I was getting in the taxi beside Faye, I turned to see my father bounding down the steps, a smile on his face and his arms outstretched.

"Sonny, I couldn't let you get away like this!"

I jumped out of the car and we embraced. I hid my face against my father's neck in confusion and humiliation, while Faye leaned out the window of the cab and warned that we would miss our plane. He lightly kissed my forehead as I leaned down to him, and then I pulled away and ducked into the car. My father stood there for a few moments, waving goodbye and watching us drive away, before he went back up the steps to rejoin his seder and his guests.

We made it onto the plane, but Faye started crying even before the heavy turbulence over the Rockies. She turned away from me and pushed her face against the window. "I don't understand what's wrong," I pleaded. "You wanted to leave, and so we left. You wanted me to come along, so I came along."

"But you're only here physically," she insisted. "Your heart is back with them. You wish you were with your family, celebrating your holiday."

I made no attempt to argue with her but also refused to acknowledge that she was right. Eventually, she fell asleep (despite the bumpy ride), and I took out a yellow legal pad to scribble a long letter to Uncle Moish. I felt too angry, too damaged, to write to my parents but I knew my uncle would share my case with them. I argued that my father's tough, take-no-prisoners position regarding Faye represented a shameful breach in the kindly standards of behavior I had always associated with Judaism.

Soon after I returned to my New Haven apartment, I received a letter from Uncle Moish which asserted that Jewish tradition cared more about truth than comfort, more about long-term survival and continuity than short-term ease. We continued the argument by mail and occasionally by phone. I argued that the whole "chosen people" concept and its implications for Jewish exclusivity amounted to a xenophobic distortion that betrayed the best elements of our tradition, contradicting all the precious assumptions of American pluralism. Unfortunately for me, my uncle's rich knowledge of Jewish history and culture so vastly exceeded my own that I felt I had to work through a few introductory books to frame more informed arguments. As a result, for the first time since my Bar Mitzvah some nine years before, I spent time reading about my own religious heritage. I felt especially moved by Max I. Dimont's *Jews, God, and History*, which focused on the illogical, unprecedented survival of our tiny people through some "near miraculous" (and perhaps supernatural) life force. Herman Wouk's incomparable *This Is My God* provided rational, wise, unfailingly eloquent explanations for all those Jewish quirks and rituals that I had previously dismissed as ancient (and irrelevant) exotica. I also followed my uncle's recommendation and began making my way through an excellent, annotated translation of *Pirkay Avot*, or "Sayings of the Fathers"—by far the most accessible volume of the Talmud.

These chewy, poetic maxims, compiled from some sixty rabbis who all lived more than eighteen hundred years ago, made such a deep, instantaneous impression on me that they began rattling around my consciousness and popping out at odd, inappropriate times. I might be sitting in a Chinese restaurant with Faye, for instance, feasting on sweet-and-sour pork, when I'd feel a need to recite: "You want to hear something amazing? Listen to these questions from Rabbi Ben Zoma. He asks, 'Who is wise? He who learns from every person. . . . Who is mighty? He who conquers his own passions. . . . Who is rich? He who rejoices in his portion.' Isn't that good?" She particularly hated it when I cited Rabbi Hillel, who used to say, "The more flesh, the more worms; the more property, the more anxiety." She also disliked it when I insisted on going through long explanations for kosher laws I had yet to make any attempt to follow. "That whole business with separating meat and milk—it's fascinating," I would say. "It's there to teach you to emphasize the difference between life and death. Milk is life— it's a gift, like life itself, from the mother animal to sustain her new babies. But meat is death—it's dead flesh. Both are okay under the right circumstances, but Judaism wants you to keep them apart."

My new enthusiasm for educating myself on basic Jewish concepts certainly pushed *us* apart: Faye began to feel as if I talked so incessantly about this material in a deliberate attempt to drive her away or, worse yet, to try to convert her. Her disillusionment with her own Catholic background left her suspicious of organized religion in general, and our ill-fated visit to LA hardly inspired fresh curiosity about the potential rewards of Judaism. Nevertheless, she became convinced that some form of Jewish identification or conversion might represent her only hope for saving our faltering relationship. She insisted we consult with the Hillel director at Yale to get authoritative answers on some of the unresolved questions about conversion. (It is an indication of the level of my prior Jewish commitment that I had spent nearly six years in New Haven and had never met this quietly intense Reform rabbi before.) When the rabbi tried to gauge the level of Faye's independent interest in Judaism, she broke into tears, candidly confessing that the only basis for her curiosity about Jewish involvement was her determination to stay close to me. The rabbi brought the meeting to an abrupt close with an unexpectedly decisive conclusion: he could sense a tremendous strain between us, and at this point he didn't think Faye was an appropriate candidate for conversion. Walking out of his office into a breezy spring night, I felt an overwhelming sense of relief and liberation.

My relationship with Faye broke up a few weeks later. An utterly unnecessary argument about grilling steaks on a windowsill hibachi provided the trigger, but she blamed the split on my unstoppable Jewish "fanaticism." By this time I had already renewed contact with my parents on a more or less normal basis, speaking by phone at least once a week. I never mentioned Faye or alerted them when we had stopped seeing each other, but even without formal notification, they understood instinctively that the relationship that had posed such a worrisome threat to family harmony just a few months earlier had now sunk into oblivion. About a week after my breakup, I received a carefully packaged shipment of books from my mother: she had selected her own favorite volumes about Zionism and Judaism and wanted to share them with me.

Within seven years of these baby steps toward Jewish commitment, I had become president of a synagogue, founded two different religious schools, took on the obligations of Orthodox observance, and delivered scores of lectures about traditional Judaism in temples and community centers across the country. One of the questions that comes up most frequently after all such speeches involves the impetus for my personal Jewish revival. "So, what happened to you?" a curious member of the audience may ask. "You weren't raised Orthodox or observant. You said you had zero Jewish connection when you were in college. So what was it that turned you around?"

The best answer to that messy and complex question centers on the courage and integrity of my parents. They shocked me with their display of stubbornness and consistency when I brought Faye home for their inspection; the unexpected passion and depth of their Jewish commitment forced me to consider that identification with my own people might be more than a shrug-of-the-shoulders matter of guilt or habit.

Conventional wisdom today suggests that parents should hide their unease and disappointment when confronted with the prospect of intermarriage. With half of all Jews choosing spouses outside the faith, the common argument maintains that it's better to accept the inevitable and to maintain a cordial association (even including congregational membership) between the newlyweds and the community. According to this accommodationist strategy, that connection may intensify as the years go by, particularly when children arrive on the scene.

My parents chose the opposite approach of unbending resistance and they knew even then it was a gamble. "It was a horrible, horrible time," my mother recalled in a richly emotional conversation a few years before she died. "I was so scared. We thought we had lost you. We thought we would lose your respect forever. But we knew one thing: it was better than losing respect for ourselves." In the end, they probably sensed that I wouldn't willingly give up on my whole family, my whole history—not for that girl, not at that time.

The breakup with Faye hardly marked the conclusion of my religious debates with my parents, but after that milestone, our roles and positions shifted decisively. In 1971 I might berate them for their benighted Jewish insularity, for their backward refusal to accept higher principals of universal brotherhood; by the end of 1972, while reveling in my own newfound traditionalism, I began to criticize them for their assimilationism, their compromises, their casual attitude toward timeless religious obligations. If you're young, it's hard for your parents to get much of anything right. Mark Twain remarked, "When I was a boy of fourteen, my father was so ignorant I could hardly stand to have the old man around. But when I got to be twenty-one, I was astonished at how much the old man had learned in seven years."

In my case, I felt amazed not just by my father's very real growth and learning, but by my own unlikely, unanticipated ability to come home.

LESSON
17

You *Can* Go Home Again

As spring edged toward summer in 1971, I felt played out on politics and finished with Faye; I wanted to go home to California, but Thomas Wolfe wouldn't let me.

Like everyone else, I knew the title *You Can't Go Home Again,* but unlike everyone else, I'd actually read (and loved) the book. I had eagerly devoured all of Wolfe's novels, in fact, convinced by the innocent coincidence of a shared birthday (October 3) that we'd been linked forever by some profound and mystical bond. *You Can't Go Home Again* tells the story of a writer made suddenly famous by a scandalous novel and rejected by the citizens of his old hometown who recognized themselves in its pages. I hadn't finished (let alone published) my own scandalous new novel so its thinly disguised characterizations had not yet offended anyone, but the prospect of going home still seemed impossible or, at least, inappropriate. No practical obligations kept me tethered to New Haven—I had let another deadline pass without reenrolling in Yale Law School—but in the absence of countervailing motivators, inertia and familiarity easily carried the day.

Aside from the continued pursuit of my impassioned but informal fascination with Judaism, my literary ambitions consumed most of my energies and hopes. I had begun working on a shamelessly commercial political potboiler, a dramatic departure from my previous novel, *This Time Around*, which had failed precisely because of its lack of plot or propulsion. The basic concept of the new project, *The Lesser Evil*, involved a race for the presidency in which the Democratic frontrunner, a well-meaning, wealthy senator from Ohio, relies on his ambitious, charismatic oldest son (a former congressman) to manage his campaign, only to see the boy betray him as the result of various overlapping and diabolical conspiracies. Not surprisingly, all my characters closely resembled prominent people I had encountered in politics: Al Lowenstein, Joe Duffey, Gene McCarthy, Tom Dodd, Spiro Agnew, Lanny Davis, John Kerry, Anne Wexler, Joe Lieberman, Al Donahue, and dozens of others.

Plugging away at this project satisfied any temptation I might have felt to involve myself once again in real-life politics. While friends went off to work on the presidential campaigns gearing up to challenge Nixon in '72, I replaced my three-piece campaign suit with jeans and sweatshirts, let my hair grow, and even attempted a beard. While I devoted my evenings to the typewriter, I spent most days hiking Connecticut's marvelous trails. Occasionally, I felt guilty about devoting the majority of my days to such unproductive activity, but I reassured myself by singing at the top of my voice on forest paths, endlessly repeating one of those infectious Yiddish classics I had learned to cherish from recordings I savored in my Jewish explorations, *"Hulyet, Hulyet Kinderlach"* ("Frolic, My Little Ones"):

> *Frolic, play my little ones*
> *While you're young and gay*
> *Now it's spring, but wintertime*
> *Is but a jump away*

In New Haven, I tried to avoid friends, hoping to skip annoying conversations about my breakup with my former girlfriend, or my sudden interest in unfashionable ethnicity, or, worst of all, the progress of my former classmates at Yale Law School, who now prepared to enter their final year. No wonder that part of me felt the pointlessness of suffering through another sticky, sweltering East Coast summer and vaguely yearned for the beaches, palms, parents, and broader horizons of Southern California.

I found the excuse I'd been seeking one drizzly morning when I hurried over to Temple Street to drop off my laundry and literally collided with a woman wearing stylish boots and a bright yellow slicker. It turned out to be Anna, the object of a long-standing crush. I'd known her three years before during one of my summer tutoring programs and, like at least a dozen other guys of my acquaintance, I'd developed a fascination for this exotic Eastern European (she'd immigrated with her parents from behind the Iron Curtain) who spoke six or seven languages and displayed a cutting sense of humor to go along with her smoky gray eyes, aquiline profile, and lovely legs. Alas, she'd been involved with another guy—a Yale hockey star, no less—when I knew her before.

But now, she agreed to go out for coffee and then pleased me even more when, after the rain had begun to clear, she impulsively came along on that afternoon's hike. The next day we walked three miles into the hills and on the way home held hands. I would have celebrated a magnificent new romantic focus in my life except for the massively inconvenient fact that she was still fully involved with the hockey star. To add an odd touch of symmetry and irony, their rocky relationship represented one more example of that ubiquitous Jewish-Irish attraction that I had recently escaped by breaking up with Faye. This meant that I could try to appeal to Anna as a landsman—a fellow countryman and comrade—as well as a means to richer, more fulfilling Jewish identity. But I had only nine days to make this case—she had committed herself to a trip to Europe (that continent I had always loathed) to visit her old hometown, and after that she would fly to California to begin graduate work at Stanford.

The time limit gave our brief days of talking and walking an altogether unnatural and fatally appealing intensity. Shortly before her departure she asked me to meet her in California; initially, she may have meant only that I visit, but I immediately committed to moving west permanently in order to pursue her. The two of us pledged to suspend all attempts at communication but to meet at the stroke of noon on a specific Monday in September at the main entrance to the Hoover Institution tower on the Stanford campus. An outsider might consider it childish and irresponsible to share this sacred determination to arrange our next date more than three months in advance, but everything about our connection made instinctive sense to us. I actually felt enormously proud of this flamboyantly romantic gesture and made the mistake of telling my parents; my mother once again panicked over her perception of my manic state.

Nevertheless, my parents welcomed me into their home after I made the cross-country trek (with a significant detour in Yellowstone) in the sturdy Mustang convertible. I planned to spend the summer with them before heading up to Stanford in September, and I was delighted to have a chance to reconnect with my brothers, who, ranging in age from fifteen to ten, had begun to emerge as fascinating people in their own right. Shortly after my arrival, however, my Uncle Moish insisted on dragging me off to a session of religious brainwashing and propaganda: a gala Chassidic concert and *ferbrengen* (get-together). He assumed that my newfound curiosity about Jewish tradition would make me an eager participant, but I resisted, even resented, his invitation. For one thing, this heavily hyped "Encounter with Chabad" involved the same fervently Orthodox group that ran the New Haven Hebrew Day School and exploited my free teaching services for a full academic year; I felt no desire whatever to delve deeper into their isolated, alien world. My uncle admired this irrepressibly energetic, vaguely cultish group, which had managed to transplant itself from Russia to America and had recently begun the absurdly ambitious project of installing Chabad Houses in virtually every community across the country. The Lubavitchers struck me at that time as simple-minded, rule-obsessed automatons, and it bothered me that Uncle Moish assumed that my own Jewish journey in some way connected to their extremism.

Nevertheless, I went along with my uncle to avoid provoking an argument or hurting his feelings. During most of the program I felt bored and skeptical, fidgeting during the musical performances (which lacked the story-telling richness of the Yiddish songs I loved) and the speeches (which argued that the Jewish tradition provided a deeper truth). During the intermission my uncle explained his strong feelings about the proceedings. "When I was a boy in Russia these people were everywhere—Chassidic people, religious people, who spent every minute trying to get closer to God," he recalled. "But then the Communists came and they tried to get rid of them because they were inconvenient and counterrevolutionary. And then Hitler came and he tried to kill them all. And here in America, every-body just took it for granted that the old ways were dead and they could never come back. So this is a miracle, what you see tonight. A miracle, that here in Los Angeles, this sect that goes back two hundred years comes back to life and draws a big crowd. Even if you don't like the singing and the speeches, this miracle is what you should remember."

Before we went back to our seats for the second half of the program we strolled through the lobby and passed various tables where members of the Chabad movement offered books, tracts, records, or Sabbath candles. At one table, a red-bearded rabbi called to me: "Hold on a minute, you! Yes, you! Come over here—just a minute." He beckoned for us to approach him and immediately shot out an oddly assorted series of questions. "Just a couple of things to ask you: Do you care about the peace of Jerusalem? You want to strengthen our brothers who're defending the Jewish people? Did you put on tefillin today?"

I had no idea what he meant, but his warmth and heartiness drew me into conversation, as Uncle Moish stood behind me, bemused but approv-ing. Tefillin—known in English as "phylacteries"—are the little wood and leather boxes that religious Jewish males wear on their arms and foreheads as part of daily prayer. I had, of course, seen these strange contraptions in photographs and paintings—particularly the kitschy artwork of pious sages and scholars that my mother and other nostalgic Jewish homeowners often displayed on their walls. I had never worn tefillin, however, or even been in the same room with someone who did.

The fast-talking rabbi with the red beard tried to explain his mission. "You care about what's going on in Israel, right?"

I confirmed my family's strong feelings about Israel and Jerusalem, where both of Uncle Moish's daughters had moved and married. At the time, the Israelis had just concluded the bloody War of Attrition with Egypt, which claimed more than 1,500 Israeli lives—double the death toll suffered during the nation's sweeping victory in the Six-Day War some four years before, and a vastly greater proportional loss than America suf-fered in eight years of Vietnam. The jovial rabbi, who introduced himself as Shlomo Schwartz but insisted that everyone knew him as "Schwartzie," argued for a mystical means of expressing concern for Israel's ongoing agony. "Whenever there's danger in Jerusalem," he explained, "this mitz-vah—this specific commandment—of putting on tefillin becomes particu-larly important. That's what the sages say, and there's a *medrish*, a teaching, going back more than two thousand years. So if you want to give strength to our brothers and sisters who are protecting Israel, then you can do something right here by putting on these tefillin—today, and every day."

Out of curiosity more than obligation, I agreed, and there, in the crowded lobby, I performed for the first time in my life one of the daily du-ties of Jewish devotion. The rabbi helped me put on each of the two phy-lacteries—the first box applied to the muscle of my left arm, then the long leather strap wrapped seven times around my forearm, before pronounc-ing a blessing: "Blessed are you, O Lord our God, King of the universe, Who has sanctified us with His commandments and has commanded us to put on tefillin." Then the second box went onto my forehead, with the leather straps encircling my head and a knot resting at the nape of the neck. Under the rabbi's prompting, I pronounced a second blessing. Then, finally, he showed me how to wind the arm strap around my middle finger which represented, he said, the attachment of a wedding ring. I then re-cited in Hebrew and English words from the Biblical book of Hosea: "I will betroth you to Me forever, and I will betroth you to Me with right-eousness, justice, kindness, and mercy. I will betroth you to Me with fidelity, and you shall know the Lord."

With both tefillin now fully attached, I stood there feeling totally ridiculous, as Schwartzie asked me to recite the simple *Shma* prayer—"Hear O Israel, the Lord is God, the Lord is One"—the one short sentence of Hebrew liturgy unmistakably familiar to me (and to most Jews, no mat-ter how detached from their faith). Finally, he led me through a special blessing, the *Shehechiyanu*, to note the fact that this brief transaction repre-sented a new milestone for me: "Blessed are you, Lord our God, King of the universe, Who has kept us alive, sustained us, and allowed us reach this season."

The red-bearded Chassid and my Uncle Moish both joined in a loud, emphatic "Amen!" and the rabbi clapped me proudly on the back. During most of the five-minute experience of winding straps and repeating words, I had felt too self-conscious to note if I had received some sort of supernat-ural charge, but when reciting the *Shma* prayer about God's oneness I had experienced an intensely physical tingling sensation as I closed my eyes, almost sexual in its pleasurable electricity, spreading from my head down to the torso and on through all four limbs before it dissipated. I didn't know what this meant, and I still don't—even though I receive the same wave of warmth and goose bumps on rare occasions when I manage to pray with special focus and intensity.

My first encounter with tefillin hardly featured that sort of prayer: at that time I wasn't even sure I believed in God, so I tried to understand why this ancient ritual had produced an irrational sense of satisfaction and solidarity. Back at my parents' house, I began pulling books off the shelf to read about the background of what I'd done. I learned that the boxes I had bound to my arm and my forehead contained little pieces of parchment hand-inscribed with four Biblical verses from Deuteronomy and Exodus, including "You shall love the Lord thy God with all your heart, and all your soul, and all your might." The tradition insisted that when attaching the tefillin, you must bind your arm *before* you bind your head, because the Jewish approach stresses changing behavior as a way of changing your thoughts and your mind, rather than the other way around. In other words, directing the work of your hands, of your arm, toward purposes of goodness will instill, rather than merely express the presence of, inner goodness in your mind and soul. Herman Wouk, popular novelist (*The Winds of War, The Caine Mutiny*) and peerless Jewish teacher, explained the process in a way that I grasped immediately. "We have here a ceremony dedicating arm and brain to God," he wrote in *This Is My God*. "The act does not then and there make a man good, but if the imagery takes hold in his mind, it ought to make him a better man, provided he is improvable."

I wanted desperately to believe myself improvable, and the next morning as various Medveds puttered around the kitchen fixing breakfast, Uncle Moish came up to me and silently handed over a royal blue velvet bag the size of a hardcover book. "What's this?" I asked.

"It's my tefillin," he said. "I don't use them anymore. Maybe you would. After yesterday, I thought you would be interested."

After breakfast I found a quiet corner of the busy house, put on the phylacteries, and read from a prayer book in the halting Hebrew left over from my Bar Mitzvah. And every morning for the rest of that homecoming summer I made the same choice, getting more proficient every day at the

Hebrew blessings and the mechanics of attaching the boxes and leather straps to my arm and head. I never felt impelled to attend synagogue or to try to pray with a group of pious Jews; my experimentation remained so personal that I even felt uneasy when other members of the family saw what I was doing. I couldn't have explained myself in any coherent or rational style. Rabbi Schwartz had suggested that this consecrated daily activity somehow strengthened the Jewish people as far away as Israel. Against all logic, I felt stronger myself and sensed that I contributed in some indefinable spiritual way to an overall toughening and quickening of our identity.

During those weeks at home, we also began to celebrate the Sabbath more substantively and regularly—with my dad making a point of coming home early on Friday nights, leading the blessing over the wine at a big sit-down meal, singing and arguing and laughing with his four boys, his wife, and his silver-haired brother, Moish. I knew that my mother welcomed this greater emphasis on Shabbat as a response to my own freshly minted and somewhat suspicious religiosity. Here I was, in her house, praying every day like her Orthodox grandparents, but she still worried about me. I held no job (though I continued to make slow progress on my political novel), refused to return to law school, and still planned to move out at the end of the summer to chase some mysterious woman in the Bay Area. My mother could only hope that my new Jewish commitment might prove to last longer than all the other fads or fleeting fascinations that regularly commanded my attention.

I tried to reassure her, telling her on several occasions that I felt happier, more fulfilled than at any time I could remember. I believed at the time that the basis for this joy was my expectation of imminent reunion with Anna or my increasingly self-confident steps toward a life of Jewish commitment and authenticity. Unfortunately, I missed the biggest, most obvious reason I felt so good so much of the time: I simply loved living at home, getting to know my brothers, spending time with my brilliant, demanding Uncle Moish, and reconstructing a loving relationship with each of my parents. I had left this boisterous home six years earlier at the ridiculous age of sixteen because of the inane unwritten rule that says that all ambitious middle-class kids must strike out on their own as soon as they graduate from high school. This absurd superstition rests on the illogical assumption that when a child approaches the age of eighteen, a mother and father can do nothing more to advance that individual's development and maturation. At this point, in other words, the vulnerable adolescent should turn from his parents to his professors (what a horrifying thought) or, more likely, to his collegiate peers as the main source of guidance and enlightenment. The belief that this shift represents the sort of benign, inevitable progress made no sense to me, and remains equally irrational when applied to my daughter, who, in 2004, left our loving home at age seventeen for educational advancement some ten thousand miles away.

In leaving my own parents (again!) at the end of my homecoming summer of '71, I didn't have the excuse of making academic progress, and based the entire move on a childish, prearranged romantic meeting at high noon on the Stanford campus. Even if that potential intimate relationship never worked out—and after three months of separation, I had little confidence that it would—I knew several friends who had recently settled in the San Francisco area. To arrange my life as close as possible to those friends and not *too* close to Anna if the relationship faltered, I decided on Berkeley, an hour's drive from Stanford. I found a studio apartment just a mile from the University of California campus in that woodsy, artsy, countercultural community. I also walked in off the street and managed to talk my way into a job as a clerk at Record City, a crowded hole-in-the-wall shop on funky Telegraph Avenue, Berkeley's main drag, famously populated by drug dealers and homeless messiahs and street performers and busy students. Perhaps this employment represented something less than an ideal opportunity for a guy with a Yale degree and some high-level political experience, but I still felt delighted to work in a familiar environment (after three years of part-time record store work in New Haven) where I could indulge my passion for music. According to my careful calculations, my meager salary—only a few pennies above minimum wage—would bring in just enough to cover my modest rent and limited food expenses while I spent all my free time finishing my novel.

Two days later, on a sweltering September afternoon, I drove down to Stanford for my fateful appointment with Anna. Sweating and fretting as I fought the ridiculous traffic, I worried that I'd arrive late for our sacred appointment. I entertained visions of my gray-eyed friend fitfully checking her watch, then making a tearful departure from the scene moments before I arrived—like a Thomas Hardy heroine consigned by chance and mis-understanding to some crushing destiny. As I tried to focus more rationally on my situation, I concluded that odds and logic dictated that she wouldn't show up at all, and I'd be the one waiting in vain for a faithless sweetheart.

She did keep me waiting for nearly fifteen minutes, but then she appeared, looking sheepish and stressed while, to my surprise, taking long, hungry drags on a cigarette. (It was a nasty new habit she had picked up during her three months in Europe, she said—which I noted as yet another reason to curse the despised Continent of Death.) We wasted little time with small talk before she dropped the bomb that I had half-expected all along: she had used the time of our separation to decide we could never build a happy relationship because the impassioned intensity that ruled us both would result in mutual combustion. In place of the tears or pleas generally associated with such moments of melodrama, we both seemed to feel an odd sense of relief. We agreed that it would be best for both of us if we never saw each other again, but two weeks later she gave me a call and drove up to Berkeley for an edgy visit. After that interchange, we made the goodbyes stick. She is today a distinguished academic with a tenured, prestigious position and five well-received books—including published volumes of her poetry. Anna, for the record, is not her real name.

After the abrupt termination of our tentative romance, I had no further excuse for living in Berkeley, but I'd already placed a deposit on my studio apartment and secured a record store job so I decided to stay for a few months at least. I explored San Francisco at night when I got off work, flirted shamelessly with any vaguely eligible women who ventured into the record store, and tried to connect with Jewish life on the Cal campus. My first Friday night I visited the Chabad House for a community *Shabbes* dinner, hoping to feel uplifted by the same outreach-oriented Chassidic group that had introduced me to tefillin a few months before. Unfortunately, the dingy atmosphere at the Berkeley establishment scared me away, with the other guests including Hare Krishna devotees in saffron robes, a few rank-smelling homeless wanderers who seemed entirely unaware of their whereabouts, and a smattering of cynical, wise-cracking students more interested in free chicken and sweet kosher wine than any spiritual sustenance.

While Chabad initially struck me as a refuge for lonely losers, I felt vastly more comfortable with another campus group called the Radical Jewish Union. Despite its resounding revolutionary title, the organization actually served a counterrevolutionary purpose: challenging the increasingly anti-Israel emphasis of the Berkeley left and trying to instill some national pride in wavering students who might otherwise feel more devotion to Mao than to Moses. During that fall semester, Jewish activists at the University of California protested the use of student money and facilities for the screening of a vicious Palestinian propaganda film called *Revolution Until Victory*, which featured crude footage of chanting guerillas calling for Israel's destruction as they waved Kalashnikovs in the air. They also objected when the student union held a program featuring the bearded Bob Scheer, an editor of *Ramparts* magazine and a failed antiwar congressional candidate in 1966, who asserted that the same colonialism that led to American "genocide" in Vietnam led to Israeli suppression of the peace-loving, generous-hearted Palestinian people. Scheer, now a prominent liberal columnist for the *LA Times*, made much of his Jewish ancestry and unforgettably asserted, "If Moses were alive today, if Elijah were alive today, they'd pick up submachine guns, put on Kafiyehs, and join the PLO! Long live the Palestinian revolution! Revolution until victory!"

In general, the political agenda of the Radical Jewish Union (despite its avowedly socialist perspective on "economic justice" issues) placed the little group at odds with the overwhelmingly "third world" slant of the Berkeley student body. For the first time ever, I found myself participating in an organization tagged as "right wing" or even "fascist" by the local arbiters of "progressive" values. Meanwhile, I quickly discovered that the mindless and self-righteous Berkeley support for any murderous cause identified with revolutionary violence—whether the locally popular Black Panthers, Castro's Cuba, Mao's China, Ho Chi Minh's Vietnam, or even (for some pompous, America-hating fools) Brezhnev's Soviet Union—made Yale's radicalism look genteel and moderate. At the time, though, I was less focused on challenging left-wing intolerance than on joining the Friday night communal dinners that the Radical Jewish Union hosted. These gatherings featured affectionate nods to traditionalism (the standard blessing on the Sabbath wine, the patient chanting of the Grace after Meals) along with innovations peculiar to that time and place. For instance, instead of slicing and distributing the braided and fresh-baked egg bread (challah) after one leader pronounced the blessing, we all placed our hands on the huge loaves, simultaneously recited the words, and then tore off our individual pieces of the whole.

I connected with other centers of religious energy in the East Bay, as well. Berkeley Hillel, the mainstream Jewish organization on campus, had recently employed a bright and engaging Orthodox rabbi, and I began attending Sabbath afternoon classes at his home. He stressed the spiritual significance of even the most difficult to comprehend details of meticulous observance. At his suggestion, I began purchasing thick, white Sabbath candles and lighting them at sunset on Friday night, offering a blessing in my Spartan apartment before driving off to Shabbat dinner parties. At times, I'd return to my dark home to find the twin flames still burning; on those occasions, I'd keep the lights off and watch the candles hiss, thinking about how my grandmothers on both sides lit these same flames, every Friday night of their lives, wherever they found themselves in the wounded world. I thought of W. H. Auden's famous poem commemorating the first day of the Second World War:

> *Defenceless under the night*
> *Our world in stupor lies;*
> *Yet, dotted everywhere,*
> *Ironic points of light*
> *Flash out wherever the Just*
> *Exchange their messages.*

I hoped to exchange such messages, to count myself among the Just, and to show my own "affirming flame."

Meanwhile, the lights went out on my fading dreams of novelistic glory. During visits with David Wallechinsky, an old high school friend who had recently relocated to Berkeley, I'd heard about a literary agent in New York (a friend of David's father, best-selling novelist Irving Wallace) who had just set up shop and wanted promising clients. I spoke to Artie Pine on the phone and sent him a copy of my mostly completed novel, *The Lesser Evil.* Artie, with his thick New York accent, expressed burbling and infectious enthusiasm for the book but over the next several weeks had no success selling it to publishers. When he sent back the manuscript I first blamed Artie for my failure (not even dreaming that he and his son and business partner, Richard, would work as my agents for the next three decades). After spending an hour reading over my own work, however, I experience an intense spasm of disgust, and seriously considered flushing all three hundred pages down the toilet except for my concerns about costly plumbing damage I could ill afford.

I told no one about my literary train-wreck, continuing to portray myself to my friends and new acquaintances as a novelist on the cusp of greatness who worked only temporarily as a pathetically paid record store clerk. Most importantly, I kept my parents in the dark about this embarrassing setback for fear of their sensible demands that I return home immediately or reenroll at law school. I began to feel guilty about playing an imposter's role in my busy but unfocused Berkeley life.

As Christmas season approached, I thought about getting back into politics. I knew I could get a job with either Senator Edmund Muskie or Senator George McGovern as they prepared for their presidential campaigns, but neither candidate inspired me. Uncertain and self-pitying, I accepted an invitation to a potluck Hanukah party at the apartment of a friend from the Radical Jewish Union. I immediately focused my attention on one particular guest, Nancy, a student at the California College of Arts and Crafts in neighboring Oakland, who glowed with sex appeal and self-assurance. We spent the evening sitting cross-legged in a corner, flirting and laughing. It felt like old home week talking to Nancy: her parents lived in Beverly Hills, only a few miles from my parents' home, and her father served on the board of the same Conservative congregation my folks had joined when they first moved to LA. She told me she had rebelled as a teenager against her family's narrow-minded Jewish identity and had only recently begun coming back to affiliation with her own people. I told her my own zigzagging tale of rediscovery and return, urging her to deepen her commitment as a precious daughter of Israel.

The next day I kept calling Nancy (in that Mesozoic era before answering machines) until I finally found her at home. After some hesitation she agreed to meet me for coffee, just hours before she planned to board a plane to visit her parents in Beverly Hills. During our brief minutes together, I spoke to her rhapsodically about her coffee-colored eyes, while admiring her olive skin and wild, kinky black hair. Grabbing her hand, I started reciting Shakespeare more or less at random, for no particular reason battering her with Act V, Scene I of *The Merchant of Venice:*

> *How sweet the moonlight sleeps upon this bank!*
> *Here will we sit and let the sounds of music*
> *Creep in our ears. Soft stillness and the night*
> *Become the touches of sweet harmony.*

When we parted, I feared that I had overdone it, but she took my calls when I phoned her at home and expressed her eagerness to see me when she returned to Berkeley. Unlike the other women I had passionately pursued (Lynn, Faye, Anna), she had no pretensions or qualifications as an intellectual, but she took such hot-blooded pride in her own quirkiness and creativity that it hardly mattered. At California College of Arts and Crafts she specialized in gallery-quality fabric sculpture and silk screen printing, and I felt pugnaciously proud of all her work even if I never claimed to understand it.

Just six weeks into our relationship, we flew together to Los Angeles to meet her family. As soon as she met me, her effusive, hyperenergetic maternal grandmother concluded that we were engaged and welcomed me to the family with embraces, wet kisses, shrieks of joy, tears, and mazel tovs. In fact, I had not explicitly proposed to Nancy, but we had already jointly and tacitly assumed that we would marry, so we did nothing to discourage the notion that we'd become engaged. My parents also felt delighted with the match, though my father worried about my tender age. I was twenty-three; Nancy was twenty-one. I reminded Dad that he had been two years younger than I was when he married my mom, but given the often rocky course of their partnership (particularly in its early years) he hardly considered the argument conclusive.

Above all, Nancy's parents made the idea of our marriage seem appropriate, appealing, even inevitable. For nearly thirty years they had enjoyed their own richly romantic relationship, with Nancy's elegant mom focused on maintaining her home as a showplace of hospitality and style, while her gruff, kindly poppa earned a lavish living as a real estate developer (and gave with a free hand to Jewish charities). Compared to the over-the-top emotional intensity of the Medved household, Nancy's family seemed normal, functional, reliable. Despite my lack of immediately apparent prospects, they eagerly adopted me as their new son and began planning a sumptuous wedding. I welcomed the wedding as the ultimate act of home-coming—home building, really—and Jewish affirmation, while feeling especially lucky with the fortuitous way the nuptial plans intersected with my new political priorities.

Judaism Is a Better Religion
for Jews Than Liberalism

"**J**ust when I thought I was out, they pull me back in!" groaned Michael Corleone in the most celebrated line of *Godfather III,* mourning his inability to avoid a reluctant return to the corrupt, dangerous life he had hoped to leave behind.

I felt similarly trapped in the spring of '72 (some eighteen years before the release of that final installment of the cinematic mobster epic), dragged with great trepidation into a raging political war I ardently wanted to avoid. By citing the famous lament of a fictional crime boss, I don't mean to equate the antiwar activist/New Politics network that compelled my involvement with the New York Mafia, but the two operations did boast a number of common features. Like organized crime, the liberal "peacenik" wing of the Democratic Party deployed its tentacles everywhere through dedicated little cells, linked by a sense of common purpose, ruthless determination, and a misleading but reassuring notion of "family." Leftists and mobsters required a similar willingness to sacrifice for the sake of the organization, while indulging blood feuds among bitterly warring factions and promoting an arcane code of honor improbably fused with a win-at-any-cost amorality. The bosses of the embattled McGovern for President campaign knew how to work the levers of guilt, obligation, nostalgia, and menace as skillfully as any Mafia don. In terms of antiwar politics, I counted as a made man, a wise guy, and in a situation of total war the capos couldn't allow me to turn my back on my old comrades in arms.

In part my desire to avoid the political scene stemmed from my scant personal attraction to George McGovern as a candidate. I viewed the South Dakota senator as a nonentity deployed as a convenient (if largely empty) vessel by our ongoing McCarthy-Kennedy movement; I used to make fun of the senator's clenched-teeth, prairie-flat, nasal delivery, and how he looked like a much less flamboyant version of "the People's Pianist," Liberace. More importantly, a frenetic new political gig hardly seemed the ideal way to begin married life with Nancy; my prior political experience had taught me that the all-consuming toil of an itinerant gypsy campaigner conflicted in obvious, inevitable ways with my determination to establish a stable, rewarding, mature, monogamous marriage. Nancy herself was utterly indifferent to the outcome of the Democratic primaries, while my prospective in-laws looked upon the McGovern campaign with undisguised dread, considering this trendy cause a simultaneous threat to their daughter's nuptial plans and the survival of the Republic.

By late spring, the race for the Democratic nomination had come down to a two-man duel between McGovern and former vice president Hubert Humphrey. Two former colleagues from the Lowenstein campaign called to insist that I go to work for McGovern, saying that the struggle for the future of the party had come down to one climactic winner-take-all primary in California—and Jewish Democrats had emerged as a crucial swing vote. Although wealthy Jews from the most fashionable circles of New York and LA represented such a heavy percentage—indeed, perhaps a majority—of McGovern's top financial backers, the McGovern high command had learned that outside of Park Avenue and Beverly Hills, Jews with a more serious religious (or at least ethnic) commitment looked with skepticism if not outright suspicion at the South Dakota senator. Humphrey, in contrast, had established an intense emotional bond during his three previous campaigns for national office. Unlike McGovern, whose neoisolationism left him wary of the U.S. commitment to Israel, Humphrey had become one of the nation's most outspoken advocates of American suppor for the Jewish state. In debates, Humphrey pointedly needled McGovern over his uncertain affinity for Israel, and polling data showed that these attacks had begun to make an appreciable impact in California's substantial Jewish community.

As much as McGovern left me lukewarm, I listened to my friends' entreaties because Hubert Humphrey looked incalculably worse—disgraced in my eyes as a longtime apologist for LBJ's Vietnam policy and the big-city machine candidate who had blocked the late Bobby Kennedy's path to the Democratic nomination. I became more tempted when I learned that the McGovern campaign wanted me to move temporarily to LA, the site of the statewide headquarters and the teeming center of Jewish population in the Golden State; this relocation would make it much easier for Nancy and me to work out the intricate details of our August wedding. Finally, a surprisingly generous offer of payment for one month of political consultant work sealed the deal: no matter how much my future in-laws might despise McGovern, I felt more entitled to their respect by instantly quadrupling my record clerk's salary.

As it turned out, the McGovern campaign brought with it a series of family fringe benefits, including a greatly enhanced relationship with my brother Jonathan, the oldest of my three siblings. During my seven years away from home, he'd grown up from a roly-poly, precocious, and self-consciously adorable tyke to a burly, self-confident, explosively energetic, widely accomplished teenager. Having worked as a volunteer advance man in the 1970 senatorial campaign of John Tunney in California, Jonathan eagerly embraced the opportunity to work alongside me in the McGovern campaign, often cutting class during his final weeks of high school to find his way to our "Conversion of the Jews" headquarters on Fairfax Avenue. To our conspiratorial delight, we discovered that we sounded exactly alike on the telephone—same inflections, same verbal patterns, same pitch to our voices. This enabled me to accomplish twice as much in dealing with the various calls that filled my days, since my kid brother authoritatively handled routine conversations as "Michael Medved." Thirty years later, I began inviting Jonathan to join me on my radio show in his role as one of Israel's leading venture capitalists and political commentators, which provokes regular comments from listeners on the eerie resemblance in our on-air presentation.

During the California primary battle of '72, my father took inordinate pride in the feverish politicking of both his sons, viewing the McGovern cause as a means for completing the unfinished work of the Kennedy campaign of four years before. My Uncle Moish, however, expressed nothing but contempt for our involvement in a cause he despised and took every opportunity to remind us of his enthusiastic support for Humphrey. My uncle's contempt for our candidate arose not only from McGovern's indifferent attitude toward Israel but also from the South Dakotan's advocacy of a foreign policy which Moish considered "appeasement and surrender." He remained implacably opposed to that deadly and contagious "Scarlet Plague"—the disease of international Communism—about which he had warned me more than a decade earlier. He barked out that McGovern qualified as one of those simple-minded fools who harbored secret sympathies for the Marxist barbarians. We hooted at such warnings, with their echoes of discredited McCarthyism, and cringed when Moish pledged that if McGovern won the Democratic nomination he would abandon our family's traditional party allegiance and cast his precious vote, as a naturalized and patriotic American, for Richard Nixon.

Even in the midst of the all-absorbing primary battle, I understood that the cunning president had established a radical new context for all conversation about the war. Nixon had already withdrawn hundreds of thousands of Americans from Southeast Asia in pursuit of the policy he called "Vietnamization," turning over more of the fighting to our South Vietnamese, anti-Communist allies. With high-profile peace talks under way in Paris, the United States now fought for precisely the sort of diplomatic compromise and negotiated settlement that Kennedy and McCarthy once demanded in their antiwar campaigns. Most importantly, Nixon ended the practice of drafting young Americans to fight in Vietnam, relying entirely on volunteers while moving decisively toward today's professional army of willing warriors. When my Yale acquaintance John Kerry testified to the Senate in April of 1971 as leader of Vietnam Veterans Against the War, he carefully phrased his famous question to adjust to the new realities. "How do you ask a man to be the last man to die for a mistake?" he declared—using the term "ask," not "order" or "force" or "compel." The voluntary nature of Southeast Asian service helped strip the antiwar movement of its moral force. Meanwhile, McGovern's demand for immediate withdrawal and his ultimate campaign slogan of "Come Home, America" leant credence to charges of naive isolationism. "You're spoiled, you boys," my uncle used to say to Jonathan and to me. "You've had it too easy all your lives. You don't understand the way the world works. You don't understand the way the Communists think. If you're dealing with bullies, with violent and angry people, you don't make yourself safer by running away or giving them what they want. That just makes sure they hit you again and again."

Meanwhile, Jonathan and I hit unsuspecting voters with defiant assertions of Jewish nationalism, transforming a neighborhood campaign headquarters into the "McGovern Jewish Center"—the very heart of our shameless effort to wrap a WASPy, white-bread candidate in so many layers of schmaltzy ethnic identity that nervous voters wouldn't pause to ponder the uncertainties of his Middle East policy. At our offices, we installed a little portable record player and pumped out a selection of traditional Israeli and Yiddish music (including my favorite album of folk songs by Theodore Bikel), blaring nostalgic melodies all day and most of the night through remote speakers onto the busy street. I also dispatched my brother and several other volunteers to make phone calls to every rabbi of any denomination we could find anywhere in California, in order to compile a massive "Rabbis for McGovern" list that we could use in any ads or leaflets aimed at Jewish voters. Predictably enough, the names of endorsing rabbis came disproportionately from the Reform movement of Judaism— the most liberal branch, both theologically and politically. When Hubert Humphrey's campaign hit us with a full-page ad in all the local Jewish newspapers designed to make McGovern look like a peacenik and appeaser (which, in fact, he was), contrasting his calls for a more balanced, "even-handed" Middle Eastern policy (and his one-time support for an "internationalized" Jerusalem) with Humphrey's robust, unwavering support for Israel, I responded by designing a two-page spread under the optimistic headline SCARE TACTICS WON'T WORK WITH THE JEWISH VOTER. This included a handsome photograph of the skyline of the Old City of Jerusalem, accompanied by ringing endorsements of McGovern from Jewish celebrities and communal leaders (including, of course, the Rabbis for McGovern) and a series of pleasant platitudes by Senator McGovern pronouncing his passionate admiration for Israel as the only democracy in the Middle East.

I wrote most of these reassuring declarations, getting them approved at Washington headquarters.

I have no idea to this day whether McGovern ever personally saw these ardent affirmations released to the public in his name. Even at the time, I felt vaguely embarrassed by devising such over-the-top propaganda, especially when I saw that some of the rabidly pro-Israel rhetoric I had crafted began making its way into McGovern press releases for the New York primary. I considered this sort of exploitative, patronizing politics both silly and necessary, given the visceral attachment that many Jews (particularly of the older generation) felt toward Israel.

Despite my cynicism toward pandering politics, my daily immersion in this communal combat subtly deepened my own sense of ethnic identification. Following up on a passing suggestion from my McGovern-hating Uncle Moish, I arranged for the famous neo-Chassidic, spiritually energized, guitar-strumming rabbi and revivalist Shlomo Carlebach to perform for us at a McGovern rally. I had attended one of Reb Shlomo's performances at Yale and seen how he electrified a mixed audience of Jews and gentiles with his ecstatic singing, dancing, and storytelling. In return for a carefully negotiated cash contribution to his burgeoning "House of Love and Prayer," the legendary teacher and troubadour agreed to fly to Los Angeles. A few hundred enthusiasts turned out for a noon street-corner rally, and Shlomo, with his kindly bug eyes, graying beard, portly form, and rainbow-hued guitar strap, got everyone singing along with his seductive *niggunim*, or wordless melodies. He also adopted traditional texts to produce his own inspirational songs, repeating the same phrases ("The whole world is waiting / To sing this song of *Shabbes*! You and I are waiting / To sing this song of *Shabbes*!") with often hypnotic effect. We clapped, we jumped, we danced, we linked hands, singing praises to the Creator on a sweltering day late in May while the TV cameras rolled and the newspaper photographers clicked. That press coverage represented the only real justification for the event—showing a group of young people in energetic, rapturous song, affirming their Jewish heritage in response to a charismatic holy man, all only tangentially connected to the McGovern campaign. One of my fellow political operatives nudged me as I sang myself hoarse, commenting that our event resembled "some Come-to-Jesus camp meeting" more than any ordinary electioneering event. That felt fine with me, and I embraced Rabbi Carlebach with real emotion after he finally acceded to my request and concluded his performance with some vague remarks about the candidate.

The national campaign planned a very different Jewish event in Los Angeles. "The Stars Come Out for McGovern!" promised a huge rally at the Fairfax High School football stadium, featuring an odd assortment of Hollywood celebrities and the senator himself, who would deliver a major address on America and Israel. But as it happened, the stands were only about a third full, and much of the program was uninspiring, including McGovern's speech, in which he offered, in his bland, perfunctory style, precisely the sort of condescending clichés about Israel's "sacred right to exist" that I had written in his ads. Most of the "stars," meanwhile, were B-list actors like Sally Kellerman (who had played "Hot Lips" in the movie version of *M*A*S*H*) and Jack Klugman. But the climax of the show came from Joel Grey, the hyperkinetic song-and-dance man who had won a well-deserved supporting actor Oscar for his role as the Master of Ceremonies in *Cabaret*. Grey introduced a Yiddish number as an emotional tribute to his father, Mickey Katz, the creator of the Jewish novelty act "The Borscht Review," which once delighted Catskills crowds in upstate New York. "So maybe some of you know what I'm about to sing," Grey told the crowd. "It was made famous a long, long time ago by the great Aaron Lebedeff. Here it is . . . *Rumania! Rumania!*"

A knowing, approving murmur went through the oldsters in the previously indifferent crowd, and as I stood at one side of the stage I found myself moved and stirred in a way I never expected by Grey's affectionate, finger-snapping performance. The song begins with a slow, melancholy, richly tuneful, immigrant recollection of a lost homeland:

> *Oy! Rumania, Rumania, Rumania, Rumania, Rumania, Rumania!*
> *Es gib amol a lant, a zeese a shayna!*
>
> O! Rumania. . . .
> Once there was a land, a sweet one and beautiful!

The singer recalls the culinary treats of the old country—a pastrami, a spicy sausage, and glass of Rumanian wine—saying, "Oh, it is a life-giving joy, nothing can possibly be better! Oh, it's a sweet pleasure, to drink

Rumanian wine!" He then goes ahead to a leaping, high-kicking performance of nonsense syllables (*eye-dicka-dicky-dom-dicky-dicky-dom!*) with the orchestra playing faster and faster and the singer fairly exploding with joy and energy. The crowd went wild at Fairfax High School, and after the rally I went directly to a Jewish music shop to secure a copy of the Aaron Lebedeff original, which I played incessantly in our headquarters thereafter. We had only a few days left till the primary, and as we looked toward the end of our operation the inevitable aura of anticipatory nostalgia began to set in. This time, however, I wasn't simply thinking of my ties to my fellow campaigners; as I listened again and again and again to Aaron Lebedeff crooning about his vanished Rumania, I wondered where my own yearning, my dreams of home, might focus in the future. Where would I identify my "Rumania, Rumania"? I had left Philadelphia before the age of six, and San Diego had never been spicy or colorful enough to inspire that sort of longing. New Haven? I had left that college town behind more than two years ago, and many of my friends from that period had already vanished.

In the last hours of the McGovern campaign for the California primary, I came to realize with a heart-tugging emotional jolt that my own old country, my far away homeland, would always be right here, on tacky, tangy Fairfax Avenue. That neighborhood of modest Spanish-style bungalows with a few palms and fruit trees, of four-unit, two-story apartment buildings, of street-corner synagogues and bearded beggars in side curls and broad-brimmed black hats, of quarreling immigrants from Russia and Israel, of aspiring actors working as waiters, of ethnic markets and delis and kosher bakeries and religious bookstores—that neighborhood had begun to feel like home to me. Maybe it was a home from collective memory, or a previous life, or the remembrance of my long-departed grandparents in South Philly. But every morning as I arrived for work at headquarters, I stopped into Schwartz's Kosher Bakery (which opened at dawn) to buy a fresh-baked prune Danish—and then started buying two, so I'd have one to give to Mrs. Appelbaum, the gray-haired yenta in the floral muumuus who came in each day to stuff envelopes and schmooze. At lunchtime I'd duck into the Chabad-Lubavitch center down the block, to reassure the boys who lurked in the doorway, waiting to assault passersby, that yes, I had put on my tefillin today. At night, often very late a night, I'd go into

Canter's Deli to enjoy the incomparable fragrance of the cured meats and sour pickles, wolfing down a mountainous sandwich of kosher-style pastrami on rye. Nancy stopped in to visit me at the office on a few occasions, and I introduced her proudly to everyone—my *Yiddishe maidel*, my Jewish maiden, soon to be my bride in a ceremony that would be just as traditional as we could make it. Walking those streets, savoring my role as the McGovern ambassador to a kingdom of Jews, I felt so comfortable, so fulfilled with my own Jewishness that I didn't want to leave, I didn't want to go back to bizarre, hippy-dippy Berkeley, I didn't want to acknowledge the inevitable fate of that neighborhood finding its distinctiveness dissipated and diluted (as, indeed, it has some thirty years later).

In short, I had gone native: having arrived in Fairfax to perform missionary work on behalf of the alien McGovern movement, I'd taken on the flavorful folkways of the locals, feeling far more kinship with their *kvetching* and gabbing and old country attachments than with the electoral agenda of the outlanders who had hired me. McGovern won the primary (and with it, largely wrapped up the nomination). But despite all our rabbinic endorsements and campaign literature translated into Yiddish, Humphrey overwhelmed us in the most ethnically identified Jewish enclaves. This gave my entire experience with the campaign a decisively bittersweet flavor, particularly as I dealt with the sudden and unavoidable dismantling of the campaign world that had been my focus for several unforgettably intense weeks.

As a kid, I'd enjoyed a 1930s novel by James T. Farrell called *Can All This Grandeur Perish?* He meant his title ironically, since the harsh Irish-American world he described hardly counted as grand, but I thought of that phrase two days after the election when I walked into the now largely abandoned and empty headquarters to clean out my files. When Mrs. Appelbaum came in for her daily visit I had no prune Danish to give her and no tasks to assign. She worried about another absence. "What happened to the music?" she wanted to know. "You took the record player away. What happened to all that beautiful *Yiddishe* music?"

Liberal Heroes Aren't All Heroes

With my wedding just a few weeks away, I turned down a flattering offer to continue in my well-paid position with the McGovern Jewish desk through the New York primary and then the Democratic Convention in late July. Instead, while Nancy and her mother focused on planning the ceremony, I headed back to Berkeley to set up the details of married life. With that in mind, I rented the bottom floor of a rambling, turn-of-the-century house in the leafy South Campus neighborhood across from the lush, green square block of Willard Park. At the time, the local left had already begun calling this pleasant enclave, favored by dog walkers and Frisbee throwers, Ho Chi Minh Park in honor of the North Vietnamese Communist leader who initially inspired the struggle against the French and then the Americans. At first I found it amusing and quirky to tell people that everyone referred to our neighborhood recreation area as a memorial to the goateed revolutionary who remained a deeply despised figure in the nation called America that continued to flourish beyond Berkeley's borders. By the time we left Northern California in 1975, however, I felt deeply ashamed—personally guilty, in fact—even to allow my dog to do her business in a city square called Ho Chi Minh Park.

Shortly after renting our new place, I got an unexpected phone call from a famous Berkeley lawyer and activist who helped lead the radical faction of the local Democratic Party. Like many of the area's leading leftists, John lived a comfortable life in a fashionable home in the sylvan hills above the Cal campus, but he identified himself as a tireless crusader for the downtrodden masses (many of them African-American) who lived in the shabbier, vastly more crowded "flats" that extended down toward Oakland and the San Francisco Bay. This genial, neighborly idealist told me on the phone that he'd heard great things about me from the national McGovernite network and asked me to take on a high-ranking position in the reelection campaign of the first-term congressman from Berkeley and Oakland, Ron Dellums.

Two years earlier, this strikingly charismatic African-American social worker and hard-left member of the Berkeley City Council had earned national headlines with his successful primary challenge to a well-established white moderate Democrat. Dellums, who quickly drew attention in Washington with his commanding height, towering Afro, drooping Fu Manchu mustache, and angry diatribes against American "colonialism and militarism," remained a stylish favorite among all those "beautiful people" who eagerly (if incoherently) desired revolutionary transformation in the United States. Despite his national stature and a tidal wave of campaign contributions, Ron (everyone referred to this coolest congressman—and comrade— by his first name) faced some problems with his reelection drive which some of his wealthy backers believed I could help solve. Thanks to redistricting by the fascist Republicans and diabolical establishment Democrats in the California legislature, this Castroite crusader for the "dispossessed" among Oakland blacks, Berkeley student radicals, and posh old lefties who fought the revolution from their hillside mansion barricades suddenly found himself in a new congressional district that looked notably more white, more suburban, and potentially more Republican. He had also drawn a formidable opponent—a glib, persuasive, moderate-sounding advertising executive named Peter Hannaford (who later achieved a formidable reputation as a speechwriter for President Reagan).

As John described the situation, I realized this veteran of countless "social justice" struggles was too sensitive and enlightened to say why he really needed me: Dellums had just inherited a bunch of upwardly mobile Jews who might feel more than a tad nervous about his openly expressed sympathy for anti-Semitic radicals both at home and abroad, from the Black Panther Party to the Palestine Liberation Organization. "You know, some of these new voters, they don't know Ron, and they might not understand where he's coming from, on certain emotional issues about American foreign policy, if you know what I mean," John explained.

I naturally felt wary of taking on a new assignment as the smiling Jewish, suburban face of the angriest black radical in Congress, but I liked the idea of participating in one of the nation's most exciting and attention-getting congressional battles without straying far from the new home I planned to establish. My semiofficial recruiter also readily agreed that I should take three weeks off for my wedding and honeymoon; he even expressed enthusiastic approval when I told him I had begun thinking about trying to avoid working on the Sabbath—which would take me out of the political pressure cooker from sundown Friday till full dark on Saturday night. "No, Michael, that's not a problem. In fact, we want you to do that— we'd encourage it!" he chortled, relishing (I imagined) an unanticipated ability to trot out not just any Jewboy to represent the campaign, but a Sabbath-observing Jewboy—as a rare token (the appropriate word, no doubt) of Ron's commitment to diversity and coalition-building.

The promised salary (which came with the lofty title campaign manager) helped seal the deal, but as I began integrating myself into the ongoing operation, the vaunted Dellums juggernaut proved far less formidable or focused than I had anticipated. My first contacts with the campaign operation, in fact, revealed a chaotic, overconfident crowd of arrogant amateurs who seemed far more concerned about one-upping one another with their poses of radical righteousness than working together under any conventional notion of political organization. The reelection campaign reflected all the long-standing fissures of the Berkeley left, with rich, tweedy, wine-sipping Old Lefties lavishing their patronizing approval on the swaggering, smoldering black nationalists, who in turn resented the Age of Aquarius, psychedelic squad from the campus, while the old-line

Democratic apparatchiks with their gritty organized labor background hated virtually all of the newcomers as a bunch of fruitcakes, dilettantes, and pinkos who would soon tire of their electoral adventures and leave the party to its rightful, long-term proprietors.

They all managed to unite on one point, at least: their common hostility to the latest unwelcome intruder—me. Of the first five meetings I scheduled, two participants stood me up entirely, and the other three turned up an hour or more late. Each of the three latecomers gave an identical but cryptic explanation for keeping me waiting. "CPT!" they insisted, and only when I demanded a translation did they laughingly expound on the concept of "Colored People's Time," elevating a pattern of sloppiness to a principle of cultural authenticity. Since two out of the three latecomers who used the excuse of "CPT" happened to be white, I viewed their attitude as unconscionably racist. Wasn't it racist to expect less of black people—in terms of achievement, decency, or even punctuality—just because they were black? Wouldn't it be even more racist to expect less of white people, just because they happened to represent a black guy with an attitude?

Ron's campaign displayed several other peculiar and worrisome features, including an odd habit of paying for everything—printing, office supplies, reimbursements, and salaries—in cash. I received my first payment (on time, exactly one week after I began my meetings) in a little paper bag with my name scribbled on it, with the twenty-dollar bills carefully bound by a rubber band. The funds that fueled the fledgling operation appeared to arise spontaneously, from no centralized source; some of the veterans referred to their resources as "walking-around money." I also became increasingly uncomfortable with the open drug indulgence (marijuana and cocaine, exclusively) by several stalwarts, who seemed to consider taking a snort for energy as normal as gulping a cup of coffee. I understood that Berkeley qualified as one of the national centers of the drug culture I despised, but this was still a campaign for a sitting member of Congress. In all my prior campaign experience, the individuals who chose to get high did so in private and in secret, understanding the incompatibility of their illegal habits with the overriding determination to succeed in mainstream politics. In Ron's campaign, however, the stoners felt proud of their defiance of middle-class mores and the law—as if drug use provided one more signal of their candidate's unique status as an elected revolutionary. Years later, in 1982, a doorkeeper in the House of Representatives charged that Dellums himself had abused cocaine, but a fifteen-month formal investigation failed to generate conclusive evidence.

I finally met Ron some two weeks after I began working in the campaign, hoping to feel reassured by personal contact with the candidate. He certainly made an unforgettably intense impression, with his heavy brows and perpetually scowling countenance, his lithe, coiled-spring athleticism, his penetrating gaze and snarling, hyperdramatic, singsong voice. The biggest surprise came from his light complexion—perhaps a shade more pale than my own swarthy skin—so that I wondered if his carefully tended, hugely intimidating, already graying Afro might not have resulted from a perm. It also occurred to me that the exaggerated ghetto cadences and inflections in his speech, with its distinctly southern twang, could qualify as an affectation—considering his middle-class, richly educated, Northern California background and prestigious Cal-Berkeley degrees. I later crossed paths with his bubbly and warm-hearted mother (a former schoolteacher) and she certainly spoke with no identifiable ethnic accent.

I wanted desperately to like Ron and to feel reenergized about working in his campaign, but everything about him seemed to rub me the wrong way. He came across as one of those handsome narcissists who take an almost physical pleasure in the sound of their own voices and speak to even intimate groups as if addressing a multitude of cheering admirers in a jammed stadium. The aloof self-absorption, the totally self-conscious projection of "charisma," reminded me of another tall, lanky, hugely ambitious, humorless pol I had known (and disliked) years before: John Kerry.

In my first conversation with Dellums, he asked me about my experience with the Jewish desk at the McGovern campaign, then seemed impatient and disdainful when I tried to answer him. "I've just got one message to the Jewish community in this district," he growled. "Don't expect me to jerk you off! Don't expect me to kiss your ass. I'm going to tell you the truth. I'm going to tell it like it is! I don't take orders and I'm not going to tell you what you want to hear. But I'm going to say what you *need* to hear." I couldn't tell for sure whether he was speaking about black-Jewish relations in this country, or questioning American support for Israel, or alluding to some other passionate conflict I couldn't even imagine. It struck me as crazy and counterproductive that he should sound contemptuous toward Jews (who had provided him with overwhelming support in his previous race) and angry at the new suburban voters in his district before they even had a chance to cast their ballots in his reelection bid. He also disturbed me with a long, emotional, maddeningly incoherent discourse about the need for the redistribution of wealth, and a sweeping restructuring of society, the establishment of a whole new basis for every kind of human relationship, and so forth. During one hard-to-follow detour in this zigzagging diatribe, he made admiring reference to Fidel Castro and the achievements of the Cuban revolution, and I thought immediately of my uncle's warnings about the infectious danger of the Scarlet Plague. In the midst of the congressman's odd little lecture (Was it meant to impress me? Educate me? Test me?), I began to wonder if he even remembered my name or recalled why I was there.

I came out of this meeting with a pounding headache and a growing sense of resentment, wondering how I could continue accepting my little bags full of cash to work for this pompous creep. I knew that many of those who had known Ron for years in Berkeley considered him a warm, generous, fun-loving, even noble human being, and in the late '90s, by the time he finally retired after twenty-eight years in Congress, several colleagues who had served with him in the House (including a few Republicans) hailed him as a dignified, dedicated, compassionate public servant. Nevertheless, in 1972 he came across to me as an icy, impossible, egotistical ideologue, and I left for my wedding in Los Angeles feeling painfully uncertain whether I would go back to the campaign when I returned.

I certainly preferred the joyous family atmosphere surrounding the celebration of our marriage. Nancy and I didn't meet face-to-face during the week before the wedding, following our halting understanding of Jewish tradition, though we nevertheless engaged in romantic late-night conversations on the telephone. The ceremony took place at Sinai Temple in Westwood, a prominent, prosperous congregation representing the Conservative movement of Judaism—the middle branch that attempted to split the difference between the rigorous strictures of Orthodoxy and the undemanding, do-your-own-thing approach of Reform. When we met with the rabbi, we made it clear that we wanted a strictly traditional service, but at that early stage in my Jewish development I wasn't even sure what that meant.

We spent the first night of our marriage in a Beverly Hills hotel room and woke up the next morning to drive to our honeymoon in the scenic Monterey Peninsula. Before we left, we called Nancy's parents, who were hosting a big Sunday brunch for the clan members on both sides. On the phone, we effusively expressed the unexpected desire to delay our departure to join them for the added family occasion. Somehow, it felt far more appropriate to begin life as a married couple surrounded by the people from three generations who meant the most to us rather than locked into a long freeway ride on the way to an isolated romantic vacation. Only later did we learn that Jewish law actually corresponded to our instincts—frowning on the artificial separation of the honeymoon and mandating that the first week for a newlywed couple should feature communal celebrations for all seven nights. Alas, our parents also remained ignorant of this beautiful tradition, and insisted that we leave them behind and find our way to Monterey.

By the time we finally arrived back in Berkeley and moved into our new flat, we had reached the joint decision that I should cut my contact with the Dellums campaign. On a Monday morning I went in to tell those colleagues I could find that I had decided that I had little to offer the congressman's reelection effort. I had worked with them only three weeks, but it was long enough to realize that I didn't fit in with the candidate who, I assured them, would win easy reelection whether or not I participated in his campaign.

I was absolutely right about that: despite their initial sense of insecurity over the redistricting and the divisions among Democrats, Ron swept to victory in a landslide and even did well in the new suburban communities (Orinda, Moraga, Lafayette) that had been added to his constituency. He went on to win a staggering total of fourteen consecutive victories in his congressional races and even rose to the incongruous post of chair of the Armed Services Committee (despite his undisguised hostility to the military establishment and his advocacy of radical cuts in the defense budget) before the Republicans seized control of both houses of Congress in the Gingrich revolution of 1994. On Election Day of 1972, I couldn't bring myself to vote for Dellums, but I felt guilty, even queasy, about the thought of casting a ballot for his Republican rival, so after considerable agonizing, I wrote in the name of Jeffrey Cohelan, the organization Democrat whom Dellums had knocked out of office.

I still supported McGovern, however, and cringed as I watched his faltering, marginalized campaign collapse into ineptitude and irrelevance in the weeks before the disgusted voters finally went to the polls. I kept in telephone contact with a few friends in the national campaign and their last, forlorn hope was the Twenty-Sixth Amendment: this was the first presidential election in which all eighteen-year-olds could vote. McGovern supporters simply assumed that a stealth army of youthful, first-time voters would come out for their candidate, since we antiwar activists associated exclusively with friends who shared our values and since the mass media regularly characterized all Baby Boomers as "the peace and love generation." We remained shockingly ignorant of the other voices among American youth—pro-military, conventionally patriotic, and resentful of all the countercultural propaganda. Nixon, in fact, won a majority among voters between the ages of eighteen and twenty-nine, 52 percent to McGovern's 46 percent.

This result should serve as a correction to one of the most common misconceptions about my generation: despite the warped, rose-tinted memories of aging anti-establishmentarians, the peace demonstrators never came close to representing all, or even a bare majority, of young people in our cohort. During the one election in which these youthful cadres enjoyed their clearest chance to support a self-proclaimed peace candidate, a majority of Boomers preferred to sustain Richard Nixon in the presidency. For all the hype about the "commitment" and "engagement" of the '60s and early '70s, most young people of the time remained moderate (or confused), placing themselves safely in the mushy middle, equally distant from gung-ho Green Beret heroes who committed body and soul to the war in Southeast Asia and from the anti-American radicals who burned draft cards or waved Viet Cong flags.

Most of my fellow liberal activists felt crushed and devastated by the McGovern disaster (the Democrat carried only Massachusetts—barely—

and the District of Columbia), but my recent efforts to distance myself from politics and the joy I felt in my new married life helped soften the blow for me. Perhaps most importantly, as we began our life together, Nancy and I had chosen to embrace more of the essential elements of traditional Judaism. We now wanted our home to stand aside as different—different from the other apartments and houses and crash pads in the dysfunctional zoo known as Berkeley, and different from the circumstances of our life when we were single. Keeping kosher, with special dishes and restricted food consumption, served to accomplish that purpose, as did our determination to observe the Sabbath.

Keeping kosher involved getting two sets of dishes to facilitate the painstaking separation of meat and dairy (reflecting the distinction between death and life) and limiting our at-home meat consumption to Biblically stipulated kosher animals, slaughtered in the humane, instantaneous manner prescribed by Jewish law for millennia. The word "kosher" doesn't mean "pure" or "healthful" or "sacred" or "blessed by a rabbi"—it means, simply, "appropriate" or "proper." (Contrary to popular belief, a rabbinical official reciting some magic formula over a food item cannot make it kosher—nor does the lack of such rabbinic pronouncement make such food nonkosher. The "kosher marks" that frequently appear on mass-marketed grocery items refer to rabbinic *inspection*, not blessing—and indicate that designated monitors have certified that the ingredients and production process avoided nonkosher elements.) In Genesis, God creates the universe by making distinctions, between the waters above and the waters below, the heavens and the earth, light and dark, man and animals. The Godly element of our human condition leads us to separate, to divide, to set aside, to distinguish aspects of reality in a way no beast ever could. Kosher laws raise us above animal nature by forcing us to make distinctions between appropriate and improper food. The purpose is character building and spiritual wellness, not the pursuit of physical health.

Similarly, by observing the Sabbath from sundown Friday until the dark of night on Saturday, we would separate ourselves from the pressures and priorities of everyday life—pulling back from driving cars or handling money or using the telephone or engaging in any sort of world-changing, creative work. Judaism recognized the nobility and significance of such work, but also believed that we could appreciate its full power and potency only when we gained perspective by temporarily putting it at a distance. Whatever happened in the world of frightening headlines and urgent alarms—or to the liberal candidates we had built up as false gods—Shabbat arrived every Friday at dusk, the candles cast their familiar, reassuring glow, and end-of-the-world edginess gave way to Sabbath peace.

LESSON

20

"Affirmative Action" Is a Racist Scam

"**W**hen the going gets weird," writes the drug culture sage Hunter S. Thompson, "the weird turn pro."

Beginning my second year in the Left Coast capital of weird, Berserk-ley, I definitely wanted to turn pro but wasn't sure how to do it. Even before abandoning my connection to purportedly idealistic left-wing campaigns, I'd made up my mind that I needed to "sell out" but discovered, much to my chagrin, that it isn't always easy to attract a buyer.

My preferred mode for selling out involved somehow inserting myself into the advertising industry since my campaign experience suggested a marketable flair for coming up with persuasive copy, press-worthy stunts, snappy slogans, and attractive layouts. I naturally felt qualified for a big-time gig that would grant me some outrageously lavish salary in the most creative corner of the business world. With this in mind, it would have made sense to consider relocating to New York City, but Nancy had re-cently transferred to the University of California to complete her degree, so I fixed my sights on the far more limited advertising opportunities in the Bay Area.

Unfortunately, the move from leftist politics to business success proved more difficult than anticipated, and I learned that the invocation of potent leftist names like Lowenstein, McGovern, Duffey, and Dellums did little to reassure potential bosses—even in San Francisco—as to my capitalist savvy. After being turned down by virtually every big firm in the Bay Area, I gratefully accepted an offer to serve as the new creative director (Creative Director!) of the largest, most powerful minority advertising agency in all of Northern California.

Only after I had begun working at this new job did I realize that Anrick Incorporated also happened to qualify as the *only* minority advertising agency in Northern California. Its proprietor, Nicholas, initially invited me for lunch at a funky coffee shop in downtown Oakland, where he boasted of his political connections (he claimed both Ron Dellums and San Francisco assemblyman Willie Brown as close personal friends) and sketched his grand dreams for empire building. Short, compact, confident, and energetic, Nicholas wore a maroon, double-breasted, bell-bottom suit with big shoulder pads, a yellow-and-red paisley tie, a pink shirt with a high white collar, and chunky gold, silver, and diamond rings on three fingers of each hand. Even with his high-heeled, black patent leather go-go boots, he stood only about 5'6" high and bore a striking resemblance to rock 'n' roll pioneer Little Richard.

In describing his business, Nicholas rightly pointed out that black people amounted to more than 10 percent of the national population at a time when most of America's top corporations made little or no effort to market their products specifically to this vast community. Only in the last few years had the big companies begun to discover the power of the black consumer, which meant millions of dollars to Nicholas and his enterprising partners at Anrick, who could help frame TV ads and marketing campaigns to appeal to the distinctive sensibilities of America's ethnic enclaves. He said they had recently received so much business that their existing staff couldn't handle it all, so they wanted a new genius to manage all the "think work" (in the boss's distinctive phrase) and to supervise the hiring of at least a half-dozen more employees. Nicholas believed that I looked perfect for the job because my brief experience with Dellums indicated my "sensitivity" to minority culture, while my Yale background suggested roots in the white establishment.

Working for an ambitious, politically conscious company imbued with black pride and dreams of social justice offered me a chance to cash in without selling out. The only reason I felt lingering guilt over leaving the Dellums campaign involved the ineradicable suspicion that my distaste for the candidate betrayed some tinge of subconscious racism. Now in my work for Anrick I could reassure myself about the depth and sincerity of my commitment to social justice. When Nicholas offered an unexpectedly generous salary, and even encouraged me to work from home (where creative people work best, he said), I eagerly accepted the job. I had only one question: how had he and his partners decided to name their firm "Anrick"?

"Oh, that's from African history!" he proudly announced, as if surprised that I didn't know. "The Anrick was what they called the great gladiators. The professional warriors, the fierce fighters with swords and shields, who used to be very popular in ancient Africa."

I tried to look up the reference when I got home but could find no mention of these historic heroes in any of my books on black history or culture. Rather than investing precious time in this esoteric investigation, I concentrated on the immediate assignment that Nicholas gave me as my first job in advertising. From his elegant leather briefcase, he'd produced a formal announcement from four leading police departments in the Bay Area—San Francisco, Oakland, Berkeley, and Richmond. These departments had jointly received a grant from the federal government through the Law Enforcement Assistance Administration (LEAA) to hire more minority officers, and they were now soliciting proposals from advertising firms for a series of public service announcements to attract new applicants from the black, Latino, and Asian communities. So my first task required designing the campaign that would win us the contract, but after struggling with the burden for several days at home—this government project demanded completion of nearly a hundred pages of forms—I called Nicholas and suggested that I consult with some of the other senior employees at Anrick.

On the phone, I sensed his discomfort with my request. "You mean to tell me, Mike, that you don't think you can handle this one on your own?" He brusquely declared that my new colleagues couldn't take time away from their high-pressure responsibilities on a series of other projects to help with this speculative endeavor. Besides, part of the gladiatorial

Anrick philosophy involved individual initiative and accountability, rather than doing anything by committee. I must soldier on alone; the only instruction he gave me was to emphasize our status as the "largest minority advertising agency in Northern California" when arguing that we should receive the contract above any other applicants. With that in mind, he also suggested that I omit my name from any of the documents that we would submit to the government agencies, since the responsible authorities might "smile a little more over our application" if it left out any mention of the company's only white employee.

I shrugged and accepted the politics of the situation, but the next week, my optimism instantly dissipated when the bank called to inform me that my first Anrick paycheck had bounced. I tried to reach Nicholas by phone but his receptionist declared him "unavailable," and, when I called back, even announced that he had gone out of town. Nicholas had requested that I keep myself isolated from the office environment in order to "focus my creative energy," but I angrily drove into north Oakland to find the address listed on the check, our forms, and his business card. I finally found the "corporate headquarters"—a little rundown print shop in an industrial area, with a small hand-lettered sign in one corner of the front window announcing "Anrick Incorpated" (with the word "Incorporated" misspelled). I knocked at the locked door and tried to look inside, seeing nothing but printing equipment, a few empty desks, and some telephones. I left an indignant note and kept trying to call Nicholas.

He finally phoned me back late that night, full of apologies and reassurance, insisting that he truly had gone out of town (to try to collect some overdue accounts owed to *him*) and promising that he would make the check good—plus a little bonus—within two weeks. For Nicholas, the most important priority involved keeping our "eyes on the prize"—focusing on the police contract that he believed we stood an excellent chance of winning. In fact, we'd been invited to make a formal presentation to high-ranking officials of all four departments at the San Francisco Police headquarters building, and Nicholas now wanted me to come along as a "special consultant" who would outline our plans. At this point, I tried to get him to admit that his entire operation amounted to a pathetic scam—that the "colleagues" and "account execs" who allegedly worked for him did not, in fact, exist—any more than the "classy, expensive advertising offices" he had once described. After long silences and much clearing of his throat, Nicholas refused to comment on the fraudulent nature of his fictions and continued to show himself utterly incapable of facing the awful fact of his own deception.

Despite this insanity, I stayed on, and I even came to feel abiding affection for Nicholas. Ultimately I appreciated, even savored, his shame-less audacity, grandiose delusions, flashy style, easy smile, infectious laugh-ter, and fierce, warm-hearted devotion to his own family: he doted on his five children, worshipped his mother, and maintained loving relationships with his twelve brothers and sisters. I also came to appreciate the opportu-nity to watch him operate.

I would work with Nicholas, against all odds, for nearly two years, and in that time I saw him spinning the same sorts of tales to others that he had initially told to me. Our big meeting with the police officials provided an example of Nicholas at his most effective. He spoke with conviction and flair about the need for ending the long, sad years of resentment and mis-understanding between police officers and minority communities, and his heartfelt desire to use Anrick's formidable corporate resources to help the necessary process of empowerment and accountability. He then turned the meeting over to me as "a special consultant with expertise in employment recruiting." Watching the faces in the room, I knew that they soon realized that I had personally written all the pages and pages of material, though they probably didn't know I had also done the rough sketches of the print ad layouts and the billboard designs (since Anrick's crack art department had been unavailable to help). As we wrapped up the presentation, the dep-uty chief of Oakland posed one last question. "That name?" he inquired. "You're called 'Anrick.' Where, exactly, does that come from?"

I graciously deferred to Nicholas, who didn't hesitate to provide the explanation. "It's from ancient Rome," he said. "At the Coliseum, with hun-dreds of thousands, the cheering multitudes, the most popular gladiator of them all was an African slave. His name was Anrick, and the crowd used to cheer his name."

We won the contract.

I couldn't blame Nicholas for the sleazy system of racial preferences that facilitated and encouraged his various dodges and scams; he simply recognized the sad fact that he could exploit his skin color more easily, more reliably, than attempting to deploy talent or hard work. Before my experience with Anrick I had automatically accepted the idea of "affirmative action" as a well-intentioned, arguably indispensable attempt to redress centuries of racist abuse. My firsthand involvement, however, convinced me that dishonest premises—such as the belief that providing undeserved plums to dubious companies identified as "black" somehow advanced the interests of an entire community—led inevitably to additional lies, and to their uncomplaining acceptance by otherwise decent people who should have known better.

Police See Reality More Accurately Than Professors

The notion that police officers deserve the public's admiration and gratitude hardly counts as a controversial proposition in the twenty-first century—especially after the terrorist attacks of September 11. Thirty years ago, however, most Americans who saw themselves as left of center expressed grave doubts, even open hostility, toward law enforcement professionals.

Black radicals and student revolutionaries regularly described cops as "pigs" and I personally witnessed demonstrations at Yale, Berkeley, and the nation's capital in which the New Left shock troops of SDS stridently chanted "Off the Pig! Off the Pig!"—openly advocating the violent death of police personnel. In part this fury stemmed from the nationwide media hand-wringing over a few bloody riots for which even mainstream liberals blamed police brutality rather than the violent defiance of "revolutionary" youth. At Ivy League bastions like Harvard and Columbia, the brawny boys in blue provoked widespread countercultural contempt when they cracked heads and shocked sensibilities after beleaguered administrators called them in to restore campus order. Most famously, the Democratic Convention of 1968 saw the Chicago cops fighting pitched battles with long-haired and proudly unwashed fanatics representing the "Yippies" (or Youth International Party); Senator Abe Ribicoff (among many others) bitterly denounced the "Gestapo tactics" of the police. A year later in Berkeley, regional law enforcement confronted the mobs of protesters who seized an empty lot which the University of California wanted to develop as part of the campus, and the "People's Park" struggle turned into another violent nightmare (ultimately involving Governor Reagan's National Guard) that killed one student and injured many others. Meanwhile, chic Black Panther leaders like Bobby Seale and Eldridge Cleaver remained profoundly popular with the liberal vanguard despite (or perhaps because of) the fact that they regularly engaged in gory shootouts with the local police.

According to "enlightened opinion" of the early '70s, cops deserved disdain as racist thugs and sadistic bullies, the storm troopers of a repressive, intolerant regime. If any progressive thinker dared to question that attitude, he need only consider the alarming fact that many (if not most) police officers expressed open admiration for President Nixon and leaned unmistakably in the dangerous direction of the Republican Party. The cops provoked additional animosity with their dutiful enforcement of unpopular laws designed to separate stylish young people from the daily doses of marijuana and other mind-altering substances that they considered their inalienable right as well as an essential requirement for their spiritual health. The enthusiastic embrace of idiot ideas—like the crazed conviction that feel-good drugs expand and enrich human consciousness—leads inevitably to even more daft delusions, like the noxious notion that law enforcement professionals represent the ultimate enemies of freedom, rather than its guarantors.

I found it impossible to view cops as the enemy, however, after many of them became my personal friends through the police recruitment campaign on which I toiled in 1973. Far from the lefty stereotype of callous, power-mad, hate-filled brutes, the police officers I got to know came across as smart, funny, worldly wise, decent, and deeply dedicated. The officers who oversaw the ad campaign quickly understood that "Anrick Incorporated," despite its stirring evocation of glorious gladiators in Africa, Rome, or wherever, amounted to little more than an affirmative action con job, but they showed enough consideration not to rag me too harshly for my status as the officially invisible white "consultant" who ended up doing all the work. They also showed a genuine and often passionate desire for that work to succeed in achieving its purpose: every white cop I met, at every level of authority and seniority, without exception expressed a fervent desire to recruit qualified minorities—black people in particular—to join them in the burdens of police work. If any of the white officers harbored the vaguest tinge of racism in their attitudes toward their African-American colleagues, they hid that prejudice and resentment extraordinarily well. The two dozen black cops I got to know over the course of the project had earned the respect and affection of their comrades for the best possible reasons: they struck me as some of the finest, most admirable human beings I had ever encountered in my life.

Ironically, I began my association with them in stark fear that they might arrest and incarcerate me. The good news concerning the Anrick advertising contract was that I would be paid regularly, with no more bouncing checks. The bad news was that I had to figure out some way to deliver credible ads for television, radio, billboards and print media, while running the considerable risk that the police responsible for paying us could discover at any moment the outrageous levels of fraud and deceit in our representations that we knew how to produce the promised materials. I didn't even own a movie camera or one of the new VHS camcorders, let alone any of the professional video or 16-millimeter film equipment our new contract specified. The fearless rascality of the whole endeavor made me laugh out loud as I drove home across the Bay Bridge and considered the immediate future: running a big con against any sophisticated executives involved obvious dangers, but I had locked myself into a prospective swindle of the top police officials in the Bay Area, not to mention the snoopy feds.

Audacious improvisation enabled me to produce billboard designs and radio ads to placate the demands of the deputy chiefs, but I could come up with no similar shortcuts for creating our eight promised television commercials, the crucial core of the entire project. I submitted scripts, which received enthusiastic endorsement from all layers of bureaucracy, but I had no idea how to produce these concepts or to pay for the hugely expensive camera work, lighting, sound recording, editing, and duplication we had budgeted to deliver. My partner, Nicholas, had already diverted the majority of the money we had received from the cops to fend off his most insistent creditors, so I began to believe that it would take a miracle to avoid some potentially felonious failure—and, ultimately, a Miracle is what I got.

Driving home one afternoon at twilight from the downtown Oakland police headquarters, I stopped to pick up a hitchhiker. Aside from my own sentimental associations with hitchhiking, this particular bystander looked absolutely irresistible: with flowing, shoulder-length locks, a blondish beard, thin frame, and sandals, he resembled a Hollywood vision of Jesus Christ.

When he got into the car, I reached over and introduced myself. "I'm Michael," I said. "Where are you going?"

"I'm heading up to Berkeley—North Campus," he explained. "My name is Jay Miracle."

I began laughing so uproariously that I nearly plowed into the car in front of me. I thought he must be kidding, or else had assumed the other-worldly name as some sort of spiritual statement in the style of that hippie-dippie era. Mr. Miracle, however, insisted that he had been born with the distinctive moniker, had grown up in the Midwest, and now worked as an aspiring filmmaker as part of a newly formed collective of like-minded souls who pooled their resources and jointly rented a house near the Berkeley campus. They'd also managed to buy some decent used equipment, and together, they'd begun learning cinematography, lighting, editing, and all the other essentials of film production. They called their little group (never more than eight people) the Berkeley Film House and hoped someday to establish themselves as a professional production company.

Despite my personal distance from Christianity, as I looked over at the bearded, beatific face of my mysterious Messianic passenger, I felt tempted to pronounce the words "Thank you, Jesus." (Whenever I've told the story of my chance meeting with the Miracle man, my listeners have assumed that it's apocryphal, or at least embellished and exaggerated, but I can certify every bizarre detail as true. Jay Miracle not only exists, but has gone on to conspicuous success in the film business, working as an assistant film or sound editor on *Star Wars*, *Apocalypse Now*, *One Flew Over the Cuckoo's Nest*, and other movies of note.)

Within hours of initially dropping him off at the Berkeley Film House, I came back for a meeting with his oddly assorted colleagues. I filled them in on our ambitious project with the local police departments, explaining the remarkable opportunity it offered to all of them. They wanted production experience and credibility: here they could create TV ads that would be seen by millions, and I would reimburse all their expenses for this grand educational venture. As tantalizing as the prospect seemed, some of the members of the group objected to the very idea of working with the hated police. Didn't the "pigs" lord over the Bay Area like an occupying army? How could the Berkeley Film House maintain its progressive integrity and communal soul by joining forces with the gun-toting, badge-wearing fascists in blue?

I emphatically addressed these concerns, suggesting that our focus on minority recruitment would provide just the sort of fresh perspective that the police departments needed to loosen their cruel grip on ghetto communities. After nearly an hour of raucous debate, the movie geeks from the Berkeley Film House agreed to join our enterprise and eventually threw themselves into the commercials with gusto. Though they never fully embraced the cops and their culture the way I did, our shared experience gave them a reluctant respect for the police force and its work that counted as unusual for that time and place.

The first part of the production process involved "auditions" for the stars of the TV commercials. A parade of black and Latino officers came in to read from my scripts while some of the Berkeley Film House crew offered their opinions of their on-camera suitability. The entire scene offered such a rollicking collision of contrasting universes that our police station conference room crackled with unlikely electricity. The crew-cut police brass with their shoulder holsters beneath their sports jackets, together with some of the Film House people in cowboy hats, *Easy Rider* mustaches, and tie-dye T-shirts, watched me trying to give direction ("Read it again, Officer McCoy, but this time a bit slower and with stronger emotion") to the succession of nervous officers who wanted to appear on TV. All my life, I'd been accustomed to meek submission in the face of police orders ("Here's my license and registration, officer. Was I really going that fast?"), but now I reveled in the opportunity to order around a succession of brawny lawmen who suddenly treated *me* as the authority figure.

Despite my responsibilities, I developed close relationships with most of my "stars," including the jocular, muscular, constantly kidding young officer who had joined the police force after completing two tours of duty with the Marines in Vietnam. He had won decorations for his courage in twice braving enemy fire to carry wounded buddies to safety on his broad back—and in both cases, by the way, those buddies happened to be white. He had already been wounded in the line of police duty while rescuing a grievously injured partner from a shootout with local thugs. Despite this valorous history, he tried to avoid talking about his own citations and medals ("It's just part of the job," he said with a shrug) and only reluctantly answered questions about his own record of selfless heroism. He spoke freely, however, about his general experience in Southeast Asia, and his uncompromising pride in the Marine Corps ("These were my brothers and I love every one of 'em") and its accomplishments contradicted every prevailing cliché about Vietnam vets as broken, remorseful, tragic souls haunted by post-traumatic stress.

And then there was Harold, a beloved black sergeant in the Oakland department who became an especially close friend. I got to know Harold during a late-night "ride-along" through some of the most dangerous urban neighborhoods in America; the command structure had invited me to go out on patrol with officers because they wanted me to gain firsthand knowledge of a cop's daily grind. A churchgoer, family man, gifted song-writer (he sometimes jotted down verse while pausing for doughnuts on patrol), guitar player, Little League coach, and opera lover, Harold loved to talk about Puccini and Mozart and Wagner (not his favorite) in between heart-stopping interactions with menacing marauders. Meanwhile, it took a crusty, foul-mouthed, hard-drinking sergeant (frequently derided as a "backwoods cracker" by his black pals) to hand me a three-year-old clip-ping about my buddy Harold, who, one Sunday afternoon, had heroically jumped into Oakland's Lake Merritt to pull a drowning little boy from the bottom, then expertly performed CPR to save his life.

Such relationships enabled me to understand, and ultimately to enlist in, the enduring American love affair with cops. (After all, little boys still dream about growing up to wear a badge and battle bad guys, and even after all the political and cultural changes of the past fifty years, TV series about dedicated police officers remain a pop-culture staple.) During a visit to LA in the midst of the police recruiting project, Nancy's bemused father listened with increasing amazement to my proud descriptions of my new cop buddies and my infatuation with every aspect of law enforcement culture. "My God, you sound so conservative!" he said, laughing. "I can see it coming: you're going to end up as the biggest right-winger in the whole family!" Since he had recently broken with tradition to cast his own presidential vote for Republican Richard Nixon, he felt warmed and vindicated by this prospect—even though I made ardent avowals of my undying liberal faith.

Despite my protests to my father-in-law, the cops provided me with an intensive education in the conservative worldview. The ride-alongs in particular (I went on three of them altogether) permanently changed my vision of the urban environment that surrounded me. Spending eight uninterrupted hours watching a law enforcement professional performing his job focuses unflinching attention on the most problematic people in any community. A cop doesn't pay much attention to the hardworking householder who plays by the rules and trudges home at dusk to enjoy dinner with his family; his real "customers" are individuals in trouble or people who *cause* trouble. The police taught me the difference between "citizens" and "assholes"—an asshole being anyone who had already broken a rule or violated an important norm, or else looked likely to shatter the public order in the near future. Naturally the cops spent the great majority of their time monitoring, intimidating, or arresting the assholes. At two in the morning, for instance, we drove through the parking lot of a small shopping center and spotted a half-dozen sullen black teenagers gathered by the side entrance of a closed sporting goods store and passing around a bottle of cheap whiskey in a brown paper bag. "All right then," the officer told me, as he turned his spotlight on the startled little group. "I think we're going to have to have a little talk with these assholes right here." After reminding them that they all looked too young for legal consumption of alcohol and strongly suggesting that they should go home before they ran into trouble, the cop got back into our car and waited for the kids to disperse before driving away. "They won't come back here," he explained, "because they know I'll be looking for 'em. But we gotta keep an eye out on where they're going next. If we see 'em again, then we search 'em for weapons." Much to my relief, we didn't see them again.

On a few occasions, I watched the police face potentially dangerous situations. One urgent radio call reported a burglary in process; the cops interrupted the burglary and chased the panicked perpetrator before he managed to disappear down a series of dark alleys. On another night, we received word of a brutal case of domestic abuse and rushed to the scene with siren and flashing lights. The officer banged on the door, shouted a warning, then pushed his way into the house, chasing away the brutal husband (who jumped out a window) while trying to comfort the badly bloodied wife and hysterically crying children until the paramedics arrived on the scene. Another patrol car picked up the fleeing asshole within an hour, though we later heard that the woman—who needed more than twenty stitches in her face—eventually declined to press charges.

Though police critics may doubt or deny it, my experience sharing patrol schedules with Bay Area officers convinced me that they possessed an almost supernatural sense for spotting bad guys. One night at four in the morning, as Harold led me away from our break at his favorite Winchell's Donut House, he spotted a late-model blue sports car parked at the far end of the parking lot, with two young toughs talking and smoking inside.

"You see those two?" he asked me. "I think I'm going to say hello. Because those two are assholes."

"But how do you know?" I asked, genuinely puzzled.

"After a while, you just know. You can smell it. Just watch the way this goes down, and you're going to see I'm right." Whistling an aria from *The Marriage of Figaro*, checking on the status of his service revolver, he approached the car. Eventually, we called for backup, and the two assholes left the scene (and their stolen roadster) in handcuffs, with a total of more than twenty pending warrants for their arrest. This episode helped persuade me of the seldom-acknowledged truth that most veteran cops have developed a generally reliable—perhaps even foolproof—asshole detector.

My new experience managed to clear my head of the fuzzy clichés that had previously dominated my thinking about crime. Like everyone else I knew, I had instinctively dismissed "law and order" politicians as racist demagogues who exploited the public appetite for simplistic solutions and denied the one obvious, unquestionable truth: that we could only reduce crime if society addressed its "root causes." Watching Bay Area cops (my friends and colleagues) risking life and health to stop criminal activity every night blew this nitwit nostrum to smithereens: these guys reduced the crime rate the old-fashioned way, by intimidating or arresting the bad guys. They didn't need social workers or psychologists or civil rights activists to help them, but they most certainly welcomed the prospect of reinforcements. They firmly believed—and easily convinced me—that the presence of more well-trained, well-armed police officers (especially black police officers) patrolling the streets of the most troubled urban neighborhoods could do more to deter predators than all the poverty programs ever devised by scheming bureaucrats.

This proposition—that a visible, vigilant cop will discourage all but the most reckless criminals from hurting people or violating property in front of him—struck me as so logical that I forgot how offensive it sounded to committed liberals. One night when Nancy and I went to dinner with another couple that she had known in high school, I began ranting about the need for more police personnel to protect us from the skyrocketing crime rate. For the first time in my life (but hardly the last) my arguments on behalf of conservative ideas ruined an otherwise perfectly pleasant (and comfortably shallow) social occasion, as our dinner companions responded to my comments with shock and awe. "You better watch yourself!" the husband warned. "I can't believe you're serious about all this racist stuff about locking 'em up and throwing away the key! You sound like George Wallace, or the Ku Klux Klan."

Of course, I hadn't even mentioned race—though I should have emphasized that the courageous cops I most admired happened to be black. It also struck me as ignorant, if not demented, that my interlocutor never acknowledged that the thugs and creeps I hated and feared preyed predominantly on precisely those vulnerable members of the African-American community for which he professed such sympathy. Why would any decent human being choose to identify with black criminals rather than black victims? On this issue, liberal opinion remains stubbornly detached from American reality. Even today, a decade after Rudy Giuliani and Bill Bratton showed the world that more vigorous policing can cut crime drastically without any sweeping social or economic restructuring, leftist orthodoxy still insists (against all evidence) that social welfare programs do more to promote a safe society than placing violent criminals behind bars.

My heartfelt dissent from this quasi-religious faith left me far more comfortable talking about issues of security and justice with tough-minded police officers than with any of my trendy, tender-minded compatriots from the McGovern or Dellums campaigns.

After our TV commercials proved conspicuously popular with both police officials and the public, running for more than a year on local stations and helping to generate the telephone calls and new applications the departments had wanted to get, I welcomed the idea of some continued association with law enforcement. My partner, Nicholas, in fact, savored our triumph and sketched grandiose plans for some vague long-term collaboration between the gladiatorial geniuses of Anrick and the local constabulary. Those schemes never materialized, largely because I terminated my own business association with him, as soon as I made sure that we had paid off our various debts and that I had received most (but not all) of the money I was owed.

Despite my assumption that I had concluded my significant association with local law enforcement, an unwelcome intrusion brought me back to intimate contact with the criminal justice system. Irving Kristol, the widely admired godfather of neoconservatism, once declared that a "neoconservative is a liberal who has been mugged by reality." In my case, it wasn't a mugging; it was a burglary.

One Thursday night Nancy and I entertained one of my old friends from Palisades High School who worked near San Jose as a schoolteacher. After dinner, we piled the dishes in the sink and took a walk up to Telegraph Avenue to show off the used bookstores that represented one of Berkeley's most celebrated cultural assets. We took along the hyperenergetic Norwegian elkhound we had adopted from the local pound and spent less than two hours strolling before we returned at about eleven o'clock. As we came up the walkway, our dog, Muki, began barking and straining at her leash, instinctively announcing that something had gone wrong; then we saw the front door, wide open to the broad porch. The window facing the street, we saw, had been forced open. As we entered our place in stunned, breathless silence, we took an instant inventory of the damage. He had stolen my electric typewriter, a clock radio, Nancy's purse, and my entire stereo system—speakers, tuner, turntable—which I had painstakingly, lovingly assembled over the years. He also left a trail of muddy footprints on our living room carpet.

We called the police, and although the officer seemed sympathetic (especially after I began dropping names and he understood my past connection to the police department), he emphasized the fact that even a small city like Berkeley experienced numerous burglaries every night and only rarely did people get their stuff back. He told us the crime could have been vastly worse—if the crook had broken into the house while we were in bed, for instance. His attempt at reassurance didn't make it any easier to get to sleep that night, or for weeks thereafter. Every creak from the floorboards upstairs, every branch blown against the window, inspired a physical chill associated with another break-in. The sense of violation, the new awareness of vulnerability and helplessness, doesn't go away even months after a crime. Even the presence of our watchful guard dog could not restore the sense of our home as a sanctified, protected space and a safe harbor in a dangerous world.

Refusing to accept the on-the-scene officer's defeatist attitude, I took advantage of my police department contacts to see if my friends might make special efforts to try to solve our burglary, and three weeks after the crime they thrilled and startled me with a phone call. They had apprehended the guy who stole our stuff; they knew it was the right guy because he still had Nancy's credit cards and ID in his car. He had tried to use some of our plastic to get a tank of gas in Oakland, but gave himself away when he signed the credit slip and totally misspelled "Medved" in childish block letters. He also didn't look very much like a "Nancy," so the alert clerk in the office took down his license plate and called the cops. Later, they searched the house where he lived with his mother and found my speakers, which I ultimately retrieved, badly nicked and scratched, from a police locker. The police also found evidence tying the break-in artist to six other burglaries and told me about his record of eight prior convictions—eight!—before he had reached the age of twenty-four (he was, in fact, just a few months younger than I was). I understood that even the most vigorous police departments managed to arrest perpetrators for only a tiny fraction of the total number of reported break-ins, so it seemed safe to assume that this particular perp had committed scores of crimes (perhaps even hundreds) beyond those eight old convictions and the seven new charges.

After the return of my speakers (we never recovered the rest of our property), I wanted to put the entire episode out of my mind, but to my annoyance and horror the burglar's public defender insisted on taking a deposition from me as he approached a trial date. I reported to a grim little room at the local courthouse, with a court reporter dutifully typing a transcript of the resulting interview. Astonishingly enough, the defense lawyer seemed determined to intimidate me as she paced back and forth in that cramped space. Scowling behind her black harlequin glasses that drooped to the edge of her nose, she badgered me with her heavily accented Brooklyn bray, trying to suggest that the burglar was an old friend of mine and I had only loaned him my property.

"When exactly did you first meet the defendant?" she asked.

"I've never met him," I said.

"How is that possible? He's been in your home."

"He broke into my home!"

"That's your allegation. The court will make the ultimate determination."

She kept coming back to a line of questioning that assumed that I had once been friendly with the burglar.

"In your mind, Mr. Medved, did you ever reach a specific point at which you felt that you and the defendant were no longer friends?"

"We were never friends! This is absurd."

"Absurd? You think it's absurd that you'd ever be friends with a black man?"

"I didn't say that."

"I know something about you, Mr. Medved. You have many close associates, personally and professionally, in the black community."

"But my friends are black cops—not black criminals."

"Are you saying that my client is subhuman? Is that your opinion?"

It went on like that for over an hour as the public defender illustrated every sickening stereotype about pushy, obnoxious, whiny Jewish women. The frustrating experience of the deposition created a deep sense of dread that she'd summon me to the trial and attempt to embarrass me there. Her obvious hostility suggested that in her own mind she had reversed the roles played by me and by the lowlife who had stolen my stuff: he counted as the victim and I was the bad guy. I had recently seen the hit film *Dirty Harry* (1972), which featured Clint Eastwood as a fiercely focused San Francisco cop who breaks all the rules to bust predatory thugs and feels scarcely contained rage toward institutions and individuals who, out of misplaced compassion, protect vicious criminals. My personal experience with the pompous, sneering public defender gave me a whole new respect for Harry's point of view, while making me feel dirty myself.

To my relief, I managed to avoid the trial, but I got a full report from my police department sources. The defense attorney first tried to raise questions about the airtight evidence (including fingerprints and stolen property found in the possession of her client) by suggesting that the poor lamb had been framed by racist cops. Her closing plea to the rapt, attentive judge represented a tearful masterpiece of manipulative grandstanding. "Come with me now on a journey—a journey of the mind!" she began. "Travel back in time, not so long ago, just twenty-four years, but come along to a remote and distant place . . . a destitute place . . . in the deep piney woods of upstate Georgia. Listen! That's the sound of a wintry wind rustling through the pine needles and then below that, and above it too, we can hear the sound of a baby crying. It's a cry of bitterness, of pain, of despair, because it's the cry of a black baby, left alone in his cradle, with no one to dry his tears. He's crying for himself, yes, but this little boy is also crying for his whole people, for a history of slavery, tragedy, abuse, and oppression. And now, too proud to cry, but suffering just the same, that baby is grown to manhood and sitting before you, here, as defendant in this case."

She went on to sketch horrendous details about slave masters mutilating and castrating their rebellious field hands, along with piteous details of her client's own crippling dependence on various drugs, allegedly peddled by "the white corporate criminals who deserve to sit here as the truly responsible parties standing trial today." In the end, all the guilt-inducing bathos produced its desired effect with the sympathetic judge: she won a suspended sentence for her client, with a largely unenforceable requirement that he seek immediate treatment and counseling for his unfortunate addiction. According to the court records, my burglar had now been formally tied to fifteen break-ins, for which he has served a grand total of less than four months of imprisonment of any kind. While I tried to deal with my outrage and indignation over the laughably light punishment for his disruption of so many lives, veteran cops warned me to take special precautions, immediately, to secure my home and property; since I had refused to cooperate in his defense, the freshly liberated burglar might well redirect his larcenous attentions to a familiar venue and make an unannounced return visit to our flat.

These specific, vivid concerns about our personal security made it all but impossible for me to stop chewing over this whole sorry episode or to move beyond my fury at the smug stupidity of the system that made it possible. Of course, I could feel pity for the drug-addled loser who had invaded my private sanctuary, but the misplaced mercy of the Bay Area courts had done nothing at all to rescue him from his blighted life and had placed countless innocent homes at continued risk. I didn't feel quite ready to embrace the get-tough rhetoric of "backlash" candidates, but after the burglary I never again dismissed calls for law and order as simple-minded or racist demagoguery.

In his celebrated eulogy for William Butler Yeats, W. H. Auden wrote that "mad Ireland hurt you into poetry." Well, mad Berkeley hurt *me* into conservatism. A right-wing outlook might lack poetic flair, but it makes more sense for those of us forced to live our lives on solid ground. By the mid '70s, I'd gradually distanced myself from race-based preferences and utopian promises of the youth counterculture, while embracing traditional Judaism, entrepreneurial adventure, cops, and even Christians. In most respects, I'd already become a conservative, though it took a series of horrifying events in the wider world before I allowed myself to acknowledge it.

Everything Worth Defending
Depends on Military Power

Working closely with police officers and going through the experience of a
burglary taught me that all the joys and privileges I took for granted depended on the application of force by organizations of brave men in uniform. Even after I had absorbed that lesson on an intimate, local level, I
never bothered to apply it in global terms until forced to confront devastating wars in the Middle East and Indochina.

On Yom Kippur (October 6) of 1973, the holiest day of the Jewish
year, Egypt and Syria launched a massive, well-coordinated surprise attack
on Israeli positions in the Sinai and the Golan Heights. I heard about the
new war while attending synagogue services with Nancy's family in Los
Angeles, on one of those rare occasions when the Jewish calendar delivered
the Day of Atonement on the Sabbath. Beyond the initial sense of shock and
anxiety as the news rippled through the congregation, the members of the
synagogue seemed to unite in a surge of swaggering confidence in the certi-
tude of Israeli victory. After all, six years before, when the Arab dictatorships last menaced the Jewish state and threatened its annihilation, those
corrupt nations ended up losing huge tracts of land in the rapid Israeli tri-

umph. During a break from the worship services, some congregants engaged in jocular speculation about what Arab territory the Israelis should seize this time, rejecting both Cairo and Damascus as highly undesirable.

Unfortunately, the news reports the next day, and the next, proved that this would be a radically different sort of war. The Egyptians overwhelmed the Israeli lines through sheer force of numbers, outnumbering the defenders at points along the Suez Canal by as much as fifteen to one. Worst of all, the Arabs had received deadly new surface-to-air missile batteries from their Soviet sponsors, and they used these weapons to cripple Israeli air power. In the first four days of conflict, the Israelis lost more than a fifth of their 500-plane air force, and simultaneously saw the destruction of a third of their 650 tanks. By the end of the epic three-week struggle, 2,522 Israelis had died in action; as a percentage of the population, this loss equated to more than double the U.S. death toll over eight years in Vietnam.

With my parents and in-laws in Los Angeles, and then back in our own home in Berkeley, I followed the news from the Middle East with mounting horror. Both of my first cousins, the daughters of Uncle Moish, had lived in Jerusalem for years and they sent their reservist husbands into the thick of battle. When the Israelis began to mount counterattacks to turn the tide of the war on both the Egyptian and Syrian fronts, the Russians began resupplying their clients at a rate as high as five hundred tons of military equipment per day, including planes, tanks and more missile batteries. To balance this tidal wave of materiel, Israel needed immediate assistance from the United States in the form of spare parts and replacement equipment.

That lifesaving resupply depended on Richard Nixon, a president almost universally despised by Jewish liberals, who counted among his most implacable pursuers at the height of the Watergate scandal. Like most other Jewish Democrats at the time, I watched "Tricky Dick's" travails with self-righteous glee. Even while armies battered one another in the Middle East, the American press downplayed the bloody conflict to focus on a very different sort of massacre: the infamous "Saturday Night Massacre," in which the president effectively fired the Watergate special prosecutor along with the attorney general and his deputy. Less than a year after Nixon's landslide victory that crushed my man McGovern, I yearned for his disgrace and destruction, even while the war in the Middle East threatened the vastly more cataclysmic destruction of Israel. I remained willfully oblivious to the inconvenient fact that the arch-villain Nixon divided his time between fending off his prosecutors and persecutors and working decisively behind the scenes to make sure that Israel received the equipment its forces needed for their survival.

According to Jonathan Aitken in his authoritative Nixon biography, "Nixon had absolutely no doubt or hesitation about what he must do. He told [Secretary of State Henry] Kissinger to 'let the Israelis know that we would replace all their losses' and instructed him to work out the logistics for doing so." The Pentagon feared that the deployment of too many transport planes would alienate the Arabs and the Soviets, but Nixon angrily told his defense secretary to stop worrying about international reaction. "We are going to get blamed just as much for three planes as for three hundred," the president declared, announcing his willingness to take responsibility if the Arabs retaliated by cutting oil supplies. He reportedly exploded to Kissinger, "Goddamn it, use every one we have. Tell them to send everything that can fly."

The president's determination produced an electrifying impact on Israeli morale and military capability. While American liberals remained blinded by our partisan obsessions, Israeli peaceniks couldn't afford to make the same mistake. The perennially dovish Cabinet member Shimon Peres, later a prime minister and Nobel Peace Prize winner, said, "As someone said to me this morning—a left-winger, no less—'Thank God for the reactionary United States!'"

The war ended with daring, dramatic Israeli advances on all fronts (led in the South by the dashing, audacious "Patton of the Middle East," General Ariel Sharon) until Kissinger and Nixon negotiated the cease-fire that led, five years later, to peace with Egypt under the Camp David Accords. The Israelis prevailed over their adversaries, but the bitter cost of their success permitted no sense of jubilation concerning the final outcome. Launched on the sacred and solemn Day of Atonement, this painful struggle became known as "The War of Atonement" in Israel—a necessary corrective for the overconfidence and arrogance surrounding the rapid victory of the Six-Day War.

For Americans who chose to consider the situation with open eyes, the course of the war conveyed inescapable lessons. For instance, the decisive role of America's emergency resupply exposed the dishonesty in the left's traditional argument that conventional military equipment counted for nothing in a nuclear age. In countless debates of the era, Pentagon critics insisted that the destructive power of the hydrogen bomb made lesser weapons obsolete and irrelevant: we didn't need to waste our money on technologically advanced tanks, planes, or aircraft carriers since intercontinental ballistic missiles could destroy any conceivable enemy many times over. During the October war, however, Israel's very existence depended on the airlift of precisely those "useless" tanks and planes we had always derided. Had it not been for Nixon's timely resupply turning the tide of battle, Israel might have confronted an unthinkable doomsday choice between accepting defeat and unleashing nuclear weapons.

For leaders determined to avoid global incineration, battlefield hardware matters, and it matters a lot: survival may well depend on both its quality and its quantity. Peaceniks might cherish the image of an invading enemy stopped in his tracks by flower-power demonstrators placing daisies in gun barrels, but in the real world a well-equipped tank battalion will halt aggression more reliably.

Despite President Nixon's commanding role in leading the United States through the world crisis in October, the cease-fire that ended the distracting war allowed America's liberals—including Jewish liberals—to get back to the serious business of hounding him out of office. Whenever the president's defenders cited his role in rescuing the Jewish state, his attackers dismissed it as a reflection of Tricky Dick's vestigial anti-Communism. "He doesn't really care about Israel—in fact, he's an anti-Semite!" I heard on many occasions. "The only reason he helped the Jews was that the Russians were against them, and he's always been obsessed with beating the Soviet Union."

Even at the time, I couldn't understand why anyone would think that some sentimental attachment to Jews provided a stronger basis for supporting Israel than hardheaded calculations of Cold War real politik. In fact, it seemed to me that the war offered a potent reminder of the reckless adventurism of the Communist superpower, since the Soviets had played such a prominent role in planning, equipping, and encouraging the Arab attack. In disregarding the idea that the Middle East conflict represented just one front in the fateful, ongoing global struggle between the United States and the Soviet empire, my liberal friends wanted to show that they had liberated themselves from the "outmoded" paradigm of the Cold War. No one I knew ever expressed much affection for the Soviet Union, but many otherwise intelligent people did mouth idiotic "moral equivalency" clichés. According to this line of reasoning, the USSR might indeed constitute a brutal, imperialist power, but so did the United States: just consider the American role in Vietnam, or the oppression of black people, Native Americans, and other victims of our incorrigibly racist regime.

By the end of 1973, such arguments not only struck me as unpersuasive but downright offensive. America's flaws didn't mean that our wonderful country, which had so abundantly blessed my family and countless others, deserved no support in its struggle to defend itself against Communist dictatorships committed to our destruction. The suggestion that people of goodwill couldn't choose between an imperfect United States and the nightmarish brutality of the Soviet Union made as much sense as saying that a patient should express no preference between the prospect of contracting a common cold and developing colon cancer since both conditions involved some form of illness.

Many years earlier, my Uncle Moish had warned me about the Scarlet Plague, and now he helped me come to terms with the depth of that sickness when he gave me a copy of the first two volumes of Alexander Solzhenitsyn's harrowing masterpiece, *The Gulag Archipelago*. I was riveted, almost hypnotized, by Solzhenitsyn's oddly lyrical, deeply ironic, scrupulously documented accounts of Stalinist oppression, sadism, torture, slave labor, madness, and murder on an unimaginable scale. At Yale, my Russian history professors had treated the Bolshevik Revolution's purges, executions, and forced starvations as just another cruel episode in the long, bloody history of mother Russia, comparable to Ivan the Terrible's wanton killings in the 1500s, or the random slaughter of the Time of Troubles at the beginning of the seventeenth century. Suddenly, Solzhenitsyn, having himself survived eleven excruciating years as a prison camp inmate in the "Worker's Paradise," provided an alarming new perspective: the vast suffering under Lenin, Stalin, and their successors wasn't so much typical of Russia as it was typical of Communism. After all, the pattern of brutality and hypocrisy had repeated itself in every nation that enshrined

Marxist-Leninist ideas, from China to Czechoslovakia to Cuba. The Soviet Union wasn't just another corrupt, inefficient, highly militarized nation state, but rather an inevitably monstrous outgrowth of an inherently monstrous system.

My father-in-law, who had already predicted that I would one day qualify as the most right-wing member of the family, decided to hasten the process by buying me a Hanukah gift subscription to *Commentary* magazine. Published by the American Jewish Committee and edited by the former Trotskyite intellectual and now fervent anti-Communist Norman Podhoretz, *Commentary* later became famous as the house organ for the neoconservative movement, but when I began reading it obsessively in the mid-'70s none of its star writers (Podhoretz, wife Midge Decter, Daniel Patrick Moynihan, Jeane Kirkpatrick, and colleagues) had yet embraced Reaganism or even left the Democratic Party. Living among angry anti-American radicals in my Berkeley neighborhood (Patty Hearst got kidnapped in 1974 from an apartment less than two blocks away from my home), I welcomed the monthly arrival of *Commentary* with the guilty thrill of some Russian Refusenik receiving a jealously guarded packet of samizdat literature and eagerly devoured it, cover to cover. The magazine captured my imagination and shaped my political perspective; most importantly, it highlighted the appalling hypocrisy of Jewish liberals who voiced passionate support for Israel while simultaneously obsessing on cutting the U.S. defense budget so as to "reorder" our national priorities. As defense expert Edward Luttwak argued, "It is entirely illegitimate to press for drastic cuts in the scale of the American military effort on the one hand, and then try and squeeze what Israel needs out of what remains." I tried to make this case with my remaining friends from the Radical Jewish Union, who clearly loved Israel (many of them later chose to live there permanently) but still harbored unshakable leftist suspicions about the U.S. defense establishment. At the same time, these ever more lonely Jewish activists tried to ignore the increasingly obvious anti-Semitism from Black Panthers, SDSers, and other leftists they persisted in viewing as their allies.

While eminent intellectuals like Podhoretz and Solzhenitsyn helped move me to the right in political terms, more homey, intimate influences served to shift my religious orientation more self-consciously toward traditionalism. During our frequent visits to Los Angeles, I began accompanying Nancy's grandfather to the Orthodox synagogue he had supported for many years. Everybody else in her family as well as my own identified with the moderate Conservative movement in Judaism—which incorporated nostalgic elements of old-country practice and liturgy without making any behavioral demands on its members. For upwardly mobile suburbanites of my parents' generation, Orthodox identification looked like an utterly irrelevant alternative: as a child, my mother explained to me that Orthodoxy was "dying on the vine" and appealed only to "immigrants and old people who don't speak English and don't want to play any part in American life." Nancy's Orthodox grandfather fit the immigrant, Yiddish-accented part of that stereotype, but his worldly success (he'd earned a bundle in the real estate business in New York and LA) and personal sophistication contradicted the rest of it. And everything about the explosively vibrant synagogue to which he took me—Beth Jacob Congregation in Beverly Hills—rebutted the idea of Orthodoxy as an exotic, withering branch of American Judaism.

With membership of nearly a thousand families, Beth Jacob boasted standing-room-only crowds of fashionable young and middle-aged people, along with hordes of joyous kids, every Saturday morning. The rabbi, Maurice Lamm, who had written eloquent best-sellers explaining Jewish tradition to the general public, delivered impassioned sermons of prodigious learning and intense personal relevance. For the first time, I began to enjoy attending synagogue services: the so-called Modern Orthodox approach at Beth Jacob felt vastly more accessible, more comfortable than the Chassidic, "lost souls" services at the Berkeley Chabad House within walking distance of our home. While we didn't feel ready to shock both sets of parents by identifying ourselves as Orthodox, we had definitely begun moving in that direction.

By the same token, I couldn't openly acknowledge the fact that I'd become a political conservative even though I'd traveled a vast, obvious distance from my McGovernite roots. On issue after issue, I felt more identification with the right than with the left, though I found it difficult to break away from my instinctive association between the "liberal" label and positive values like compassion, generosity, enlightenment, and integrity. In other words, I refused to give up on thinking of myself as a liberal because I didn't want to stop seeing myself as a good person. Only after the grim conclusion of the Vietnam War did my disillusionment spread from disgust over certain personalities (Ron Dellums) and disagreement over specific issues (affirmative action, support for the military) to a general rejection of an entire movement for its corruption, callousness, and hypocrisy. After Nixon's resignation in August 1974, the left wing of the Democratic Party (with which I had strongly identified for many years) dictated the new direction of American foreign policy, and this sweeping political victory produced a horrifying humanitarian catastrophe.

The Watergate scandal led directly to one of the most lopsided congressional elections in history; the Republican Party collapsed and the Democrats added huge numbers (forty-nine in the House, five in the Senate) to their already overwhelming majorities. Many of these new arrivals felt determined to "finish the work" of the antiwar movement, even though more than two years had passed since American troops fought directly in Vietnam. They demanded the elimination of all aid to the pro-Western forces in Vietnam to make more money available for sweeping social programs at home—even though this "reordering" would involve betraying the South Vietnamese allies we had solemnly sworn to protect. In the 1973 Paris Accords formally ending American involvement in the war, the Communists had promised to respect the territorial integrity of South Vietnam, and the United States had provided a separate guarantee to deliver "unlimited military replacement aid" to our allies in order to enforce that pledge. It was precisely this aid that the triumphant congressional Democrats were determined to deny. In fact, the increasingly militant "Peace Movement" made undisguised efforts to coordinate its demands directly with the implacable generals in Hanoi.

Encouraged by unmistakable evidence that the Americans would do nothing to stop them, the North Vietnamese Communist armies (with new hardware from their Soviet sponsors) launched an invasion that required a mass evacuation of the whole of central Vietnam. Eyewitnesses described heart-rending scenes in which more than a million terrified refugees fled in the face of the Communist onslaught, seeking safety in the southern capital of Saigon. If Nixon had been able to survive in office, he might have found a way to face down a hostile Congress and defend the Paris Accords, but the new president, Gerald Ford, wielded little power or influence. The Democrats arrogantly disregarded him and made light of

My two grandfathers in their naturalization photos

Harry Medved *(left)*, my father's father, emigrated from Ukraine and worked as a barrel maker for more than thirty years before finally achieving his dream of American citizenship in 1943. Saly Hirsch *(right)*, my mother's father, served in the Kaiser's army and built a successful business in Germany before fleeing Hitlerism in 1934 and becoming a citizen in December 1942. Their European experience (helplessly enduring the death of five children, losing property to persecution) was normal for their era; their American blessings were not.

A new family visits a new nation, 1949

My absurdly young parents (my dad twenty-three, my mom a year older) pose for a passport photo as they prepare to take me, at age six months, for an extended adventure in the newly established State of Israel. Frustrations, homesickness, and educational opportunities at home led them to return to Philadelphia earlier than expected.

Three generations in Philadelphia, 1952

With my mother, Renate Hirsch Medved, and my grandmother Bella Hirsch (my adored "Oma," the dominant figure of my early childhood), gathered behind Oma's little variety store on Chelten Avenue.

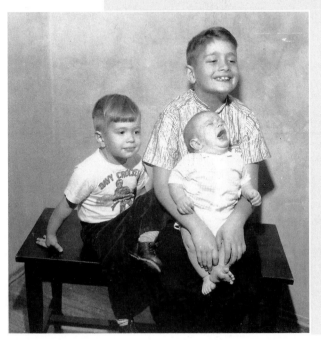

Trying for the suburban mainstream, 1958

The three oldest Medved boys, freshly scrubbed, attempt to sit still for a respectable photo in our San Diego home, with two-year-old Jonathan wearing a Davy Crockett shirt that signifies his preparation for life on the California frontier. Newborn Ben expresses his displeasure with the proceedings, while at age nine I'm squinting slightly since my mother forcibly removed my glasses for the sake of the picture.

Quiz team triumphs, high school and college

My participation in televised general knowledge showdowns demonstrated the brute power of publicity and TV's ability to alter everything. Our arrogantly undefeated Palisades High School team *(above)* won the 1964 Southern California Championship of *Scholarquiz* on CBS's L.A. affiliate. Four years later, our Yale team crushed archrival Harvard (230 to 80) on the *GE College Bowl* on NBC. That achievement earned me more acclaim than any of the far more substantial endeavors of my university years.

CHATZIE KIRK   DAVID MANNIS   MIKE MEDVED   MARK HOWSON

CAPTAIN

YALE DAILY NEWS

Uncle Moish, 1972

Twenty-one years older than my father, Moish lived with my parents for the last decade of his life and held our raucous family together through the sheer force of his personality. He inspired all four of his nephews to take Jewish identity more seriously and gave me an unforgettable education about the very real dangers of the "Scarlet Plague."

A generation gap with role reversal, 1968

My forty-two-year-old dad manages to connect with the hip, mellow, experimental spirit of the times, while his notably uptight son impersonates a straight arrow to provide effective service to the Bobby Kennedy presidential campaign.

The "Children's Crusade" that captured Connecticut, 1970

As a twenty-one-year-old head speechwriter, I confer with Joe Duffey, our thirty-seven-year-old antiwar, insurgent candidate for the U.S. Senate. Staffed by students and recent college graduates, our underdog campaign won a stunning upset in the Democratic primary but lost the general election. I may have been able to control the candidate's words, but I proved utterly incapable of controlling my hair, which followed a will of its own in rising from my head.

Bestselling Boomers on *The Tonight Show*, 1976

With coauthor David Wallechinsky (and guest host David Brenner), I look happily dazed by the unexpected success of our bittersweet where-are-they-now book about our high school, *What Really Happened to the Class of '65?* NBC later attempted to capitalize on the national obsession with Baby Boomer navel gazing by turning the book into a weekly series, but the embarrassingly awful adaptation survived for only thirteen weeks.

Oceanfront wedding, 1985

According to Jewish tradition, wedding guests celebrate the bride and groom like a king and queen at their coronation. After the ceremony at the Pacific Jewish Center "Shul by the Beach" (the congregation I had led as president since its founding), our friends and family danced Diane and me to the Venice boardwalk for a short ride (in an antique convertible) to the banquet hall.

Four dancing bears

The Brothers Medved ("Medved" means "bear" in Russian) celebrate my wedding. From left, my frequent coauthor and long-time housemate Harry (then twenty-four); Bay Area therapist (and die-hard liberal) Ben (twenty-seven); Israeli venture capitalist and political activist Jonathan (twenty-nine); and the happy bridegroom (thirty-six).

The Sunshine Girls, 1991

The three charismatic women in my life—Sarah, age four; Shayna, age two; and Diane—can light up any room. Becoming a parent relatively late in life, after frustration and miscarriages, helped persuade me that children count as a gift, not a choice.

Father and son, at last, 1992

At age forty-three, I finally welcome a baby boy—Daniel Joshua—into our family. He arrived just weeks before the publication of my book *Hollywood vs. America,* and he proved to be far less controversial.

Three former liberals, 1992

Former president (and one-time New Deal Democrat) Ronald Reagan meets conservative fire-brand (and one-time Berkeley Marxist) David Horowitz along with a repentant staffer (me) for the likes of George McGovern and Ron Dellums. I felt profoundly exhilarated to talk (briefly) with one of the nation's greatest chief executives.

Movie mavens, 1993

With my cohost (and friend) Jeffrey Lyons on the set of *Sneak Previews*. My nearly twelve years with this nationally broadcast PBS movie review show demonstrated that the job of a film critic is neither as glamorous nor as powerful as the public assumes. (© *Window to the World Communications, Inc. All rights reserved. "SNEAK PREVIEWS" is a registered trademark of WWCI.*)

Rabbi Daniel Lapin, 2004

Author (*America's Real War*), radio host, father of seven, peerless teacher of Jewish substance, friend, and Seattle neighbor. For more than a dozen years we shared leadership of the Pacific Jewish Center community in Venice/Santa Monica.

A boyhood dream comes true, 2004

No, I'm not pitching for the Phillies, but I am working from their mound—throwing out the ceremonial first pitch during "Michael Medved Night" (sponsored by our local radio affiliate, WNTP Newstalk 990) at Philadelphia's gleaming new Citizens Bank Park.

The valedictorian and her fan club, 2004

Sarah, seventeen, graduates from Yeshiva High School and delivers a memorable speech about "the courage to be different," supported by brother Danny (eleven), sister Shayna (fifteen), and her emotionally overwhelmed, slightly numbed parents. Our determined, idealistic firstborn illustrates the way that personal commitments work better than mass movements in changing the world, modeling the potent force of Do-It-Yourself Conservatism.

warnings of atrocities on a grand scale as the Communist invasion proceeded unchecked.

I became obsessed with the nightmarish dispatches from Saigon that marked the tragic culmination of eight years of American blood, valor, and sacrifice. One typical dispatch in the *New York Times* (April 27, 1975) read: "Countless babies were thrust at departing Americans by mothers who hoped at least to send a little emissary to the golden world across the Pacific. A C5 Galaxy transport plane loaded with 242 'orphans'—most of them children whose parents were abandoning them to save them—crashed on takeoff at Saigon's airport, killing most aboard. A Vietnamese air force officer watching the tragedy bitterly remarked . . . , 'Never mind, we have plenty more to send you.'"

In response to such scenes, the so-called antiwar movement did nothing to facilitate a negotiated settlement, a lifesaving compromise, or a nonviolent solution to the conflict: they simply and unmistakably wanted the other side to win. When President Ford warned of "a massive shift in the foreign policies of many countries and a fundamental threat . . . to the security of the United States," Congress ignored him. As the Communists advanced, President Nguyen Van Thieu of South Vietnam, emotionally announcing his resignation, blamed U.S. aid cuts for the military debacle.

On April 30, the *Times* reported, "Americans left Saigon yesterday by helicopter after fighting off throngs of Vietnamese civilians who tried to go along. . . . Large groups of other Vietnamese clawed their way up the 10-foot wall of the embassy compound in desperate attempts to escape approaching Communist troops. United States marines and civilians used pistol and rifle butts to dislodge them." I read these reports at the time, feeling guilty and heartsick for my country and for the so-called peace movement in which I had played such an active part. As British historian Paul Johnson recalled in his magisterial *A History of the American People*, "It was indeed the most shameful defeat in the whole of American history. The democratic world looked on in dismay at this abrupt collapse of American power, which had looked so formidable only two years before. . . . But it was the helpless people of the region who had to pay the real price."

According to James Webb, Vietnam vet and future secretary of the Navy, more than a million former South Vietnamese soldiers were sent to concentration camps, more than 56,000 of them to die there, 250,000 to stay more than six years, and some for as long as eighteen. In Cambodia, at least 1.7 million civilians—a third of the population—died at the hands of the fanatical Khmer Rouge.

During the Holocaust, most Americans received only sketchy and incomplete reports of the scale of the slaughter, but in the 1970s the American public had no such excuse. Those of us who cared about the fate of the defenseless masses of Southeast Asia could find detailed and vivid stories about suffering and genocide. Of the 200,000 who tried to escape Vietnam on rickety boats, for instance, at least half of them were killed by pirates or sharks.

At one point I came up with the idea that those of us who had played a prominent role in the Vietnam Moratorium should sign a joint statement and raise money for an ad demanding that the U.S. government intervene to rescue the innocents from the Communist butchers. I called four of my former colleagues to try to enlist them in this effort but they treated me with patronizing indulgence, as if I had lost my mind and begun babbling about UFOs. Despite the all-too-real bloodbath in Vietnam, Laos, and especially Cambodia, these one-time peace activists would not speak out because they believed that the atrocity stories might well be exaggerated, planted by the CIA; that the United States could do nothing without risking another major war; and that any agitation over Communist excesses would only strengthen the conservative, reactionary elements in American politics that we had always opposed.

During long months of brutality and liquidation, easily equaling the depravity Solzhenitsyn had so memorably described in *The Gulag Archipelago,* most Hollywood leftists actually applauded the Communist warlords who imposed their tyranny on all of Indochina. On April 8, 1975, at the Academy Awards celebration, the motion picture industry selected *Hearts and Minds* as Best Documentary, choosing to honor a strident piece of anti-American propaganda crafted with the same sort of balance and restraint more recently associated with the various masterpieces of Michael Moore. On receiving his Oscar just three weeks before the final Communist entry into Saigon, producer Bert Schneider (at the time the live-in lover of Hollywood princess Candice Bergen) came to the microphone and casually observed, "It is ironic that we are here at a time just before Vietnam is about to be *liberated*." He then pulled out a telegram from the Vietnamese Communist representatives in Paris, proudly passing on greetings and congratulations to the comrades in the entertainment industry.

Watching such displays of folly and depravity, feeling profoundly alienated from both my Berkeley present and my peacenik past, I experienced an overriding surge of gratitude that I'd managed to disentangle myself from the toils of liberal politics. It hadn't yet occurred to me that active involvement in the conservative movement represented the only appropriate corrective for the mistakes of my misspent youth; instead, I reacted to my changed perspective in the mid-'70s by resolving to watch all future struggles in politics and culture as a skeptical spectator rather than a participant. For the most part, I wanted to escape for a while from ideologically charged arguments and confrontations, and in my nearly limitless naiveté I got the odd idea that academia offered the perfect refuge.

Truth Is More Profitable Than Fiction

Graduate programs in creative writing take odd pride in the fact that the M.F.A. they offer—a Master of Fine Arts—constitutes a "terminal degree." What they mean by invoking this grim phrase is that no one presents doctorates for composing poetry or scribbling fiction, so that this odd little diploma they confer amounts to the end of the line.

I had enrolled in one such dubious program shortly after finishing my advertising work with the Bay Area police departments. At the time, only two dozen universities offered graduate degrees in creative writing, and San Francisco State provided the option closest to my Berkeley home. I pursued the degree in the hope that it might equip me for a teaching job even if all my literary ambitions failed. Whenever I heard the credential for which I strived described as a "terminal degree" it inevitably called to mind the phrase "terminal disease"—as if the certificate they awarded signified an incurable condition and a hopeless case. Given the practical uselessness of an advanced credential in writing, a dire diagnosis seemed appropriate.

Nevertheless, I enjoyed the program itself, particularly the long, rambling, chummy seminars in which we analyzed the work of great authors of the past. I also relished working on my master's thesis, a collection of short stories under the title *The Yiddish Theater in America*. My lead story depicted a frustrated, fidgety graduate student in Jewish history trying to complete a massive dissertation on the glory years of the New York Yiddish stage at the turn of the century. While he yearned desperately to connect with the vitality and sense of community that characterized that lost world, his wife's family—practical, warm-hearted, unpretentious, earthy, and life-affirming Jewish business people—effortlessly enjoyed the engagement and authenticity that eluded the diffident, elitist, Ivy League–educated intellectual. Most of my other stories similarly highlighted the hollowness and loneliness of leftist agitators, artistic bohemians, and adolescent romantics while depicting the greater satisfaction, manliness, and decency of practical, traditionally observant Jews who built families and businesses. With so many modern writers concentrating their contempt on the bourgeoisie, I determined to defy literary convention by exalting the middle class and its much-maligned values.

The loving, generous, utterly endearing entrepreneurs in my stories of course reflected my real-life relationships with members of Nancy's extended family and my own. During one visit to Southern California, I made a side trip with my father-in-law to San Diego County that provided new appreciation of the challenges of his work. For nearly ten years he'd been trying to develop a shopping center on a vacant tract of dusty land cluttered with weeds, garbage, and rusting, abandoned cars. He'd spent literally hundreds of thousands of dollars in submitting plans, pulling permits, and winning approval from a long series of temperamental agencies and arrogant governing bodies. While I watched his latest presentation to the local planning commission, he faced a new, almost comical obstacle in the person of a young activist with a nearby Indian tribe who had filed a complaint that the new shopping center could damage priceless Native American relics, and demanded that my father-in-law pay for a massive archaeological expedition to locate any artifacts that might exist. I found myself stunned and appalled by the truculent questions from a group of officious yahoos who seemed insanely determined to stop a creative businessman from delivering hundreds of jobs and significant economic growth to a remote section of the county. Eventually my father-in-law dropped all plans for the ambitious development altogether, allowing the puffed-up local officials to continue their debates about the possible existence of Indian artifacts while litter and tumbleweed continued to accumulate on their ugly empty lot.

My own dad, meanwhile, launched a new and startling phase of his career as a risk-taking entrepreneur. He had worked as a college professor, NASA experimenter, aspiring scientist astronaut, defense industry engineer, and research director for a high-tech division of Xerox Corporation, but he had grown weary of devoting his brilliance and creativity to enterprises he couldn't control. Much to my mother's chagrin, he committed our family's life savings to starting his own company, known as MERET Corporation—an undertaking devoted to development of his numerous patents and state-of-the-art approaches to fiber optics and lasers. MERET stood for *ME*dved *RE*search and *T*echnology, which sounded impossibly grand for a fledgling enterprise that existed for many months only in my dad's study and our family garage. Working eighteen-hour days, however, my father built an institution of lasting significance, eventually renting a lab and production facility and hiring nearly a dozen people. His dedication to every facet of business ("If I don't get this done, then nobody gets paid," he used to say) helped shift the values of all of his four sons in a decisively pro-business direction.

In the '70s, even my kid brother Jonathan caught the infectious appeal of capitalist capers and unleashed his own business ambitions as our new neighbor in Berkeley. After he enrolled at the University of California, he launched a twenty-four-hour-a-day food delivery service for hungry students in the Berkeley dorms. I watched with bemused admiration as Jonathan achieved instant success with the delivery service, which he called "The *Meshuggeneh* Brothers" ("The Crazy Brothers" in Yiddish). It was just another reminder of the entrepreneurial spirit that animated so many of our family members.

Surrounded by all this intoxicating entrepreneurial energy, I contented myself with writing about it in my master's thesis short stories, hoping that my literary endeavors would somehow lead to their own commercial jackpot. The possibility of that outcome increased substantially thanks to precious career counseling from my faculty adviser, Wright Morris, a novelist and critic who had achieved worldwide fame and earned major prizes (including a National Book Award for *The Field of Vision*).

Affably avuncular behind his gray handlebar mustache and Western string tie, he expressed general enthusiasm for my fiction even while pointing me in a different direction. "You'll get your degree and get a teaching job somewhere," Professor Morris assured me, "but if you want to succeed with your own writing, Michael, you ought to consider nonfiction or journalism. That's where you show your flair—reporting and recording, not imagining or inventing. It's not every writer who's cut out for the novelist's game."

This counsel arrived at precisely the moment that I'd begun earning a few regular, reliable dollars writing just the sort of nonfiction articles Wright Morris suggested. During my years in Berkeley I'd kept in touch with David Wallechinsky, whom I'd known at Palisades High School under his previous name David Wallace. The son of best-selling novelist Irving Wallace, he had recently declared his independence from his father's formidable reputation by taking on the Eastern European name his grandparents had abandoned when they arrived at Ellis Island. In high school I'd gotten to know Irving, whose unassuming, professorial, pipe-smoking manner contrasted with the scandalous atmosphere that surrounded his superheated international blockbusters (*The Chapman Report, The Fan Club*), which had sold some 92 million copies worldwide. His son David, deeply influenced by the experimental and utopian ideas of the 1960s counterculture, set out to build a different sort of creative career.

David and I lived only a few blocks apart from each other in Berkeley, and we remained good friends despite our sweeping disagreements on most cultural and political issues of the day. I had, of course, become an enthusiastic supporter of the military and America's cause in the Cold War, while he remained a committed pacifist who distrusted governments and armies of every sort. I embraced Orthodox Judaism with its specific rules and timeless traditions, while he favored a free-wheeling New Age spirituality that honored ancient paganism and drew inspiration from all religious systems. For instance, I followed kosher laws, but David developed his own, more radical strictures for the preparation and consumption of food, insisting on a tightly limited organic, mucous-free, no-wheat-or-animal-product diet. Most significantly, while I looked askance at the shaggy, stoned, experimental, tie-dyed world of Bay Area psychedelia, David embraced it: as a student at San Francisco State's highly rated film program, he made a ninety-minute documentary which showed a group of our mutual friends getting high by sucking on a huge tank of nitrous oxide (laughing gas), then taking their clothes off and trying (without spectacular success) to make love. Still, I always felt stimulated by David's truly indefatigable curiosity, an almost childlike sense of wonder that led him to intensive reading and research on an eccentric array of odd and absorbing subjects.

Eventually, David found a way to harness his curiosity for a practical purpose and in the process changed my life as well as his own. One afternoon he informed me that he had just won a major contract to edit a new reference book alongside his famous father. *The People's Almanac* represented a huge undertaking meant to revolutionize forever the information industry. As they ultimately explained in their introduction to this 1,500-page volume, "This is a reference book to be read for pleasure . . . to look up facts but also have fun." David's plans for the project also honored his countercultural roots, as the book promised to "break a few molds, create original forms, and give you alternative information from what you've always accepted as complete." As I listened to him talk about his bold intentions to shatter convention and upend entrenched institutions, it struck me as slightly contradictory that his entire enterprise relied on one of the most distinguished firms in the publishing establishment (Doubleday) and the coauthorship of the world's most bankable novelist.

To fill the crowded pages of *The People's Almanac,* the Wallaces planned to rely on some two hundred staff members and freelancers, and I eagerly accepted their invitation to write as many chapters as possible on U.S. history and the American presidents. Knowing me since high school, David understood my passion for trivia and storytelling about the national past and gave me first opportunity to make real-world use of my Yale degree in American history. The remuneration remained pathetic, even painful, but still opened an additional income stream to supplement the money I received from teaching at the Jewish Discovery Center, an afternoon school for privileged Jewish kids I'd launched in Contra Costa County, at the behest of a left-leaning, millionaire businesswoman who had heard about me through my brief involvement with the Ron Dellums campaign. Most importantly, the articles I wrote for *The People's Almanac* enabled me to apply the sage advice of Professor Morris: rather than toiling on short stories and novels that might never see the light of day, I was focusing my literary efforts on nonfiction featured in a high-profile publication.

For the most part, I concentrated on the presidential portraits, following a format that Irving had devised. In addition to the usual features ("Vital Statistics," "Before the Presidency: Career and Personal Life"), the almanac articles included distinctive headings like "His Person" (a detailed physical description), "Psychohistory," "Little Known Facts," and a "Pro and Con" analysis of the chief executive's term of office. I loved researching and writing this material, securing every available source on Franklin Pierce, for instance, from libraries and used book stores, ferreting out the most telling and intriguing nuggets (such as the habit of the beautiful but unhinged Mrs. Pierce of wearing black every day in the White House and spending most of her time writing letters to one of her three dead sons). I also wrote colorful articles about "Footnote Characters in American History"—Amazonian temperance crusader Carry Nation; cynical Tammany Hall boss George Washington Plunkitt; Indian mystic and military genius Tecumseh; robber baron, indulgent gourmand, and world champion eater Diamond Jim Brady; ill-favored, promiscuous, and brutal Western heroine Belle Starr—as well as a detailed description of novelist Upton Sinclair's radical (and nearly successful) California gubernatorial campaign in 1934 that first mobilized the political power of Hollywood (in hysterical opposition to Sinclair). I ended up selling the Wallaces an appalling total of more than 450 pages of manuscript.

When *The People's Almanac* soared to the top of the best-seller lists in 1975, spawning several sequels (including the even more celebrated *Book of Lists*), I felt proud of my role in the achievement, even though no one beyond my closest friends and immediate family knew anything at all of my significant role in a major publishing triumph. The text identified the authors of each article with initials rather than by name, and when one writer provided many pieces in a row (as I did with all the presidential profiles), his initials appeared only at the very end of the sequence.

Nevertheless, even the modest fees I earned for my work, which amounted to less than a penny a word, helped reduce the financial pressure of paying our bills while the completion of my "terminal degree" in creative writing promised definitive deliverance from the ongoing grind. My academic ranking at the top of our program argued that if anyone could actually get a teaching job in the field, it would be me. To my surprise and chagrin, however, I got almost no response after sending résumés to more than a hundred colleges and universities across the country. Gradually I gave up on my fantasy of living graciously in some leafy New England college town, creatively inspiring generations of well-scrubbed, gifted students while pursuing my own earth-shaking literary endeavors in the attic study of my Colonial home as the village church chimed midnight under the moonlight. I realized that this idyll might never materialize, but I felt vastly encouraged by the last-minute emergence of a prestigious teaching prospect at the University of Wisconsin.

All right, it wasn't the *real* University of Wisconsin—not the famous, world-class campus in Madison, even though I let my parents and in-laws think that it was. The invitation I'd actually received came from a branch institution known as the University of Wisconsin, Stout, in Menomonie, a town of 13,000 about ninety minutes west of Minneapolis. Formerly known as the Stout Manual Training School (after its founder, a local businessman named James Stout), the Menomonie institution provided "focused programs related to careers in industry, technology, and home economics." This concentration hardly suggested a free-spirited nurturing of creativity or the arts, but I convinced myself that a scenic small town in the upper Midwest offered a preferable, wholesome alternative to the dreary, decadent, dysfunctional, drug-infested demimonde of Berserk-ley.

In a flurry of encouraging phone calls and letters, the hale and hearty people at the Menomomie campus invited me for an interview with the entire liberal arts faculty. The university even agreed to pay for my trip—that is, on the condition that I accepted the job if offered, or that they decided after the interview not to give me the job. If they made me the offer but I turned it down, I would have to pay my own way to wintry Wisconsin. I gladly agreed to this arrangement, since Stout's late-blooming interest in hiring me represented my only real chance for the teaching job I coveted.

Unfortunately, my trip to the Midwest seemed to go wrong from the beginning. I took a red-eye, Saturday night, post-Shabbat flight to Minneapolis, where I found it impossible to rent a car. At the time I stubbornly refused to apply for any sort of credit card (concerned that carrying plastic might encourage my wife or me to spend more than we earned—a cardinal sin according to the value system that my German-Jewish Oma had instilled in me); this seemed reasonable to me, but it made no sense to Hertz, Avis, Budget, or the other companies at Twin Cities airport who refused to rent a car to anyone without a credit card. Eventually, a supervisor arrived at the Hertz counter and accepted a check for a thousand dollars, plus all three hundred dollars of my cash, as security for a flimsy Ford Falcon.

I arrived in snowy Menomonie several hours later than expected and followed the directions to the home of the dean, who had hospitably suggested I come for lunch. As I got out of the car, the stabbing cold represented the first shock and then I recoiled, physically, at a horrifying sight on the front steps to his house. Blocking my path to the door were the bloodied, frozen carcasses of five furry animals. As a newcomer to the Midwest, I knew nothing about the appropriate etiquette of entering homes by jumping past orderly displays of dead creatures. Could they be beavers, I wondered. Muskrats? Badgers, the state animal? I didn't want to come close enough to find out, so I simply stood there in the snowy street bellowing up toward the front door. "Hello! Hellooo! It's Michael Medved—I just arrived!"

The dean came out and hollered for me to come up. I winced, pointing at the corpses at my feet, but he insisted that I just step past the chilled and lifeless critters. "Yeah, look at that! We had a big day, didn't we?" he laughed. "My son and I went hunting early this morning. That's what you do in Wisconsin in the wintertime. You like to hunt?"

I didn't answer, but walked into the warmth of his neat little ranch-style home, where the aroma of ham overwhelmed me. I hadn't eaten since the peanuts on the plane, but I'd been keeping kosher long enough (four years) to feel queasy over the sweet, pungent odor of fresh-cooked pig flesh. During the meal with the dean and his wife, I simply passed on the main course rather than offering some extended explanation of the Jewish dietary laws. I did ask an important question, though: did they know of any sort of Jewish synagogue or temple anywhere in town? They looked at each other sheepishly. "Jewish?" the beefy, bespectacled dean said. "We had a Jewish guy on the faculty a few years back. Really nice fella, too. Him and his wife used to go to the Catholic church in town."

After a tour of campus, he delivered me to the room in a men's dormitory that had been arranged as my overnight accommodation. Even in the late afternoon, the noisy brawling that echoed through that hallway reminded me of some Hollywood prison movie in which the frightened new inmate quickly realizes the danger of his situation. My room adjoined the group bathroom for that floor, and despite my determined attempts to ignore the ruckus, I couldn't shut out the noise of snapping towels and smacking flesh in the Sunday evening showers, or the shouted arguments about the relative size and fragrance of the defecations that the eager students had produced. When the dean arrived to take me out to dinner, it came as deliverance, especially since he had promised a "super deluxe meal" with the chairman of the English department at the "finest restaurant in all of Dunn County."

To my amazement, they had named this elegant enclave after a dog: the Bolo Inn honored a famous Black Labrador who had won International Grand Championships in the 1920s. Every wall, every corner, every hallway, even the restrooms of the restaurant featured some image of the long-deceased but presumably immortal Bolo; many of the images were full-color oil paintings that infused their canine subject with the sort of reverent luminosity usually reserved for devotional art.

Back in the men's dorm that night, I began feeling seriously ill. I thought for a while that I might have reacted badly to the bony, underdone baked perch I had consumed back at the Bolo (the only item on the menu I could eat), though the abundance of unpleasant noises and smells that greeted me in the dormitory probably did more to turn my stomach than anything I had swallowed. On this particular Sunday night, the guys blared their music, shouted obscenities at one another, ran up and down the hall, and banged against the walls. In general, the natives had progressed from towel fights in the shower and disputes over their bodily functions to drunken revelry complete with the noise of shattered glass and enthusiastic vomiting.

By two in the morning I had concluded that I had to do everything in my power to avoid moving to Menomonie. I couldn't imagine dragging my wife away from California to a frozen, fading town in which the most popular restaurant had been named after a dead dog. In the abstract, I still liked the challenge of kindling some creative sparks in the brawny, beer-guzzling industrial arts students at Stout, but as I tried to sleep in that noisy dorm with my queasy stomach, I couldn't face the reality of spending years of my life paddling against the current at a place that didn't even offer an English major. To be sure, I longed to escape the leftist lunacy and pseudo-intellectual posturing that characterized every aspect of Bay Area life, but I realized that I felt just as alienated from the stifling, Jew-free, small-town atmosphere of Menomonie (where even some of the locals joked about "Monotony, Wisconsin"). In the end I saw no reason I had to elect either extreme: giving up on my comfortable fantasy of teaching writing on the college level didn't mean that I must work forever at poorly paying odd jobs at Berkeley.

Meanwhile, I faced the immediate imperative of finding a way to flunk my formal interview with the faculty hiring committee on Monday morning. If they awarded me the job and I turned them down, I would be forced to eat the expense of my whole frustrating trip—more than six hundred dollars for airfare and car rental, which amounted to a huge sum for me in those days. When I crawled out of bed after a restless night, I began planning to present myself in a manner so obnoxious, so disturbing, so utterly distasteful that any self-respecting faculty committee must feel forced to reject me. First, I abandoned my suit and tie for faded jeans and work shirt. Then I courageously resolved on a course of minor self-mutilation: while shaving, I sliced a long, nasty gash along my chin, then blotted the blood onto my shirt. Growing gleeful at the appalling results, I grabbed a First Aid kit and used iodine, a gauze pad, and adhesive tape to make my self-inflicted wound look incalculably worse than it was. I also wound the adhesive tape around the left lens of my glasses to suggest shattered specs. Blinking at the horrifying reflection in the mirror, I felt proud and satisfied: I looked like a homeless psychotic. No university could possibly hire me. Even the dean and the other faculty member who had seen me in my more respectable guise the day before would have to seriously wonder about my sudden deterioration—whether I'd gotten into a fight, or suffered the debilitating effects of a hangover, or experienced some psychotic break.

With my grooming carefully adjusted, I made my way over to the administration building for the fateful appointment, making a point to arrive ten minutes late. Despite my tardiness, the dozen people who assembled in the boardroom warmly greeted me. The dean made a worried gesture to the iodine-soaked bandage taped to my jaw. "What happened there, Michael?" he solicitously inquired. "Looks like you just ran into a lawn mower!"

I paused, trying to come up with some spontaneous, offensive explanation, but then decided that the path of least resistance sounded ridiculous enough. "I cut myself shaving," I said. "For some reason, it happens to me a lot."

Rather than delve further into my apparently oddball personal habits, the chairman of the committee began the interview. "Just to give us some idea of what you really want with this job, let me start out with a tough question. If you were forced to give a one-word answer of what you want most to bring to the University of Wisconsin, Stout, what would that one word be?"

I paused for a moment, hoping to come up with a single pronouncement that could instantly erase my already dwindling chances. I finally burst into a broad smile as I came up with the ideal response. "If you want one word, if it has to be one word, then I'd have to say that word would be . . . 'drugs.' "

"Drugs?!"

"That's right—*recreational* drugs. Marijuana, hashish, cocaine, maybe a little bit of LSD. You see, I've been struck since I've been here with how behind the times, how conservative this place seems to be. Remember, I'm from Berkeley, which is probably the opposite extreme. So if you want your students to begin to catch up with big trends in academia, you're going to need much more of a drug culture here on campus. Not that anyone should get addicted. But to try to get the creative energy flowing, there's no substitute for a little mind-altering experimentation. Maybe we could use nitrous oxide, or laughing gas, for a class experiment. That one is mostly legal. I have a friend back in Berkeley who made a film about a bunch of kids who do laughing gas together, then have a big orgy. Anyone know a dentist in town who can help us get the gas?"

They greeted my little discourse with a long, pained silence, and glared back at me with open mouths—like the stunned audience in Mel Brooks's *The Producers* after their first encounter with "Springtime for Hitler." I went on in a similar vein (with a bloody shirt as my visual aid) for the rest of the interview, talking about the need for more political activism and student dissent, for more sexual experimentation, for more of the countercultural values that had taken hold everywhere else to begin sweeping away the traditionalism of Menomonie. I actually enjoyed the role playing, as I gave insipid, even sickening explanations for advancing ideas I actually hated. At one point a committee member protested my rambling presentation. "You sound very different today than you sounded in the material you sent us with your application. It says right here that you're deeply committed to 'traditional Jewish values.' It doesn't sound very traditional; all your talk about sex and drugs."

"Well, actually, I should have made myself more clear in my application," I replied. "I'm a member of a very radical sect in Judaism, very hedonistic, very controversial. We sort of combine Jewish elements with the sensual wisdom of the Far East. Do you want me to talk to you a little bit about Tantric Yoga and my plan to share it with some of the students?"

Fortunately, no one called my bluff and demanded an exposure of my appalling ignorance of Eastern mysticism, but even if they had, further babbling about trendy nonsense could only confirm the impression that they had brought a demented, dangerous blowhard to their stolid campus. I kept waiting for them to stop the process, for the referee to call the fight and (you should pardon the expression) stop the bleeding, but they encouraged me to chatter on about nothing in particular. When we finally concluded after an hour, the dean asked me to step into the adjoining office and wait for him while the committee discussed their reactions to the interview. I sprawled into a chair near his secretary, who eyed me warily, as if expecting me to steal something off her desk. I felt satisfied and confident, knowing that I had given the pleasant, perplexed middle-aged faculty members the worst impression I knew how to convey. Now I longed to flee from Menomonie and all its attendant humiliations.

After about fifteen minutes, the dean emerged from the boardroom with a big smile and an extended hand. "Well, Michael," he beamed. "I think congratulations are in order. You got the job. Now we can start talking about trying to help you move."

I tried hard to hide my shock and horror. "I got the job? You're making the offer? Actually, I was afraid that some people might react poorly to some of what I had to say in there."

"Oh, you were controversial, all right. Two of the faculty members thought we were crazy even to consider you. But for most of us, we think we need some controversy. This can be a pretty stodgy place. We're trying hard to send out a message that we're not just about industrial arts. Some of your ideas—about politics, the sexual revolution, all the rest of it—would really start to shake things up. Michael, you'll be a breath of fresh air."

I fought for breath myself and realized that my uneasy stomach had returned along with my vision of six hundred dollars in travel expenses pointlessly withdrawn from our already paltry bank account. On the flight back to Berkeley, I knew that I faced further travel in the near future. I could no longer resist the heartfelt and altogether logical pleas of my in-laws and, most notably, my mother, who insisted that I correct a mistake I'd made more than six years before. They dearly wanted me to return to my legal education at Yale, or some other prestigious lawyer mill, and I knew I had only a last, forlorn chance—a single desperate, Hail Mary play—to continue to defy them and to avoid the fate I dreaded as one more parasite taking his place in the swarming plague of superfluous attorneys already infesting America.

For the Most Part, Conservatives Are
Both Nicer and Happier Than Liberals

On the radio show I've hosted since 1996, no subject provokes more anger from callers across the country than my contention that conservatives aren't just more astute and practical than their liberal counterparts, they are also happier, more fulfilled in their lives and their work. This argument doesn't suggest that conservatives start off as better people, but it does make the case that they benefit from better ideas.

The Gallup Poll provides statistical backing for this conclusion. According to a Gallup press release from January 2004, "In recent years, Republicans beat Democrats in happiness each time it was measured except in 1996, when about an equal percentage of both parties said they were very happy." Concerning the most recent survey, the Gallup organization declares "that Republicans may have found the keys to happiness, even after taking marital status and income levels into account. Sixty-two percent of Republicans surveyed say they are very happy compared with only 50 percent of Democrats." Professor James Lindgren of Northwestern University reported similar conclusions in July 2003: "In the National Opinion Research Center General Social Survey (a standard social science database, second only to the U.S. Census in use by U.S. sociologists), the GSS asks the standard survey question about happiness in general. In the 1998–2002 GSS, extreme conservatives are much more likely to report being 'very happy' than extreme liberals—47.1 percent to 31.5 percent. Earlier years show a similar pattern. . . . Conservatives usually tend to report less marital unhappiness than liberals. . . . Earlier General Social Surveys found that conservatives were more satisfied with their health, their friendships, their family life, and the city or place they live—all in all, a remarkably consistent picture."

Skeptics may dismiss this contrast between conservative contentment and liberal unease as a simple reflection of the greater wealth of those on the political right, but the data specifically contradict that interpretation. Even adjusting for economic and marital status, and making direct comparisons between respondents with similar financial resources, Gallup found that a conservative orientation correlated powerfully with greater happiness. According to the polling organization, "Deep happiness is found in roughly equal measure among a majority of adults living in most household income groups." In other words, high income doesn't predispose a family toward reporting happiness, but a conservative outlook does. The current prominence of bitter, angry, fabulously wealthy liberals illustrates the proposition that cheerfulness and optimism connect more reliably with political philosophy than with personal riches. Financier George Soros may control some seven billion dollars, but in the fall of 2003 *Fortune* described him as the "world's angriest billionaire" for his acrimonious and obsessive drive to force George W. Bush from office. John Kerry himself, my one-time Yale colleague, may live in one of the nation's wealthiest households (worth more than $500 million), but no one possibly could describe his personality as sunny or ebullient.

Over the years, I've concluded that the obvious contrast between gloomy, dour liberals and cheerful conservatives has less to do with the reassuring influence of right-wing ideas than it does with the unfailingly depressing impact of leftist thinking. Over the past thirty years, the liberal project has emphasized national guilt over past American atrocities; competitive claims of victimhood from various aggrieved groups; reports of impending environmental disaster threatening the future of the earth itself; the helplessness or ordinary people in the face of cruel corporate elites; the impossibility of racial justice without preferential treatment for oppressed minorities; the doomed, outmoded nature of traditional marriage, conventional religious faith, and other sources of common comfort; and a constant sense of dire crisis which justifies the sweeping, radical governmental initiatives that the left considers our only hope. Good news and self-confidence present existential threats to "progressive" activists. If people feel happy in their private lives and personal arrangements, then why would they need the thoroughgoing transformation of society and its fundamental institutions that left-wing agitators invariably demand? For the true believers of the liberal faith, discontent, restlessness, and rage amount to far more than useful political tools; they provide the very basis for their philosophical orientation.

For the first quarter century of my life, I stubbornly embraced that liberal faith without recognizing its corrosive, destructive impact on my own success and happiness. Even after I began to recognize the corrupt, illogical elements in leftist thinking (criminals deserve more sympathy than cops; weakening our defenses will make us safer from dangerous enemies; government should punish its most productive citizens and reward its most indolent), I failed to replace this idiocy with a more functional, coherent system of ideas. Instead, I tried to distance myself from politics altogether, assuming that the frustrations and disillusionments I'd experienced in liberal activism would extend to electoral involvement of any kind.

My prevailing distaste for politics encouraged me to resist the increasingly intense demands from all sides of my extended family that I return to Yale Law School as soon as possible. I knew that no academic environment on earth boasted a more feverishly political atmosphere than the august institution I had deserted, but I also knew that the pleading from my mother and my in-laws made a great deal of practical sense. Nearly six years had passed since I went on "leave of absence" from Yale to work in the Duffey campaign, and despite varied and frenetic efforts during that period of exile I'd made little headway in establishing a career or providing for the children we hoped and expected to soon welcome to our home. I could hardly deny the argument that I'd reached a point where I owed it to my wife and to myself to return to the nation's most prestigious law school and to complete a degree that would all but assure my future professional success.

Unfortunately, the time limit had already expired (after five years of leave of absence) for my automatic admission so I had to reapply to Yale and retake the Law School Admission Test (LSAT). To my enormous relief, I scored slightly higher on the test than I had when I took the exam as a senior in college, and my old friends at Yale admitted me once again, even restoring my generous fellowship. While Nancy, my in-laws, and my parents celebrated, and Nancy began to arrange our move to New Haven, I still yearned to find a way to squirm out of imprisonment in a legal career. I dreaded the prospect of dressing up in a suit and reporting every day to some government office or big firm for the purpose of framing other people's arguments. My embarrassing (and costly) experience in Menomonie convinced me that I could never earn an easy living as a teacher of writing, but I refused to give up on my long-standing conviction that I could somehow beat the odds and make enough to sustain for myself as an author. At the same time I reapplied to law school and continued toiling at my articles for *The People's Almanac*, I started working on one last book project, in the forlorn hope that getting a contract with a significant New York publisher would remove the pressure to resume my legal education.

In choosing a subject for this final fling at fame, I childishly decided to follow my passion: classical music. I came up with a title (*Goodbye Beatles, Hello Brahms!*) and a concept (guiding people to classics they would cherish based on their taste in rock 'n' roll) that seemed original and trendy enough to generate some commercial interest. I meant to strip away the stuffy, elitist veneer from the greatest music ever created by human beings. If you love the Beatles, I argued, you should try Brahms; those who prefer the Stones ought to sample Beethoven and Stravinsky; Simon & Garfunkel devotees, Mozart and Schubert; fans of the Who, Mahler and Shostakovich; and so on.

I toiled happily on the project, spending hours and hours listening to music on my stereo and making fateful decisions about the finest available interpretations. Unfortunately, my agent, Arthur Pine—who continued to promote my prospects despite a shockingly consistent lack of success—had no luck pitching this manuscript, either. An associate editor at William Morrow, who warmly praised the book, summed up the problem from the publishers' perspective: "There just do not seem to be enough people around who are willing to buy classical music records, let alone a book telling them how to buy classical music records." At this point, my long-suffering agent suggested a different approach. "The problem is you write these big books—you finish the whole thing before you show 'em to anybody," he said. "If you really want to get a book contract, you don't need to do all the work. Just write a description of the book you're going to write, and then send it to me. You've already done all those articles for *The People's Almanac* so they know you can write. So just put down ideas, even stream of consciousness. Write it as a letter to me, and then I can take the letter and show it to publishers. Come up with a lot of different ideas and maybe one of 'em will work."

I took the advice to heart and wrote out a twenty-page single-spaced letter to Artie that briefly but energetically described six very different book ideas. The first was a logical follow-up to all my *People's Almanac* work on the presidents. While researching my least favorite chief executive, LBJ (a dishonest, loathsome, hugely dangerous megalomaniac I had foolishly admired as a teenager), I read *The Tragedy of Lyndon Johnson* by Eric Goldman, one of Johnson's long-suffering White House aides, which provided a fascinating insider's view of the excitement and frustration of working every day as part of a president's staff. I realized that a comprehensive history of presidential staffers—toiling in the shadows while their bosses changed the world—would make a fascinating book. In my letter, I pushed this "secret history of the chief executives and their top aides," laying out an ambitious plan to visit every presidential library and to conduct personal interviews with surviving top staff members going back to the Truman administration.

Though I felt most passionate about that project, which I called *The Shadow Presidents,* I pitched five other book ideas in this life-altering letter to my agent, including, as an afterthought, a loving, tongue-in-cheek, coffee-table tribute book honoring *The Fifty Worst Films of All Time.* I felt altogether certain that no publisher would ever touch that idea. After all, they didn't want a great project about classical music because they said that nobody bought classical records, so why would they ever go for a book about bad movies that nobody saw?

After he had read my letter, Artie called me collect (as he always did at this point—after all, I had earned him nothing in four years) and expressed breathless enthusiasm for my book concepts, telling me he was confident that he could get some sort of contract on at least one of my ideas before I reported for my scheduled sentence of at least two more years hard labor at law school. I particularly disliked the notion of finding myself suddenly surrounded by students several years younger than I was; the awareness of my rapidly advancing age had begun to trouble me because of the approach of my ten-year reunion from Palisades High School. I talked about that upcoming event with Roger Friedland, a former classmate who had passed through Berkeley on a visit and now offered me the chance to ride with him back to LA to rejoin my wife, Nancy, who had flown south for one of her family's regular big occasions. During the five-hour ride with Roger (who today is a sociology professor at the University of California, Santa Barbara), we began talking about the people we remembered from Palisades High, many of whom had taken strange, tortured, often self-destructive paths over the past decade. The quarterback of our football team (and also "The Most Likely to Succeed") made his living as a massage therapist and a minister in a truly bizarre religious cult. A tightly regimented "grind" had taken too many drugs in college and now lived in a psychiatric facility. A soft-spoken math student had gone on to UCLA but now begged at street corners with the Hare Krishnas. Our head cheerleader and Homecoming Queen had earned a Ph.D. and a job teaching women's history at Princeton. We gasped and laughed over these stories on the whole trip to LA, wondering what shocking tales we might find from classmates we didn't know about.

Even before Roger dropped me off at my parents' home, I realized that the subject of our conversation represented the strongest possible basis for a marketable book. The night I returned to Berkeley I went over to see my friend David Wallechinsky and proposed that we collaborate on a "where are they now?" book about our high school class. David knew more of our classmates than I did, since he had grown up with them since kindergarten, whereas I had not moved to LA until junior year in high school; he also had begun working as a leader of the reunion committee, so he had a much better idea about how to track down our targets. Moreover, the explosive success of *The People's Almanac* had made him a hot literary property, with agents and publishers clamoring for his next project.

Wallechinsky embraced the idea, and through an agent he knew, David Obst—another hip, bearded Baby Boomer, who had recently gained fame as the agent behind Bob Woodward and Carl Bernstein's Watergate book, *All the President's Men*—we quickly made a deal with Random House based on a book proposal we wrote in a single afternoon. Our brief proposal emphasized a *Time* magazine cover story that had appeared our senior year and focused on our high school as one of two upper-middle-class schools to illustrate the theme of the article: "TODAY'S TEENAGERS: On the Fringe of a Golden Era." The stories that we collected highlighted the irony in that optimistic vision and made it painfully clear that for most Pali graduates of 1965, the era they'd experienced since high school hadn't proved golden at all. From the beginning, I consciously saw the book as a means to expose the emptiness and folly in the "liberating" promises of the counterculture. We decided to title the book *What Really Happened to the Class of '65?* because the real—and rather sad—story of our generation had remained obscured by so much stylish puffery, self-serving apologias, and premature nostalgia.

Although my share of the advance money we received from Random House hardly counted as a windfall, I now held a contract with a leading publisher and needed to concentrate on the book through the summer and fall. I tried, therefore, to tell my mother that I couldn't possibly return to New Haven, but she pleaded against the very idea that I might turn away from a place at Yale Law School a *second* time. We continued this argument through costly long-distance phone conversations for several days before I got an early-morning ring from Artie Pine—shocked that for the first time he hadn't called me collect. He congratulated me, telling me that he had just sold the *Shadow Presidents* proposal to New York Times Books. Suddenly I had not one but two book contracts—and of course two books to write.

When I phoned my distraught mother with this latest development, she resigned herself to the fact that I would never go back to law school and would scrape along for the rest of my life as "a starving writer." Within weeks, however, my literary horizons expanded even further: Artie Pine came back with another contract, committing me to the project I'd never taken seriously—*The Fifty Worst Films of All Time*. An editor at Popular Library Press (a division of CBS Publications) had bought the book based on a few snide paragraphs in my letter to Artie; he understood that his book stood third on the Medved dance card, but he felt it would be worth the wait.

For the remaining months of 1975, I worked at a frenetic pace to advance, as far as possible, all three projects simultaneously. With David Wallechinsky continuing his whirlwind publicity for *The People's Almanac*, the burden of conducting tape-recorded interviews with our classmates fell primarily on me, while Nancy dutifully transcribed the tapes. Of course I enjoyed the entire process of reconnecting with people we hadn't seen in years—especially since David and I very consciously sought out the most desirable females we could remember, many of whom we wouldn't have dared speak to in high school. Our preference for beautiful women constituted only part of the elaborate process we used to select our thirty subjects out of some six hundred members of our graduating class. We chose the most dramatic stories and also tried for broad representation (featuring a Vietnam veteran, a suicide survivor, a successful businessman, a married couple with kids, plus a generous sampling of burnouts, commune members, cultists, rebels, and head cases). Recognizing that every high school features a similar cast of characters, we identified our classmates in terms of the timeless roles they had played as teenagers: "The Quarterback," "The Intellectual," "The Surfer," "The Bad Girl," "Homecoming Queen," "The Goof-Off," and so on.

For me, the most important interview centered on the classmate we appropriately designated as "The Idealist": my old friend and fellow teenaged intellectual Jamie Kelso. We had shared a number of irresponsible adventures in high school, including the hour we spent together in the local jail in San Clemente, California: busted for allegedly "resisting arrest" after Jamie threw the book he was reading (*The History of Western Philosophy* by Bertrand Russell) at the cop who asked us to move our sleeping bags from an unauthorized state park campsite. After high school, Jamie had bummed around Europe and then briefly attended UCLA before dropping out. In 1971 I had called his parents to try to find him and they sent me to a ramshackle, communal living facility near downtown LA in which Jamie served the Church of Scientology as part of their elite, paramilitary corps of missionary shock troops, "The Sea Organization." During a brief, disturbing conversation he told me he had signed a "billion-year contract" binding himself in this and all future incarnations to the Scientology movement and its "enlightened" leader, L. Ron Hubbard. Jamie struck me at the time as deeply delusional, in fact floridly insane, though charming, energetic, good-natured, optimistic, and dedicated as always.

Four years later, when it came time to locate him for *The Class of '65,* I called the Church of Scientology, since my calculations indicated he still had some time left to serve on his contract. To my surprise, the operator at the main switchboard transferred me to four different offices before I found one that admitted any knowledge of Jamie. "That's a name we're not supposed to talk about," said the businesslike voice at the other end of the line. "He ran away two years ago, double-crossing the organization. If you locate him, be sure to give us his address."

I had no intention of ratting out Jamie to the New Age Nazis of Scientology, and through his younger brother I managed to track him down to a farmhouse near Kansas City. After extensive telephone negotiations, I persuaded him to travel out to California to sit for an interview with me and to visit his parents and brothers. During his visit, we ended up spending a great deal of time together in a series of ridiculously intense, free-flowing, mind-opening late-night conversations—memorable exchanges that amounted to my first ever substantive contact with a friend who described himself as a political right-winger. Jamie, in fact, had joined the John Birch Society and planned a race for Congress as the nominee of the fiercely anti-government American Independent Party. After exhausting years of deep involvement in various religious cults (in addition to Scientology, Jamie had played prominent roles in Transcendental Meditation and Nichiren Shoshu Buddhism), he had discovered the writings of Ayn Rand and (in his own words) "finally emerged from the shadows of mystic-collectivist dogma and entered the brilliant sunlight of reason and individualism." He had read and reread every word that Ayn Rand had published. "She is, without question, the greatest novelist in human history," he told me.

At Jamie's insistence, I also began making my way through *Atlas Shrugged,* and while I couldn't share his assessment of Rand's unparalleled brilliance as a novelist, I did find her arguments persuasive and energizing. Reading Rand played an unexpectedly important role in challenging me to fill in holes in my personal outlook. Rand, for instance, emphasized the "virtue of selfishness"—the idea that the honest pursuit of personal profit benefited rather than exploited your neighbors, since it created new wealth and offered them goods or services they wanted to buy. In her view, a free economic exchange between private citizens represented a far better way to influence behavior than governmental force or coercion. These notions reinforced my instinctive enthusiasm for the entrepreneurial effort that flourished in all corners of my family, and Rand's book also provided an ideological underpinning for explaining how all this energy and daring benefited society as a whole.

Most importantly, the encounter with my nonconforming high school friend shattered the stereotype that described all right-wingers as mean, grim, grumpy, and old. Regardless of how one might react to his ideas or his organizational affiliations (I've never felt any special warmth for the dour conspiracy theorists at the John Birch Society), no one could deny Jamie's personal warmth, wit, cheerfulness, youthful energy, and soaring optimism. In fact, some of his words in his tape-recorded interview with me sound downright prophetic. "I'm taking bets that inside of twenty years, I will live on a planet where Communism, socialism, Big Brotherism, collectivism, fascism, and all variant systems of terrorizing free men will repose on the scrap heap of history," Jamie said—a full fourteen years before the destruction of the Berlin Wall, and seven years before President Reagan predicted that Communism would one day reside on "the ash heap of history."

A few months after my memorable reconnection with this visionary friend from high school, I got the chance to interact with a number of nationally prominent Republican leaders who further opened my eyes to the fundamental decency of conservative ideas and personalities. At this point in the narrative, a reader might reasonably expect some touching anecdote about the late Ronald Reagan, who inspired so many young people with his personal example of warmth, kindness, and optimism. Unfortunately, I didn't meet President Reagan until eighteen years later, long after he had completed his two epochal terms as president and I had begun playing a conspicuous role as a Republican partisan. During the years of disaffection between my rejection of Democratic politics and my ultimate discovery of a new ideological home in the GOP, Reagan—alas—played little role in my consciousness.

Instead, I found myself personally impressed and engaged while spending time with three hugely controversial figures from the Republican establishment: Sherman Adams, former governor of New Hampshire and Ike's scandal-tarnished chief of staff; Bob Haldeman, the Nixon aide whose determination to protect the president during Watergate led him to a term in federal prison; and Dick Cheney, who once served as top aide to President Ford and more than two decades later would polarize the public with his conservative leadership as vice president. I conducted intensive, moving, surprisingly intimate interviews with all three of these gentlemen as part of my research for *The Shadow Presidents*, which I began working on as soon as I'd finished my tape-recorded conversations for *Class of '65*.

I had approached Sherman Adams with trepidation; after all, he qualified as an ancestral enemy—the indispensable assistant to the same Dwight Eisenhower whom my parents had taught me to despise as a boob, an ignoramus, and a spineless disgrace. Nevertheless, when I finally got to speak with Adams (after much resistance by the former White House aide), I felt deeply impressed in spite of myself. He spoke with growling force and ice-sharp clarity (even though he was approaching eighty) and compelled respect and sympathy. In 1958, he had resigned his post under an ethical cloud, though the controversy looks shockingly trivial by today's standards: he had accepted some expensive gifts (a vicuna coat, an oriental rug, free hotel rooms) from a New Hampshire industrialist and long-time personal friend who ended up the subject of a congressional investigation. To his neighbors in northern New England (who spoke with me freely when I visited), the charges against "Sherm" counted far less than the vision and leadership he displayed after he retired from government, developing a beautiful lodge and ski resort at Loon Mountain that provided scores of jobs and a jolt of economic energy to a remote, fading section of the state.

Bob Haldeman also forced me to reevaluate my prejudices during the two full days I spent with him in his home in Los Angeles, just months before he went away to serve his eighteen months in a federal minimum-security facility. He had been widely caricatured as a latter-day Nazi, a fanatical enemy of the Constitution and every element of human decency, but the Bob Haldeman I got to know headed a loving, vibrant, richly cultured, deeply patriotic family that exemplified the wholesome values that most Americans, liberals as well as conservatives, professed to honor. While everyone I knew expressed hatred and contempt for Haldeman, I came to see the Watergate catastrophe through his eyes and to feel sympathy for the ruin that rewarded his lifetime of hard work and his idealistic devotion to President Nixon. I learned that if leading media outlets could be so biased in their characterization of a figure like Haldeman, I should look skeptically at their evaluations of any power players who dissented from their trendy leftist nostrums.

Dick Cheney, who performed with understated but undeniable effectiveness as chief of staff in the Ford administration (taking over that post from his friend and mentor Don Rumsfeld), drew scant criticism from the press because he attracted so little attention. Only thirty-four when he took on the vast responsibility of supervising the 480 members of the White House staff (in the midst of an underdog election campaign, no less), Cheney displayed decisiveness and administrative skill that impressed all his colleagues. He also impressed me with his direct answers, wry sense of humor, knowledge of historical trivia (he'd been a history graduate student at University of Wisconsin before coming to Washington), and future promise. No politician I had ever met struck me as more intelligent, more capable, or more pleasant company than Dick Cheney. We got together during several of my subsequent trips to Washington and I also developed a strong attachment to his feisty, brilliant wife, Lynne. At the time, Dick Cheney remained a little-known figure at the fringes of power, but he counted as the first Republican leader who personally inspired me. In some of the press interviews for *The Shadow Presidents*, I became the first commentator anywhere in the country to make the eccentric prediction that Richard Bruce Cheney (at the time below the age of forty) would one day receive serious consideration for the nation's highest office.

My friendship with the Cheneys, along with my renewed acquaintance with my old friend Jamie, removed the last obstacle to my identification as a conservative, exploding the supposition that I'd always feel closer and more comfortable with liberals. As I toiled away at my multiple book projects, I found little time for political reflection; still, conservative, even pro-Republican messages seethed and bubbled just below the surface of both *The Shadow Presidents* and *What Really Happened to the Class of '65?* (and occasionally even rose to the surface), reflecting the ongoing transformation in my perspective. The next step, impelled by family tragedy, emotional need, and unexpected fame, involved a new commitment to the oldest approach of true conservatism: changing the world by means of intimate arrangements and self-sustaining communities, and emphasizing the necessary deployment of the "little platoons" of society.

Transforming a Neighborhood—and Building a Community—Work Better Than Top-Down Change

All my life I've struggled with a love-hate relationship with the great American metropolis of Los Angeles, and under the ridiculous work pressures of the summer of '75, that confusion became especially acute.

As a kid growing up in San Diego, I'd always looked at LA as our ugly, domineering, decidedly decadent big sister to the north. When my parents moved us there in my junior year in high school, I continued to express exaggerated contempt for our new hometown despite the fact that I obviously flourished in the more competitive, worldly atmosphere of Palisades High. After going away to Yale I became an East Coast snob for years, and then a big-time Northern California snob once I moved to Berkeley, all the while refusing to acknowledge that many of my most significant and rewarding experiences (wedding, political assassination, connection with Jewish Orthodoxy) occurred when in LA.

The tasks associated with the completion of *What Really Happened to the Class of '65?* also drew me back to the Southland, despite my continuing hesitations about the quality of life. Most of our classmates still lived in the LA area, so it made far more sense to base our operations there while conducting interviews and transcribing and editing the tape-recorded material. Wallechinsky and his girlfriend, Flora Chavez, had already abandoned Berkeley and moved into his parents' spacious and elegant Brentwood estate, so Nancy and I packed up our absolutely essential possessions (including our pampered Muki), locked up our Berkeley flat, and moved into my mom and dad's basement for the duration of the book project.

As it turned out, we arrived at an especially dicey moment in the long, troubled history of my parents' marriage. They'd separated on a few previous occasions but had always come back together for the sake of the children. Now, three of their four sons had left home: I was married, Jonathan was pursuing his undergraduate studies at Berkeley, and Ben was planning to enroll at the University of California, San Diego. Only the most sensitive and dreamy of the kids, fourteen-year-old Harry, remained to occupy the emptying nest—Harry and my irrepressible Uncle Moish, who spoke out avidly and openly against the possibility that his kid brother, my dad, might actually decide to break up the family. On several occasions, he regaled us with his notorious lecture about "the dog and the railroad track." Addressing my father, he would say, "You remind me, Davey, about the dog who fell asleep on the railroad track, so a train came along and cut off a piece of his tail. He was okay at first, but then he put his head on the track to see what had happened to his tail. And then, naturally, the back wheels of the train came along and cut off his head. And the important thing is the moral of the story: you have to be a very dumb dog to lose your head over a little piece of tail!" We all laughed at the corny punch line— even my father—but I understood that the situation wasn't that simple. Just months away from his fiftieth birthday, enjoying the challenges of his increasingly successful business, watching the boys he adored one by one going off on their own, my father had begun to get serious about making changes for what he hoped would be the second half of his life. He appreciated my mother for her devotion, brains, and fierce family loyalty, but her high-strung, often angry temperament produced a contentious atmosphere in the home that contrasted with my dad's ceaselessly sunny, occasionally oblivious attitude.

Despite the obvious tension in my parents' house—or perhaps because of it—we all savored that summer as a rare, perhaps fleeting interlude: all four boys (and my wife, and my dog), along with my parents and my always-opinionated uncle, were living together again under the same roof, possibly for the last time. The home assumed aspects of a particularly high-voltage college dorm—with the various residents engaging in bull sessions late into the night, arguing over politics, movies, philosophy, religion, or the leftovers in the freezer, with different subgroups often caucusing at odd hours (frequently over tea and cookies) in various corners of the sprawling house. As observers of the Sabbath and the kosher laws, Nancy and I functioned at a different level of religious practice from the rest of them and on one Saturday afternoon in August that observance gap became a painful issue.

We engaged in a ridiculously complicated, multifaceted argument over Jonathan's desire to bid an early farewell to the Sabbath so we could indulge in a nostalgic family basketball game in nearby Crestwood Park. My Uncle Moish indignantly insisted that the Havdalah ceremony marking the end of the Sabbath and the beginning of the new week meant nothing if performed prior to the appropriate hour (when three stars appeared in the Saturday night sky). Inevitably, Moish prevailed, so we waited for the proper time to take out the braided candle, and the wine cup, and the spice box, as we formed a little circle in the living room and I led the ceremony. We concluded, as usual, with the singing of *"Eliyahu HaNovi"* ("Elijah the Prophet"), indicating the hope that the new week ahead might see the long-awaited arrival of the Messiah and the healing of all pain. Just as we finished, extinguishing the candle in the wine, Uncle Moish mumbled a few words about feeling uncomfortable, started walking toward the bathroom, and then, in front of the assembled family, collapsed onto the floor with a horrifying crash. Paramedics arrived almost immediately and made determined efforts to revive him, but his stricken face made clear that he had already died—the victim, at age seventy, of a massive heart attack.

The incident devastated all of us, and in the days that followed we became sorrowfully aware of how much our cantankerous Uncle Moish had provided the glue that kept our fragile family together. My father, freed from his older brother's scolding influence but struggling with his own burden of guilt and loss, moved out of the family home (and the scene of death) to get his own apartment in a huge complex that specialized in young singles. My brothers Jonathan and Ben went away to their university campuses when the school year started in September. Nancy and I wanted to play a constructive role with my badly wounded, often hysterical mother and with my brother Harry, but the atmosphere in that suddenly empty and haunted house made us profoundly uncomfortable. We continued to toil over *Class of '65* so we couldn't consider returning to Northern California; it made far more sense to get a place in LA so we could move all our stuff and stop paying rent in Berkeley. To some extent, my uncle's death dictated our choice of location.

During the last years of his life, Uncle Moish had become heavily involved with the struggling community of Jewish senior citizens in the bohemian beachside enclave of Venice. During the neighborhood's glory years in the 1920s and '30s, when eager crowds of tourists and thrill-seekers took the trolley every day to enjoy the boardwalk's bingo parlors and carnival attractions, thousands of immigrant Jews settled in the area. They established small businesses of every kind along with a dozen synagogues, before ill-planned urban renewal and the inevitable decline in tourist traffic (why visit shabby "Bingo Beach" when you could go to Malibu—or Disneyland?) decimated their community. By the 1950s, bearded, bongo-playing beatniks and other beach bums had largely taken over the run-down neighborhood, leaving the Yiddish-speaking old-timers isolated and impoverished. They established a last redoubt in an oceanfront building known as the Israel Levin Senior Adult Center, where they gathered to play checkers or *kibbitz* every day of the week.

Even though he'd never actually lived in the Venice neighborhood, my uncle began making regular trips to the beach in an effort to enhance the programming at the Israel Levin center and to win increased attention and support for the elderly people who frequented that institution. He eventually became president of the Levin center, and used that position to badger rabbis from every denomination to donate their time for visits to the center. He also invited an anthropologist from USC named Barbara Meyerhoff to observe and research the exotic tribe of Jewish beachside survivors who thrived so improbably in Venice, and the professor became entranced with the spicy, occasionally elegiac, old-country atmosphere. Her interviews and observations eventually provided the basis for her award-winning book *Number Our Days* and even a TV special on PBS which won the 1976 Academy Award as Best Documentary Short Subject.

Long before this high-powered publicity for the elderly Jews of Venice, my uncle had tried to get me involved, too, inviting me for the center's crowded, joyous Shabbat program on Friday afternoons, and even trying to persuade me that I should help "reclaim" a fading Jewish neighborhood. Noting that oddball Venice already exerted a powerful attraction on hippies, surfers, and other young people, he argued that committed Jews of the younger generation should begin settling in the area alongside the remaining old-timers. That way, the senior citizens could teach the youngsters Yiddish and provide them with a living connection to Eastern European Jewish culture, while the kids could offer their surrogate grandparents a sense of continuity and community, assuring the beleaguered elderly of the survival of their institutions and traditions.

Unfortunately, I never took his idea seriously until after he had died, but at that point a potent force of guilt, yearning, and coincidence pushed me toward a new home by the beach. Just hours after I attended a solemn, crowded memorial service for my uncle, one of the Class of '65 graduates I had interviewed for the book called to offer me the chance to rent her pleasant little bungalow five blocks from the beach in Venice. The unexpected emergence of this opportunity to honor my uncle's wishes so soon after his demise felt both providential and irresistible.

Nancy and I moved during the September season of Jewish high holy days, and on the afternoon before Yom Kippur—the solemn Day of Atonement fast—my father left work early to come take a look at our new place. He and I went for a walk along the Venice boardwalk to talk about the family situation, his new life on his own, and the impact of my uncle's death. As the sun began to fade toward the Pacific, signaling the approach of twilight and the commencement of the year's most intense day of prayer and introspection, a tiny old man in a battered gray hat, carrying the red-tipped white cane of the blind, tap-tapped an unsteady, zigzag route toward us. He spoke in a hoarse, heavily accented voice: "Excuse me, but we need two more men—two more Jews—for a minyan. It's *mincha*—the afternoon service—before Yom Kippur. You're Jewish? Maybe you can help us, please?" Given the man's impaired vision, I couldn't understand how he had picked us out of all the hundreds of people swarming or lounging around the Venice oceanfront. Did my father and I give off some sort of vibe that the old man picked up, identifying us as members of the tribe with religious inclinations?

In any event, we dutifully followed his slow steps for a half block down the boardwalk to a quaint storefront shul, or synagogue, with its doors opening directly out onto the beach. The peeling paint and musty interior spoke of long decline and communal neglect. For this particular afternoon service, the blind old man (identified later as the president of the congregation) had assembled the minyan: the precise minimum of ten adult Jewish males required under religious law—my father, myself, and eight slow-moving gentlemen well beyond the age of eighty. They assured me that for the main Yom Kippur *Kol Nidre* service later that night they would draw a much bigger crowd—more than fifty people—welcoming many of the elderly people from the area. During the rest of the year they convened services every four weeks on a Friday night.

The unexpected encounter with the Shul by the Beach helped cement my emotional, almost mystical investment in my new neighborhood, though the synagogue's thin schedule of services forced me to turn elsewhere for my primary religious needs. I was the only member of the family in a position to commit myself to saying kaddish (the memorial prayer) every day for eleven months in honor of my Uncle Moish. Jewish tradition dictated that this ancient Aramaic formulation—proclaiming the greatest, majesty, and eternity of God, in order to ease the transition to the next world of the soul of the departed—needed a public service with a minyan for its proper recitation, so I quickly found the only daily service in Venice.

This occurred at the other surviving synagogue in Venice, a huge building with white pillars in the front known as Mishkon Tephilo (Tabernacle of Prayer). Unlike the tiny Shul by the Beach, Mishkon Tephilo featured the services of a rabbi—a recently hired, black-bearded, 5'4" spark-plug who tried to demonstrate his hipness and accessibility by designating himself "Rabbi Manny." The product of an irreligious home, he had discovered God as a teenager and defied his parents to go away to ultra-Orthodox "Black Hat" yeshivas (seminaries) in New York and Israel. Though he nurtured a fervent desire to drag indifferent and unaffiliated Jews toward a more engaged attitude toward Jewish tradition, he settled for pathetic part-time positions with dying congregations in dingy neighborhoods. In that context, Rabbi Manny viewed me as a gift from God—the only other member of his daily minyan below the age of sixty-five and an unembarrassed idealist full of dreams about building up the Jewish community by the beach. We schemed together to create a new "Commotion by the Ocean": providing an open-to-all-comers Friday night experience, complete with wine, food, singing, fellowship, and free-ranging discussion. During my first year in Venice, these gatherings welled from a bare prayer quorum (10 men, with no women) to mixed crowds of 50, 75, and ultimately more than 150.

Some of the visitors provided memorable moments of madness. On one occasion a school bus pulled up in front of our synagogue disgorging a white-robed, barefoot, self-proclaimed Messiah with flowing brown locks accompanied by six female followers (including his elderly mother). At another Friday night free-for-all, a swarthy newcomer with soiled, torn clothes startled the assembled celebrants by introducing himself as a "hit man for the mafia"; I wrote him off as an out-of-work actor trying to do some corny scenes, but enough people took him seriously to leave the building in a panic.

In addition to the freaks, weirdoes, and lunatics who passed through our open doors, consuming our sweet wine and trying to join in singing the traditional signs, the Commotion by the Ocean also attracted more normal customers. Within a year of launching the weekly "Shabbat Happenings" and other efforts to invigorate the moribund congregation, Mishkon Tephilo more than doubled its official membership, with fifty new families and individuals agreeing to pay the modest dues. More importantly, a dozen people—mostly singles, but also one young couple with a child—moved into the Venice neighborhood to participate in the congregation. To facilitate our growth we downplayed the Orthodox orientation of our part-time rabbi and the most active members, advertising the services as open to "Orthodox, Conservative, Reform, Agnostic, and Any Jew That Moves!" This deliberate fudging of ideological orientation—based on the overconfident, even arrogant assumption that the joys of Jewish authenticity automatically would push all participants in a traditionalist direction—made for significant problems later in the organization's development.

While I enjoyed considerable success in luring various strangers and family members (especially my kid brother Harry) to take part in our congregational programs, I never managed to pull in my friend and coauthor David Wallechinsky, who viewed my deepening religious involvement with the same bemused tolerance with which he approached the various cultists (Movement for Spiritual Awareness, Hare Krishna, Scientology) we wrote about in our book. Given his indifference to my community-building efforts, I felt stunned to see him at a Mishkon Tephilo prayer service one Saturday afternoon in September. A sudden urge for worship had nothing to do with his appearance; instead, he took me aside and proudly held up a copy of the next day's edition of the *Los Angeles Times* book section, pointing to the best-seller list, which—contrary to all logic and expectation—showed *What Really Happened to the Class of '65?* in tenth place among nonfiction titles. I grabbed the paper from him and stared in disbelief, deliberately freezing the precious moment in my memory: we hadn't even reached our official publication date and yet here I was, a few days shy of my twenty-eighth birthday, officially designated a best-selling author.

Our "where are they now?" approach to writing about the impact of the '60s clearly struck a nerve and led to a flattering flurry of national publicity. David and I appeared together on ABC's *Good Morning America* (which treated our view of our heartily hyped generation as a major news event) and got the thrill of three separate appearances on NBC's *The Tonight Show*, the nation's leading late-night show. We also did literally dozens of radio shows, local TV programs, and newspaper interviews, giving commentators in every medium an excuse to discuss the odd course of the counterculture. All of the publicity paid off, as our book stayed on the *Los Angeles Times* best-seller list for several weeks, rising as high as the number three position; later, we also made it to number three on the New *York Times* list of paperback best-sellers.

I reveled in all the promotional attention, especially when we toured major cities (Boston, New York, Washington, Chicago, San Francisco) and I got my first taste of the intoxicating luxury and elegance of five-star hotels (at the publisher's expense). David, having gone through a previous book tour for *The People's Almanac* and grown up as the son of a famous author, felt far less thrilled with the process than I did. As a result, I joyously carried the entire burden for the far more extensive paperback tour (twenty cities) and developed assurance and skill in talking with the media. I especially enjoyed the call-in radio shows, on which listeners lit up the lines with accounts of their own experiences in high school and the years that followed, finding parallels with each of the portraits we had drawn. On one important Atlanta station the response proved so over-whelming that they extended my scheduled one-hour interview to two full hours. When I finished, I hurried down the hall toward a waiting car and my next appointment, but the program director ran after me. "You've got a real gift for the radio!" he breathlessly declared. "You ever thought about doing your own show? If you move to Atlanta, I'll get you on the air right away. That's a promise!" I knew I loved radio—the crackling pace and the immediate, surprisingly intimate contact with the callers—but I had an-other book to write (two, in fact) and couldn't even consider walking away from the Venice Jewish community that had become such an important focus for my life. Another nineteen years passed before I got another radio offer that I seized with unhesitating enthusiasm.

In addition to selling our book, I used all the publicity appearances to promote our synagogue in California, even extending a Sabbath invitation to America during one of the appearances on *The Tonight Show*. Literally scores of curious worshippers responded, some traveling from as far away as Cleveland to sample our homey, unpredictable Shabbat program. All the media attention to *Class of '65* not only helped to grow the congrega-tion but also changed its essence by providing a new patina of trendiness and excitement. Most notably, the increased traffic of visitors and re-porters puffed up the previously humble and hardworking Rabbi Manny, who suddenly discovered an appetite for the spotlight. As attendance swelled, he became a far more flamboyant performer, singing and dancing or pulling pensively at his beard, making corny jokes, and sometimes, when attempting to convey important content, dropping into a trembling, whispery voice with his eyes half-closed. He also learned to generate his own publicity with his peculiar hobby of spending hours locked in his synagogue office, talking to truckers and others on his Citizens Band radio—this at a time, pre–cell phones, when CB communications looked high-tech and exciting, allowing people to speak with strangers as they drove along the highway, enjoying a brief vogue (remember the hit song "Convoy"?). The media picked up on the bizarre image of a bearded rabbi broadcasting to good ol' boys in eighteen-wheelers ("Breaker, breaker, this is CB Rabbi, ready to talk Torah"), and he even earned a guest shot on the game show *To Tell the Truth*.

Unfortunately, it quickly became clear that Rabbi Manny himself found it difficult "to tell the truth." His unraveling began when he reported the theft of his beloved CB radio and made a tearful plea during a Saturday morning sermon for congregants to help replace his equipment. Several volunteers rushed forward; in fact, Rabbi Manny accepted money from at least three different synagogue members to buy a new radio, keeping each donor in the dark about the other contributions. After we began investigating this scam, the rabbi ultimately confessed that he had not only "stolen" the radio himself but also pilfered hundreds of dollars from the charity box (or *pushke*) that we used during weekday services. We eventually learned that he had received counseling for a record of kleptomania leading all the way back to high school. The scandal paralyzed our growing congregation and divided our newly elected board, with a "compassion caucus" that sought to provide Manny with "one more chance," allowing him to continue in his position while receiving intensive therapy to address his emotional problems. As the official president of the congregation, I tried to steer a middle course: I didn't want Manny to go to jail, but I wanted him to go away. After a lengthy, emotionally wrenching meeting, we unanimously agreed to invoke the "moral turpitude" clause for the termination of the rabbi's contract.

I thereafter found myself personally in charge of a large and growing synagogue community that needed to hire a replacement rabbi as quickly as possible. As we had built our organization from next to nothing, it had made sense to solicit support from "any Jew that moved," but in selecting a qualified spiritual leader we needed to concentrate on one of the three established branches of Judaism (Orthodox, Conservative, or Reform). Along with most of the younger members of the community, I wanted an Orthodox Rabbi who could encourage growth in a more traditional direction while working with congregants at all levels of observance, but many others feared that an Orthodox leader would prove too rigid and judgmental, particularly regarding the sensitive issues of female participation in the services. The tense and divisive "audition" process took so much time away from my writing responsibilities that I felt tempted to abandon the entire endeavor, but recent changes in our living situation kept me focused on the synagogue's survival.

Just weeks before Rabbi Manny's exposure, Nancy and I used the first royalty check from *Class of '65* to purchase a ramshackle 1924 farmhouse that placed us permanently within walking distance of the Sabbath services. A dozen fruit trees and a detached guesthouse made the property appealing, but the long-neglected home with subpar electricity and plumbing required extensive work to make it even vaguely habitable.

We supervised that work even while we welcomed as house guests the parade of rabbinical applicants who sought our plum position. Just days before Hanukah, one highly touted Orthodox candidate infuriated me by pulling up to our street an hour late, allowing barely enough time to make it down to synagogue for the scheduled services. Even worse, he brought with him a packet of photocopied, untranslated pages of the Talmud and announced that he would hand them out at synagogue. "I thought I told you that this was a very mixed crowd," I said to him as we rushed toward the Sabbath program. "Many of these people don't even know how to read Hebrew. They're going to be totally turned off by a page of Talmud that they can't understand."

"Please don't worry," the visitor assured me in his plummy, aristocratic British accent. "I believe that I can find a means to make the material intriguing and enlightening to everyone." By the time we walked through the doors of the synagogue I had already written off this latest candidate as yet another rabbinic embarrassment. I took one of my friends aside and warned him of an uncomfortable evening ahead. "This one is a stuck-up, arrogant S.O.B. He's going to get everybody completely ticked off."

Of course, the visitor—Rabbi Daniel Lapin—proceeded to make a liar of me by dazzling the assembled celebrants with a presentation by turns witty, challenging, profound, mystical, and altogether mind-blowing. He used the pages of Talmud to probe inner meanings by calling attention to the shapes of letters and the resemblances between words so that even those who couldn't recognize any part of the Hebrew alphabet shared in the experience of working with an ancient text. His erudite references to quantum mechanics (he currently taught physics at a local Jewish high school), the migrating habits of birds, the works of Shakespeare, and Roman history all worked to serve the same purpose: convincing the Sabbath crowd that God exists, and continues to communicate to his children through the sacred authority of Biblical truth. More than two dozen members of the synagogue mobbed Rabbi Lapin after he had completed his talk, probing him with questions, demonstrating an unprecedented appetite for continued teaching.

After our rocky start, we also hit it off on a personal basis. He had been a fan of *Class of '65* since its first release, and the prospect of meeting its author had helped bring him to the beach. Born in South Africa, educated at prestigious seminaries in Great Britain and Israel, Lapin had built an international reputation as the rebellious, black sheep of one of the world's most distinguished Orthodox rabbinic families. While his two younger brothers followed their father's example as pulpit rabbis of conspicuous distinction, Daniel felt drawn to the business world—making big money in his twenties as a manufacturer of audio boom boxes and, later, a builder of luxury yachts. After cashing out, he came to the United States with the dream of creating an elite Jewish prep school, before disputes with the board drove him to Southern California, where he lived most of the time on his sailboat in Marina Del Ray.

For our unconventional congregation in Venice, he looked like the perfectly unconventional choice, though simultaneous problems with his family and my board worked to block his selection. His father, the beloved, gray-bearded scholar Rabbi A. H. Lapin, refused to sanction his son's employment by any congregation that failed to honor the requirement under Jewish law that men and women sit separately during prayer. Contrary to common distortions, the basis for this division has little to do with women's power to distract men, or their status as "unclean" (a miserable mistranslation) during a few days a month, but rather it stems from the definition of Jewish prayer as an intimate encounter between the individual and the Almighty. When a husband and wife appear together at a social or business occasion, the people they meet will judge them as a unit; the relationship between male and female is so close ("and they shall be one flesh" says the Book of Genesis) that a man can be evaluated based on his wife's virtues, or a woman on her husband's. The only time when it's *in*appropriate to rely on your spouse is when you approach God in prayer and you can expect a separate, personal reception. Praying alongside members of the same sex may create a feeling of community, but it never provides the sense of blended identity that you experience when sitting beside your spouse. When discussing the matter with Rabbi A. H. Lapin, I felt no hesitation in committing myself to moving toward that arrangement at our synagogue in Venice, in no small part because I had already developed a preference for separate seating at prayer, having witnessed the dramatically higher level of energy and intensity at Orthodox services. Based on that assurance, the Lapins decided that Daniel could work with us, but only under the condition that he took no payment. If he was listed as an employee, it might look like he had compromised his family's principles for the sake of financial gain.

I brought this proposal to the board of directors, assuming a unanimously favorable reaction. After all, we could now work with the rabbi most of us wanted, without having to pay for his services. To my surprise, most of my fellow congregants opposed the idea of a volunteer rabbi, arguing that a rabbi who received no salary from the congregation could never work hard enough or feel accountable to the board. Many also protested an apparent "Orthodox conspiracy" between Rabbi Lapin and me to try to change the easygoing, nondenominational flavor of the community. After a series of stormy meetings, my colleagues insisted that we ask Rabbi Lapin to wait another ninety days while we continued the painful, unsettling audition process, thereby undermining my elaborate negotiations with the Lapin family.

At that point, I had come to realize that the synagogue involvement that began for me as a joy, an inspiration, and an attempt to honor the memory of Uncle Moish had become a source of deep aggravation and a huge distraction from my work. After discussion with Nancy, I wrote a letter announcing my resignation as president of the congregation while signaling my intention to continue attending services as a "civilian" worshipper. I felt liberated, exhilarated, once I informed the leading board members that I had quit but I hesitated over conveying the news to Rabbi Lapin. To my surprise, however, he sounded utterly delighted when I told him of the developments.

"Yes, it's wonderful news," he insisted. "Now we are free to start fresh and do it the right way." He came over the following Shabbat as our houseguest and at his suggestion we held services in our home. A surprising number of Mishkon Tephilo veterans turned up for the gathering, and over the next three weeks we continued to meet in living rooms around the neighborhood. To my delight, my dad played a conspicuous role in these early get-togethers and developed a particularly close friendship with Rabbi Lapin. He respected "the Reb" as a fellow physicist (and a fellow adventurous spirit) while the opportunity to join us for weekly Sabbath meals provided a warmth of family feeling that he'd largely missed since separating from my mother. He also helped come up with a scheme that could allow our little group to grow into a viable congregation with a sanctuary of its own, as he recalled the experience that he and I had had three years earlier on the eve of Yom Kippur when the blind old man led us into the shabby little synagogue on the oceanfront. The elderly and isolated proprietors of that long-neglected building might welcome an infusion of youthful energy and provide a home for a new congregation.

I arranged a meeting with the blind president of the Shul by the Beach and listened to his lengthy, impassioned Yiddish conversation with Rabbi Lapin. The old-timers, who hadn't held weekly Friday night services for many years, felt skeptical of our promises of an influx of young people, but they ultimately said they would try anything and agreed to the installation of a modest, down-the-middle cloth divider between men and women. The first week, twelve of us joined them in their run-down little building on the busy boardwalk and one of the old men wept openly, declaring over and over that he had witnessed *Moshiach's tzeiten*—"the time of the Messiah." Shortly thereafter, we attempted to secure the utopian future of our endeavor by incorporating as a new nonprofit religious organization in the State of California.

I picked the name "Pacific Jewish Center" to allude to our location immediately adjoining Venice beach and to project a significant role for our operation in an ongoing, regional religious revival. From the beginning, we pledged to function differently from ordinary congregations: with a rabbi who accepted no salary, we required no membership dues and made no attempt (unlike all other congregations of every denomination) to sell tickets for the High Holy Days. We welcomed (and needed) donations, of course, but we left it to each individual to determine how much to pay. As the unpaid head of our operation, Rabbi Lapin meant to lead the congregation instead of just serving it. He modeled his role on an independent proprietor rather than a bureaucratic hired hand, viewing the participants as his customers, not his bosses.

Our founding rabbi chose to designate me as "the president," and although the title vaguely embarrassed me (I joked that it sounded like the "president for life" honors that tinhorn dictators such as Papa Doc Duvalier bestowed on themselves), I felt proud to be playing a role in the stunning growth of our community. The only way to join the congregation involved regular attendance at Rabbi Lapin's intensive Torah classes, and quickly we signed up nearly a hundred devoted students; within a few years, the number of regular participants exceeded four hundred. We even set up a full-time parochial school serving kindergarten to sixth grade—the first ever all-day Jewish school in the Venice–Santa Monica area. We purchased eight different apartment buildings on a nonprofit basis and converted them to condominiums for observant new arrivals in the neighborhood. Eventually, we bought a plant nursery and converted its three acres (again, on a nonprofit basis) into the site of eight luxurious homes for the most prosperous members of our burgeoning community. Rabbi Lapin performed more than ninety weddings, and the great majority of those couples established homes in our neighborhood. The rabbi himself, single when we began this venture, eventually followed the powerful family-building trend after I persuaded him to make an exception to his strict rule against dating congregants when it came to a lithe, brilliant live wire from Brooklyn named Susan Friedberg. (In 2004 they celebrated their twenty-fifth anniversary, with seven children and one grandchild so far.) Pacific Jewish Center became famous for its hospitality: no one could attend Sabbath services either on Friday night or Saturday morning without being invited to a home in the community for a festive Shabbat meal.

Though we never courted publicity for Pacific Jewish Center with the same avidity Rabbi Manny had sought attention for the Commotion by the Ocean, our anomalous location assured that we attracted attention. Every Saturday at the conclusion of morning services, the congregation streamed out our doors and onto the boardwalk, suddenly providing a sea of dark suits, long dresses, and well-groomed children in the midst of the hordes of bikini-clad roller skaters, T-shirt and incense vendors, panhandling street musicians, and chainsaw jugglers (yes, chainsaw jugglers) who otherwise populated the Venice oceanfront. We took great pride in the vast cultural gap that separated our hardworking, religiously devoted families from the stoned, stunned, sun-drenched lost souls who shared the neighborhood with us, but we couldn't permanently avoid the influence of the mighty entertainment industry that dominated most aspects of Southern California life and ultimately touched even our vibrant Orthodox enclave on the shores of the Pacific.

You Cannot Escape Hollywood

In the mid-'70s, nothing about my background or passions suggested that I might spend much of the next quarter century working as a movie critic. If anything, I looked down on most products of the popular culture and took perverse pride in my isolation from the media.

Since leaving my parents' home at age sixteen, I'd lived without regular access to a TV set. They didn't permit televisions in our Yale dorm rooms, and after I got my first apartment on my own I neither wanted nor needed the tube to keep me company. I hardly found the time to do what I needed to do even without squandering the nearly thirty hours a week the average American spends watching TV, nor did I feel artistically impoverished because I never saw an episode of such ornaments to our civilization as *Three's Company* or *Charlie's Angels*. After I became a published author, I naturally welcomed the opportunity to appear on the tube to promote my books (just as I had enjoyed my session on the *GE College Bowl* as an undergraduate), but I never relished the idea a regular job in the television industry.

Meanwhile, I looked on motion pictures as a superior form of entertainment (with special affection for classics from Hollywood's Golden Age by John Ford, Frank Capra, and Preston Sturges) and that preference helped shape our decision-making in selling the rights to *What Really Happened to the Class of '65?*

With our book riding high on best-seller lists, we suddenly received a series of competitive offers for media adaptation of the project, and I persuaded my coauthor, David, to turn down an especially generous deal from a production company aligned with CBS that wanted to adapt the book into a TV series. Instead, we accepted a proposal from Universal Pictures because of the opportunity to work with the great movie director George Roy Hill, who had previously created *Butch Cassidy and the Sundance Kid, The Sting,* and other distinguished films. When we met with Hill, I felt vindicated for steering the project his way, since he seemed to understand the project's essentially negative, inescapably conservative spin on the countercultural fads that afflicted our generation. But Hill promptly moved on to other worthy projects (*Slap Shot, A Little Romance*) and we never heard from him again. I assumed that the prospect of a dramatic adaptation had evaporated—that is until one morning, more than a year later, when I began receiving congratulatory phone calls and press inquiries over NBC's surprise announcement that it planned a weekly TV series based on *Class of '65.*

Having sold the property to Universal, we had no power whatever to alter this utterly idiotic plan, which arose due to the network's last-minute need to fill a hole in their fall schedule. When affiliates at a national meeting reacted badly to a proposed series called *The Bionic Dog,* representatives of Universal Studios suggested their "hot property" *What Really Happened to the Class of '65?* as an alternative (even though it had become decidedly lukewarm at that point). The gathering of TV executives seemed duly impressed with this effort to connect with the all-important Baby Boomers, even though the network planners proposed nothing more than an intriguing title based on a best-selling book.

Unfortunately, the NBC masterminds still needed to transform a downbeat nonfiction property into a fanciful, nostalgic fantasy (think *Happy Days*) that could fit the preternaturally chipper world of network TV. The final product, hurriedly and haphazardly thrown together by veteran producer Richard Irving (father of starlet Amy Irving, future father-in-law of Steven Spielberg), embarrassed everyone associated with the project. The scripts featured totally fictional characters who bore no relation to the portraits in our book. The producers invented a smug character named "Sam" (played by suave Tony Bill) to unify the show as narrator; he was supposed to be a Class of '65 graduate who came back to teach at the bland, altogether invented "Bret Harte High School." An assemblage of attractive young stars (Annette O'Toole, Meredith Baxter, David Birney, Tim Matheson, Kim Cattrall, and many others) delivered energetic overacting in the midst of soggy, silly stories that had been hideously decorated with tinkly synthesized Muzak versions of rock 'n' roll hits of the '60s. After thirteen weeks of tediously tacky torment, the ratings for the show had dwindled to such an extent that NBC performed a mercy killing on the ambitious but ill-considered series.

Though everyone assumed that David and I had played some consultative role in the production, we had never been invited to the set or to script meetings of any kind, nor had we even been allowed to screen episodes before they aired. I assumed that public association with such a dorky disaster would permanently damage my reputation, but I didn't understand that the low quality of "our" series meant much less to Hollywood than the all-important fact that it had actually aired on NBC. A number of movie agents approached me with the intention of selling my services as a scriptwriter—regardless of the fact that I'd never attempted a screenplay in my life and knew nothing of the craft or even the format of writing for film. When I met with the venerable H. N. Swanson (universally known as "Swannie"), a folksy, gravelly voiced, red-suspendered Southerner who registered as a Hollywood institution at age seventy-eight, he assured me that my lack of experience hardly mattered; after all, in a previous generation he'd gotten some plum screenwriting assignments for two other fairly talented book writers with no background in the movies— William Faulkner and F. Scott Fitzgerald. I couldn't possibly turn down an agent who had actually worked with some of my literary heroes, so I quickly became one of Swannie's newest (and youngest) clients, making myself available for unfamiliar tasks in the film factory that inspired more curiosity than fervent desire on my part.

Instead of fantasizing about screenwriting prospects, I concentrated on my responsibilities in the book business, but even those contractual commitments conspired to bring me right back to the heart of Hollywood. While I struggled to complete *The Shadow Presidents* (New York Times

Books insisted that I cut a full third of my unwieldy manuscript), my editor at Popular Library Press began pressuring me to make progress on my other promised project, *The Fifty Worst Films of All Time*. Given the modest (in fact, pathetic) advance I had been promised by the publisher, I wanted to bail out on this particular book. After the success of a serious book like *Class of '65*, such a sleazy, marginal undertaking seemed to me a bad idea. But I had already gotten my kid brother excited about the promise that I'd give him a chance to work with me in writing it. At age fifteen and the youngest of the four Medved boys, Harry qualified as the only real movie buff in the family, and he'd developed a special fascination for the cheesy sci-fi movies of the '50s and '60s (*Robot Monster, The Horror of Party Beach*) that would play a prominent role in any anthology of the most embarrassing cinematic achievements. While I felt oppressed by the idea of writing a book about bad movies, he relished the opportunity to take his mind off the demands of high school (where he'd never achieved any notable stardom) and the sad circumstances of my parents' separation.

I knew he would feel disappointed when I told him that I couldn't go forward with the project, so I broke the news in person in the big empty house above Sunset where my sensitive brother now lived alone with my embittered mom. My little brother listened attentively, but his soft hazel eyes grew moist and mournful. "It's okay, Mike," he sighed, wiping away tears. "Maybe you'll want to do another movie book someday and I'll still get a chance to work with you." Driving home that night I felt crushed with guilt for disappointing the youngest, most vulnerable member of our fractured family, so that by the time I got home I had changed my mind. I picked up the phone and promised Harry I would go forward with *The Fifty Worst Films*, provided that he took responsibility for actually finding and viewing all of the miserable movies.

My kid brother kept his word, but in that era before the proliferation of VHS and DVD, we faced a dire challenge when it came to watching the filmic fiascos we needed to write about. *TV Guide* provided significant assistance—with Harry skipping school or waking himself at three in the morning to watch any promisingly putrid picture that had been scheduled for broadcast. We also went to a film catalog and rented a 16-millimeter projector and unbelievably wretched titles—including *Santa Claus Conquers the Martians* and *The Terror of Tiny Town*, a 1938 musical western with an all-midget cast. Meanwhile, my mother dutifully chauffeured Harry to the UCLA Film Archives, the Los Angeles County Museum of Art, and other venues where his persuasive powers enabled him to secure special screenings of immortal stinkers.

Despite these heroic efforts, we faced a difficult time completing the book. Desperate for help, we recruited my wife's cousin, UCLA student Randolph Dreyfuss (who has gone on to a long career as a character actor, appearing in *Erin Brockovich, ER,* and many other TV and movie releases). Even with Randy's inspired aid, we had to scramble to meet our publisher's final, nonnegotiable deadline; falling about a half-dozen movies short of the fifty we needed, we carelessly filled up the list with films that happened to appear on TV's *Late, Late Show* during the last two weeks (*Twilight on the Rio Grande, Jet Attack*) and that more properly qualified as merely mediocre rather than immortally awful.

For the most part, I felt embarrassed by the book (which ended up costing me more to produce than I had been paid by the publisher) and so I readily agreed to the suggestion of my agent, Artie Pine, that I take my name off the cover. I kept sole possession of the copyright, but the credit line billed the book as the work of "Harry Medved, with Randy Dreyfuss"—a clever expedient that also allowed the publicists to exploit the promotional value of my precocious teenaged brother as its irreverent author. On the eve of publication, he appeared on the *Today* show with Gene Shalit and delivered such a glib, accomplished performance (including his hilarious imitation of John Wayne playing Genghis Khan in *The Conqueror*) that our childish, humiliating little project quickly began selling out of bookstores and went back for massive second and third printings. *The Merv Griffin Show* invited Harry to appear alongside Burt Reynolds— the clumsily singing, dancing star of another movie we had savaged, *At Long Last Love.* When Burt defensively asked my teenaged brother to provide his definition of "a really bad movie," Harry cheekily and unforgettably replied, "You ought to know, Burt. You've made so many of 'em." The studio audience gasped and roared.

We continued to receive an altogether unexpected level of media attention, and at my mother's insistence, I accompanied my brother to promote the book in major cities across the country. During one interview with the already celebrated movie critic for the *Chicago Sun-Times,* Roger

Ebert, we spontaneously came up with the idea of presenting a sort of anti-Oscars called "The Golden Turkey Awards," complete with categories for "Worst Actor," "Worst Actress," and so forth. This jolly discussion made its way into Ebert's widely distributed article and I soon got a call from a major publisher who wanted to bring out a book version of "The Golden Turkey Awards." We began work immediately—at the same time that I finally completed the arduous final work on *The Shadow Presidents*.

Even in its severely edited form, my book on White House aides ran to more than four hundred pages of forbiddingly small print and won mostly glowing reviews as a "definitive, comprehensive" history of the White House staff. New York Times Books sent me out on an exhausting, four-week book tour, in the course of which I found that many of the reporters or interviewers who spoke with me preferred to talk about our bad movie books rather than discussing, say, the amazing story of Joseph Stanley Brown—the plucky, poor boy assistant to President James Garfield who ended up marrying the boss's beautiful daughter. I felt gratified by the warm response from political insiders who embraced *The Shadow Presidents* (Mike Deaver, future aide to President Reagan, called it "invaluable," while Richard Reeves wrote a featured review in the *New York Times* in which he declared, "I loved this book"), but the sales never lived up to expectations, despite my tireless touring. The public didn't seem to share my fierce fascination for historical trivia and political minutiae—even in the decisive final year of the Jimmy Carter presidency as the race to succeed him intensified.

I had already made up my mind that I could never vote to reelect Carter (my description of his slapdash, inept, and haughty White House staff amounted to one of the most scathing chapters in my book). When Senator Ted Kennedy (whose boozy, boorish behavior I vividly remembered from the Duffey campaign) challenged Carter for the Democratic nomination, the choice looked so appalling that I took the bold step of changing my registration to the Republican Party. My new friend Dick Cheney (whom I saw again in Washington during the promotional tour for *The Shadow Presidents*) spoke warmly about a former congressman and CIA director named George Bush who had mounted an underdog primary battle against Ronald Reagan. I'd first heard good things about Bush at Yale, where he served as one of the university's trustees; he had a smart, personable nephew in my graduating class and a son (George W.) in the class one year ahead of mine. By 1980, I'd come to admire Reagan's clearly articulated ideas—particularly regarding the need to enhance our military power to confront the Soviets in the Cold War—but I decided that the former California governor seemed too old, and sounded too conservative, to win the swing voters he'd need to knock the worthless Jimmy Carter out of office.

I may have learned enough about life and politics to alter my affiliation to the GOP, but my judgment of candidates remained highly suspect: it's hardly a point of pride to recall that I began my career in the Republican Party with the confident conviction that George Herbert Walker Bush could connect with the majority of Americans more effectively than Ronald Reagan. By the time Reagan had secured the Republican nomination, however, I marveled at the slick, sure-footed way that he and his staff positioned themselves for the fall campaign, and I developed a warm admiration for his seamless transition from Hollywood to politics. In a sense, I prepared to take Reagan's journey in reverse: he had shifted from making his living on silly movies to an idealistic involvement in the process of government, while I had moved away from my idealistic political obsessions to a new career making my living on silly movies.

Contrary to expectations that lampooning bad films would destroy any chance for employability in Hollywood, the publicity surrounding *The Fifty Worst Films* and *The Golden Turkey Awards* actually earned me my first major screenwriting assignment. Ray Stark, the powerful producer of *The Goodbye Girl, The Way We Were, Somewhere in Time,* and other acclaimed films, summoned me to his impressive suite of offices at Columbia Studios, where he startled me by saying that since reading about my work, he'd become fascinated with creative and commercial possibilities of using the title *The Worst Movie Ever Made* as the basis for a raucous new comedy. If I could come up with a viable way to develop that idea, he'd like to hire me to write the screenplay.

The concept I pitched involved a group of losers and underdogs at a fictional college of unimpressive academic standing (vaguely inspired by a certain campus I'd once visited in Menomonie, Wisconsin) who enter a new competition for a prestigious million-dollar award for the best student film in the country. The leader of the inevitable band of misfits notices that the sponsor of the award, and chief judge, earned his millions as a producer of low-budget schlock-buster exploitation films, so the students recycle the most endearingly awful elements from the old man's body of work.

All right, so it wasn't Chekhov, but what can you expect from a project built around the title *The Worst Movie Ever Made*? Mr. Stark and his numerous associates loved my approach. Matters proceeded swiftly and profitably (with singer Randy Newman slated to make his acting debut as my lovable lead) until we hired a brilliant but impossibly temperamental director—who promptly insisted on changing everything in my script. The whole effort eventually collapsed into chaos and entered that purgatorial state known as "turnaround"—where the company reserves the rights to take the stalled picture off the shelf but it's not bloody likely that they'll ever resume working on it prior to the arrival (or, for Christians, the return) of the Messiah.

While disappointed that my hard work never made it onto the big screen, I soon learned that many screenwriters manage to fail upward, and I resolved to follow their example. My work for Ray Stark qualified me to join the Writers Guild and set me up for other assignments. The Swanson agency put me together with a sophisticated and literary-minded independent producer who had secured commitments for the first-ever on-screen collaboration between Jane and Henry Fonda. He asked me to adapt a thirty-year-old novel by a blacklisted Communist screenwriter, so I made a point of keeping quiet about my own political orientation: I imagined that if "Hanoi Jane" found out that the young screenwriter hired for her project had recently registered as a *Republican*, I might have been victimized by another sort of blacklist. In any event, while writing my version of the script I took sadistic glee in making the Jane Fonda character particularly unattractive, and also created a violent, babbling, drug-addled psycho to accommodate the producer's desire for a part we could offer to Jane's *Easy Rider* brother, Peter. While I got paid for my contributions, the project fell apart after the aging Henry hurt his hip and became uninsurable. The producer wanted to replace him with Charlton Heston, but Jane (predictably) balked. A few months later, Henry recovered sufficiently to realize his dream of working with his daughter (and with Katharine Hepburn) on the far more ambitious and worthy project *On Golden Pond*, which won the Golden Age icon his only Best Actor Oscar.

My brief, intensely concentrated, and ultimately frustrating efforts as a screenwriter never quite qualified me as a "Hollywood insider," but they significantly enhanced my credible status as a namedropper—especially after my agents put me together with Barbra Streisand. She had recently begun the agonizing preproduction process for her directorial debut, *Yentl*, so it made sense for her to make contact with perhaps the only writer in the business who was also a synagogue president and had immersed himself in precisely the Orthodox Jewish world she intended to invoke. At our first meeting (where I was struck by the way her tiny, quiet, and understated presence contrasted with her big, bold, brassy image on screen), we spoke mostly about my Jewish involvement and my synagogue at the Venice oceanfront, and they followed up by sending me several screenplay versions of the story "Yentl the Yeshiva Boy" by Nobel Prize winner Isaac Bashevis Singer. The story focuses on a bookish girl in nineteenth-century Eastern Europe who studies Talmud with her saintly and scholarly father despite the general prohibition on females concentrating on those texts. When he dies, she disguises herself as a boy so she can continue to learn in a religious academy, and ultimately she falls in love with her manly study partner. This odd tale naturally appealed to Streisand's feminist inclinations but also lent itself to insulting caricatures of Jewish religiosity. The drafts that I reviewed (including a particularly clumsy and crude effort by the great Singer himself, full of extraneous and warped sexual references) struck me as stilted, implausible, and poisonously hostile toward our faith tradition. This attitude presented a gigantic problem for the movie: how could the audience admire a heroine who made huge sacrifices to study a religious faith that looked silly and outmoded onscreen?

I discussed my reaction with Streisand first on the phone and then in a full-day meeting at her sunny, elegantly appointed "cottage" near the beach in Malibu Colony. She jotted down notes as we went over my objections and suggestions concerning the screenplays I had seen (she ultimately commissioned a half-dozen additional drafts, hiring some of the most celebrated writers in the industry before writing the final script herself). I kept expecting to catch a glimpse of the demanding, demented diva of Hollywood legend, but the Streisand I saw remained unfailingly warm, polite, and considerate. In the course of the afternoon, I also met her twelve-year-old son, Jason Gould, and we began talking about her desire that he should receive a Bar Mitzvah—the official welcome-to-manhood ceremony that loomed much larger in suburban American Judaism than in ancient tradition. Jason expressed his contempt for the procedure and ran out of the room, but I tried to sell Streisand on the idea that she should stage the Bar Mitzvah at our unpretentious, idealistic congregation in Venice, rather than selecting one of the glittering Bel Air or Beverly Hills "Temples of the Stars" that other celebrities favored.

At my urging, she met with Rabbi Daniel Lapin, who agreed to take responsibility for preparing Jason for his Bar Mitzvah but only under the condition that Barbra would make time to participate personally, sitting with her reluctant son in all study sessions. I assumed that the very act of placing audacious demands on one of the planet's biggest, busiest stars could only discredit the rabbi in her eyes and destroy any chance of her future relationship with Pacific Jewish Center. To my complete surprise, and to her eternal credit, Streisand readily agreed to devote a considerable chunk of time to studying the basics of Jewish tradition alongside her son. She also accepted an invitation to attend Friday evening sunset services at our picturesque beachside congregation, and to join us afterward for a festive Shabbat dinner at my house. For this grand occasion she brought along Jason (the perpetually bored Bar Mitzvah boy); her ex-husband (and Jason's father), Elliott Gould (who dressed in OshKosh overalls that only partially covered his shirtless, hairy chest); her boyfriend, former hairdresser and current movie producer Jon Peters; and her fidgety but delighted mother, Diana Kind.

At our table, Barbra displayed an intense curiosity about all aspects of traditional observance and admitted that she had received shockingly scant prior exposure to any religious elements of her Jewish identity. Her determination to arrange a Bar Mitzvah for her son, as well as her passionate desire to make a movie version of *Yentl*, both derived from an emotional, almost mystical need to connect with her father, a purportedly devout Hebrew teacher named Emanuel Streisand, who died before his daughter's second birthday. She came across as vulnerable and insecure over the fact that she knew so little about either her father or the faith that he practiced. At age thirty-seven, she also feared that she might die suddenly before her fortieth birthday, as had both her father and grandfather. Her non-Jewish boyfriend, Jon, expressed vigorous support for her enthusiasm to study and reaffirm her heritage, while ex-husband Elliott spent most of the evening in his own world, lost behind a blissful grin.

Today, like other conservatives, I find Barbra Streisand's smug, leftist rants ill-informed and offensive, but they don't erase my recollections of a gracious, frequently sad, incongruously shy, but very serious lady who evinced a sincere desire to connect in some substantive way with the Jewish people. On several occasions, Streisand called me to talk about some detail involving *Yentl* and I always responded, though I never became one of the official writers on the project. Streisand listened to me respectfully, though I think she felt uncomfortable with my lack of reverence for I. B. Singer as the last word in Jewish authenticity; I tried to stress for her that his often inaccurate portrayal of traditional laws and practices arose out of his own tormented, often embittered relationship with that tradition. I particularly loathed one scene he had created in his screenplay in which pious rabbinic students go to the village *mikva* (ritual bath) and masturbate together while they spy through a peephole on the naked married women immersing themselves. I also had the temerity to suggest that she change the name of the central character, since *Yentl* sounded uncomfortably close to "yenta"—a Yiddish word for a gossipy, meddlesome woman that had become known to millions through Yenta the Matchmaker in *Fiddler on the Roof*. I could tell that such suggestions made Streisand uncomfortable, since she viewed the original Singer short story as something akin to holy writ.

Nevertheless, she continued to listen to my outspoken advice and to drag her consistently complaining son to attend Rabbi Lapin's politically incorrect Bar Mitzvah classes. One night Barbra even summoned me to talk politics with some of her influential friends. The call came in at about ten-thirty, but like most people in Streisand's circle I instinctively (and unquestioningly) did her bidding. When I arrived at the homey and tastefully appointed mansion of her good friends, Oscar-winning songwriters Allen and Marilyn Bergman, I found that the assembled grandees (including much of the top brass at Warner Brothers, along with Stanley Sheinbaum, the wealthy and well-connected head of ACLU) had settled back with their after-dinner drinks, waiting to hear me talk about the White House secrets I had uncovered in *The Shadow Presidents*, a copy of which I had given Barbra. I began relating intriguing anecdotes about the intimacy between presidents and their chief aides (for example, Harry Hopkins and FDR shared adjacent bedrooms, while First Lady Eleanor slept far down the hall), but the Hollywood honchos wanted more relevant material.

"What about Jerry Ford?" one of them interjected. "Isn't it true that he's borderline retarded? I've heard that he couldn't even write a letter, let alone a speech."

"And Reagan—tell us about Reagan. He's a complete phony, right? It's just a bunch of rich people who control everything he does, who make all the real decisions. I heard someone say that he isn't even smart enough for White House janitor, let alone for president."

It now became clear what they wanted to hear: stories that could confirm their most cherished liberal prejudices, to lend support to their bedrock conviction that all conservatives amounted to dimwitted, bigoted boobs. To them, the title *Shadow Presidents* invoked the notion that twilight figures (often associated with the source of all evil, the CIA) secretly controlled the empty, amiable idiots who inexplicably captivated the unsophisticated public. I didn't want to ruin my relationship with Barbra by getting into an embarrassing argument, but they questioned me so aggressively that I couldn't avoid honest answers that struck them as naive, ill-informed, even dangerous.

"Actually, I don't think it's fair to write off President Ford as some kind of clumsy moron. Do you know he graduated from Yale Law School, with solid academic standing? And that *Saturday Night Live* stuff about his stumbling and clumsiness—he's actually the most accomplished athlete to ever become president. He played football at the University of Michigan and got offered a pro contract with the Green Bay Packers, but turned it down to go to Yale."

"But the people around him—around most of the Republican establishment—you met those people, didn't you? And they're very scary, right?"

I paused and sighed, before describing my admiration for Ford's first chief of staff, Don Rumsfeld, and my warm friendship with Rumsfeld's even more capable successor, Dick Cheney. They listened in stunned, stony silence—as if I were delivering an especially ludicrous but vivid description of alien abduction. Actually, they might have accepted UFO tales far more sympathetically than my insistence that Ford, and Rumsfeld, and Cheney, and even Reagan (whom I also tried to defend) were decent people with patriotic instincts who wanted to help the country. I made the argument that, prominent political leaders of both left and right crave love, admiration, and a positive verdict from history, and they can't win those things by betraying their country, or oppressing ordinary citizens, or engaging in conspiratorial schemes. Even if a politician is deeply misguided on his approach to the issues, he'll try, according to his own lights, to do the right thing and improve the lives of his constituents.

Despite my patient efforts to get them to accept the good intentions and dedication of the Republicans they hated, these Hollywood bigwigs indignantly closed their minds to logic, and I began to wilt in the heat of their obvious disapproval. By the time I excused myself to get back home to my wife, I knew that I had disgusted my hosts with my unwillingness to affirm the liberal pieties—and had caused Barbra at least minor embarrassment in front of her influential friends.

She nonetheless went forward with the Bar Mitzvah plans while trying to keep the prying press in the dark about all dates and details regarding the big event. We decided to perform the ceremony at Saturday afternoon prayers, rather than the more standard (and much more heavily attended) service on Saturday morning. The occasion went off without a hitch; Barbra and her group sat uncomplainingly in the women's section of our Shul by the Beach despite her public status as a fiery feminist. Later that night, after the conclusion of the Sabbath, Jason got a party much closer to his adolescent desires—complete with disco diva Donna Summer igniting the A-list Hollywood crowd with her singing and dancing.

After the Bar Mitzvah, she continued to talk with Rabbi Lapin from time to time (he eventually received credit as a "technical adviser" on *Yentl*), but I lost all contact with her as she began traveling to Europe to focus on her film. She did come through with a major donation to Pacific Jewish Center (Rabbi Lapin had, characteristically, refused any personal payment for teaching her son), and she showed up at a well-publicized dedication ceremony when we renamed our hundred-student Jewish day school "Emanuel Streisand School" in honor of her late father.

At the same time, my brother Harry and I busied ourselves with a less idealistic project, as we promoted our second "bad movies" book, *The Golden Turkey Awards: Nominees and Winners—the Worst Achievements in Hollywood History.* This time we arranged specific categories in the style of a reverse Academy Awards, describing five or more nominees for "The Worst Title of All Time," "The Worst Performance by an Animal," "The Most Unerotic Concept in Pornography," "The Worst Performance by an Actor as Jesus Christ," and so forth. We also devised a sadistic little gimmick that featured a "Warning Label" prominently displayed on the back cover, declaring: "Over 425 actual films are described in this book, but one is a complete hoax. Can you find it?"

Over the years, literally thousands of readers have contacted me to see if they have found the hoax, many of them guessing that one of our nominees for "Worst Performance by a Politician" (Leon Trotsky in *My Official Wife*) or for "Worst Blaxploitation Movie Ever Made" (a 1937 singing western called *Harlem on the Prairie*) couldn't possibly be real, but both these films (and so many other mind-boggling miscues) are indeed authentic movies, accurately described in our text. In the interest of clarifying the historical record, I now stand prepared to expose the actual hoax movie for the first time: it turns up under "Worst Performance by an Animal," with our nomination of "Muki the Wonder Hound" for her performance in *Dog of Norway*. Muki, of course, was my own beloved Norwegian elkhound. Much to my amusement, I've fielded scores of inquiries over the years from movie fans who want my assistance in their desperate quest to see the immortal *Dog of Norway*, but they can't seem to locate a copy of the silly old B-movie. For obvious reasons, I've never been able to help them—until now.

To our delight, *The Golden Turkey Awards* became a smash hit not only in the United States but also in Japan, Germany, and especially the United Kingdom and Australia. I traveled twice to London to host gala "Worst Film Festivals" inspired by the book, and Harry and I cohosted a similar but even more ambitious event that played to sold-out (and raucous) crowds for six nights at the Beacon Theater in New York City, complete with the glamorous presence of Cheryl Rixon, the *Penthouse* Pet of the Year, in a tribute to cross-dressing director Ed Wood. Two youthful producers (who also happened to be brothers) bought the rights to *The Golden Turkey Awards* as well as *The Fifty Worst Films of All Time* in order to make an anthology film that featured funny excerpts from the horrible movies we described. Although Harry and I got credited as consultants on the finished film (released under the title *It Came from Hollywood* in 1982), we felt discouraged by Paramount's refusal to allow the Golden Turkeys to gobble for themselves. The studio honchos ruined the original concept by inserting painfully unfunny skits and narration featuring big comedy stars of the day—Dan Aykroyd, Cheech and Chong, John Candy, and Gilda Radner—trying in vain to upstage such absurdity as robots from the moon wearing gorilla suits and diving helmets in the cherished classic *Robot Monster.*

As a result of all the media attention, our phrase "Golden Turkey Awards" became part of the national discourse, used without attribution on numerous occasions—by magazines naming the worst local restaurants, for instance, or radio psychologists designating destructive behaviors. The buzz behind the book even facilitated my graduation to a new position: film critic. The freshly launched cable service CNN had just started a late-night entertainment hour hosted by one-time sportscaster Lee Leonard. They booked me on the show to "talk turkey" (and to try to sell books, of course), and the segment went so well that they asked me for a second and then a third appearance. At the end of my third on-air session with Lee Leonard, the show's producer, Eddie Madison, approached me with an offer.

"You know, Lee loves working with you," he enthused. "We all love working with you. Have you ever thought about reviewing the new movies every week?"

"Not really," I replied with a shrug. "But I'm sure I could do it." I instantly agreed to come back each week, eagerly embracing the opportunity to promote my books on a regular basis. It never even occurred to me that I'd actually get a paycheck for appearing on TV and talking about my reaction to new movies. When I began receiving that payment, I felt as if I'd won some lottery—even if the remuneration remained modest or, more accurately, minimal. During the three years I worked with CNN, that struggling new cable system hadn't yet emerged as a dominant force in global news and everything about our Hollywood studios remained cheesy and low rent. Nevertheless, I enjoyed my weekly visits to the studios on Sunset and my regular connection to the energizing bustle of live TV. In the show's green room, I had the opportunity to fraternize with the odd collection of stars and wannabes who cycled through our show, from Lauren Bacall (a nasty, snarling piece of work) to the busty, giggly leading ladies of the deathless classic *Malibu Bikini Shop* to the motor-mouthed, wise-cracking star of a lame TV show called *Bosom Buddies*; this young actor, Tom Hanks, considered himself a major fan of *The Golden Turkey Awards*.

I've always formed strong opinions on my encounters with art and entertainment, pronouncing self-confident snap verdicts on paintings in art museums, performances in concert halls, political candidates, novels, sermons, plays, and, of course, movies. Thanks to my gig at CNN, these judgments took on a new significance and provoked reaction from the wider world. Though I only reviewed a single movie per week, my commentary occasionally elicited strong reaction. I hated *Conan the Barbarian* (describing it as a "sweaty stinker") and made fun of its muscular star, suggesting that the Austrian bodybuilder seemed to assemble his lines phonetically with no understanding of the meaning of the English words he spoke. The review provoked a call from an angry TV producer who claimed to speak for Mr. Schwarzenegger. The producer cursed me out, furious not just at my disparagement of the budding star's English language abilities but, more importantly, at my pronunciation of the former Mr. Universe's name, which he said was a crude, unforgivable display of racism. I had voiced the moniker in the authentic German manner as "*Shvartze*-negger," unwittingly invoking the old Yiddish term of derogation for individuals of African heritage. I protested that I had merely pronounced Arnold's name as his neighbors back home in Graz might have said it, basing my approach on the proper Teutonic vocalization as learned from my beloved German Oma. I refused to apologize, although I did make a point for the future of carefully pronouncing the future governor's name in its bland, Americanized fashion as "Sch*W*arzenegger."

Though producers or publicists might occasionally protest a particular review, no one ever challenged my credentials or authority to review movies. The fact that I appeared once a week on CNN automatically qualified me as an expert—"Our Movie Maven," as Lee Leonard always introduced me. If anyone bothered to question my right to evaluate motion pictures, I stood ready to assert a crucial qualification: unlike most other critics, I had personally worked on big studio film projects (with two of my books turned into TV or motion picture productions, generating mixed results) and established myself as a member of the Writers Guild. Some of the best known movie commentators on television (Gene Shalit, Jeffrey Lyons) had attended law school just as I had (briefly), and few critics had ever pursued some academic course of study on motion pictures. For the most part, the people who write reviews for leading newspapers get their jobs because of their journalistic, rather than Hollywood, backgrounds—they start out as regular reporters and simply seize unexpected opportunities to begin writing about film. At least I had cowritten two popular books about bad movies before I ever began talking about motion pictures on TV.

During my years at CNN, I still considered myself a book writer, not a film critic, and I eagerly pursued literary projects far removed from the world of Hollywood. One of my friendly acquaintances at Pacific Jewish Center had suffered a horrible nervous breakdown (in which he took off all his clothes and began stopping traffic on a major freeway) and together with another leader of the congregation, I helped bring him home from the police station and arrange psychiatric help. Because the young man in question worked at a prominent hospital as an obstetrician, and resumed his busy practice within forty-eight hours of his life-threatening psychotic break, I developed a strong new interest in the psychiatric problems and daily stresses of medical professionals. I decided to write a book on the subject, choosing to interview the staff of an important teaching hospital to reveal their relationships with one another and the emotional costs of their work. For this project—which Simon and Schuster would publish under the title *Hospital*—I received more money than for both of my movie books, combined with all three years of salary at CNN. My dabbling in Hollywood commentary, in other words, had little to do with financial rewards.

I realized, however, that talking about movies and the entertainment industry connected me with more people in a more emotional way than my other areas of interest. Many Americans happily ignore politics and, until they become seriously ill, pay scant attention to the medical profession, but none of us can escape the pervasive impact of Hollywood. To my chagrin, I discovered that the public remains more fascinated by conversations about the "Worst Two-Headed Transplant Movie of All Time" than by any discussions about the worst (or best) White House chiefs of staff. I might feel more excited by my personal acquaintance with Sherman Adams or Dick Cheney, but most people I met greatly preferred to hear accounts of Barbra Streisand or Elliott Gould. Every year, press and public focus with greater intensity on analysis of the Oscar election for Best

Supporting Actor than they will in any evaluation of the choices for the House of Representatives in their own congressional district.

My work in reviewing movies and hosting Worst Film Festivals around the world (in addition to London and New York, we presided over events in Australia, Canada, Austria, and Belgium) allowed me to remain casually linked to the world of Tinseltown glamour and creativity. I focused far more time and emotion on my continuing role as a synagogue president, not to mention my ambitious literary projects. It might be comfortable and convenient to blame the subversive impact of "Hollywood values" for the personal setbacks that coincided with my intensifying work as a film critic, but it wouldn't be true; in the end, I can blame only myself for my most notable failure.

LESSON

27

No Marriage Is Solid Enough
to Take for Granted

While I began concentrating on my next big book, *Hospital*, my wife wanted us to focus—together—on the more ambitious project of starting a family.

That goal presented challenges well beyond the need to carve out time for physical intimacy—which for us, an affectionate young couple, never amounted to much of a problem. The more formidable tests required the reorientation of my priorities, and the abandonment of a lifelong bad habit of giving precedence to the urgent over the important. Nancy understood long before I did that all my frenetic activity could only cover, but never correct, an essential emptiness in our home.

When we first married, neither of us wanted to think about children, since we felt like kids ourselves (I was twenty-three, Nancy was twenty-one). We used birth control to protect our perpetual adolescence—despite the fact that blocking conception is authorized by Jewish law only under special circumstances that probably didn't apply to us. Eventually Nancy came to acknowledge her growing baby hunger, but only after we got out of Berkeley did I come around to her way of thinking. While we worked together on my books, our marriage felt rewarding, stable, dependable, and eternal. We had launched a religious community in Venice and bought a home, so it seemed to make sense to trust in our love—and in God's plan for us—when it came to the prospect of welcoming a child into the family.

For a while, we felt exultantly conscious that each night of private affection might produce a new human being, and we expected to delight our parents at any moment with an announcement about their first grandchild. A year passed, then two, but nothing happened. Nancy sought medical help; the doctors assured us that we faced no insurmountable physical obstacles to our hopes for offspring and provided advice to help us produce the child we wanted. We quickly discovered that millions of American couples faced similar challenges: according to authoritative figures from the National Institutes of Health, between 20 and 25 percent of all married couples at one time or another seek medical assistance in treating infertility. At the urging of a brilliant obstetrician we admired and trusted, we began to arrange our sex life in response to calendars, charts, pills, and thermometers that revealed the perfect moment to maximize our chances for conception. Naturally, this emphasis subtracted from the spontaneity and passion, the friskiness and fun that previously characterized our connection.

By this time, all ambivalence had disappeared in my attitude toward parenthood. I now viewed the effort to make a baby as a challenge, a measure of my competence and determination that required the same single-minded focus I'd apply to any other significant test. Rather than dreaming together about the long-term meaning of our endeavor and visualizing the joys and responsibilities of raising an actual child, we concentrated on the process of producing one.

Eventually we gained admission into the USC Medical Center's world-renowned program for the new, cutting-edge technology of in vitro fertilization, but the new effort to produce a "test tube baby" only took us further away from the joys of normal sexuality. Our long, frustrating years of struggling for conception also cast a psychic shadow on the remaining occasions for unscheduled, informal marital intimacy—suggesting that something about our sexual relationship remained incomplete, dysfunctional, broken.

Ironically, our impassioned daily involvement in the leadership of a fervently pro-family Orthodox Jewish community only made our situation more painful and precarious. Over the years, literally scores of our single friends in the community (including Rabbi Lapin himself) found their soul mates, staged festive marriage ceremonies, and quickly began producing progeny—so much so that Pacific Jewish Center became known as "Prolific Jewish Center." Nancy became increasingly uncomfortable with the Baby Boom that surrounded us. According to a touching old-country tradition, one of the honors at a bris (circumcision ceremony) goes to a couple in the community that desires God's help in producing a baby: the barren husband and wife get the privilege of walking the eight-day-old infant from his mother's arms to his father and the mohel (circumcisor), who will welcome the little boy into the covenant. After a while, our role in escorting literally dozens of babies came to feel humiliating: we imagined our friends and neighbors watching us with pity, feeling sorry for the poor, childless Medveds.

At the same time, Nancy became fanatically committed to a variety of athletic endeavors, devoting a significant part of every day to running, cycling, or skiing. Though she never said so explicitly, it seemed obvious to me that her sudden passion for developing her strength and endurance stemmed at least in part from our fertility frustrations. While most of the women in our world spent the majority of their time cuddling or nursing their soft, defenseless infants, Nancy pounded through miles of park and pavement every day, building up to competitive ten-kilometer runs and, eventually, to frequent marathons.

We pursued separate recreational priorities—I never attended her marathons, and she never went to my games with our synagogue softball team—but it never seemed to matter until skiing became an issue between us. Her parents (and especially her younger brother, who served on ski patrol) loved the sport, but when we went along on their ski vacations I felt bored and annoyed with the long lines for lifts and the crowded slopes with reckless showoffs threatening at every moment to knock you down. An orthopedic surgeon I interviewed for *Hospital* told me that skiing injuries provided him with half his practice, vividly describing the horrific physical damage resulting from that chic winter activity. Like all devotees of high-risk sports, Nancy brushed off concerns about injury by saying that "you can also get run over when you're crossing the street"—ignoring my logical comeback that crossing the street often represented a practical necessity, while going away on costly ski vacations remained entirely optional.

In part, her newfound enthusiasm for winter escapes represented a response to my own travel schedule. I'd begun hitting the lecture circuit after the success of my books, delivering at least a dozen speeches a year for colleges, synagogues, or community organizations. My wife rarely accompanied me on these trips because they often involved red-eye flights and hectic schedules with little chance for touring or pleasure. Also, like other childless couples, we doted on our pets (having by that time acquired a second Norwegian elkhound), and we felt reluctant to pack our pampered pooches off to kennels. Whenever possible, one of us stayed home to take care of the dogs, so I went off to speeches by myself, and Nancy began to travel alone for ski trips with her family.

Far more seriously, I made three trips to London without my wife. The first one centered on promotion of *The Golden Turkey Awards* and the hosting of a hugely successful Worst Films Festival at the Scala Cinema, a funky art house especially popular with hip, young movie fanatics in the United Kingdom. Stephen Woolley, the pony-tailed proprietor of this profitable establishment, came up with the idea of creating a TV series called *The Worst of Hollywood* in which I would appear before a rowdy live crowd, just as I had at the Scala, to introduce the same endearingly awful movies to a national television audience. In later years, Stephen went on to appropriate acclaim as one of Britain's most accomplished producers (*Mona Lisa, The Crying Game, Interview with the Vampire,* and more than twenty other films), but our showcase of bad movies on Channel 4 (the UK's new commercial network) became his first creative credit—and first hit. I wrote the series and got involved in every aspect of the production, and developed my own exciting London life and my own circle of friends and associates, from which Nancy felt callously excluded.

Amazingly enough, it never occurred to me that our frequent separations placed a serious strain on our marriage—especially at a time when my wife felt acutely pained by the repeated failure of our attempts at in vitro fertilization. At a time when offspring looked like an increasingly remote possibility, I flew across the country and around the world while she stayed home and transcribed my tape-recorded interviews, took care of the dogs, attended Torah classes in our community, and continued to build up her already formidable abilities as a runner.

Shortly after I returned from London, Nancy went off for one of her family ski trips but returned after a few days, when my in-laws delivered her at two in the morning—with crutches and a cast on her leg. She had taken a nasty fall on the slopes and torn up her knee, necessitating two complex and delicate arthroscopic surgeries. She couldn't blame me for her terrible accident but she quite naturally hated me for having, in effect, predicted it. Visiting her during her hospitalizations, I brought flowers and resisted the powerful temptation of "I-told-you-so," but her sense of vulnerability and shame, along with my well-established negativity about skiing, made it difficult for me to provide the unconditional support she needed. Shortly after she came home from the first surgery and began her taxing program of rehabilitation, she announced her intention to leave our home and spend an undetermined period of time with her parents.

I felt stunned and resentful. Unlike my parents, we had no history of bitter fights. We worked together smoothly on everything—book projects, the Pacific Jewish Center community, remodeling our house, even our ridiculously indulged dogs. As I reminded her while she packed up a suitcase in preparation for driving off to her parents' home, our friends and acquaintances considered us a model couple. Literally hundreds, perhaps more than a thousand people had received their first exposure to a traditional Sabbath experience as guests in our house, while enjoying one of Nancy's delicious Shabbat meals. We played an important joint role in the ongoing Jewish revival and the dynamic growth of our community. If she left me, I argued, she would do serious damage to the Pacific Jewish Center experiment she had worked so hard to advance, since our separation would show the failure of traditional practice and observance in keeping a committed couple together. Looking back years later, I realized how stupidly I had missed the point: Nancy didn't want to hear me talk about how our marriage mattered to the community; she wanted to know that it mattered to me. Instead of telling her that her departure would hurt the Jewish people, I should have told her that it would hurt me—that I passionately, personally, needed her to stay.

I made elaborate efforts to keep our separation secret, even from my parents, though I did tell Rabbi Lapin about what had happened, hoping he could use his influence over both of us to persuade Nancy to come home. When we met with him on his sailboat in the Marina Del Rey at sunset, Nancy stunned me with her anger and hostility, crying and complaining about the selfish way I had taken her for granted, treating her like a convenient component in my life rather than a separate human being with a life and priorities of her own. She observed (with considerable justification) that I spent more time talking to relative strangers who happened to visit our community than I ever spent speaking with her. I responded that she had become more and more withdrawn, preoccupied with her running (before her accident) and her novels (which she loved to read). The rabbi sided mostly with my wife: if I had shown greater consideration, provided her with greater respect, he argued, he couldn't imagine Nancy taking such a radical step as moving out of the house.

To my enormous relief she returned home a few days later, while insisting that we see a marriage counselor. The therapist we tried actually succeeded in bringing us closer together—by producing a shared disgust at her neohippie platitudes. Without counseling, we did manage to talk more substantively, to travel together more frequently, and to grant each other more "space," according to Nancy's wishes. I attempted to treat the marriage more as an end in itself than as a means to an end (impressing other people, building our Jewish community, achieving literary success), while providing conspicuous verbal support as my wife continued her frustrating process of physical rehabilitation for her damaged knee and returned to the hospital for her second major surgery.

Above all, I wanted our relationship to return to its "normal" sense of predictability and friendliness, and I hated the idea that emotional turmoil might stand in the way of my honoring the contractual deadline for completing the manuscript of my book. My original title for that project, *Vital Signs*, had to be junked because the same name had been employed just a few months earlier for an identity crisis novel by a struggling poet and nutritionist from Berkeley named Michael Weiner—who is now one of my most controversial colleagues in conservative talk radio under the synthetic designation "Michael Savage." Simon and Schuster eventually forced me to accept their title, *Hospital*, despite my warnings (amply justified, as it turned out) that the public would confuse our nonfiction book with the critically acclaimed recent film by the same name starring George C. Scott.

Despite my disappointment over the title, I threw myself into the publicity campaign for *Hospital* and made an appearance on *Nightline* with Ted Koppel (and the president of the American Medical Association) to discuss the breakdowns and substance abuse experienced by alarming numbers of physicians. During another interview, an otherwise enthusiastic reporter in New York City confided to me that he found himself surprised by my project's pro-physician point of view. "Nearly all the doctors I know are right-wing Republicans," he said. I paused for a moment, coughing and clearing my throat, before posing a modest question: "Do you really believe that if somebody is a conservative, that means he can't be a good human being?" The angry tirade that answered this inquiry lasted for nearly ten minutes, before I managed to steer the conversation back to the subject of the book I was trying to promote.

Hospital drew the best reviews of my career and earned strong, steady sales—rising all the way to number three on the *New York Times* list in its paperback edition. *Time* magazine ran a glowing, featured review; the *Washington Post* described the book as "a revelation"; and the *LA Times* listed it among their top recommended titles. Because of Nancy's hard work in transcribing the interviews that provided the basis for the book, I wanted to make sure that she shared in the reassuring glow from its success. Even at the time, I noted the irony of my situation: the book offered sobering accounts of medical professionals whose devotion to work and their needy patients hurt their relationships with the people who mattered most in their lives, while I similarly (but far less justifiably) concentrated on serving relative strangers (editors, agents, journalists, the amorphous public) above caring for my own hurting wife. I invited her to come along on most of the stops for the new book tour, but she shrugged off the prospect of punishing travel itineraries and opted to stay with our dogs and maintain her demanding rehabilitation regimen.

We brought new energy into our home when we invited my brother Harry to move into our guesthouse. He and I had begun work on a follow-up to *The Golden Turkey Awards*—collaborating this time on *The Hollywood Hall of Shame*, which focused on the biggest financial flops in movie history. Nancy welcomed Harry generously and enthusiastically, and his natural sweetness, consideration, and good humor made him easy company at our Sabbath table and, schedules permitting, during the rest of the week. He knew nothing about our previous, short-lived separation, and I thought that his addition to our household might help fill the enduring empty spaces associated with our continued childless status. I wanted to convince my wife, myself, and the world that whatever her lingering sense of grievance and dissatisfaction, we now constituted a big, happy family.

Another injury accident abruptly intruded to shatter my complacency: one afternoon, Nancy failed to return as scheduled from one of the grueling bike rides that helped her maintain her strength and build up her knee. I phoned her parents, her friends, and ultimately the police to try to locate her, and had grown desperate by the time I received a late-night call from the hospital. She had crashed her bike on a steep downhill in the Malibu Mountains, suffered a concussion, and remained unconscious until passersby called the paramedics. When she came home, badly banged up, we argued with unprecedented bitterness. Hating the thought of my wife lying—out cold—on a remote road, I said I couldn't abide, or understand, what I viewed as a self-destructive pattern of behavior.

In August of 1983 we celebrated our eleventh anniversary with Nancy's parents at a glamorous, expensive restaurant, and though my wife seemed slightly quieter than usual, the evening felt loving and encouraging. I spoke excitedly about my upcoming trip to London: in just a few days I would leave for nearly a month for the taping of our thirteen weekly episodes of *The Worst of Hollywood* for British TV.

The next day, with a bare minimum of drama or disagreement, Nancy announced that she needed another separation. This time she intended to get her own apartment and planned to vacate our house by the time I returned from England. I felt more resigned, more worn out, by this turn of events and simply accepted her insistence that she felt absolutely sure of her course of action, even though she couldn't explain the basis for her decision in terms I would understand. Rather than pleading for her to reconsider, I responded with an irrevocable decision of my own: since she planned a long-term separation (why else establish your own apartment?), I wanted to move immediately toward a definitive break—a Jewish religious divorce (a relatively easy process) followed by a division of our property and (I hoped) an amicable legal conclusion to our marriage. I've always hated loose ends, confusion, clutter, uncertainty, but Nancy saw my preference for a quick, decisive resolution as one more example of the way I undervalued her.

The trip to London provided three weeks of searing, exhilarating, bittersweet intensity: I loved my work, my charming flat in the Swiss Cottage neighborhood, my attendance at world-class symphonic and operatic performances nearly every night, the ability to explore the galleries and neighborhoods of that glorious city, the partnership and friendship with creative young people. At the same time I remained painfully conscious of the fact that my life six thousand miles away had fallen apart: here I was, with dozens of producers and technicians and executives depending on my capacity to sound witty and enthusiastic on the silly subject of bad movies, reminding myself literally every hour that I would eventually come home to deal with the miserable realities of divorce. The very idea of marital breakup still felt disgraceful, even dangerous to me—as if I'd suddenly entered the strange, unpredictable life of someone else.

By the time I returned home, however, I'd begun to feel excited, even energized by the prospect of that new life. Nancy also seemed notably sunnier in disposition, proud and pleased with her independent success in setting up her new apartment. I agreed to buy out her share of the appreciated value of our property so I could stay on that Santa Monica hillside near Pacific Jewish Center, and, working with two attorneys from our synagogue, we arranged an equitable division of our assets. We then scheduled a session with the Orthodox religious court, or *Bet Din*, in order to finalize our divorce according to Jewish law. The key element of a get, or traditional bill of divorcement, involves both parties appearing before a panel of three rabbinic judges and declaring in clear, unequivocal terms their mutual decision to end the marriage. If a man refuses to cooperate with the process, it can't even begin; if a woman refuses to accept it, it can't conclude. In the court that day, Nancy wept openly as she listened to the proceedings. Before we completed the ceremony, the presiding judge, a kindly, worldly-wise, European-born rabbi in an old-fashioned bow tie— took me out of the room for private, informal consultation. "It's obvious she doesn't want this!" he pleaded. "Wouldn't it be better to wait?"

I patiently explained that she had moved out of the house for a second time and that we had agreed a clean break represented the right thing; we had even begun working with attorneys on our civil settlement.

"But you've been married eleven years. And what about the children?" he asked.

When I assured him that we had no children, he sighed with resignation, put a reassuring hand on my shoulder, and led me back to the main room, where we finished the procedure.

As I drove home with my dad (who had finalized his own Jewish divorce with my mother just a week before), we talked about my brief, private conversation with the presiding rabbi and its deeper meaning. For two millennia, Jewish law has mandated that after ten years of childless marriage, a husband and wife must reconsider their relationship. Divorce isn't absolutely required in that situation, but it is, to some extent, expected. My breakup with Nancy didn't stem from any conscious effort to follow this ancient prescription, but it did reflect the essential truth and wisdom behind the tradition.

While I expected to slog through weeks of depression and remorse following our religious divorce, my mood actually brightened with the new clarity in my situation: I faced the oddly exhilarating prospect of starting over. I initially dreaded informing all my friends and neighbors about the demise of our purportedly perfect marriage, but I felt deeply touched by the concern and support from the members of our Jewish community. People came over to check on my mental state, bringing lovingly prepared meals, little gifts, and offers to introduce me to indescribably wonderful, unattached, observant Jewish women. I appreciated the affectionate attention, but mostly ignored the food. For the first month after Nancy's departure, I survived on adrenaline, ice cream, and beer, thereby managing to lose more than twenty pounds and getting down to my lowest weight since high school. I began exercising furiously every day (pushups, sit-ups, free weights) and going down to the beach for bodysurfing every afternoon. I derived new enjoyment from my weekly movie reviews on CNN, and in the green room, I met a rising blonde starlet who appeared on our show to promote her new high-school sex comedy. We went out to dinner the next night—representing my one and only date with a Hollywood actress. In what I could have read as a definitive message about the need to shun such temptations, our nightly CNN entertainment show received a sudden cancellation notice the next week—bringing an abrupt end to my three years of movie reviews on the cable network.

Much worse news arrived in a more intimate arena that placed a new perspective on my divorce. One evening at dusk, I discovered that our older elkhound, Muki, had disappeared: a repairman had carelessly left the side gate open. After getting in the car and making a fruitless search for Muki throughout the entire neighborhood, I finally called Nancy, who maintained a huge emotional investment in both our dogs. She went out herself to try to find the missing pet but came to the house at 2 A.M. to express her desperation and anxiety; naturally she blamed me for the gate left ajar and for the disappearance of a dog we had cherished for more than ten years. After midnight on the second night since Muki's departure, I got the call I dreaded most: "I think I found your dog," said a worried lady with a thick Spanish accent. "And she's hurt really bad." I called Nancy and we converged on the site. Muki had been hit by a car and died before we could get her to the vet.

This sad development hit me with disproportionate and devastating force. I had to go out of town for a lecture in the Midwest the day after Muki's death and I found it difficult to function, or to stop crying. On the plane, I sobbed so obviously that the flight attendant tried to comfort me. I knew that my exaggerated grief made no rational sense: our clever, endearing dog had already lived a reasonably long life in canine terms. My pain arose from the contrast between the wretched reality of a bloody, dead animal and the silly, childlike fun and affection that Nancy and I had always invested in Muki. As newlyweds, we had adopted her as a puppy from the Berkeley pound, and now her death came to symbolize the death of our marriage. I hadn't felt mournful or wounded over our divorce, but now all the deferred, denied emotion overwhelmed me. I felt inconsolable, especially since the only individual who possibly could understand my pain had chosen to abandon our marriage.

I knew that I wanted to marry again, and determined to pursue that goal in a sensible style. I discovered that within the observant Jewish world—where eligible women greatly outnumber the eligible men—an imposing array of attractive females showed interest in a possible connection with a successful author who owned his own home, appeared regularly on

TV, served as synagogue president, and possessed a full head of hair. When I returned to LA, I got an unexpected visit from an elegant, imposingly sophisticated lady journalist I had befriended in London. A certified aristocrat, distantly related to the royal family, she had heard through the grapevine about my divorce and came to California to spend time with me. While flattered by all the attention, I determined to take my time. In fact, I looked forward to several years of self-sufficient bachelorhood, indulgently exploring every conceivable alternative before I made a fateful new commitment. I might have managed to honor that resolution had I avoided a quick trip to the beach one Tuesday afternoon in the fall.

LESSON

28

Love at First Sight Is Implausible
but Not Impossible

In the weeks following my divorce I made a special point of swimming at Santa Monica Beach as often as I could, devoting most of my weekday afternoons to riding the waves on a newly acquired "boogie board"—a cunningly designed styrofoam float that shot through the surf at prodigious speeds and provided some of the exhilaration previously reserved for serious surfers. This almost ritualistic activity provided an abundance of psychic rewards, making me feel healthy, young, even childish, offering a reassuring reminder that I might still expect many more years of adventure and change. The boogie boarding meant so much to me, in fact, that I continued regular expeditions to the beach even after the advance of autumn, when the drop in the water temperature and the thinning of the crowds left me at times in sole possession of a significant swath of empty strand.

One windy afternoon I arrived at about three o'clock, planted my towel on the sand, and spotted another hearty soul in the water, an athletic-looking girl who wore a brief bikini and body-surfed with evident expertise. I took off my shirt and glasses, grabbed my boogie board, plunged into the bracing brine, and headed out in her general direction. We rode one wave into shore more or less together before I accessed the impertinence to try to begin a conversation. I began paddling toward her, and opened with a nonthreatening inquiry: "So, what do you do that allows you to come out to the beach on a Tuesday afternoon?"

"I'm a writer and a psychologist," she answered.

I privately snickered at her response; she looked to me like a teenager, or perhaps a student at Santa Monica City College, and certainly too young to qualify for the accomplishments she claimed. I couldn't see her clearly without my glasses, but felt acutely conscious of the dazzling blue eyes and gleaming smile that indicated that she defined herself based on ultimate ambition, rather than present occupation.

"A writer? Really? Are you working on screenplays?"

"No, actually I write books."

"Are you looking for a publisher?"

"No, my second book just came out. With Bobbs Merrill. You can find it in most bookstores."

This announcement left me shocked at my own good fortune as we splashed and bobbed over the waves breaking far from shore. What were the odds against meeting a bathing beauty in a snug bikini who was also a published author? It seemed appropriate to try to impress her with some of my own credentials.

"You know, it's an amazing coincidence meeting you in the middle of the ocean, because I'm also a book writer. How many people make their living that way? In any event, I'm working on my sixth book right now, and it's scheduled to come out with Putnam's next spring."

She asked me what I wrote about and I told her I tried to cover disparate, even disconnected subjects, keeping in mind the old saw that it's always harder to hit a moving target. I mentioned that I'd done two books about movies, plus serious nonfiction projects about growing up in the '60s, the White House staff, and the medical profession.

She swam a bit closer and began laughing out loud. "That means you must be Michael Medved. Right?"

I felt astonished, flattered, prodigiously thrilled that this attractive stranger knew both my work and my name. I asked her why and she explained that during her final years of psychology grad school she had worked as a staff writer for the *LA Times* and in that capacity had reviewed

The Golden Turkey Awards. When she told me her name—Diane Elvenstar—the awkward memories came together: I remembered that odd byline attached to the single most contemptuous notice we received on our otherwise popular project. "You know, I remember your review. How could I forget? It always stood out as the worst review we got from anyone."

"It wasn't that bad," she said with a laugh. "The review was mixed." We interrupted the conversation to catch another wave, as I steered the boogie board to ride toward the shore just a few feet away from her lithe body. When we headed back out into the drink, splashing and floating and treading water, I asked about her book projects. The current release bore the intriguing title *First Comes Love: Deciding Whether or Not to Get Married.* Her first book, adapted from her Ph.D. dissertation at UCLA, was called *Children: To Have or Have Not.* Hoping to advance our flirtatious conversation, I posed the obvious, provocative question: "So, what have you decided for yourself. Have—or Have Not?"

She answered without hesitation that she had made up her mind long ago that she'd never want children: she enjoyed her life too much to allow huge disruptions for the sake of little strangers who didn't yet exist—and never needed to exist. Despite her unequivocal words, I refused to accept that her dismissive attitude represented her final position on the subject.

"I know you're the expert, and you wrote the book," I offered, "but I'll bet that at some point you're going to change your mind, and you're going to end up with kids." My years of frustrating effort trying to conceive with Nancy left me finely attuned to the elemental, universal power of baby hunger. "Sooner or later, just about everybody decides they want children. When you get older, you'll probably feel different."

"That's one of the most arrogant assumptions I've ever heard! You know me for maybe ten minutes, and you think you're ready to make big predictions about my future?" Fortunately, she seemed more amused than offended by my audacity. We continued to banter as we walked out of the water and onto the beach. I gathered up my towel and my tote bag, and with her permission followed her along the sand to spread out my stuff next to hers. With my glasses on and both of us out of the ocean, I got a much better look at her as she settled down onto her towel, stretched out on her back, and luxuriated in what remained of the afternoon sun. Raising myself on one elbow, looking down at the droplets of water drying on her sleek golden form, I felt slightly intimated but hugely excited by her movie-star glamour. She projected an aura of unshakable self-confidence, cheerful strength, and effortless charisma. I told her she reminded me of a young lioness and she laughed, having been born, she said, under the Zodiac sign of Leo.

We spoke for several minutes about agents, since she felt that her literary representative had dropped the ball in the preparations for her latest book. I told her about my own long-standing and gratifying relationship with Artie Pine, and with his son Richard, who had recently joined the old man in the family business, and I suggested that she approach them about representing her in the future. She found that prospect intriguing enough that she asked me to write down my phone number so she could call me for further information. I thought about asking for her phone number but hesitated, worried that if I did so I might make my interest too obvious.

Before I could summon the nerve to ask, she checked her watch and announced she had to go. As I watched her striding across the sand to the parking lot, I felt mournfully certain I'd never see her again. Nevertheless, that night I jotted down her name on the calendar where I recorded the highlights of each day. I wrote simply: "Met Diane Elvenstar at the beach. Danger. Danger! Danger!!" I suppose that my categorization of her as double-exclamation-point dangerous stemmed from the combustible, spontaneous, vaulting nature of my attraction. I suspected that her improbable combination of attributes—a Ph.D., no less, with those legs— might make it harder for me to feel excited about other women who didn't measure up. I also assumed that she wasn't Jewish, which, given my communal responsibilities, represented danger enough in itself. Nevertheless, I looked up her number in the phone book, and wondered if I could come up with an acceptable excuse for making the call.

To my enormous relief, I didn't have to produce a justification for pursuing her: she called me the next day. After I gave her my agents' contact information, she suggested that we get together to spend a few minutes talking about the book business. I agreed to come over to her apartment, and the moment she opened the door to greet me with that electrifying smile, I knew I was lost, captured, hopelessly and instantly infatuated. What became of my worthy resolution to remain cautious and calculating in approaching new relationships? Seeing her for the first time in street clothes (snug jeans, turquoise blue sweater), I found her even more formidable: her long straight hair, which had been wet, dark, and matted on the beach, now assumed its normal blonde radiance with rich highlights. She prepared blackberry tea; I sipped, watched her, and felt intoxicated. We talked about music, and she expressed enthusiasm and gratitude that I knew so much about it, since she had recently decided to educate herself on the classics. She played a Chopin tape, and for a few seconds, I squeezed her hand during the *Ballade in F Major*. A blinding, white glow seemed to come off her sun-kissed skin: like Marlene Dietrich in one of Josef von Sternberg's classics, it looked as if a smitten director had lovingly illuminated her in every scene with her own bank of lights to invest the star with an almost supernatural force field.

We've now been married twenty years and I'm still knocked out by the way Diane lights up a room. It's not my imagination, either: I've asked other people about it and they, too, can sense her electrifying energy, that warming, undeniable glow. How could I possibly fight against that? On innumerable occasions, we've been asked how we met and we've gotten good at dodging the question. We usually say, "We got to know each other through our Jewish community in Venice." That's true enough as far as it goes, but it doesn't reveal the bizarre and embarrassing reality that our first encounter occurred amidst the waves of the Pacific Ocean—several years after she had just happened to review my book for our local LA newspaper.

That first afternoon of brief handholding and blackberry tea, she talked for a while about her background. To my amazement, she came from pioneer Jewish stock: her grandfather, Lionel Edwards, founded the first Jewish newspaper in Southern California (*The B'nai B'rith Messenger*) in 1897. On her mother's side, the family connected to the Mayflower, veterans of the Continental Army (and members of the Daughters of the American Revolution), and eighteenth-century German immigrants to the Shenandoah Valley. With her Jewish father and a mother raised in Christian Science, the family compromised: she had attended Congregational Church as a girl, but still found her way into participation in Jewish youth organizations (including B'nai B'rith Girls). Under Jewish law, she would need an Orthodox conversion to count as a full member of the community, but I felt powerfully drawn to her tangled roots that combined German

Jewish immigrants and hearty patriots of the Colonial period. Her own odd name, Elvenstar, reflected neither side of her ancestry. She had gotten married at age eighteen—barefoot, in a meadow, with flowers in her hair— and shortly thereafter she and her doting husband had invented their own magical moniker to suggest fairy tales and enchantment.

Now that name (with her recently completed "Ph.D." proudly attached) appeared on her handsomely packaged new book, *First Comes Love: Deciding Whether or Not to Get Married.* On a Sunday afternoon she invited me to drive her to an important hour-long, taped radio interview promoting her project. I sat just outside the studio, watching Diane through the glass, listening to her warm alto voice fielding every question with crisp assurance. I felt so explosively proud of her that I wanted the people at the station to think we were involved, even though I still had no idea about our real status. Was I just a friend, riding along for moral support? Significantly younger than I was, she had accomplished so much in such a short time: all those degrees (and two teaching credentials, to boot) from UCLA, while publishing more than two hundred articles (in publications including *Ladies Home Journal, Glamour, LA Magazine,* and the *LA Times*) to support herself through school. Looking at the dishy blonde Doctor of Psychology in her businesslike brown suit cut just above the knee, watching her speak authoritatively into the microphone as she crossed and uncrossed her long, perfectly sculpted legs, I felt suddenly seized with the breathless, heart-racing knowledge that I couldn't live without her. She continued speaking about her book, with its theme, as stated in the jacket copy, that "romantic love is still very much alive and well, but it is now more likely than ever to be tempered by mature, realistic forethought when a lifelong commitment is considered." I didn't feel at all "mature" or "realistic," but I irresistibly—irrationally—considered a lifelong commitment.

The next day I flew to Las Vegas for a Jewish Federation lecture about the '60s generation, and when I got back to the hotel I couldn't sleep at all. At two in the morning I sat by myself at a little table in the largely deserted casino, nursing a beer and writing a long, rambling, confessional love letter to Diane. After I returned home she presented me with a bundle of letters of her own—witty, perceptive little masterpieces that amounted to more than twenty pages about her family, her childhood, her conservative values, her romantic history (there wasn't much of one, since she had been a teen-aged bride), and her religious development.

When Diane came over to meet my brother (and housemate) Harry, for the most part neither she nor I could speak: we sat for an hour in the sunny dining room of my Santa Monica house, holding hands, staring into each other's eyes, occasionally laughing and stammering. At dusk, I got a ladder out of the garage and led her up to the roof. We clambered to the peak and sat down to watch the sun going down over the Pacific. I didn't have an agenda for the conversation but I sensed she shared the emotion of that sunset moment. "You remember our first conversation? When I was telling you that I thought you'd end up having children someday? Well, I think, Diane, you will be the mother of my children."

She looked shocked, but not horrified. She made no effort to with-draw her hand from mine, and instead snuggled against my shoulder. I took this reaction for assent, and that rooftop encounter—on only the sixth occasion we ever set eyes on one another—amounted to my proposal and our agreement, tacit though it might be, to bind our lives together. Before reaching a formal engagement, however, we knew we had to overcome a series of daunting obstacles, most of them concerning religious affiliation and practice.

Diane welcomed the opportunity to embrace a generalized Jewish identity—with her mixed ancestry, she already felt like a Member of the Tribe—but she remained skeptical about committing herself to the Ortho-dox life I had chosen. She found it difficult to imagine giving up spending time at the gym, or taking a drive in the country, or going out to the shop-ping mall, every Saturday for the rest of her life. Nevertheless, she wanted to confront the intellectual basis for traditional observance and so planned to attend all available classes at Pacific Jewish Center. To give formal focus to this effort, she won an assignment from *Los Angeles Magazine* to write a massive report on "The Jewish Revival in Los Angeles"—an article that would reflect the results of her classes and her interviews with leading rab-bis in all branches of Judaism. Three nights a week she dug into Biblical and Talmudic analysis, and she started learning Hebrew with a tutor every weekday afternoon. The members of the Venice community happily wel-comed her as a glamorous visitor, but not the "girlfriend" of the president, since we went to considerable lengths to avoid public acknowledgment of our involvement.

Nonetheless, I confided in my friend and teacher Rabbi Lapin, and to my surprise he reacted to Diane almost as positively as I did. I had expected that he would discourage me strongly from involvement with a divorcee with no prior grounding in Orthodox religiosity, but after he met with Diane he looked beyond her superficial disqualifications. "She is extraordinary," he told me. "It's not an easy situation, but she seems to have the strength and the substance to make it work." My parents also responded with unexpected enthusiasm to the possibility of welcoming Diane into the family: my mother and father agreed on almost nothing, but they both liked the blonde with the infectious optimism, the easy laugh, and the high-octane energy.

Diane applied that energy, along with her formidable strength, intelligence, and intensity, to the task of completing her conversion in record time. She began studying with Rabbi Joseph Feinstein, a gentle, faithful soul who specialized in working with those who wanted to convert to Judaism under Orthodox law. According to our tradition, a convert (even one with a Jewish father) must develop an independent, personal connection to the people of Israel—an association that in no way depends on the romantic desire to wed a prospective spouse. For several months, therefore, we had to stop seeing each other (except for the times we attended the same synagogue services), though we continued to engage in lengthy yearning conversations every night on the phone.

Diane made unprecedented progress with her conversion studies—mastering the basics of the Hebrew language, familiarizing herself with daily and Sabbath prayers, studying all the key Biblical passages, learning about the complex ins and outs of Jewish law. In less than a year, Rabbi Feinstein presented her to the religious court—with the same kind-hearted rabbi who had presided over my divorce serving as the chief judge. The three officials asked a series of probing questions to test the depth of her knowledge and, more importantly, to evaluate the sincerity of her commitment to honor Jewish law and attach herself to our people. Deeply impressed by her occasionally tearful responses, they sent her with praise and encouragement to the final stage of the process—full immersion in the *mikva,* or ritual bath. This ancient Jewish practice (from which the Christian ritual of baptism clearly derived) is associated with rebirth and clean slates and fresh beginnings, and here it marked the commencement of Diane's new life as a daughter of Israel. We announced our engagement the next week during Sabbath services at our synagogue, surprising (and thrilling) most members of the congregation, who erupted into song and applause, providing hugs, backslaps, even high-fives for the prospective bride and groom.

A few weeks after that public announcement and in the midst of the frenetic preparations for our wedding, I got an unexpected Sunday morning phone call from Nancy. After the normal exchange of "how're-you-doing" pleasantries, she got right to the point. "I wanted to tell you I'm getting married this afternoon," she declared, without emotion. I hadn't even known she'd been seeing anyone, so her revelation shocked me into silence. She had arranged an intimate family wedding to her former trainer, a prominent, well-respected track coach more than twenty years her senior who had helped prepare her for marathons and supervised her rehabilitation after the knee injury. With several grown children from his previous marriage, he felt no compulsion to build another family—freeing Nancy, as I understood it, from any further pressure or pain over the issue of offspring. To the best of my knowledge, she's still happily married and enjoying conspicuous success in a challenging business position she took on as part of her new life. I haven't seen her for more than fifteen years: without children to mandate permanent, regular contact, there's no practical reason (and several obvious downsides) for maintaining a connection with an ex-wife. Though we no longer enjoy even a casual relationship, I still feel grateful to her for the many ways she blessed me—not least with the timing of her own second marriage. By the end of our brief conversation just hours before her wedding, I had begun laughing with excitement, not only pleased to hear about her satisfaction but also exhilarated over the welcome sense of liberation for myself.

Every aspect of our wedding arrangements with Diane underscored the difference between this new ceremony and my prior experience. Instead of the bride's parents assembling a social occasion aimed primarily at their friends and other members of the older generation, we took charge of every detail ourselves. As the founding president of our youthful synagogue, I'd played a prominent role in literally dozens of Orthodox weddings and become intimately familiar with all the ancient traditions— timeless customs we could now apply to our own fresh start. Best of all, my marriage to Diane occurred within a conscious context: our intention to create a *Bayit Ne'eman B'Yisrael,* a "Faithful Home within the People of Israel." From the moment of our engagement—from our first conversation on the very day we met, in fact—children represented an explicit focus of our relationship, giving us a sense of purpose, of destination.

The wedding ceremony took place on a sun-drenched January afternoon in 1985 in the quaint oceanfront synagogue we had rebuilt and restored. The more than two hundred guests who had jammed the synagogue for the ceremony then surged out onto the beach to dance the newlyweds to the antique convertible that drove us to the banquet hall. There we all feasted on a lavish six-course meal, danced with athletic abandon in two separate circles (one for the men, one for the women), and listened to emotional toasts from our various rabbis, my brothers, and my father. My dad felt especially swept up in the ecstatic nature of the occasion; he had recently bought a condo a half mile away from our beachfront synagogue and only six blocks from the home where Diane and I would begin our married life. Dad joked about our family now including another "Dr. Medved" (since Diane—despite the fact that she had published two prior books as "Elvenstar"—had affirmed her new marital identity by changing her name) and tearfully hugged her as the daughter he never had. Diane's parents, meanwhile, watched the proceedings with amazement and growing delight: despite his Jewish ancestry, my father-in-law, a former major in the U.S. Army and a career civil servant for the state of California, had never attended an elaborate Orthodox wedding.

During the course of the evening, it struck me that the whole grand affair arose out of a coincidence—except that religious people don't like the term "coincidence." In a nonrandom, purposeful universe, everything unfolds according to some plan, even if we enjoy only limited success in discerning its outlines. I've wondered on many occasions about the timing of my visit to Santa Monica Beach on that autumn afternoon. What if I had delayed my boogie-boarding expedition by an hour? What if I had selected a different stretch of sand? At the moment that you're intentionally linking yourself for eternity to another human being, it's difficult to conceive that such a significant passage can count as the result of a happy accident.

In the first week of our marriage, we honored the ancient custom of *sheva brachos*, or "seven blessings"—going to a different dinner party in our honor on each of those seven nights. Surrounded by family and friends, honored and pampered by the people who meant the most to us, we went home each night with a charge of jubilation and exaltation— at last authorized, and in fact encouraged, to share a bed, embraces, and a future. Those days provided such spectacular joy, such a flood of love and laughter, that I felt that I'd received a foretaste of heaven itself— strengthening us both for the unexpected challenges and changes that lay just ahead.

The Job of a Film Critic Is Neither as Glamorous Nor as Powerful as It Looks

In the midst of the hyperemotional and melodramatic run-up to my marriage to Diane, I took time out to promote the release of my new book, *The Hollywood Hall of Shame*. This interlude forced me to take note of the glaring contrast between the serious, consequential issues I faced in my personal life and the essential frivolity of my work. While I privately sorted through questions about love, destiny, religious identity, and the future of my family, I spoke in public about the amusing embarrassments behind the biggest commercial bombs in motion picture history. Contrary to all reasonable expectations, even my half-hearted engagement with this trifling topic ultimately brought me back to the big problems of providence, observance, and permanent priorities.

From the beginning, my brother and I viewed *The Hollywood Hall of Shame* as a slightly more substantive undertaking than our previous books on bad movies. By focusing on financial disasters rather than aesthetic atrocities, we shifted our attention from incomparably inane monster movies of the '50s and '60s (*The Attack of the Mushroom People, From Hell It Came*) to ambitious but ill-considered projects featuring major stars

(*Mohammad, Messenger of God* with Anthony Quinn, or *Inchon* with Laurence Olivier woefully miscast as Douglas MacArthur). We felt particularly proud of the new light we managed to shed on especially appalling episodes in cinema history, including the 1944 Nazi extravaganza *Kolberg*, a grandiose melodrama about the Napoleonic Wars featuring 187,000 Wehrmacht soldiers as battlefield extras (they had been borrowed from the crumbling Eastern front) and personally supervised by the movie-mad Dr. Joseph Goebbels.

In assembling our book, we made a conscious and cunning bid to connect with comedienne Joan Rivers, who served at the time as Johnny Carson's "permanent substitute host" for the all-important *Tonight Show*. Rivers had recently devoted much of her act to a nasty and hilarious vendetta against Elizabeth Taylor, calling cruel, constant attention to the bloated form of the once svelte and sexy superstar. With this feud in mind, we designed an entire "Elizabeth Taylor Wing" for our Hollywood Hall of Shame and larded it (you will pardon the expression) with corny fat jokes deliberately designed to appeal to Rivers. The strategy worked beautifully when we sent her an early copy of our book (and I reminded her that we had appeared together during my promotion for *Class of '65*), provoking a quick response from Bob Dolce, the *Tonight Show*'s legendary guest coordinator. He wanted me to appear for an extended on-air conversation with Ms. Rivers during the two weeks in April she had been designated to pinch-hit for Johnny, but our struggle to agree on a suitable date wound up wielding a profound, unexpected influence on my career. I sighed with frustration when he threw out his first suggestion for my guest shot on the show.

"Bob, you know I'd love to do it, but the night you want is the second night of Passover. It's a major Jewish holiday. I'm afraid I can't do it."

He assured me that I could enjoy the best of both worlds—attending the early evening taping of *The Tonight Show* and still making it to the seder. In response to Bob's good-natured insistence on my participation, I hated having to explain why Jewish commitment demanded more than merely turning up at a family meal: I wouldn't be able to ride in cars, talk on phones, or handle money (let alone appear on TV) at any time between sunset on the first night of the holiday until full dark at the end of the second day. He might have been slightly incredulous to hear about my level of traditional involvement, but he cheerfully promised to get back to me shortly with an alternate date.

The next day he called to suggest another night—exactly five nights after the first date he had mentioned. I checked the calendar with a queasy sense of dread, and then tried to explain the problem. According to our tradition, the last two days of the eight-day Passover festival, like the first two days, are full religious holidays: no work, no riding in cars—and no appearances on *The Tonight Show*. Bob admitted that he'd never before heard anything about this second round of Passover limitations. In fact, he called back the same afternoon to report on his conversations with Jewish members of the staff, who pronounced that I had either made some silly mistake while examining the calendar or else had fabricated a holiday. The guest coordinator had begun to wonder if I harbored some secret, unstated reason for trying to avoid appearing with Joan Rivers on the show.

I assured him of my respect for Ms. Rivers and my eagerness—even desperate eagerness—to return to *The Tonight Show*. I even got out my Bible and provided the specific citation (Leviticus 23, verse 8) that established the seventh day of the Passover festival as a "holy convocation" on which "laborious work" was prohibited. The fact that a vast majority of American Jews did not observe—or even know about—this holiday (formally known as *Shevee'ee Shel Pesach,* or "The Seventh of Passover") couldn't absolve those of us (the few, the proud) who did know.

Bob sounded so dubious when he hung up the phone that I assumed I had obliterated, forever, any possibility of a *Tonight Show* appearance. Considering the horrific martyrdom (death, dismemberment, dispossession) my ancestors experienced for the sake of their faith, this small sacrifice seemed utterly insignificant, but it still left me feeling sour. The Hollywood establishment displays fawning respect and accommodation for any expression of unconventional religiosity—Scientology, Kabbalah, Transcendental Meditation, generalized New Age nonsense—but when it comes to the time-honored practices of Judaism (a faith that a disproportionate number of industry movers and shakers at least nominally share), the general response has always been impatience and incomprehension. If I had told the guest coordinator that his suggested date conflicted with a special fast day in honor of my meditation guru, I would have felt far more confident at getting an alternate invitation.

Despite my spasm of self-pity and premature indignation, Bob Dolce did call me back two days later with yet another date for my appearance, and after a quick glance at the calendar I shouted my grateful acceptance. The resulting interview qualified as one of my most enjoyable and amusing TV appearances, and while I was pleased with the enthusiastic response from the studio audience, my proud publisher, and friends and family, the most important feedback came in a phone call the next day from a senior producer at the Chicago PBS station, WTTW. John Davies wanted to talk about my possible involvement with *Sneak Previews*, the nationally televised movie review show he helped produce.

Even without a TV set at home, I knew something about this program, which had made celebrities of Roger Ebert and Gene Siskel and become the highest-rated regular series in PBS history. In 1982, Ebert and Siskel (who had been selected, after auditions, by the WTTW producers to fit into a format the station had devised) left public television for a much richer contract in commercial syndication, where their new venture, *At the Movies*, slavishly replicated every aspect of the original show. Meanwhile, the PBS brass in Chicago determined to keep their franchise alive, but as producer Davies candidly conceded to me on the phone, the program was now struggling under its new hosts, dapper Jeffrey Lyons and bearded Neal Gabler. Based on the segment he'd seen on *The Tonight Show*, Davies thought that my humor, energy, and easy conversational manner might help reinvigorate *Sneak Previews*. He offered me a free plane ticket to fly to Chicago to talk about it.

During the ensuing visit I met the station brass, toured the studios, looked at tapes of recent *Sneak Previews* (discussing possible improvements with producers), and formed an instantaneous bond with John Davies—an edgy, hyperkinetic, hypercreative hipster in tennis shoes, with a perpetually amazed expression behind his thick round glasses and shock of blond hair. He came up with the idea of launching my association with the show by introducing a regular "Golden Turkey" segment in which I presented clips from the most amusingly incompetent recent releases and offered my cutting commentary. In addition to adding spice to the program, the highly produced packages would introduce me to the viewing audience—and, more importantly, to the executives who ran the various stations in the public television system. If they responded well to my televised presence, I could make an easy transition to the coveted position of cohost of the already venerable program.

I came home from the flattering meetings in Chicago with a powerfully appealing deal: getting decent payment for an extended on-the-job tryout. As the opportunity unfolded, I found that I thoroughly enjoyed my monthly trips to the Midwest to write and shoot the "Golden Turkey" sequences with Davies, collaborating on the slick, selective editing of quick scenes from various duds and exploitation films (including highly dubious mess-terpieces by Sylvester Stallone, Chuck Norris, and my old pal Arnold Schwarzenegger), to which I applied ironic voiceover analysis. We taped the introductions to these segments in the projection booth of a real movie theater in suburban Chicago, with Mike Hagerty of the famed improv troupe Second City (who later became a much-used character-actor in Hollywood) playing the silent, blue-collar projectionist "Moose" in a Cubs jacket and hat, who reacted to my wisecracks and ostentatiously threaded the cinematic stinkers into the machine for our brief consideration.

This silly but spirited addition to a staid PBS show drew the enthusiastic audience embrace that allowed the *Sneak Previews* producers to proceed with their plans to try out a new pairing of critics. Dumping the distinguished but dour Neal Gabler (who has gone on to write a series of influential and important books that I greatly admire), they announced that I would now occupy the aisle seat opposite Jeffrey Lyons. I welcomed the challenge of bringing new edge and electricity to the program, knowing from the beginning that people tuned in not just to get information and opinions about new movies (there were many other sources for that) but also to watch me bickering with Jeffrey in an amusing manner. We couldn't possibly compete with Ebert and Siskel in terms of their complex, prickly, sincerely hostile but oddly codependent relationship, honed over many years of cross-town rivalry as Chicago film critics. After all, the first time I sat down on the *Sneak Previews* set I knew Jeffrey not at all and couldn't even pretend to dislike or resent him. As we did get to know each other, any attempt to project personal antagonism became even more unthinkable: Jeffrey remains one of the kindest, most generous media professionals I've ever encountered, full of an infectious, boyish infatuation with celebrities, movies, and the Boston Red Sox (his one true passion).

In fact, his cheerful relish for his job provided me with the opportunity to define the essential conflict that came to characterize our collaboration: simply put, Jeffrey enjoyed most of the new movies, and I emphatically did not. Even with the most wretched or mediocre releases, he tried to find something nice to say, having lived since childhood (as the son of legendary *New York Post* entertainment columnist Leonard Lyons) surrounded by the glamorous and creative people whose work he now reviewed. Jeffrey repeatedly recalled the advice that actress Ruth Gordon (best known from *Harold and Maude*) gave him before he began his critical career. "Just remember, you're reviewing somebody else's work. Put yourself in their position for a moment. And before you attack them, remember that they probably tried to do the best they could."

While I could admire my cohost's humane and compassionate approach, I couldn't endorse it—especially in light of my growing indignation at the hours and hours I wasted in the dark with utterly worthless exercises in celluloid excrescence. During my three years at CNN, we covered at most two titles each week (and frequently covered only a single big release), so my screening schedule offered a generally welcome diversion and never became an uncomfortable burden. On *Sneak*, however, we covered five new films every week, and with Sabbath observance taking Friday nights off the table and my plane travel to and from Chicago usually eliminating another two nights, I frequently watched two or three movies in a single day, rushing from one studio screening room to another.

Movie critics enjoy many advantages over the general public (seeing big blockbusters ahead of time, and for free), but those of us who take the job seriously can never exercise the sacred, inalienable right retained by civilian film fans: walking out on the most appallingly awful offerings. During my first years with *Sneak*, I began to sense my life slipping away as I struggled to remain attentive to *Porky's Revenge, Missing in Action 2—The Beginning, Sheena* (with former *Charlie's Angel* Tanya Roberts), or *The Perils of Gwendoline in the Land of the Yik Yak* (with the incomparable Tawny Kitaen). When I made the weekly trek to Chicago to talk about such material, I didn't need to feign hostility toward Jeffrey since I often felt genuine annoyance toward the movies I had seen. This righteous indignation provided the show with a new sort of energy, as Jeffrey most often searched for some redeeming element in an inept opus while I angrily, satirically slashed and trashed the hapless title and all affiliated personnel. In summarizing our verdicts on the movies we covered each week, we voted either straightforward "Yes" or grumpy "No" (Roger and Gene had taken their celebrated Thumbs with them); I quickly emerged as "The Abominable 'No'-Man," while Jeffrey cheerfully became the Will Rogers of movie criticism—he never met a film he didn't like.

Each taping of *Sneak Previews* required several hours of preparation, while Jeffrey and I looked over the package of clips prepared by our staff and wrote the precisely timed introductions to those scenes. After a full morning setting up the show and readying copy for the Teleprompter, we went out to the set, recorded the canned segments, and hoped for the best with the "cross-talks"—the few minutes of interchange or argument in which we made our case for or against each movie. The production staff tried to prevent us from discussing the films in advance so our interaction on the show could feel fresh and unrehearsed, and for the same reason we always tried to make these cross-talks work on the first take.

I flew into Chicago each week from the West Coast, while Jeffrey made the much shorter journey from his home in Manhattan. He always stayed overnight with his in-laws in Chicago (his wife, Judy, had grown up as the daughter of one of the city's tough-but-tender career cops), while I rattled around regular rooms in local hotels. After my first two years as co-host of the show, I found the weekly travel schedule (four hours each way in coach class; this was PBS!) too grueling to sustain, so I persuaded the producers to switch to a system in which we'd come in for two days every other week, knocking off two different shows during each visit. This change allowed me a few extra hours a month to live a life apart from airplanes and screening rooms. On several occasions, I talked with the management of WTTW about the possibility of moving with my wife to Chicago, but the producers always discouraged the notion of relocation, knowing that our show remained on shaky financial ground, renewed only for a year at a time and always, it seemed, in imminent danger of collapse. As it happened, I worked on the show for twelve years, eleven of them as cohost—logging over a million airline miles.

On many of these flights, my fellow passengers began to recognize me as my face became more familiar on television. Their comments and conversation followed predictable patterns: "You're much taller than you look on TV!" almost always emerged as part of any exchange. I've never understood this universal assumption that I'm a vertically challenged shrimp, since I've been 6'1" since my freshman year of college. On *Sneak Previews*, I never got up from my seat—in fact, we ended each show with the tagline "And until next time on *Sneak Previews*, don't forget to save us the aisle seats!"—so perceptions of height proceeded from no rational basis. Because I lack Jeffrey's long, thin, angular face, viewers never guessed that I was actually several inches taller and some pounds lighter than he was. In any event, I've come to accept the fact that the television medium that I've always banned from my home performs some malevolent transformation on my person that makes me seem diminutive.

After expressing their surprise about my actual stature, the strangers I met on planes usually wanted to talk to me about my fascinating profession. "What a great job, working as a film critic! You get to watch movies, and get paid for it!" became the most common opening, followed almost immediately with the oddly contradictory observation, "But aren't the movies just terrible today? It's unbelievable when you think about all the trash." Few people made the obvious connection between the second statement and the first, unable or unwilling to recognize the inevitable fact that the low quality of motion pictures detracted in a serious way from the excitement and satisfaction of my vocation. At times, my work made me feel like a glorified sewer inspector. Considering the dreary, brain-dead nature of so many major releases, I spent years trying to avoid identifying my primary occupation as "film critic"—even after I began spending by far the majority of my work time on my responsibilities with *Sneak Previews*. I wanted to continue describing myself as a writer (who just happened to host a weekly movie review show), and in order to maintain that designation I overcame my trepidation about the demands on my time and signed a new book contract for another "bad movies" volume with my brother.

Son of Golden Turkey Awards offered twenty-three new categories for aficionados of fatuity, ranging from "The Worst Nude Scene in Hollywood History" to "The Worst Beach Party Movie Ever Made," from "The Worst Performance as a Nazi Mad Scientist" to "The Worst Performance by Ronald Reagan"—a frankly affectionate chapter that drew grateful phone calls from some of the president's pals, who appreciated our full-throated defense of *Bedtime for Bonzo*. Despite the fact that Harry and I enjoyed the process of putting together the best researched and most cleverly written of our four collaborations, we feared from the beginning that this new venture might count as ill-considered and excessive; having mocked Hollywood mercilessly for its diseased tendency to milk tired ideas beyond any point of utility or sanity, we had fallen victim to our very own case of sequelitis. Compounding our embarrassment, sales proved disappointing, thanks in no small part to the garish, crudely drawn cover and the wholly inept publicity campaign orchestrated by our new publisher, Villard Books. When the feeble results became painfully obvious, Harry sheepishly returned to UCLA to continue his slow, stately progress toward an eight-year B.A., while I refocused my attention on *Sneak Previews* and the ongoing challenge of keeping the show alive.

The process of funding and scheduling the ambitious programming on public television remains mysterious even to those who have toiled for years within the system. Unlike the commercial alternatives, PBS isn't so much a centralized network as a loosely affiliated collection of powerful local stations, each of which hopes to produce original programming that will air around the country. WTTW viewed *Sneak* as a major source of national prestige and credibility, distributing the program to more than two hundred stations free of charge and relying on contributions from corporate underwriters to pay the cost of production. Since the very essence of PBS involves its refusal to sell commercial time, companies who support a show or a station get a few seconds of precious underwriting announcements ("This show made possible by a generous grant from the Gigantor Corporation . . .") at the beginning and end of a program. During the ongoing struggle to pay our bills, I learned of cunning ways to stretch the rules so that these "announcements" began to seem strikingly similar to advertisements. For instance, one season Ford Motor Company made a major commitment to pay for our show, in return for which a stentorian voice proclaimed: "*Sneak Previews* made possible by a grant from Ford, makers of the new Thunderbird. It's a beautiful day for 'Bird' watching." During this brief declaration, the screen showed a beautiful new T-bird driving along a twisty country road and pulling into full, glorious view. Unfortunately, we discovered that this image violated one of the arbitrary rules of public television: showing "turning wheels" while the car moved. According to the regulations of underwriting announcements, a company could show a stationary automobile, wheels and all, or else depict a moving car without showing those pesky wheels, but for some reason visible, turning wheels remained strictly taboo. When the national officials at the Corporation for Public Broadcasting demanded that Ford alter its scandalous imagery, the automotive giant abruptly pulled its grant (the most generous we ever had).

I got personally, passionately involved in the constant scramble for donations, speaking directly to various executives and major foundations in order to keep our program on the air. At several points we improvised: one season we sold the show to the Lifetime cable network while it continued to air on selected public TV outlets; another season we changed the focus to video rather than theatrical releases (because Hollywood already made more money on renting and selling videos than in playing movies in theaters). One way or another, we kept the show going, and during most of our seasons we continued to reach in excess of a million weekly viewers.

One motivation for this stubborn struggle for survival was the spirit of competition with Siskel and Ebert, who had left behind a definite aftertaste of resentment and envy when they abandoned public television. Four years after leaving *Sneak Previews*, the critical icons jumped again, starting a new show with the Disney company (*Siskel & Ebert & the Movies*) while their former syndicated program (*At the Movies*) hired Rex Reed and Bill Harris to replace them. For a while, America sustained three different critics programs (and I transcended the embarrassment of strangers thinking I had partnered with Rex Reed), but we soon could take pride in the fact that we lasted on the air a full six years longer than the ill-fated, inept *At the Movies* extravaganza. Meanwhile, we knew we could never effectively challenge Roger and Gene, who enjoyed a huge head start in public recognition, vastly greater financial resources behind them (with salaries literally ten times what we received), and strong newspaper platforms (as principal critics for the *Chicago Sun-Times* and *Chicago Tribune*, respectively) that I got only near the end of my *Sneak Previews* run. Within the tight, incestuous world of Chicago media, they also benefited from their status as the "hometown boys" while Jeffrey and I remained a pair of interlopers who only intermittently appeared in the midwestern metropolis that had oddly emerged as the capital of televised movie criticism. Though we appeared with Siskel and Ebert for one big "confrontation" at a heavily hyped Chicago press luncheon, and I later debated Roger before an audience of a thousand black-tied dignitaries at a Palm Beach banquet, they never accepted us as colleagues, or even as competitors who deserved to contend on the same playing field.

In addition to all the negative factors uniquely associated with my ongoing job at *Sneak Previews* (exhausting travel, ridiculous screening schedules, a constant need to beg for underwriting), I also faced the indignities and discomforts encountered by everyone who appears regularly on TV. After my first two weeks as cohost of the show, the producers announced their vehement objections to my thick glasses, upset at the way the massive lenses reflected the intense lighting on the set. I've needed a big correction for my myopia since the age of five, and without specs I couldn't recognize Jeffrey sitting two feet away from me—let alone read a Teleprompter or avoid tripping over lighting cables. To cope with the problem, I secured contact lenses for the first time in my life and proudly presented myself for the next two shows with a new, glasses-free face. Unfortunately, the audience reacted badly to this change: we received letters and phone calls from ordinary viewers, as well as a few local public TV executives, complaining that I looked "weird" (or at least radically unfamiliar) without my glasses. In response, the station forced an obnoxious "compromise" on me: I would wear my contacts, but I would also wear dummy glasses (with no distracting lenses in the frames) to reassure the nervous audience with my well-established, four-eyed look.

For eight long years I went along with the glasses imposture, but I finally rebelled by deliberately reaching through the empty frames to rub my eye or scratch my nose while on camera. At that point the producers relented, letting let me appear on air without glasses. I also showed a defiant streak in dealing with the officious wardrobe and grooming consultants they employed from time to time in futile efforts to upgrade our appearance. I refused to go along with an attempt to dress me in a series of earthtoned sweater vests and bow ties, and Jeffrey joined me in standing up against stylishness. The other two movie review shows (particularly Rex Reed's) might win public plaudits for their showy sweaters, but we maintained our curmudgeonly commitment to sports jackets and ties. Jeffrey, in fact, wore precisely the same blue blazer for every episode in the eleven years we worked together.

The annoying emphasis on superficials during my long tenure with *Sneak* only confirmed my contempt for the TV medium in general and left me proud and gratified that the Medved household remained one of the rare American homes with no television. This made it easier to resist the temptation to overestimate my overall impact on pop culture simply because my mug turned up every week on somebody else's little screen. I tried to avoid the solemn self-importance of so many of my fellow movie critics, keeping in mind at all times the strictly limited nature of our influence on any film's success or failure. I thoroughly despised the first *Batman* movie, for instance, and pleaded with the audience to avoid that ugly and mind-numbing experience, but it went on to become one of the top-grossing blockbusters in history. That film may have earned its share of (undeservedly) enthusiastic reviews, but the so-called critical community did achieve rare unanimity in its contempt for the various installments of Sylvester Stallone's *Rambo* saga, even as the masses eagerly defied our verdict to make those movies into muscle-bound hits. On the other hand, Jeffrey and I both anointed *Enchanted April* as the best film of 1992, but despite our rhapsodic enthusiasm for great performances by Miranda Richardson, Joan Plowright, Alfred Molina, and Jim Broadbent, almost no one bothered to see the film.

The strongest evidence for the irrelevance of most movie criticism comes from a quick comparison of the "Year's Best" honor roll from any well-known reviewer and the catalog of the top moneymakers at the box office: at most, you'll find two or three titles (movies like *Titanic* or *The Lord of the Rings* trilogy) that qualify as both critical and commercial favorites. This doesn't mean that truly disastrous reviews (like the justly savage response to the Ben Affleck–Jennifer Lopez atrocity *Gigli*) can't hurt a film, or that critics can't help some obscure but worthy work (*You Can Count on Me* and *In the Bedroom*) from winning unexpected public and even Oscar attention. But in the tradition of the Great and Powerful Oz, the occasional demonstrations of the magical clout of movie critics owe as much to accident as effectiveness.

That never stopped publicists and production companies from pursuing us ruthlessly for prerelease endorsement quotes to use in their advertising material. Those breathless blurbs ("I laughed! I cried!"; "The best musical Pirate buddy comedy of the decade!") that ornament the newspaper layouts for even the most miserable movies didn't just emerge unbidden from sincerely enthusiastic members of the commentariat; a busy squadron of flacks and hacks works overtime to coax a few timely words of praise from those critics who've displayed a preternatural fondness for seeing their names in movie ads—any movie ads. In this endeavor, print critics (who display a general reluctance to tip their hand before the formal publication of their written reviews) offer far less assistance than those of us who ply the trade on TV and radio. After a critic has attended an advance screening, the publicist who arranged the showing will often follow up with a call. If the promoter wants to display old-school courtesy she'll first ask, "What did you think?" and then pretend to listen attentively while the pompous critic rattles on about his reaction. Eventually, no matter what the reviewer's response to the masterpiece in the docket, the press aide will cut to the proverbial chase with the inevitable question, "So, do you think you can give us a quote?"

In response to that inquiry, I make an effort to avoid an outright no. Usually, I declare, "Sure, I've got a quote for you. How about 'The most muddled and mediocre movie mess of the year!' or 'Not as bad as Madonna in *Swept Away* but she ought to be stranded on the same beach!'" At times, publicists prove so slow on the uptake that they will painstakingly write down my nasty, satirically minded blurb. I can just imagine some eager beaver running into her boss's office and proudly announcing, "Hey, I don't believe it! I got a quote from Medved. He says, 'An unforgettable experience that fits somewhere between root canal and chemotherapy!'"

Jeffrey, of course, expresses his genuine kindness, congeniality, and beneficence by showering the studios with effusive encomiums in his well-established role as one of the most prolific blurb-meisters in the business. I used to tease him about the appearance of his name in five, six, or seven movie ads simultaneously. Often, these endorsements followed his favorite, familiar formats, such as "*[fill in the blank]* explodes across the screen!" or "*[fill in the blank]* gives a towering performance" or "I haven't laughed so hard in years." In the course of a single year, Jeffrey provided the same enigmatic quote for three different movies, declaring—with Zen-like layers of meaning, no doubt—"I grabbed my seat and held on!" We used to banter and bicker about such rhetorical flourishes during the interminable light checks as we sat on the set of *Sneak Previews*.

But at least Jeffrey counted as a real movie critic with literally millions of viewers (he now serves as film and theater critic for NBC in New York

City, playing a prominent part in America's top-rated local newscast). Many of the names featured regularly in movie ads don't really qualify as reviewers at all, with only a scant presence on some ultraobscure radio outlet or, even worse, a trivial gig on the Internet. Several years ago, the entertainment press discovered that Columbia Pictures had been using the name of a critic who didn't even exist, except within the imagination of the publicity department. At least those inventive flacks found one way to avoid wasting time with uncooperative wiseacres like me.

On occasion, they've also used other nefarious means to mislead the public about bad reviews, including quotations taken outrageously out of context. *Sneak Previews* made it easy for the studios to do that by providing them with written transcripts from each show. In 1987, for instance, a transcribed cross-talk with Jeffrey showed me lamenting a recent setback to a gifted actress whose work I'd always liked. Concerning her participation in a sultry stink bomb called *Summer Heat,* I declared, "Lori Singer is one of the most beautiful, magnetic, and riveting actresses . . . so it's a shame her performance is wasted in a movie with no plot or substance." The next Sunday, newspapers featured a full-page ad with my words (and my name) above the title in huge lettering that declared, "Lori Singer is one of the most beautiful, magnetic, and riveting young actresses." It took more than a dozen furious phone calls, and a full two weeks of intense annoyance as they continued to run ads implying my endorsement of a movie I disliked, before they finally managed to draft a new layout without my name.

Even the formidable Disney Company at times tried similar tricks. In 1997, I gave a mixed review to their tongue-in-cheek cartoon epic *Hercules,* declaring, "Unlike Disney's recent, more ambitious animated offerings, *Hercules* doesn't even try to qualify as a masterpiece." Inevitably, perhaps, they used my name at the top of their initial ads with the simple triumphal proclamation: *"A MASTERPIECE!"—Michael Medved.* At least the crack publicity department at the Magic Kingdom managed (in response to my vigorous complaints) to get some Fairy Godmother to wave a wand and lift this distortion almost immediately.

In light of all the embarrassment and inconvenience associated with *Sneak Previews,* my growing skepticism about Hollywood, and my long-standing distaste for TV, it seems irrational, at best, that I should devote so many years to working as a movie critic on television. In part, that unexpectedly durable tenure stems from the sense of competition and challenge associated with any demanding job: you keep the gig going even when it's not good for you because any sort of withdrawal would look to the world like a sign of defeat. Each year, it took so much fiercely committed and impassioned activism to keep *Sneak* on the air that I never bothered to ask the crucial and obvious question of whether that effort made sense for me. This preoccupation with process plays a prominent part in the TV world, where everyone operates under the unspoken, unchallenged assumption that appearing on air is such a valuable privilege that it justifies every manner of sacrifice or humiliation. Consider the irrational allure of so-called reality programming to millions and millions of Americans: the contestants on these shows never pause to consider the bugs they will eat, the insults they will endure, or the public mortification they will suffer. To many people, getting on TV represents a lifelong dream, an absolute and unalloyed good; any collateral damage that comes in pursuit of this transformational dream is therefore acceptable.

When I was a small kid, some of the hosts that I watched on cartoon shows used to refer to "all our friends, all you boys and girls, out there in TV Land." I now know that "TV Land" referred to the world of the audience, but at the time I thought it described the through-the-looking-glass, wondrous, mystical kingdom behind the screen, inhabited full-time by all the likable, good-looking people, adorable puppets, and fantastic creatures I saw on the tube. For me, *Sneak Previews* provided a twelve-year visa to the exotic enchantment of "TV Land," and it took me a while to realize that I needed, ultimately, to return home.

My involvement with the show proved all the more addicting because of the indications that fate had intervened to make that TV connection for me—the same sense of an ordained destination, if not destiny, that I associate with all the most important elements of my life. Six years—or halfway—into my *Sneak* experience, I went to dinner at John Davies's condo to celebrate the flourishing association made possible when he spotted me one night talking about *The Hollywood Hall of Shame* on the *The Tonight Show*. Over beer and spaghetti, John emphasized his amazement at the way things had worked out: he almost never watched *The Tonight Show*, he said, and had just happened to tune in the night I appeared.

This fascinated me, since that night represented the third and final choice, with two other alternatives ruled out because of my observance of Jewish holidays. "You're sure, John, that you wouldn't have been watching any other night in that week?"

"Absolutely!" he replied, without hesitation. "I'm a hundred percent sure that's the only time I saw *The Tonight Show* that whole year!"

In other words, while I thought that my inconvenient religious commitment might cause me to sacrifice an important opportunity, by following that traditional path I ended up as a guest on the show on the night—the only possible night—when my appearance led me to an even greater opportunity that opened a whole new direction in my career. If that detour into years of intensive movie reviewing lacked some of the substantive satisfactions I craved, it still felt like part of the providential path I'd been assigned to follow, while I pursued deeper fulfillment in the more reliable arenas of faith and family.

LESSON

30

There Is No Such Thing as Planned Parenthood

As visibly affectionate newlyweds, Diane and I learned to handle an impertinent question from friends, acquaintances, and even well-meaning strangers. "So, you just got married!" they might say. "And how many kids do you plan to have?"

At first, we merely shrugged and declined to answer, or mumbled our defensive insistence that this decision wasn't in our control. My long, ultimately fruitless marriage to Nancy left me with an uncommon perspective on the childbearing process: I felt no sympathy whatever for the widespread, thoughtless assumption that you could choose the size of your family as easily as ordering appliances from a catalog. Eventually, I began responding with a combative edge to the inevitable questions about our family plans.

"Asking about how many children we want to have is like asking how many years I want to live," I might say. "Or asking me how rich I want to get. Sure, I hope for good things, but I'm not stupid enough to think that it's all up to me."

Even before I became a father, in other words, I emphatically rejected the trendy mantra of "choice" as the highest family value. The idea that parents can choose children effortlessly leads to the notion that they can discard them guiltlessly. People of faith (including most Orthodox Jews) tend to oppose abortion not just because their dogma condemns the practice, but because their belief system sees a Godly, spiritual element to any conception. A human baby—even at the very early stages of its development in the womb—represents some spark of the Divine, not just a blob of worthless protoplasm. This proposition seems so unassailable, so obvious, that there must be some deeper explanation for the stubborn refusal of so many otherwise thoughtful Americans to accept it. Why would anyone insist that a new life that had already begun to grow amounted to nothing more than a piece of the mother's body, rather than recognizing that developing fetus as a separate human possibility?

Ultimately, I'm convinced that the private history of Baby Boomers (and others) provides the best answer to the riddle of pro-choice absolutism. According to Planned Parenthood, more than thirty million American women have received a total of some forty million abortions since *Roe v. Wade* in 1973—meaning that a third of all women who've gone through childbearing years in this era must feel at least some impulse to legitimize a procedure they personally have experienced. Though some of those millions of abortions no doubt took place without the participation or awareness of the men most intimately involved, it's safe to say that a substantial percentage of American males have also accumulated some direct knowledge (and potential guilt) regarding the termination of pregnancies.

Fortunately, I never went through such an ordeal myself, though my irresponsible behavior (particularly during the years as a liberal political operative) easily might have landed me in the situation of an unwanted conception. During my senior year at Yale, my girlfriend, Faye, accompanied one of her classmates from Connecticut College on a train ride to New York City to get an abortion at a time when the procedure remained strictly illegal in Connecticut. I took both women out to dinner at a Chinese restaurant upon their return, but the two of them wept so bitterly and inconsolably that they could barely eat. Long after I had come to recognize that a child represented a gift, not a choice, my recollection of this experience helped to keep me politically pro-choice. I felt pity for Faye's devastated friend, and contempt for the boyfriend who had washed his hands of the whole situation, but I couldn't imagine that either of them belonged in jail. Diane also shared the conviction of most other females of her generation that a woman "had the right to control her own body," and her first book, *Children: To Have or Have Not* clearly advanced the idea that couples could make choices about offspring.

In time, her deepening religious involvement began to alter her outlook. Six months after our wedding, we traveled to Israel to celebrate the marriage of my brother Jonathan. The journey represented my first visit to the Jewish state since infancy, and for Diane it was the first trip ever. In the days preceding the ceremony, Jonathan and my dad took us on hectically scheduled sightseeing trips across the country. Despite my determination to resist the sentimental manipulation of my brother's frankly Zionist agenda—Jon emphasized the political, nationalistic aspects of Jewish identity—I was unexpectedly overwhelmed with emotion. On a scorching hot day in the Old City of Jerusalem, we walked to the Western Wall. Jews don't call it the "Wailing Wall" anymore, since we stopped wailing after our people's return to the Biblical homeland. Nevertheless, to see and to touch the last remnant of a Holy Temple utterly destroyed by the Romans nearly two thousand years ago left my family and me awed into a stunned silence. We prayed for a while at the Wall, placing tentative hands on those enormous, ancient blocks of stone; I stood beside my father on the men's side of the divider, while Diane went on her own to the women's section. I followed the centuries'-old tradition of leaving a scrap of paper with a written plea in one of the gaps in the wall, writing out a brief request that God might grant us a child we could name in honor of the departed members of the family I remembered so vividly—my sweet grandparents, or my fondly remembered Uncle Moish. Diane stayed and prayed longer, more intensely, than we did; in view of her recent conversion, this visit represented even more of a homecoming. Through her own passion and commitment, she had recaptured her family's Jewish connection—linking with the ancestors on her father's side who, only seventy generations earlier, surely would have made pilgrimage journeys to this same Temple site. When she walked back to us from her private prayers and her shining, tearful face with the piercing blue eyes came clearly into view, I felt dizzy, breathless, filled with adoration and gratitude.

Shortly after our return to California, a visit to the doctor confirmed

the glorious news of Diane's pregnancy. We wanted to make an announcement to all members of the family but we waited. According to Jewish tradition, we follow a commonsense principle of avoiding any public talk
about a new baby until at least ninety days have passed since conception.
Obstetric statistics suggest that half of all conceptions end in natural miscarriages, though in most cases the woman isn't even aware that she was
pregnant. Among identified pregnancies, between 20 and 25 percent will
miscarry, with the overwhelming majority of these babies lost in the first
trimester. We therefore waited, and prayed, and went to the doctor for an
ultrasound; she provided us with a shiny, grainy, black-and-white image of
our healthy baby, growing comfortably inside Diane.

Three and a half months into the pregnancy, according to our best
calculations, we attended a wedding for one of our good friends at Pacific
Jewish Center. We sat at a table with my father, who took notice when
Diane turned down a waiter's offer of champagne. "What's the matter?" my
dad wanted to know. "You usually take a little bit of bubbly, so we can say
l'chaim together. You don't even want a little sip?"

My wife and I exchanged significant glances, knowing this was the
moment for the dramatic disclosure we had planned. "Dad," I began,
"there's actually a reason that Di isn't supposed to drink any alcohol right
now." His mouth opened wide as he put together the evidence. "You
mean . . . ? You mean . . . ?" my father stammered. He burst into tears, then
jumped up and grabbed his daughter-in-law, squeezing her so hard that I
worried about the safety of the baby. If anything, my mother reacted to our
news with even more overjoyed excitement and wanted to spend time with
Diane shopping for baby things. Our new addition meant the beginning of
a new generation for the family, the first grandchild on either side.

In our private moments, Diane and I saw the situation as the ultimate
confirmation of our love, a sign that God had smiled on our marriage with
this gift of new life before we even reached our first anniversary. The
atmosphere at home felt so blissful and optimistic that I felt shocked by
Diane's irritable mood one Sunday night in November. In contrast to her
normally sunny, explosively energetic disposition, she seemed edgy and
resentful as we stumbled into a stupid, utterly pointless argument—the
biggest of our marriage, in fact—about trivial scheduling details in the
week ahead. We went to bed without settling anything and slept fitfully

until Diane woke up at two in the morning, bleeding and suffering horrific pain. I rushed her to the emergency room of the nearest hospital and watched with dread as they sat her in a wheelchair and took her away.

The next four hours I sat in the waiting room, desperately worried about my wife. I stared at the glossy photos on the wall, showing barns and cows, waterfalls and forests, obviously meant to reassure the grim, hurt faces gathered in this waiting room at the small hours of the morning. I knew we faced a grave problem with the baby, but I couldn't even think about the child I'd never met; I only wanted them to bring Diane back to me, healthy and whole.

When they finally brought Diane down, she was in the wheelchair, looking small and pale, still groggy from her general anesthetic. She had lost the baby, of course, after excruciating pain—the worst in her life—followed by a D & C (dilation and curettage). A miscarriage in the middle of the fourth month of pregnancy is no minor matter, though the only permanent reminder of the baby survived in that one photo from the ultrasound. Any lingering temptation to take the process of childbearing for granted as a smooth, natural phenomenon, ultimately under human control, disappeared forever on that hazy November morning.

We tried not to think about children or conception in the months that followed, concentrating on our work and the stunning growth of our Pacific Jewish Center community. Almost exactly one year and one month after the miscarriage, we returned to the hospital at the timely, normal conclusion of a new pregnancy, throughout which Diane had been blessed with spectacular good health. As the baby finally emerged after twenty hours of labor, the doctor announced, "There it is . . . there it is . . . a beautiful baby . . . girl!" Apparently, my immediate reaction was to pronounce a startled expletive. I had been certain, confident beyond all reason, that our firstborn would be a boy. We always, inevitably, had boys in the Medved family: in our family of four brothers, we didn't know what to do with girls. But when I took the new lady in my life out of the delivery room for her first bath, I couldn't help but stare in wonder at the all-important stranger.

In a Saturday afternoon service at our synagogue, we named her Sarah: after my grandmother, the kind-hearted, blue-eyed heroine who had watched her own five daughters die in Russia before coming to the favored earth of America to begin a new life with the birth of my dad. Our

Sarah gave us our own new life, as Diane and I doted together on our chubby, adorable, willful, prodigiously gifted (which was obvious even before her first birthday) baby daughter. Our charmed little circle expanded when my brother Jonathan and his wife, Jane, moved from Israel to California so Jon could help my dad with his struggling high-tech company; the couple rented a house literally four doors up the block from ours. We shared raucous meals almost every Sabbath, with Jonathan (led in part by his brilliant, Orthodox-leaning wife) becoming more traditionally observant and active in Pacific Jewish Center. Together we celebrated the good news that Jane and Jon were expecting their first baby; Sarah would soon have a first cousin only nine months younger than herself.

Unfortunately, that baby came much too early and the grim atmosphere in the hospital, as we rallied to support Jonathan, brought back searing memories of our miscarriage. Nearly three months premature, my brother's little boy weighed scarcely three pounds and survived in an incubator, facing daunting prospects for survival. When they finally brought the little boy home, they named him Moshe—in honor of my Uncle Moish, who had inspired Jonathan as he had inspired me. Seventeen years later, this tiny, struggling infant had become my strapping, magnificent nephew, nicknamed Momo, more than six feet tall, as he prepared for service in the Israeli army. A local hero as a volunteer paramedic, Momo achieved a brilliant record at his elite religious academy and as a leader of the first Israeli national debate team to sweep the European championships. The entire world, in short, counts as a better place because a tiny speck of humanity who decided to leave the womb painfully early, managed to win his struggle for life.

Momo's birth, our own experience with delivery and miscarriage, my vain prior attempts to conceive a child with Nancy—all worked together to change my attitude on the defining issue of abortion. Momo had developed for barely six months before he entered our world, and yet the strident advocates for unfettered "choice" insist upon their right to kill precisely that sort of child. Such a baby living within his mother may face a very different, far more secure situation than my nephew in his incubator, but there is no difference whatever in the extent of their development or their essential personhood. Having endured a terrifying miscarriage (and going through two more unsuccessful pregnancies on the way to welcoming our two additional kids), we couldn't look upon the concept of "termination of pregnancy" with the same benign indifference that the pro-abortion forces stubbornly maintained.

At the same time we lived through our transforming private experiences, I engaged in an honest examination of public data that forced a total rethinking of my attitude toward abortion. One of the early slogans for pro-choice crusaders promised "Every Child a Wanted Child," suggesting that with a legally guaranteed right to put an end to an unwanted pregnancy, far fewer unwed and teenaged mothers would see their lives ruined by unplanned babies they couldn't effectively raise. Contrary to all expectations, however, the rate of single motherhood skyrocketed under the new national policy of abortion-on-demand required by *Roe v. Wade.* In 1970, before that fateful court decision, 10.7 percent of all U.S. births were to single mothers; by 1985 (the year of our miscarriage), out-of-wedlock birth had exploded, disastrously, to 22 percent; by 2000, the figure had reached an appalling 33.4 percent—more than triple the percentage from the purported "dark ages" before every woman enjoyed the sacred right to "choose."

Rather than building a new culture of conscientious choice, the abortion revolution actually encouraged the idea that you could enjoy sex without consequences. Even if young people behaved irresponsibly, "enlightened" opinion suddenly promised them an easy way that local clinics could "fix" any problem that resulted. The altered behavior that naturally followed—producing a staggering combination of some forty million abortions together with a tripling of the out-of-wedlock birth rate—suggests a truly massive, unprecedented upsurge in reckless sexuality. In any event, only activist true believers utterly blinded by irrational commitment could possibly claim that the Abortion Industrial Complex has in any way succeeded in its self-proclaimed goal of reducing the number of children thrust into unprepared, unmarried households.

Beyond rational argument or intimate family history, Jewish law speaks unequivocally on this issue, banning even early-stage abortion unless the mother faces a direct threat to her survival. Rabbi J. David Bleich, the leading contemporary expert on Jewish medical ethics, writes, "A Jew is governed by such reverence for life that he trembles lest he tamper unmindfully with the greatest of all divine gifts, the bestowal or withholding of which is the prerogative of G-d alone. Although he be master over all within the world, there remain areas where man must fear to tread, acknowledging the limits of his sovereignty and the limitation of his understanding. In the unborn child lies the mystery and enigma of existence. Confronted by the miracle of life itself, man can only draw back in awe before the wonder of the Lord."

This attitude, deeply rooted in Jewish culture and faith, may help to account for the infrequently noted fact that every study indicates that the women in our community remain far less likely to abort their babies than other Americans. Given the clear teaching of our tradition and our infrequent resort to the termination of pregnancies in the real world, the overwhelming Jewish support for the pro-choice side of the national debate looks painfully mystifying. Like so many other puzzling aspects of current Jewish existence, the strangely sympathetic attitude toward abortion arises out of a deep fear of Christian faith rather than any affirmation of our own—an irrational, paralyzing fear, in fact, that I became increasingly eager to combat.

A More Christian America Is
Good for the Jews

Many—if not most—American Jews harbor the stubbornly irrational conviction that a Christian revival in this country would threaten their security and survival. To them, religious faith amounts to a zero-sum game so that any strengthening or intensification of Christianity leads inexorably to a diminution of Judaism.

This argument pointedly ignores the evidence of the recent past: in the 1950s, the Jewish community experienced an unprecedented wave of suburban synagogue construction, along with vastly increased rates of congregational affiliation, all at precisely the same time that the Christian community went through its own surge of church attendance ("The Family That Prays Together Stays Together") and public activism (the insertion of the words "under God" in the Pledge of Allegiance). Two decades later, the dynamic, much-discussed *Baal T'shuvah* ("Return") movement in Judaism coincided with the explosive growth of Evangelical and Pentecostal Christianity—in both cases led by young people from disaffiliated or casually engaged homes who passionately embraced more fervent and traditional forms of religiosity than their parents ever practiced. There's no logical or empirical basis to assume that a trend which sees Christians taking their own faith more seriously will somehow force Jews to move in the opposite direction and to discard our traditions more thoughtlessly. In fact, it's easy to argue that more respectful attention for Christianity (in its various manifestations) will likely spill over to encourage Jews to look more carefully at the substance of our own ancient creed.

A more Christian America need not menace Judaism (or any other minority religion), but it does threaten secularism—and despite confusion on the part of left-leaning agencies in the Jewish community, the interests of secularism and Judaism do not count as identical. It may weaken Christianity, for instance, if large numbers of our fellow citizens claim no religious affiliation, but that disaffiliation in no way can be said to strengthen Judaism. An individual who rejects the Messianic claims of Jesus of Nazareth may exclude himself from the Christian community, but that simple act of rejection hardly qualifies him as a Jew. Our faith centers on the affirmation of its own time-honored teachings and demands, not merely denial of the beliefs of the nation's Christian majority. For years, demographers and Jewish leaders have warned that assimilation and intermarriage harm our community's long-term prospects far more seriously than anti-Semitism, and secularism facilitates both those debilitating forces. If, for instance, my Catholic girlfriend during senior year at college had felt a deeper personal commitment to her own faith tradition, our relationship never would have gone as far as it did and precipitated a withering family crisis. It's an irreligious, secularist approach that erases the distinctions between Christians and Jews and strips our people of any basis for a continued independent existence.

These logical arguments enabled me to avoid the suspicion and wariness that most Jews feel toward outspoken, zealous Christians, even before I began working closely with serious Evangelicals and Catholics. It helped that my personal interaction with religious Christians of every denomination had always been pleasant and positive, beginning with my membership in a Boy Scout troop that met every week in the basement of the red brick Presbyterian Church in the Point Loma neighborhood of San Diego. Even though I grew up in a community where Jews represented only a tiny minority, I never felt pressured or persecuted, and experienced only a single incident of anti-Semitism (a couple of cigarette-smoking, tough-guy creeps throwing pebbles at me and calling me "Hebe" one awful afternoon as I walked home from junior high). At Yale, I not only attended Reverend Coffin's chapel services but also came to appreciate "The God Squad," a group of bright and personable undergraduates fervently dedicated to evangelism, who stood out for being clean-cut and courteous in the ragged and rebellious '60s. Some of my classmates felt threatened by these missionaries—who would sit down with you, uninvited, in the dining hall to talk earnestly, respectfully, about the need to find a personal relationship to Christ—but I pointedly preferred their good manners and self-discipline to the far more aggressive proselytizing of the rank-smelling SDSers and other minions of the trendy left. A few years later, in Berkeley, I formed a friendship with my upstairs neighbors, Doug and Debbie Krieger, an unfailingly friendly couple who were trying to "plant" a church amidst the heathen hippies; their wholly supportive interest in learning about my Jewish observance confirmed my positive attitude toward serious Christians. When we were revitalizing Congregation Mishkon Tephilo in Venice, my next-door neighbor, a retired Presbyterian pastor named Reverend Lees, did everything he could to assist and encourage us. And when the Pacific Jewish Center's day school outgrew its temporary home in a Reform Jewish Temple, the Ocean Park Christian Church allowed us to move into its unused school building virtually rent-free until we purchased our own property, pleased to help an educational institution that encouraged reverence for God and meticulous Bible study.

In short, my personal encounters with Christian believers over the years introduced me to a group of people who came across as kind, upbeat, productive, sincere, down-to-earth, and consistently respectful—if not outright supportive—of my own Jewish religiosity. I strongly suspect that nearly all my fellow Americans have had similar interactions with serious Christians. This doesn't mean that you won't run across more than a few oddballs, hypocrites, crooks, or fanatics among the tens of millions of people who identify themselves as people of faith, but the overall level of decency, of unalloyed niceness, remains high enough within the Christian community that it's hard to understand why so many skeptics look on these fervent believers with fear and resentment. In most cases, I'm convinced that such negativity—especially on the part of my fellow Jews— stems more from negative media imagery than from any real-world experience. Typical Americans spend far more hours in the week watching TV, DVDs, or movies than they do interacting with their actual friends and neighbors, which means that abrasive broadcast presentations by controversial evangelists, or Hollywood's frequent, fictional portrayals of crazed, corrupt Christian clergymen, easily overwhelm the pleasant impressions left by flesh-and-blood casual acquaintances.

During my first months on *Sneak Previews* I got the chance to express this long-standing concern about antireligious stereotypes in movies when we reviewed a heavily hyped Jane Fonda project called *Agnes of God*. The movie opens with the uplifting spectacle of a disturbed young nun played by Meg Tilly giving birth in a convent, apparently murdering her baby, and then flushing the tiny, bloody corpse down the toilet. Anne Bancroft portrays the stern mother superior with appallingly medieval ideas, who wants to cover up the crime, but Fonda plays a probing psychiatrist determined to get to the bottom of the case. Columbia Pictures promoted the duel between the two strong women as a dramatization of "the eternal struggle between science and faith," but with the morose and mediocre movie so squarely on Fonda's side it never feels like an evenly matched battle. When we discussed the film on the air, Jeffrey Lyons praised the accomplished performances while I slammed its shallow, one-sided dismissal of religious faith and its tired recycling of anti-Catholic caricatures. During our cross-talk (the brief, unscripted exchange about the movie under discussion) I added, "As you know, I'm not a Catholic, but it doesn't matter what your religious orientation, everybody's got to be a little bit tired of all of the Catholic bashing out of Hollywood. In one movie after another, you've got lecherous priests or pregnant nuns or corrupt cardinals, and it's never balanced by anything positive. It's really become a form of religious bigotry, it seems to me, and I don't think it's fair."

To my surprise and satisfaction, the weeks that followed brought an avalanche of mail supporting my position and thanking me for speaking out against the entertainment industry's increasingly blatant anti-Catholic bias. I received a particularly touching letter from a monsignor in St. Louis who worked with the homeless and destitute; he wrote that he had cried tears of gratitude when he heard my brief remarks, having become heartsick over the way movies and television had made the public notably more suspicious of those who dedicated their lives to serving Christ and the

Church. Deeply encouraged by the public reaction to my passing comments, I pushed for the chance for a more extensive exploration of the issue of the overall relationship between the movie business and organized faith.

After several weeks of badgering, Jeffrey and our producers agreed to follow my lead in broadcasting a *Sneak Previews* special on Hollywood's grudge against religion. Every fourth week, we faced the challenge of creating a "trend show" that focused on a broader topic in the movie world rather than reviewing the new releases (these "evergreen" episodes could then be rebroadcast during the summer hiatus). Before my arrival, the trend shows focused mostly on retrospectives of important directors or stars, or revealed the personal taste of the cohosts with dueling lists of favorite comedies or love stories or mysteries. I pushed hard to use the trend shows to take on social and political issues, examining the impact of movie messages. We eventually put together challenging programs called "Kids Know Best" (about Hollywood's contemptuous attitude toward parents), "Sex for Sale" (about the movie fascination with prostitution), "Does Hollywood Bash Big Business?" (the answer was obvious), "Hollywood's Afterlife" (which featured a recent spate of sex-after-death movies), and other topics that provoked strong response, both positive and negative, from the audience.

The first of these issue-oriented trend shows, "Hollywood vs. Religion," remained our most influential and popular, receiving several rebroadcasts. I even fought and won a battle to include a brief scene from a well-crafted dramatic film by the Billy Graham organization (it was called *Cry from the Mountain*) to show that the religious community had become so frustrated with hostility from the mainstream media that it had begun making its own faith-based alternatives. We received a few angry phone calls from executives at scattered public television stations who considered it somehow inappropriate that our show would consider a project with an openly evangelical agenda, as if even the slightest recognition of an openly religious film betrayed the PBS mandate and played into the hands of some unspecified enemy. I began to discover the power of any religious discussion to mobilize passions on all sides, while ongoing debate over recent changes in movie characterizations of religious believers helped me develop my distinctive voice in the national conversation about media and values.

That conversation became something of a shouting match in the summer of 1988 with the explosive controversy over Martin Scorsese's embattled adaptation of the Nikos Kazantzakis novel *The Last Temptation of Christ*. Even before the film's opening, more than 25,000 demonstrators gathered at Universal City, California, in the largest protest ever mounted against the release of a motion picture. Though characterized by one typical commentator (for the *Detroit Free Press*) as "sour, fun-loathing people" representing the "know-nothing wacky pack," the leaders of the protest included Hollywood insiders (like a former vice president of Disney) and a courageous Reform Jewish rabbi and Holocaust survivor. MCA/Universal, the vast conglomerate distributing the film, treated all questions about its contents with arrogant indignation and made no attempt whatever to ease the concerns of the demonstrators. When one minister from Atlanta, Richard G. Lee of Rehoboth Baptist Church, collected 135,000 signatures opposing the film's release, he repeatedly called Universal to ask that a company representative take ten minutes to formally receive the documents, but the public relations executives refused to cooperate. Pastor Lee recalled: "In our last conversation they told us, 'We don't care about your petitions. Leave them with the guards, and we'll put them in the dump.' They were saying, 'We don't care about the opinions and the heartbeat of a hundred and thirty-five thousand Americans.'"

In this roiling controversy, I felt instinctive sympathy for the Christian leaders who expressed a sense of violation and outrage over Universal's callous disregard of their concerns. It struck me as hypocritical in the extreme that the same Hollywood establishment that eagerly consulted with gay activist, environmental, or animal rights groups before filming any vaguely sensitive script should fail to draw input from representatives of the nation's majority religion when it came to a movie questioning the very nature of their Lord. After its release, the film drew condemnation from the National Council of Catholic Bishops, the National Catholic Conference, the Southern Baptist Convention (with fourteen million members), the Orthodox Church of America, the archbishop of Canterbury (head of the worldwide Anglican Church), the archbishop of Paris, the Christian Democratic Party of Italy (the nation's largest political party), and Mother Teresa of Calcutta, among many others.

Nevertheless, I tried to keep an open mind about the movie's aesthetic quality because of my respect for its director, Martin Scorsese, who'd crafted some of the most challenging films of the 1980s (including *Raging Bull,* chosen in a poll of film critics as the greatest film of the decade). Two weeks before the much-debated release of *Last Temptation,* I gathered with a dozen other reviewers to see the picture at a weekday afternoon showing in a small screening room at the Universal lot. Unfortunately, as the simultaneously accursed and acclaimed film unreeled before our attentive eyes, it became clear almost immediately that Scorsese might have retitled his magnum opus *Raging Messiah.* Within the first five minutes came a scene in which Jesus (Willem Dafoe) inexplicably assists the Romans in crucifying some innocent Jewish victim. As they nail the poor man's feet to the bottom of the cross, blood spurts out and covers Christ's passive, poker-faced cheek. This scene only marked the beginning of the film's general portrayal of Christ as delusional and dislikable. This radical retelling of the story of Jesus of Nazareth culminated in the scene that generated most of the controversy and condemnation—the "temptation" scene, when a child-like angel takes Jesus down from the cross and shows him a vision of what his life could be like as an ordinary mortal if he survived the crucifixion, including a graphic sex scene with Mary Magdalene (Barbara Hershey).

In its painfully padded two-hour-and-forty-minute length, the movie delivers an almost endless stream of ludicrous and incompetent elements. Harvey Keitel, for instance, plays the crucial part of Judas with his Brooklyn accent firmly intact, braying out his lines like a minor Mafioso trying to impress his bosses. He looks as if he accidentally wandered onto the desert set from a very different Martin Scorsese film, and appears for some reason in a flaming orange fright wig that makes him look like a Biblical Bozo. The picture is crammed with such idiotic touches—from Jesus reaching into his chest and pulling out his bloody pumping heart to the resurrected Lazarus answering a question about the contrast between life and death by mumbling, "There isn't that much difference." In response to its memorably miscalculated moments, some of my normally restrained colleagues at the critics' screening at Universal began snickering, hooting, and laughing aloud midway through picture's all-but-insufferable length.

When we finally staggered out into the light of day, blinking our eyes and shaking our heads in disbelief, a TV camera crew from a national entertainment show approached a few of the recognizable reviewers and asked for our instantaneous responses. I told them, "It's the height of irony that all this controversy should be generated by a film that turns out to be so breathtakingly bad, so unbearably boring. In my opinion, the controversy about the picture is a lot more interesting than the film itself."

That comment forever ended my chances of making Martin Scorsese's Christmas card list, since it was widely quoted in the national media as part of the continuing debate over the new motion picture and its significance. I remain convinced that any impartial appraisal must conclude that the movie constituted an artistic disaster—and it certainly qualified as a financial disaster, drawing sparse audiences despite all the publicity. Nevertheless, *Last Temptation* earned largely positive reviews (and a ridiculously undeserved, surprise Oscar nomination for Best Director) because of Hollywood's circle-the-wagons mentality. In response to the angry denunciations from the Christian community, many commentators fiercely defended the film in the name of "freedom of expression" without confronting the evidence of its aesthetic incompetence. For instance, the one critic who had snorted the loudest and clucked most derisively at the afternoon screening we attended together later provided a report to the public that featured glowing praise and only the most minor reservations. When I called him to ask about the contrast between his privately expressed contempt and his on-the-record admiration, he cited the need to rally for "artist's rights" and to support the beleaguered genius, Scorsese. "He's under attack, so I can't hit a good man when he's down," he said. "Besides, if I slammed the picture, then people would associate me with Falwell— and there's no way I'm ready for that."

Of course, I'd already associated myself with Christian conservatives in their critique of Hollywood's ongoing antireligious bias, so I felt no hesitation in speaking out freely and forcefully about this movie in numerous interviews with print and electronic journalists. I tried to draw the essential distinction between imposing censorship and questioning sponsorship: it didn't amount to "book burning" or fascism for Christian leaders to ask why a major entertainment company elected to spend millions to produce and promote a misbegotten project sure to offend hundreds of millions of believers. If a big studio chose to make a film biography of Martin Luther King that concentrated on dramatizing reports of his irresponsible and kinky womanizing, would anyone question the right of the black community (and many others) to express their indignation? Does it make sense for a society in which more than 85 percent identify as Christians to treat Dr. King, as great as he was, as a more sacrosanct figure than Jesus?

The angry dispute over *The Last Temptation of Christ* didn't initiate Hollywood's hostility to religion, it merely called attention to it; sadly, the film's underlying attitudes were typical rather than exceptional. I got a chance to expand on this point of view when I received an invitation to deliver a series of lectures at Hillsdale College in Michigan in March 1989. Hillsdale had recently become famous among conservatives when it defied federal "civil rights" directives to classify all its students according to race; as one of the first academic institutions in the country to admit African-American students (a decade before the War Between the States), the school refused to abandon its long, proud tradition of color blindness. As a result of this battle, the small liberal arts college (with an enrollment of 1,500 students) lost all governmental support; its students were even prohibited from applying for federal loans and financial aid. Hillsdale's courageous battle for educational independence drew impassioned and generous support from leading figures on the right and led to ambitious lecture programs that drew a procession of world-famous figures (Ronald Reagan, Margaret Thatcher, Jeane Kirkpatrick, William F. Buckley, Bill Bennett, Tom Wolfe) to its remote but picturesque campus among the farms and fields of South Central Michigan.

My trip to Hillsdale not only began a long-standing and fruitful association with the school but also brought greatly enhanced attention and support to my arguments about Hollywood's disconnect from the general public. Hillsdale published a transcript of one of the talks during my visit ("Hollywood vs. Religion") in its journal *Imprimis*, which at the time reached 300,000 readers (it now boasts a circulation approaching 2 million). A few months later, *Reader's Digest* (the nation's top circulation magazine) ran a slightly edited version of the same lecture. My presentation not only covered the popular culture's hypocrisy in coping with *The Last Temptation of Christ* but also described a series of mostly wretched recent films (*The Runner Stumbles, Mass Appeal, Monsignor, Crimes of Passion, Light of Day, Salvation, Riders of the Storm, Pass the Ammo, Poltergeist II,* and, yes, *Agnes of God*) that provided the public with a sad series of extreme and ugly caricatures of Christian believers. I made the point that these projects remained mostly obscure (despite the presence of big stars like Dick Van Dyke, Michael J. Fox, Christopher Reeve, Kathleen Turner, and many more) because they proved to be resounding flops at the box office. "Taken together, these pictures lost hundreds of millions of dollars for the people who made them," I declared. "Hunger for money can explain almost everything in Hollywood, but it can't explain why ambitious producers keep launching expensive projects that slam religion. . . . It is hard to escape the conclusion that there is a perverse sort of idealism at work here. For many of the most powerful people in the entertainment business, hostility to traditional religion goes so deep and burns so intensely that they insist on expressing that hostility, even at the risk of commercial disaster."

I recalled a revealing private conversation with an influential film executive concerning the notorious 1985 fiasco *King David* starring Richard Gere—an insipid epic that cost $30 million to make and attracted less than $5 million in domestic ticket sales. Beyond the bizarre casting (industry wags referred to the project as *An Israelite and a Gentleman*), the film advanced the revolutionary (and entirely unsupported) notion that the embittered Biblical king freed himself from his primitive, religious delusions at the end of his life. One of the concluding sequences shows the suddenly enlightened David violently rejecting God as he smashes, in excruciating slow motion, a scale model of the holy Temple he had planned to construct in Jerusalem. A few weeks before the film's release, I spoke with one of its producers, who, knowing of my Jewish commitment, felt particularly proud to tell me all about his movie's "fresh, daring" take on its well-known subject matter. "We could have gone the easy way and played to the Bible Belt," he said. "But we wanted to make a film with guts. With integrity. We don't see David as a gung-ho, Holy Joe, Praise-the-Lord kind of guy. We wanted to make him a richer, deeper character." In his mind, in other words, secure religious faith counted as incompatible with depth of character.

His comments highlight one of the most important, often overlooked, motivations for countless Hollywood moviemakers: the desire to be taken seriously. The ever-present urge to make a buck isn't the only factor shaping creative and business decisions in the popular culture. Actors, executives, producers, or directors who've achieved enough power to launch or block major projects don't need to worry about where their next meal is coming from—or their next Mercedes, for that matter. They do, however, yearn for the respect of their peers, which is why Oscars and dozens of other laughably trivial awards loom so large for the Tinseltown community. Consider the well-established pattern of popular glamour girls or muscular action stars taking outrageous risks in edgy little pictures to play suffering or villainous characters: potential artistic acclaim means more to them than surefire commercial success. Steven Spielberg crafted many of the top-grossing movies all time (*Jaws, E.T.,* the *Indiana Jones* and *Jurassic Park* series) but only after he began making darker, less populist fare about the Holocaust and slave rebellions did he receive the respect—and Oscars—he had long craved (and deserved). On the other hand, Woody Allen and, yes, Martin Scorsese remain two of the most admired and celebrated directors in the business, inspiring several generations of eager film-school imitators, despite the fact that both geniuses have released an almost unbroken series of financial flops and box office disappointments.

This means that it's absurd to assume that when Woody Allen inserts poisonously insulting, resentful references to the Jewish religion in his films (*Everything You Always Wanted to Know About Sex, Radio Days,* and many others), or when former Catholic seminarian Scorsese portrays a raving, delusional Christ in *Last Temptation,* they're motivated by a drive to make more money or build personal popularity. They're making, rather, the sort of "personal statements" that may offend the general public but will earn applause for courage and audacity from a creative community that shares, almost unanimously, a contemptuous attitude toward traditional faith. If religious organizations and media watchdog groups condemn their work, all the better: as the *Last Temptation* flap unforgettably illustrated, such condemnation only enhances the inside-the-industry prestige of the problematic project. Religion offers the one subject, above all others, which everyone acknowledges as fundamentally serious. Therefore, antireligious references—no matter how silly, abusive, or downright hostile—can lend a misleading air of importance even to the most trivial projects.

I concluded my Hillsdale presentation with a cautionary word about boycotts, letter-writing campaigns, and other protests: since Hollywood trashed organized faith in order to defy, rather than flatter, the values of the movie-going masses, angry denunciations only validated the underlying agenda. The best way to make a difference, I argued, involved less complaining and more creating. Too many traditionalist denominations (unfortunately including Orthodox Judaism) had discouraged participation in mass media as a corrupting process, abandoning the field to one side of the religious-secular divide. The presence of more people of faith within the entertainment establishment would not only facilitate more projects sympathetic to Christianity and Judaism, but would also undermine some of the lingering antireligious stereotypes. Decision-makers in the industry elite might participate in various New Age cults (Scientology, the Kabbalah Center, Richard Gere's preferred forms of Tibetan Buddhism), but they rarely attended church or synagogue, and seldom knew friends who did. If important media executives began to encounter fervent believers as their colleagues and coworkers, they couldn't so easily write off religion itself as a deranged, fanatical force that preyed on the ignorant. With this goal in mind, I specifically applauded Christian organizations that had begun producing feature films "in order to create an alternative source of movie entertainment—providing motion pictures that reinforce family and spiritual values. . . . In the process, they may win back part of the mass audience for films that the movie industry has recently lost."

These comments produced an electrifying effect when circulated around the country through *Imprimis* and *Reader's Digest*. I instantly received invitations to speak at most of the religious organizations that had set themselves up as "movieland missionaries"—including InterMission, the Actor's Co-op, Mastermedia International, the Los Angeles Film Studies Center, and the Mormon group ALMA (Associated Latter-day Media Artists). I felt enormously energized, even uplifted, by the youthful idealism and the spirit of fellowship I discovered at these faith-based, guerilla-tactics, change-the-world operations. We also continued our energetic efforts at Pacific Jewish Center to reach out to the many unaffiliated Jews in the entertainment industry—and many prominent figures in Hollywood received their first encounter with traditional observance at our Sabbath table.

Meanwhile, Diane's work brought us into contact with the Christian counterculture that flourished in "flyover country," below the radar of the mainstream media. While nursing baby Sarah and quietly building her psychology practice, Diane had begun working on a new book about divorce, wanting to provide a practical guide on the right way to reach and implement a decision on terminating a marriage. It seemed a logical follow-up to her previous projects, *Children: To Have or Have Not* and *First Comes Love: Deciding Whether or Not to Get Married*. In the midst of her extensive research and interviews, however, Diane realized (as she wrote in her opening chapter) "that writing a 'morally neutral' book showing divorce to be just another option—a life choice no better or worse than staying married—would be irreparably damaging to the audience I wanted to help. . . . Quite simply, I discovered in my research that the process and aftermath of divorce is so pervasively disastrous—to body, mind, and spirit—that in an overwhelming number of cases, the 'cure' that it brings is surely worse than the marriage's 'disease.'" While candidly acknowledging her own divorce ("I am humiliated and mortified at failing in a relationship others at one time held exemplary") and specifying the circumstances where marital breakup is appropriate or even imperative, *The Case Against Divorce* emphasizes the most persuasive reasons to stay together, rebutting the seven most common "Exit Lines" used to justify unnecessary splits.

Praised by the *Wall Street Journal*, condemned by the *New York Times* (for its "judgmental" and "opinionated" tone), this feisty, groundbreaking volume made an important contribution to the national conversation and shortly after its publication, I happily chauffeured Diane to a Sunday evening panel discussion on marriage and divorce. The other principal panelist that night was Dr. James Dobson, though neither Diane nor I knew anything about him—which speaks volumes about the dumb, destructive divide between the secular pop culture that dominates the consciousness of most Americans and the vibrant world of Christian media and institutions. A one-time professor of psychology at USC Medical School, Dr. Dobson left academia to launch a national ministry, Focus on the Family, dedicated to preserving and applying timeless truths about marriage and children. By the time we met him, he'd already written a series of influential volumes that became big best-sellers in Christian bookstores and established himself as one of the nation's most popular broadcasters, with more than a thousand stations carrying his smart, folksy daily program. Unlike other media bigshots we'd met over the years (Diane had just finished an hour on the *Oprah* show debating her book), Dr. Dobson wore his fame comfortably, projecting the same genial, neighborly personality in private that he did in public. During the panel discussion, he enthusiastically endorsed Diane's arguments, and when we spoke with him privately after the session, he was just as generous in his praise. He also mentioned that he knew all about my work on media and religion and expressed his support for it. We gladly accepted his invitation to tour Focus on the Family's campus in Pomona and to join him as guests on his national radio broadcast.

Regardless of political or religious orientation, every open-minded observer must feel profoundly impressed by a visit to the Focus on the Family operation—either in its former command center in California or its current, vastly larger and more elaborate headquarters in Colorado Springs. Dr. Dobson proudly took us through the different components of his complex undertaking, including a vast mailroom that received some 250,000 monthly requests for help from families in trouble. Each one of these correspondents got a prompt response, often including an emergency check with the understanding that the recipient would, when possible, make his own contribution back to the ministry so others could benefit from its resources.

Our exposure to Dr. Dobson and Focus on the Family powerfully intensified our connection to the vibrant Christian community. Diane and I received invitations from churches, schools, and religious colleges across the country to deliver lectures or sermons on media and families. Diane generally declined these opportunities as our own family expanded: our second daughter, Shayna (named in honor of my mother's mother, my adored Oma), arrived in 1989, the same year *The Case Against Divorce* was published. With a growing family, I made an effort to maximize the amount of time I spent at home, but I also embraced the chance to connect with the centers of religious energy and creativity in every corner of the country. While I continued to speak regularly at major universities and at synagogues and Jewish Community Centers, I started giving higher priority to Christian colleges in out-of-the-way places—Searcy, Arkansas (Harding University); Virginia Beach, Virginia (Pat Robertson's Regent University); Steubenville, Ohio (Franciscan University); Decorah, Iowa (Luther College); Abilene, Texas (Abilene Christian University); Rexburg, Idaho (Rick's College), and scores of other little-known municipalities. I tried to convey the same message to these students as I did anywhere else:

that they shouldn't ignore the potent influence of media imagery in shaping real-world values and behavior.

Despite the demands of this trave, I cherished the opportunity to speak at these schools, not because of the money (I often spoke at religious institutions for modest or nonexistent honoraria) but because the visits to Christian colleges put me in direct contact with a healthier, more hopeful America than most people in LA, New York, or Washington ever acknowledged. All national surveys on the subject of faith reveal the deep religious commitment of everyday Americans (nearly half of us attend church or synagogue weekly; two-thirds pray regularly; nearly 90 percent believe in an afterlife that delivers reward and punishment), but members of the media elite often question these figures because they seldom enjoy personal interaction with heartland believers. While most journalists focus on self-indulgence and hedonism among the *Dude, Where's My Car?* generation, I've had the chance to meet thousands upon thousands of well-scrubbed, hardworking young people who focus more energy on the question "Dude, where's my savior?"—committed to serving God and country, to building compassionate communities and stable marriages, and to disproving the assumption that every smart student embraces slacker habits and leftist politics.

Whenever my fellow Jews question my long-standing and collaborative association with the so-called Christian Right, I try to explain to them the many ways that committed Catholics, Protestants, and Mormons actually help to ensure a vital Jewish future in this country. Most importantly, Christian revival in the United States is "good for the Jews" because it's good for America. On every significant challenge—whether it's crime or poverty or family breakdown or drug addiction or educational inadequacy—serious Christianity represents part of the solution, not part of the problem. Whether rehabilitating convicts, counseling drug addicts, feeding the homeless, facilitating adoptions, or building schools and clinics and hospices in America and around the world, people of faith play a vastly disproportionate role in trying to heal and redeem humanity. The generous heart of Christian America is so striking, and so strikingly obvious, that the fears of so many American Jews seem perplexing if not inexplicable.

For the most part, those fears arise out of the historical association between Christian fervor and violent anti-Semitism. Everyone in the Jewish community has heard the shocking tales of European pogroms and slaughters in which brutal marauders murdered, raped, and pillaged in the name of Jesus. Most American Jews can trace their ancestry to Poland, Germany, or Russia, where any increase in Christian fervor usually meant a new excuse for savage treatment of the Children of Abraham. My own grandmother, Sarah Medved, felt appropriately fearful of the local priest in her Ukrainian village because his anti-Semitic fulminations might at any time provoke violence or cruelty.

Unfortunately, Jewish leaders who apply such logic to contemporary America resemble bad generals who try to fight new battles with the strategy of the last century's war. Holding fast to the irrelevant lessons of another continent, they ignore the fact that in the more than 350 years that Jews have been in America and despite the uniquely intense Christian religiosity of the population, serious anti-Semitic outbreaks have been virtually nonexistent. The few exceptions to that rule—the lynching of Leo Frank in 1913, the Crown Heights riot in Brooklyn in 1991—reflected the work of political demagogues and street toughs rather than the religious passions of devoted churchgoers. The evidence of actual persecution or hatemongering by conservative Christians is just about nil. In fact, the few hundred fringe fanatics of the Christian Identity movement have drawn strenuous denunciation from leaders of every important denomination precisely because their anti-Semitism and racism betray authentic church teaching; when the heinous neo-Nazi David Duke ran for governor of Louisiana, no one did more to ensure his defeat than Pat Robertson, who identified him as a "false Christian."

Unfortunately, the Jewish people in the twenty-first century face more serious threats than a few delusional white supremacist skinheads in Idaho or the now-jailed "Aryan" uber-agitator David Duke. Though secular fundamentalists may prefer to focus their attention on the Catholic or Eastern Orthodox anti-Semites of yesteryear, it's hard to ignore the current reality of tens of millions of murderous Muslim extremists who menace Jewish lives and institutions in the Middle East, Europe, Latin America, and around the world. As it happens, our staunchest allies and most reliable protectors in this moment of peril are the passionately pro-Israel Christian conservatives that the liberals who dominate our community continue to fear and condemn. Ironically, the Jewish establishment feels more comfortable with the Israel-hating religious left than with the Israel-loving religious right. For reasons that defy sanity or any normal instinct for self-preservation, they express greater indignation over Christian conservatives who believe you must accept Jesus to achieve salvation than over the Christian liberals in the Presbyterian Church, USA, who in the summer of 2004 voted to block all investment of their giant portfolio (more than $7 billion) in any companies doing business with Israel. As for me, I'd rather ally myself with theological right-wingers and take my chances on the afterlife than cozy up to smug, pious, politically correct hypocrites who single out Israel as the one nation in all the world—not Sudan, Cuba, Syria, China, or North Korea—that merits economic sanctions intended to undermine its existential struggle for survival.

Of course, the Jewish left dismisses and distrusts the crucial support for Israel by Evangelical Christians because they suspect that this backing originates in a religious imperative based on an arcane understanding of End Times prophecies. It always seemed obvious to me that an alliance based on faith in Biblical truth might prove more durable and meaningful than one based merely on political expediency. Secularists in the Jewish community point with alarm to passages in the Book of Revelation that suggest a horrible fate for those Jews in the Messianic era who fail to embrace Jesus Christ, but I don't worry about such predictions; if I did, I'd be a Christian, not a Jew. Meanwhile, it's hard to see the downside in fervent believers who strive mightily to strengthen Israel because they believe it represents the fulfillment of Old Testament prophecy and will hasten the ultimate redemption.

Despite the nearly unanimous pro-Israel, philo-Semitic orientation of Christian conservatives, skeptics can't get past an ancient dispute over the road to redemption. Jewish friends invariably ask me, "How can you work with people who sincerely believe you're going straight to hell?" There's a simple, direct answer to that question: it's not a problem for me because I'm confident that they're wrong. As long as Christians don't treat me like hell in this world, or do anything to hasten my entry into the next world, why should I worry? If they don't insist that I accept their theology as the price of cooperation, how dare I insist that they accept mine?

While many Christians demonstrate an easygoing acceptance of the unbridgeable gap between their faith and ours, it's true that many others feel the need to speak to all nonbelievers (including me) about the Good News of eternal redemption through the blood of Jesus Christ. Unlike many of my fellow Jews, I've never felt offended by Christian efforts to witness to me; to Christians, the Great Commission of spreading the Gospel to the ends of the earth is every bit as natural and sacred as studying Torah, or keeping the Sabbath, should be to Jews. In any event, when a friend or acquaintance chooses to share with me the most precious gift he's ever received, I don't interpret that offer as an act of hate or disrespect; it never threatens me because I feel certain that God wants me to be a Jew and that my commitment to the old covenant, and the law, honors His will.

Christian conversionary efforts may offend many Jews (by imputing an "incomplete" or outmoded status to our faith), but on the most basic level, those missionary endeavors hardly represent a dire threat to our community. Christian conversionary efforts have met with feeble success among Jews. According to the best available figures, less than 4 percent of those Americans born as Jews currently practice some other religion—and only a tiny percentage of those converts (perhaps 15 percent, or 30,000 individuals across the country) identify themselves as "Messianic Jews," "Jews for Jesus," or members of any other specifically Hebraic Christian sect. Moreover, according to all available data, the number of born Christians who have converted to Judaism is substantially *larger* than the number of born Jews who have converted to any form of Christianity.

Christian revival doesn't endanger Jewish endurance, but secularism most certainly does. According to the American Jewish Committee, more than a million Jews—nearly 20 percent of the Jewish community in the United States—identify themselves as religiously unaffiliated; that's more than thirty times the number who say they're some form of "Messianic Jew." As my friend Rabbi Dov Fischer pointedly observed more than twenty years ago, the real problem for the future of the Jewish community isn't "Jews for Jesus," it's "Jews for Nothing." My children and grandchildren will live better and more secure lives as both Americans and Jews in a more conscientiously Christian United States. The long tradition of respectful pluralism (going back to separate colonies founded by Puritans, Quakers, Catholics, and Anglicans who needed to learn to work together in a Revolution) ensures breathing room for sects of every sort, while their continued free and open competition provides more religious vitality than in many European nations with their single official church. In this free-wheeling atmosphere, religious Jews can proudly and appropriately participate in the healthy ongoing dialogue about faith, truth, and godliness.

All my intense conversations with my Christian brothers and sisters have reaffirmed my conviction that America remains utterly abnormal in this world, with no real tradition of tormenting or oppressing religious heretics or dissenters. I soon learned that the inquisitors of the all-powerful entertainment industry, however, have devised their own means for punishing anyone who seeks to expose Hollywood's predations, prevarications, and pretensions.

LESSON
32

Hollywood Has Lost Touch
with America

On exceedingly rare occasions the process of public speaking can provide one of life's potent but inexplicable pleasures: a soaring, unexpected sense of assistance and transport by some mysterious force. In the midst of a talk, you'll suddenly notice that the words have begun to flow more easily—falling effortlessly into patterns of their own while your voice sounds alien and impressive to your own ears with its musicality and assurance. Anyone who stands frequently at a podium—from political candidates to college professors—will recognize what I'm writing about: it's a strange sensation of hitching a lift on something bigger and better than what you've planned, like catching a perfect wave on a boogie board, or feeling your hang glider lifted high off the ground by a long, smooth blast of air. You can never count on such freakishly favorable conditions, and they may last for only minutes at a time, but whenever you get them, they deliver one sweet, exhilarating ride.

In November 1990, in Orange County, California, I enjoyed about a half hour of such oddly enchanted energy while speaking to a group of about four hundred business and community leaders in what became the most important talk of my career. My friends at Hillsdale College regularly convene such regional forums across the country under the aegis of their Shavano Institute for National Leadership, and after the national impact of my previous talk for them, "Hollywood vs. Religion," they invited me to contribute to their session on "Faith and the Free Market." I welcomed the opportunity to address some of the broader pop cultural issues that seldom came up on *Sneak Previews* in the midst of our weekly slogs through the latest cinematic sludge. In fact, I began my speech with a fairly detailed description of an especially appalling picture I'd recently endured—a purportedly daring "art film" starring Michael Gambon and Helen Mirren called *The Cook, the Thief, His Wife, and Her Lover.*

The opening scene unfolds in the parking lot of an imposing restaurant, lit by ghostly neon, where a pack of stray dogs snarl over bloody hunks of rotten meat. Two refrigerator trucks pull up, loaded with dead fish and hanging pig carcasses, before attention shifts to a group of foppishly dressed thugs who tear the clothes off a struggling, terrified victim in order to smear his naked body with excrement. They force filth into his mouth and rub it in his eyes, then pin him to the ground while the leader of their merry band urinates, gleefully, all over him.

The fun proceeds in much the same spirit for two unbearable hours. We see sex in a toilet stall, deep kisses and tender embraces administered to a bloody and mutilated cadaver, a woman whose cheek is pierced with a fork, a shrieking and weeping nine-year-old boy whose navel is hideously carved from his body, a bubbling tureen of vomit-colored soup employed to scald the face of a restaurant patron, and an edifying vision of two naked, middle-aged lovers writhing ecstatically while enjoying intercourse in the back of a truck filled with rotting, maggot-infested garbage. The grand finale of the film shows the main character slicing off—and swallowing—a piece of carefully seasoned, elegantly braised human corpse in perhaps the most graphic scene of cannibalism yet portrayed in motion pictures. I told my astonished audience: "There is, in short, unrelieved ugliness, horror, and depravity at every turn. So naturally, the critics loved it. . . . The movie just made me sick, but the positive reviews made me angry."

I went on to read excerpts from the glowing notices provided by some of the nation's most influential critics. The *New York Times*'s Caryn James hailed *The Cook, the Thief, His Wife, and Her Lover* as "something profound and extremely rare: a work so intelligent and powerful that it evokes our best emotions." Ebert and Siskel praised the film as "provocative" and conferred their coveted "Two Thumbs Up" benediction. Richard Corliss of *Time* made disapproving reference to the X rating originally attached to this "splendid" work of art by an allegedly censorious ratings board, while describing *The Cook, the Thief* . . . as "exemplary, exciting, extraordinary, extravagant," and "X as in excellent."

My objections to such extreme, excessive, ex-static praise went well beyond normal aesthetic disagreements and led me to raise the possibility that my critical colleagues had committed a form of professional malpractice. While focusing on the picture's "raunchy humor" or "searing indictment of capitalistic corruption" they gave prospective moviegoers no honest indication of the intensity of the horrors they would experience if they paid their money to see the film. I made this point on a special segment of *Sneak Previews*, suggesting, "When you look at the great reviews for a loathsome little picture like this one, you can understand why so many people don't trust film critics anymore." This led to a flurry of especially hostile mail, condemning me for my "arrogance," "right-wing bias," and "moralistic bigotry." My correspondents argued that I should confine myself to evaluating the competence of a film's camera work, editing, or acting, but make no attempt to address its moral or intellectual content or to weigh the messages it might send to the movie-going public. In other words, the one aspect of a work of art that is always off-limits for a critic to consider is the one aspect that matters most.

As I declared to ringing applause in my Orange County speech: "This is the very nature of the cultural battle before us. It is, at its very core, a war against standards. It is a war against judgment. Its proponents insist that the worst insult you can offer someone today is to suggest that he or she is judgmental.

"One of the symptoms of the corruption and collapse of our national culture is the insistence that we examine only the surface of any work of art. The politically correct, properly liberal notion is that we should never dig deeper—to consider whether a given work is true, or good, or spiritually nourishing—or to evaluate its impact on society at large. Contemporary culture is obsessed with superficial skill and slick salesmanship while ignoring the more important issues of soul and substance. . . . Everywhere around us, in every realm of artistic endeavor, we see evidence of the rejection of traditional standards of beauty and worth. In the visual arts, in literature, in film, in music of both popular and classical varieties, ugliness has been enshrined as a new standard, as we accept the ability to shock as a replacement for the old ability to inspire."

The words tumbled out, offering a comprehensive, global indictment that went well beyond anything I had planned. I never use prepared text or written notes for my public presentations, since I believe that the creative process of assembling a talk for the first time before a live audience provides the occasion with an irreplaceable energy and spontaneity. This stubborn eccentricity works better on some occasions than others, but in Orange County I felt uniquely favored by an adoring audience (which interrupted two dozen times for applause, and provided a generous standing ovation) and by that precious, unpredictable sense of a favorable breeze at my back, helping voice and language to work together to say what I meant to say. I concluded with a plea to support a revolution in the entertainment industry: "As part of the continuing struggle we must do more than protest the bad, we should also begin promoting the good, and providing uplifting alternatives to the trash that currently dominates the scene. . . . Let the call go out immediately: the outnumbered good guys in Hollywood desperately need reinforcements! Keep in mind that the entertainment industry is one area of endeavor in which a few gifted individuals can still make an enormous difference . . . to make sure that popular culture will once again reflect—and encourage—the fundamental goodness of our people."

Such sentiments may have drawn wildly enthusiastic responses from the conservative crowds I addressed at various conferences, congregations, or religious campuses, but from the beginning I understood the very real career risks in my increasingly outspoken denunciations of Hollywood. Over the course of my first five years on *Sneak Previews*, I'd gradually settled into the role of controversial cultural curmudgeon—I'd moved beyond complaints about the movie industry's nasty, one-sided portrayal of religious believers to more sweeping challenges of the dark, demented nature of some of our national entertainment obsessions. My colleagues on the TV show began to worry about my outspokenness; during our unscripted "cross-talks," the producers frequently yelled "cut" and ordered retakes because I had stepped over some invisible line of nonpartisan propriety. I knew they wanted only what was best for me and for our show, and feared the consequences with PBS if I came across too unequivocally as a "shrill, right-wing fanatic." Conventional wisdom insisted that we assess movies according to some mythical standard of objectivity, but I maintained that no piece of entertainment, no matter how empty or trivial, could count as altogether "message free"; it therefore made no sense to pretend that those values, impressions, and ideas (about violence, or institutions, or success, or intimate relationships) never mattered and deserved no consideration in an honest discussion of motion pictures.

As expected, my growing determination to emphasize movie messages earned a notably negative reaction from the media and journalistic establishment. *TV Guide*, for instance, dramatically altered its assessment of our show because of new doubts about my "moralistic" tone. In May of 1986, as I completed my rookie season as cohost, the magazine had run an unreservedly enthusiastic review of *Sneak Previews*, hailing the fact that the show now rested in the "capable hands of Jeffrey Lyons and Michael Medved, both of whom are well-qualified to judge movies," and praising "the witty, perceptive, sometimes provocative comments of Lyons and Medved." Three years later, *TV Guide* reassessed the program and took particular note of my admittedly unconventional approach: "*Sneak Previews*, following Medved's lead more than Lyons', concentrates on the moral content of the films in question. Medved . . . tends to look for a homiletic hook wherever possible. He liked *Everybody's All-American* because it showed that marriage can be sexy. . . . If you're more interested in moral instruction than in movies, this is definitely the place to go."

Other publications displayed far greater hostility when they looked at our venerable PBS show. *Spy* magazine ran a large caricature of me, holding aloft a huge golden cross, and suggesting that I had personally hijacked *Sneak Previews* to serve my "Christian right" agenda. Based on "reports" from a disgruntled college intern who had worked a few weeks on our show, the article reported that I bullied Jeffrey into parroting lines that I fed him (which wasn't even vaguely true) and that my ultimate goal was to raise huge sums of money from right-wing contributors so I could run for Congress. This charge laughably missed the mark, since I've never seriously considered running for any electoral office (as a speechwriter and campaign consultant, I had gotten close enough to the political process to be turned off by its often devastating impact on marriage). Unfortunately, the story in *Spy* so disturbed the station's executives that they summoned me to appear at a meeting of top officials to promise them that I had no intention whatever of seeking political office.

Even after they accepted my assurance, I knew that they continued to worry over my high-profile image as an anti-Hollywood gadfly, especially after my allies at Hillsdale College published a transcript of my impassioned Orange County speech in their internationally circulated journal, *Imprimis*. The piece appeared under the title "Popular Culture and the War Against Standards," and *Reader's Digest* once again ran its own condensed version, this time using the headline "A noted film critic deplores . . . THE BATTLE AGAINST BEAUTY & TRUTH." I received a flood of invitations from radio talk shows across the country that wanted me to discuss the charges in my piece and from newspaper reporters who were fascinated by the story of a television film critic who had dared to challenge the mighty industry he had been covering for years. I therefore registered only minor surprise on a scorching July afternoon when Diane called me to the phone at our Santa Monica home with excited word that a *New York Times* reporter wanted to ask me a few questions.

When I picked up the receiver, a highly caffeinated newshound immediately began peppering me with aggressive but incomprehensible inquiries. "Sorry to bother you at home, but I'm under deadline, and I just need a few sentences of reaction on the whole Maitre affair, since you're obviously one of the major players. What do you think should happen to the guy?" As he spoke, I started feeling physically dizzy and unsure of my balance, like the perplexed, suddenly endangered hero in a Hitchcockian "wrong man" thriller.

"I have no idea what you're talking about. What is the Maitre affair?"

"I don't want a dissertation, nothing philosophical. Just a few words of reaction. Please, don't play games. How did you feel when you found out you were the victim?"

It took me several minutes to convince the impatient journalist that I remained honestly, utterly ignorant of my own victimization. He then explained that a prominent dean at Boston University had plagiarized twenty-five paragraphs from my lecture "Popular Culture and the War Against Standards" for his well-received commencement address. The case had made the front page of the *Boston Globe* for two days in a row, prompting calls for the dean's resignation. With the story about to explode into national news, the *New York Times* wanted to know if the perpetrator had called me to apologize.

I sat down to try to get my bearings and refused to comment until I learned something more about background of the controversy. I had never heard of H. Joachim Maitre, dean of Boston University's highly regarded college of communication, which educated students in both print and broadcast journalism. On the gala day of the commencement ceremony, I learned, he had offered an impromptu, fairly clumsy introduction urging the graduates to take action against the corruptions of the popular culture and then proceeded to read my words, without attribution and with only the most minor alterations and insertions. The speech—my speech, really—impressed the crowd so much that more than a dozen spectators called the university and asked to buy a videotape of the occasion, which the campus press office began selling after securing Maitre's approval. Finally, more than a month after commencement day, an anonymous observer analyzed the video and noted the obvious similarity between Maitre's words and my widely circulated article; the person promptly called the *Boston Globe*.

When I finally heard from Maitre, who was vacationing in Malaysia, he offered a strange, strained, five-minute apology. He insisted that he had intended to acknowledge me as the source of his commencement comments; in fact, before the *Globe* story broke, he said, he assumed that he *had* mentioned my name and praised my work. He had never intended to get away with passing off my work as his; if he had, why would he have authorized the sale of the videotape that all but guaranteed his exposure (since it clearly showed him reading from a copy of *Imprimis* while he delivered the speech)? He told me that the whole university knew of his admiration for my remarks, since he had given out free copies from a stack he kept in the dean's office. On the day of the commencement, he had taken some medicine for his heart condition and began to sweat in his heavy academic robes under the hot sun. Notified that the ceremony had started to run badly behind schedule, he felt flustered and somehow forgot to acknowledge my authorship—the most dangerous and damaging omission of his life.

In the end, I believed him and publicly and repeatedly forgave him in interviews for newspapers, magazines, and network news broadcasts. As I learned more about Maitre's background, it became clear to me that many in academia reacted with over-the-top indignation not because of his unauthorized borrowing from a single speech but because of his long-standing adherence to conservative ideology—a cardinal sin in most academic environments. Maitre, I discovered, had been a crack pilot and high-ranking officer in the East German air force but had defected to the West in a daring, death-defying flight to freedom in his MIG fighter jet; after his defection, this son of high-ranking Nazi general became a dedicated anti-Communist and a vigorous Reaganite, and he attracted more than his share of enemies in the university world. I made spirited attempts to defend the man, but to my disappointment, he resigned his powerful position as dean a week after the story first appeared, though BU president John Silber braved new howls of protest by allowing Maitre to retain his academic employment as a member of the faculty.

A few months later, I traveled to Boston for a lecture and Jo Maitre took me to lunch. We hit it off immediately: he came across as a figure of enormous sophistication and charm, with the crisp, tightly wound energy that reminded me of the bracing Germanic values of my own Oma. A few months after our first meeting, he traveled to California on business and joined us for a traditional Sabbath meal at our home. Diane found him every bit as impressive as I did, though we marveled at the strange fate that had brought us together—and the supernatural power of America that allowed the son of a Third Reich general to sit down with the son of Jewish refugees for a family meal filled with prayer and Hebrew song.

During the week that the world focused most intently on the Maitre affair, I got my first real taste of life as a media sensation—with phones ringing every moment as reporters and curious acquaintances and would-be advisers demanding "just a few moments of your time," cumulatively soaking up so much energy and oxygen that normal life becomes impossible. Even after the dean's resignation, the odd media frenzy continued, with the *Boston Globe* devoting huge space to publication of my original comments under the snide heading "The Words Joachim Maitre Never Wrote." The *Globe* also ran an editorial attacking *me*; the liberal newspaper deemed my ideas dangerous in their totalitarian essence. "The purloined paragraphs recited by Joachim Maitre," the editorial declared, "betray something more diffuse than dishonesty, less corrigible than self doubt. Bad taste was the trait. . . . Maitre's stolen text was a reactionary ragout of paranoia, false history, and internal contradictions. . . . The art commended in Maitre's plagiarized text is uplifting propaganda akin to the kitsch favored by the commissars of Kultur who once ruled his native East Germany." Since the only approving reference in my talk cited Hollywood's "Golden Age" and "the heyday of Gary Cooper, Jimmy Stewart, and Katharine Hepburn," one can only marvel that one of the nation's most prestigious newspapers would implicitly write off movies like *Sergeant York, Mr. Smith Goes to Washington,* and *The Philadelphia Story* as "kitsch" and "uplifting propaganda" worthy of Communist dictatorships.

I considered writing some response to the *Globe*'s insulting editorial but before I could do so, my plans collapsed in the wake of a new earthquake in the form of a phone call from HarperCollins in New York City. At that powerful publishing house a veteran editor named Hugh Van Dusen had been reading all about my work in the context of the Maitre controversy and asked if I thought I could expand my ideas into a major book. Soon my agent, Richard Pine, had negotiated a deal (securing the largest advance I had ever received). Though I was delighted by this opportunity, I felt some trepidation about sustaining the angry denunciations I knew the book would provoke. I even warned HarperCollins that we should anticipate a hostile, indignant response from everyone even loosely connected with the entertainment industry, but the publisher seemed to relish the commercial possibilities associated with raging controversy.

In order to focus on the new book, which I had decided to call *Hollywood vs. America,* I needed to set aside another literary endeavor that had occupied my attention off and on for more than three years. I had sold E. P. Dutton on the concept of a "where are they now?" book about the talented but tragically self-destructive individuals responsible for the movie *Easy Rider* (which I had watched in the year of its release with my law school friend Hillary Rodham), weaving together the bizarre production history of that troubled but wildly successful film with personal stories of the people who made it. For *Riding High* I interviewed Dennis Hopper, Peter Fonda (who provided sixteen hours of audiotaped recollections), and nearly all the other principals, assembling more than three thousand pages of transcribed interviews with the dozens of people involved in the film. I even went down to Morganza, Louisiana, to interview the local residents who had played the murderous, intolerant yahoos who persecuted, beat, and ultimately killed the fictional, free-spirited bikers, Captain America and Billy. It turned out that these "real live rednecks" (as director Dennis Hopper had described them) qualified as some of the kindest, most generous and hospitable people you could find anywhere in the country. In real life, they never insulted or assaulted visiting long-hairs; in fact, when local promoters experienced a disaster with a poorly planned rock festival, the good citizens of Morganza drove out to the stricken site and delivered free food and clean water to the stranded hippies. Despite all my work on *Riding High*, I finished only about half of the book and in the end I never returned to the project.

Unfortunately, I couldn't shirk some other commitments despite my fervent desire to concentrate all of my energy on *Hollywood vs. America*. Six months before I started working on my new book, a distinguished and persuasive law professor from Loyola Marymount University approached me with the suggestion that I help him as a consultant in one of the most celebrated and complicated legal battles in Hollywood history. Columnist Art Buchwald had sued Paramount Pictures, claiming that the basic concept for the hit Eddie Murphy film *Coming to America* had been stolen from a three-page treatment he had submitted to the studio more than a decade earlier. Paramount insisted that the finished film bore so little resemblance to Buchwald's sketch that he could never claim he had originated the project. The law professor wanted me to dig through the papers on the project—including Buchwald's brief story outline (which the studio said it had discarded) and the many drafts of the *Coming to America* script—and give my opinion as a film critic on the true sources of the appealing aspects that guaranteed the finished film's success.

I eagerly accepted the chance to work on this case not because of the money (which totaled only $8,000 for more than a year of intermittent, occasionally intensive labor) but because of my fascination with the issues involved and the chance for an intimate, behind-the-scenes examination of the process by which major filmmakers shaped and refined a slick commercial project. Substantively, Buchwald's case struck me as almost laughably flimsy. His concept centered on an African king deposed and exiled in a sudden coup who seeks refuge in the African-American ghetto of Washington, D.C., where the U.S. government eventually makes use of him for its own purposes. In the Eddie Murphy movie, the main character is an African prince who defies his powerful father to travel incognito to the United States to find an appropriately modern, independent-minded woman. Beyond the most rudimentary similarity in the stories—African royalty traveling to America—the plotting, characterization, humor, and themes of the Paramount romantic comedy bear no connection to Buchwald's much darker, much more political outline. I outlined my opinion in a deposition for the big LA law firm O'Melveny and Myers (representing Paramount) and agreed to appear as an expert witness in the trial. I knew that my take on the case displeased most journalists (who naturally sympathized with their esteemed colleague Buchwald), but I had already established myself as a Hollywood dissenter so I didn't worry about the consequences.

To my surprise, Court TV provided a live broadcast of my testimony and reporters outnumbered lawyers in the cozy hearing room. I went home in midafternoon feeling triumphant and satisfied, but when the newspapers arrived the next day, my intriguing little legal adventure had morphed into a career-threatening disaster. A reporter for the Associated Press had written a brief, scurrilous story, picked up across the country, suggesting that I'd been exposed and disgraced as a corrupt hack who had sold my soul to the studios. The lead in his article declared that PBS film critic Michael Medved "accepted money from studios to rewrite scripts and advised studios how to market their films." Repeating these ridiculous charges to various experts, the reporter quoted their predictable denunciations of such behavior. "I think Medved has to turn in his critic's badge over this one," opined Tom Shales, the outspokenly liberal TV reviewer for the *Washington Post*. Within forty-eight nightmarish hours, television news picked up on the story, reporting gleefully on the self-righteous, Hollywood-scolding crank who had pretended to objectivity while secretly enriching himself on the studio payroll. Some commentators connected this new "scandal" to the previous scandalous headlines on the Maitre affair, somehow suggesting that I stood culpable and humiliated in both instances (though no one could explain, if asked, why I deserved blame because a perfect stranger used a speech of mine without attribution). I shot off an immediate six-page letter to major press outlets correcting the misinformation in the AP story; much to their credit, both the *New York Times* and the *LA Times* ran corrections and retractions. Nevertheless, I came to see the horrid truth in the observation, usually credited to Mark Twain, that a lie can travel halfway around the world while the truth is pulling its boots on.

The big lie in the AP hit piece centered on the idea that I worked as a "screenwriter and script doctor" for major studios at the same time that I reviewed their products. During the first part of my testimony, one of the lawyers from our side of the argument had attempted to "qualify me"—by asking questions about why the court should accept my authority as an expert witness. I talked about my work in writing and revising scripts—but all of it performed (as I made clear in my answers) some five years before I began covering movies for *Sneak Previews*! As to the suggestion that I "advised studios how to market their films," this derived from my experience in viewing a few screenings long in advance of a movie's release (along with several other critics) and then answering questions for the producers about our reaction to its problems and prospects. I never received a dime for such conversations, though the AP story made it appear that I got rich as a studio "adviser."

Recalling the nasty slam on my integrity (with a media feeding frenzy reminiscent of the short-lived excitement over the Maitre affair), I still feel indignant, outraged in fact, over the shameful application of an obvious double standard. In *Time* magazine, Richard Corliss (with whom I had disagreed so pointedly over *The Cook, the Thief, His Wife, and Her Lover*) wrote a substantive piece attacking me for lending "expertise to a studio" and purportedly "selling out," but neglected the far closer relationship to major movie companies by some prominent colleagues. Rex Reed, for instance, briefly interrupted his career as a critic to play a starring role (as the transsexual twin of Raquel Welch) in the 1970 Twentieth Century Fox bomb *Myra Breckinridge* (one of our "Fifty Worst Films of All Time," in fact), but Reed never felt constrained about reviewing Fox projects shortly thereafter. Roger Ebert also found time during his distinguished efforts at analyzing motion pictures to write the screenplay to Russ Meyer's uplifting epic *Beyond the Valley of the Dolls* (1970). As a matter of fact, the checks provided to both Ebert and Siskel (and now to Ebert and Roeper) come from the same Walt Disney Company that produces many of the titles that the TV critics review. At the prestigious *New Yorker*, the legendary Pauline Kael briefly worked for Warren Beatty, while Penelope Gilliatt wrote the script for *Sunday, Bloody Sunday* without leaving her critical perch at the magazine. Jay Cocks of *Time* appeared on screen in *Street Scenes* (1970) and received "special thanks" from Martin Scorsese in the credits to *Mean Streets* (1973) a full four years before he stopped reviewing movies for the magazine. (Since that time, he's scripted major films such as *The Age of Innocence* and *Gangs of New York* [both for Scorsese], *Strange Days*, and *DeLovely*.) Paul Attanasio also worked as a film critic, for the *Washington Post*, before sliding over into writing (*Quiz Show, Donnie Brasco, The Sum of All Fears*) and producing and creating TV series (*Homicide: Life on the Street, Gideon's Crossing*). Ironically, the same Tom Shales who demanded that I turn in my "critic's badge" continues to review television shows for the *Washington Post* despite revelations that he hawked scripts and programming ideas to ABC TV during the same period he evaluated the network's new productions with purported objectivity.

I disagree with Shales on every conceivable political and cultural issue (in 2004 he suggested that Mel Gibson had earned himself "a parking space in hell" for directing *The Passion of the Christ*), but I don't begrudge him the right to dream that he could do better than the TV hacks he regularly reviews. I happen to believe that creative ambition and real-world production experience make a critic more qualified to do his job, not less so. In that context, and after the long, distinguished history of reviewers participating in some way in the making of motion pictures, I felt outraged by the attacks visited on me after the Paramount case. How could people pretend to be "shocked, shocked" that I made money writing scripts *before* my critical career, or that I told studios and producers about my reaction to their films (without charge) when they proved kind enough to screen them for me (and for other critics) long in advance?

The idea of Michael Medved as a studio lapdog looked especially ludicrous when the first excerpts of my new book appeared just weeks after the Paramount controversy had died down. Inserted into Sunday newspapers across the country, *USA Weekend* ran a cover story, with my photograph, over the headline: "ONE ANGRY CRITIC: On the eve of the Oscars, Michael Medved has had it with Hollywood's fixation on the dark side." I began the piece with the same sentence I later used to begin my book: "America's long-running romance with Hollywood is over." To back up my point, I suggested, "If you doubt it, ask yourself a simple question: When was the last time you heard someone you know say that the movies—or TV, or popular music, for that matter—are better than ever? On the other hand, how recently have you listened to complaints about the dismal quality of the movies at the multiplex, the shows on the tube, or the songs on the radio?"

Referring to the "assault on traditional values" I had endured as a working critic for a decade, I urged Hollywood to "begin a serious reexamination of its current directions and its relationship to the mass audience. . . . I no longer can ignore destructive trends and continue to focus exclusively on my reviews of individual films while pretending not to notice that Hollywood's 'big picture' has grown so much darker and more ominous. No matter how elegant and diverting the passing parade, someone must step forward to suggest that the entertainment emperors are wearing no clothes."

The magazine set up two different 800 numbers so readers could register agreement or disagreement with my basic point, that "Hollywood no longer reflects—or even respects—the values of most American families." Three weeks later, they reported the results: 75,000 readers flooded the lines with calls, which was "the biggest reaction from *USA Weekend* readers in our six-year history." The official vote showed an overwhelming 70 percent agreeing with me, but the magazine acknowledged that the percentage actually should have been higher: "The call-in generated so much reaction that phone lines were swamped. . . . Thousands of calls didn't get through. Hundreds more readers called the next day wanting to vote yes—which indicates that, had all calls gotten through, the yes vote would be even higher."

The next week, the magazine contacted Jack Valenti, president of the Motion Picture Association of America, for the official response from the movie business. "Hollywood is a fragmented community of 1,000 producers, many directors, etc., and each has a way of telling a story, unsuitable to some, congenial to others," he reasoned. "There's good and bad, profane and sacred."

The public, however, clearly agreed with me in seeing an unnecessary preponderance of the bad and profane. Within a week of my story's publication, *USA Weekend* reported, "nearly 1,000 letters had poured in, of which all but a handful supported the cover story by Michael Medved." The magazine ran a selection of letters, including one from W. Robert Shade of Libertyville, Illinois, who enthused, "It's about time a film critic had the guts to blow the whistle on the decadence in the film industry." Mimi Tudman of Burlington, Massachusetts, wrote, "Three cheers for Medved. I am appalled by the way Hollywood portrays the sick and disgusting."

With the publication of my book five months later I received similarly encouraging letters from literally thousands of ordinary Americans, which helped to ease the sting from the hysterically negative reaction from leading reviewers in every corner of the country. At first, Diane and I winced when we read the denunciations by prestigious publications. After a few weeks, she stopped reading press comments altogether while I felt more and more amused by the vitriolic excesses of my enemies. For instance, David Denby in *New York* magazine began his review by declaring: "*Hollywood vs. America* is the stupidest book on popular culture I have read to the end." Richard Corliss (again!) in *Time* dubbed me "The Magistrate of Morals" and suggested that I approached my work with "the fervor of a modern Martin Luther, an angry evangelist determined to nail his 95 theses not on a church door but on a movie marquee." In the *New Yorker,* Lewis Menand suggested that I played the role of a "modern day Savanarola." I felt conspicuously honored to count as the first synagogue president simultaneously compared to Martin Luther and Savanarola.

As expected, the "bible of the entertainment industry," *Variety,* ran a furious denunciation, under the headline "HOLLYWOOD HILLS ALIVE WITH THE SOUND OF MEDVED." In the course of his front-page review, editor Peter Bart declared, "The tome provides a chilling glimpse of what happens when a humorless, authoritarian mind is inundated by the noise of pop culture. Purporting to be an analysis of the state of the arts, the book reads instead like a nervous breakdown set in type. By the end, it's clear that all Medved wants is to be in seclusion someplace, watching *The Sound of Music* nonstop for the remainder of his days. . . . At the beginning of his book, he expresses the fear that the entertainment community might banish him for 'speaking out.' Much as I disdain blacklists, a case could be made to banish Medved from all future screenings, purely on humanitarian grounds. The poor guy has suffered enough. So have his readers."

Even Jack Valenti departed from his normal tone of courtly moderation (which he had employed in his previous comments to *USA Weekend*) for a full-throated denunciation of the Medved menace. "He is a singularly uninformed individual who leaps from soggy premises to stupid conclusions," he told *Los Angeles* magazine when asked about me. "A failed screenwriter who became a critic and is now raising hell because he couldn't get his scripts produced." It amazed and amused me that recognized leaders of the entertainment establishment preferred to question my sanity or aver my malevolence ("nervous breakdown set in type," "raising hell because he couldn't get his scripts produced") rather than making the slightest attempt to address the contentions at the heart of my work.

Much to my relief, I received abundant opportunities to answer such attacks in more than three hundred radio, television, and print interviews concerning the book, many of which played out as energetic debates. These engagements gave me the chance to try to correct some of the willful distortions of my positions employed by Hollywood apologists in an effort to discredit my core arguments. For instance, my opponents charged that my agenda included the irrevocable shredding of the First Amendment, but I specifically condemned the idea of governmental regulation as a means for uplifting the popular culture and provided an entire subchapter ("The Censorship Temptation") to make the case against political interference.

The most common objections to my overriding theme, that messages matter in pop culture, relied on that tired old line that "it's only entertainment"—that movies and TV offer fantasy, escapism, and pure diversion, and only a fun-hating grouch could contend that they exert some serious influence on the general public. During a daylong seminar sponsored by an association of prominent producers, I debated this proposition with talented filmmakers who insisted again and again that their work contributed nothing to antisocial behavior in the real world. These same cinematic artists lavished prodigious amounts of energy and imagination on deciding the most trivial details of set design, wardrobe, makeup, lighting, dialogue, and editing employed in their high-profile projects, but now they implausibly insisted that these carefully crafted particulars conveyed no meaningful messages to the eager audience. Movies result from a complex series of highly conscious choices, and nothing appears on screen by accident. In other words, if a trashy sequel like *Alien 3* includes a line of dialogue in which one of the brutal, sex-starved inmates in an outer space penal colony tells Sigourney Weaver, "You know, we're all fundamentalist Christians here," you can be certain that at least a half dozen decision makers (writers, producer, director) agreed to that statement.

When creative personnel insist that such decisions count for nothing, they expose the most appalling hypocrisy. They tend to take their own work with the utmost seriousness—proudly collecting "Environmental Media Awards" for a ten-second reference, say, to recycling. During the producers' seminar I attended, one of the executives responsible for *Lethal Weapon 3* criticized me for failing to acknowledge that his film saved "thousands of lives" because it offered a pointed (and amusing) close-up showing Mel Gibson and Danny Glover fastening their seatbelts before taking off on a high-speed chase. But if we're supposed to believe that a few seconds of responsible role-modeling will influence the masses, we cannot then argue that the rest of the movie's 115 minutes of gunplay, knife wounds, eviscerations, lacerations, explosions, mutilations, and car crashes will influence no one at all. Similarly, the filmmaker who receives kudos from Planned Parenthood for encouraging "safe sex" cannot maintain that a brief glimpse of a talismanic condom will magically influence behavior while at the same time arguing that the long, erotic set-up that made the prophylactic necessary in the first place will do nothing to encourage experimentation.

Most Americans invest literally years of our lives (nearly one-fourth of our waking hours) in consumption of popular culture, so it's hard to believe that this gigantic time commitment fails to play a significant role in shaping values, attitudes, and actions. In order to deny the obvious impact of entertainment, skeptics often resort to an anecdotal argument when they try to contradict me. "I grew up on all kinds of shoot-'em-up entertainment, and I still love violent movies, and I happen to watch all the bloodiest TV shows," one conservative talk show host declared on the air, "but I'm still one of the gentlest, most nonviolent people you'll ever want to meet. And I know there are millions of people just like me. You claim that Hollywood is a powerful influence, but how do you account for the fact that everybody sees violent or pornographic entertainment, but only a small minority end up behaving in violent or pornographic ways?"

That clever question enables skeptics to disregard all the persuasive academic studies proving media influence (more than a thousand of them, according to the U.S. surgeon general, and duly mentioned in my book) by distorting the entire thrust of such research. The fact that media messages fail to influence *everybody* doesn't mean that they fail to influence *anybody*. Only a tiny percentage of those who see a TV commercial for BMW will decide to buy—or even test drive—that pricey car, but this doesn't suggest that the ad is ineffective. An advertising campaign need influence only a puny proportion of its potential viewers to make a big difference to the car company, and popular culture needs to change perceptions of only a small segment of its vast audience to make a significant difference to society. Even a marginal increase in the number of participants in seriously dysfunctional behavior (violent criminality, substance abuse, property destruction, irresponsible sexuality, and so on) can damage the quality of life of—and intensify the climate of fear for—all the rest of us.

Moreover, even those who never buy a Beamer have been influenced by the ads, whether they acknowledge it or not—just as those who immerse themselves in brutal or sexy entertainment have been influenced more than they realize. The purpose of most mass media advertising efforts is to work a long-term, cumulative change in images and perceptions of a given product—to redefine a brand name as hip, sexy, and desirable. In the same way, Hollywood's continual celebration of, say, energetic sexual experimentation by fifteen-year-olds has contributed to rebranding that particular "product" for a mass audience. Repeated exposure to seductive media imagery showing glamorous people engaged in often dubious patterns of behavior helps make those patterns look normal—or even fashionable, trendy, hot. There is nothing innately attractive, elegant, or manly about male garb featuring a loose-fitting basketball jersey, baggy, low-hanging pants, black tennis shoes, and gold chains, but years of media exposure to the ubiquitous hip-hop uniform have convinced legions of young Americans that this wardrobe represents the very essence of sexiness. If images in movies, TV, and music foster new norms in grooming (as they so obviously do), then isn't it dishonest and illogical to assume that such images play no role whatever in determining more significant attitudes and actions?

In addition to all the arguments over Hollywood's influence on society, my book provoked even more embittered debate over the competence and motivation of the entertainment elite. Many critics of the popular culture have attacked the members of that establishment as bad citizens; I became notorious for attacking them as bad businessmen. As I researched

Hollywood vs. America, it became increasingly obvious to me that the sleaze and cynicism that offended tens of millions of Americans helped to keep those potential patrons away from the multiplex—and crippled the industry's all-important bottom line. This proposition seemed so self-evident, so inarguable, that it amazed me that pop culture apologists still resorted to the line that insisted "the show business moguls just give the public what it wants." Does the public demand harsh language in its entertainment? Would patrons feel cheated or disappointed if they heard the redoubtable "F-word" less frequently deployed? In panel discussions and on television showdowns, I've frequently asked my opponents to cite one scrap of empirical evidence—or a single survey, marketing study, or commercial analysis—that suggests that foul language enhances a film's appeal. They have never responded because they can't: all data suggest that at least 75 percent of the public regularly expresses displeasure at the crude language in movies of all types (with PG apparently now standing for "Profanity Guaranteed") and, increasingly, on TV. One can make an aesthetic argument for the occasional use of earthy verbiage (yes, *The Sopranos* would lose much of its energy if its characters spoke more politely), but you can't make a generalized commercial case: very few customers affirmatively seek out "F-words" when making choices about how to spend their entertainment dollars.

I became convinced that sex and violence had been similarly oversold as crowd-pleasing essentials in appealing to the public. As a critic who paid close attention to the financial fate of the movies under review, I recalled too many instances when shock value fell far short of delivering decent box office returns, while gentler offerings aimed at families fared far better with the public. Looking over *Variety*'s list of the top ten box office films of the entire decade of the 1980s revealed that only one—*Beverly Hills Cop*—drew the adults-only R rating, even though R films accounted for more than 60 percent of all titles released in this period. To help investigate this phenomenon, my brother Harry (who still lived in our guest house and relished his role as favorite uncle for our two little girls) put me in touch with an analyst he knew from the Screen Actors Guild, where Harry served as communications director and editor of *Screen Actor* magazine. Harry's colleague, Rob Cain, used a comprehensive database to analyze all 1,010 domestic releases between 1983 and 1989. During this period, all G films achieved a median box office gross of $17.3 million, PG titles did almost as well at $13.0 million, while R pictures languished with $8.3 million.

In response to such figures (featured prominently in my book), defenders of the status quo offered irrelevant excuses to justify the industry's dark obsessions. When I debated Roger Ebert in Florida, he condemned my numbers as misleading because there were so few G releases that they naturally did disproportionately well, given that they faced little competition in reaching the market for family films. I countered that he had made my point for me: the audience for more kid-friendly entertainment had been so obviously, painfully underserved that no one could suggest that the entertainment establishment simply "gave the people what they wanted." In another confrontation at a retreat for journalists and broadcasters, I sparred with Joe Roth, then president of Twentieth Century Fox (later a top executive at Disney and elsewhere). Several times, he attempted to undermine the impact of my statistics by citing R-rated releases (like *The Godfather* and *Basic Instinct*) that had achieved "fabulous success." Of course, I never suggested that an R rating ruled out a film's success; I simply argued that this designation made profitability less likely and that Hollywood's continual determination to saturate the market with adult material made no practical sense.

Several critics detected a whiff of hypocrisy in my attempt to call attention to the self-destructive aspects of the entertainment industry's edgy emphasis; they suggested that I contradicted myself by debating simultaneously as a "moralist" and a "marketeer." In a scathing piece in the *New York Times*, Walter Goodman said that for me, "the essential measure of success is an accountant's," and that I had "trouble deciding whether Hollywood is too successful at corrupting America or not successful enough." Actually, I insisted that corruption and success worked at cross-purposes: less corruption would ensure more success, benefiting both society and show business. To this day, I refuse to accept the premise that there's even the slightest contradiction in asking Hollywood to offer more wholesome, Middle American alternatives in entertainment while also pointing out that the industry could serve its own financial interests by doing so.

To my amazement and delight, this contention received potent

confirmation in an independent analysis by one of Tinseltown's most respected consulting firms just a few months after the publication of my
book. According to a detailed report for subscribers from Paul Kagan Associates, Inc., "There is an underexploited segment in the motion picture industry that could be costing the studios millions of dollars at the bottom
line: family comedies and dramas that are rated 'PG' by the MPAA. . . .
Ironically, while 'R'-rated films are less likely to score big at the box office
and are less profitable than films with other ratings . . . the percentage of
'R'-raters in the mix has increased from 50.3 percent in 1989 to 58.2 percent in 1991." In other words, Kagan's data strongly backed up my controversial assertion that the industry wasn't just disrespectful of its audience,
but also dysfunctional in its priorities.

Seven years later, in June 2000, I received the strongest possible
backing from two serious scholars I had never met: economists Arthur De
Vany of the University of California at Irvine and W. David Walls of the
School of Economics and Finance at the University of Hong Kong, who released a major paper "to investigate film critic Michael Medved's argument
that Hollywood overproduces R-rated movies." They concluded that "an
executive seeking to trim the 'downside' risk and increase the 'upside' possibilities in a studio's film portfolio could do so by shifting production dollars out of R-rated movies into G, PG and even PG-13 movies. . . . Putting
tastes and morals aside, even a casual look at the evidence does suggest that
there are too many R-movies. . . . We show that, as Medved claimed, R-
rated movies are dominated by G, PG, and PG-13 movies in all three di-
mensions of revenues, costs, return on production cost, and profits." Their
conclusion was unequivocal: "This paper shows that Medved is right."

Some ten years after my book produced so many angry, indignant reactions, even the most influential industry insiders offered confirmation
for my basic point of view. In July 2003, John Fithian, president of the National Association of Theatre Owners, told *USA Today*, "Family product
sells, and R-rated product does not."

Even before the emergence of this belated consensus, I had felt
buoyed by generous support from unexpected sources. On December 27,
1992, the Sunday after Christmas, John Cardinal O'Connor preached his
homily in Manhattan's St. Patrick's Cathedral on the subject of *Hollywood
vs. America* and voiced an impassioned endorsement of my book. "I've

never seen greater courage than the courage required to write this particular book," he declared. I also found abundant backing in the United Kingdom, where the *Sunday Times* of London ran an extensive serialization of my work under the title "Hollywood vs. Civilization." The prestigious *Guardian* newspaper, leading voice of the British left, provided me with one of my most gratifying reviews. "Just occasionally, a book changes the way the world thinks," the review began. "Michael Medved's *Hollywood vs. America* is such a book."

These words, coming from the opposite end of the political spectrum, helped to revive my faltering faith that the struggle to redeem the popular culture need not amount to a conservatives-only battle—that all people of goodwill and sanity, regardless of ideological orientation, could come together in defense of common decency. In the United States, however, new controversies in an increasingly polarized society left me more openly partisan, and more isolated from my entertainment colleagues, than ever before.

LESSON 33

Never Apologize for Partisanship

During the raging debates of recent years over the impact and accountability of the entertainment industry, the American left has been unable to develop a coherent or consistent position. On other issues, liberals display a strongly pacifist and anti-corporate streak, while proclaiming their deep devotion to feminist principles, but in their instinctive support for the Hollywood establishment these sensitive souls end up taking sides with big, greedy conglomerates that regularly exploit both violence and sexism. They explain that support with references to their commitment to "free expression" and their principled opposition to censorship, even though protests from the right almost never involve calls for governmental restrictions of any kind.

The left's illogical alliance with the princes and potentates of pop culture reflects the increasingly simplistic, bipolar nature of all cultural and political battles in the United States. Every disagreement takes place within the Us-Against-Them context of a fateful, overarching, no-compromise struggle between two sides equally convinced of their righteousness. For liberals, Hollywood producers, executives, writers, and stars all draw a pass when it comes to substantive criticism because they're ultimately perceived as "our people." Their overwhelming support for cherished leftist causes (gay rights, abortion rights, environmentalism, militant secularism) inoculates them from criticism regarding other themes (the glorification of violence, encouragement of recreational drug use, the irresponsible promotion of cigarettes and alcohol for young people) on which liberals might otherwise express concern. On the crudest level, Democratic Party activists and office-holders understand their own huge financial dependence on the leaders of the entertainment industry (as both direct contributors and reliable performers at glitzy fund-raisers) so they're not about to bite the hand that feeds them so much Brie, sushi, and Chardonnay. In the same way, sue-happy trial lawyers in Gucci loafers who become multimillionaires by exploiting the suffering of everyday Americans escape serious questioning from the left because activists understand that the ambulance chasers play an important, irreplaceable role in the liberal coalition.

When it comes to the controversies that regularly swirl around the entertainment elite, there's an even more visceral, emotional basis for leftists to indulge their instinct to defend and excuse the excesses of pop culture. Most of the outspoken warnings against the influence of Tinseltown have come from the right and—even worse from the perspective of dedicated liberals—from the *religious* right. The enlightened readers of the *New York Times* and sophisticated viewers of PBS may feel some discomfort with the current emphasis on edgy, irresponsible entertainment, but they feel outright revulsion toward any position associated with Christian conservatives. As I discovered during the skirmishes over *The Last Temptation of Christ*, some film reviewers preferred endorsing a thoroughly wretched movie to proffering appropriate criticism that might place them on the same side of the battle lines as Falwell, Robertson, and Dobson. In the fourth century at the Council of Nicaea, the leaders of the early Church rejected the perfectly serviceable and elegantly constructed Jewish calendar with the line "Better to be wrong with the sun than right with the Jews." For many Blue State liberals today, it's better to be wrong on pop culture issues than right with the Christian conservatives.

Unfortunately, I didn't understand this perspective when I first planned the publication and promotion of *Hollywood vs. America*. I naively expected that the arguments in my book—urging more emphasis on family entertainment and asking for greater balance and responsibility in the portrayal of traditional families, organized religion, and other cherished institutions—could draw support from open-minded liberals as well as my core audience of conservatives. After all, Tipper Gore, the wife of that year's Democratic vice presidential candidate, had waged a courageous campaign to call attention to the degradation of popular music, and Senator Paul Simon, the liberal Democrat from Illinois, had established himself as Washington's most thoughtful and aggressive critic of television violence. I might describe myself as a conservative Republican (I made a few Jewish community campaign appearances for President George H. W. Bush in both 1988 and 1992), but I hoped that liberal and moderate Democrats might nonetheless applaud my book and join the cause. Obviously, I had come out of the closet on our PBS show and elsewhere as a "cultural conservative," but that didn't mean that I felt ready for conspicuous public identification as a *political* conservative, let alone a Republican.

I wrote my book with that distinction in mind, avoiding any hint of a partisan perspective or agenda. I never lost sight of the extensive polling data showing that among the general public, Democrats and liberals worried just as much about the impact of popular culture as Republicans and conservatives: more than 60 percent of self-identified Democrats believed that contemporary entertainment relied too much on violence, sex, and bad language. When HarperCollins offered to send review copies of the book to a long list of opinion makers, I made a point of inserting the names of more than a dozen Democrats in the Senate, the House, and the punditocracy. I had enjoyed friendly contact with these people in the past (in most cases, the fairly distant past when I still identified myself as a liberal) and hoped that they would welcome the opportunity to embrace some of my populist, commonsense messages to burnish their own mainstream, family-friendly credentials. To my surprise and disappointment, not one of these individuals (no, not even my old pal Senator Joe Lieberman) gave me a positive response, and a few sent back snide little acknowledgment notes such as: "Thanks for the book, Michael. It doesn't look as interesting as *Golden Turkey Awards*, but I guess it shows you're living through a version of your old science fiction favorite *Invasion of the Body Snatchers* as shown by your scary transformation into one of the conservative pod people."

By this time, with a bitterly contested national election just a few weeks away, I knew that the issues raised by *Hollywood vs. America* had become inescapably politicized because of a single infamous sentence from the vice president of the United States. On May 19, 1992, several weeks after I'd turned in my finished manuscript but nearly six months before the book's October publication date, Dan Quayle delivered a significant, insightful speech to the Commonwealth Club in San Francisco in response to the recent and devastating Rodney King riots in LA. "I believe the lawless social anarchy which we saw is directly related to the breakdown of family structure, personal responsibility, and social order in too many areas of our society," the vice president soberly intoned, adding, "The intergenerational poverty that troubles us so much today is predominantly a poverty of values. . . . Nature abhors a vacuum. Where there are no mature, responsible men around to teach boys how to be good men, gangs serve in their place. In fact, gangs have become a surrogate family for much of a generation of inner-city boys." Most social commentators, including leading thinkers in the African-American community, might concur with this analysis, but media accounts of Quayle's address ignored its substance and concentrated instead on a fleeting pop cultural reference. The vice president made his central point forcefully and memorably, declaring, "Marriage is a moral issue that requires cultural consensus, and the use of social sanctions. Bearing babies irresponsibly is, simply, wrong. Failing to support children one has fathered is wrong. We must be unequivocal about this." Then came the one sentence that remains the only element of the speech anyone remembers. "It doesn't help matters when prime-time TV has Murphy Brown—a character who supposedly epitomizes today's intelligent, highly paid professional woman—mocking the importance of fathers, by bearing a child alone, and calling it just another 'lifestyle choice.'"

Inevitably, the press seized on this brief mention as if it represented the heart of Quayle's concerns and immediately lampooned the vice president, already a favorite target of derision, for his "gaffe" in delivering "The Murphy Brown Speech." Many commentators scoffed at the allegedly simple-minded Veep for his silly suggestion that "a fictional TV character caused the LA riots." The *New York Daily News* ran the attention-getting headline: "QUAYLE TO MURPHY BROWN: YOU TRAMP!" On television, some bemused observers wondered whether Dan Quayle even comprehended the fact that Murphy Brown didn't actually exist.

To the surprise of scoffing sophisticates, the vice president drew overwhelming public support for his position—precisely the same sort of populist tsunami that had flooded *USA Weekend* to back my much-discussed cover story just two months before. In his many subsequent comments on popular culture, Quayle echoed my arguments so precisely that I felt simultaneously flattered and undermined. Given the injection of these issues into the heat of a presidential campaign, I lost my last, forlorn hope for a measured, balanced, open-minded response to my upcoming book. Hollywood apologists instantly stigmatized me as part of the shameless, unscrupulous GOP campaign to blame all of the nation's ills on the entertainment industry, thereby getting the Bush administration off the hook. It didn't matter that I had completed my book before the vice president's entertaining tango with Candice Bergen/Murphy Brown, or that I had scrupulously avoided any specifically political rhetoric in my text, never praising Republicans or savaging Democrats. Whenever asked about the controversy, I expressed sympathy and support for Vice President Quayle, but also said that I wished he had avoided trying to launch a serious conversation about media values in the midst of a campaign. "I personally regret that the vice president has waded into this and made it such a political issue because it's not a left-wing or right-wing issue; it's not a Republican or Democratic issue," I told *Los Angeles Magazine.*

My reservations about employing Hollywood-bashing as an electoral tactic did nothing to diminish my personal enthusiasm for the struggling Bush-Quayle ticket, and over the summer I got a precious opportunity to express that support and admiration directly to the secretary of defense, my old friend Dick Cheney. Because my publisher HarperCollins played an important role in Rupert Murdoch's NewsCorp empire, I drew an invitation to appear as a featured speaker, along with Secretary Cheney, George Gilder, and other worthies, at Murdoch's biannual retreat for his media and journalistic executives from around the world, held in Aspen, Colorado. Cheney arrived by helicopter in the midst of the conference, and Diane and I enjoyed sharing lunch with the defense secretary and his wife, Lynne, who at the time was chair of the National Endowment for the Humanities. Later, Mrs. Cheney joined me on a program that represented one of the highlights of the retreat: a smackdown debate about media influence that also included Stephen Chao, the hip, cheeky, bespectacled, spiky-haired, Harvard-educated president of Fox Television Stations who had helped develop the sex-drenched, youth-oriented programming that had allowed Murdoch's "Fourth Network" to challenge the Big Three almost instantly. TV critics regularly commented on the contradiction between Murdoch's right-wing newspapers and the raunchy fare on his fledgling TV network.

On the day of the showdown with Chao, a standing-room-only crowd of more than two hundred guests jammed the small theater at Snowmass, expecting some rhetorical fireworks. I tried to oblige them with my assertive opening statement, offering a concise version of my case that major entertainment companies—including Fox—hurt the country and their own bottom line by paying no attention whatever to the traditional values of Main Street Americans. I pushed for greater balance, for more programming aimed at the often assaulted and insulted family segment of the audience, rather than endorsing any formal restrictions or even self-censorship. Lynne Cheney, blonde, diminutive, effervescent, and feisty, followed me with conclusive arguments about pop culture's undeniable impact on children, for better or worse. Her husband (having not yet discovered the virtues of "secure, undisclosed locations") watched her proudly from a seat in the front row, just below the stage, eagerly awaiting Stephen Chao's presentation in defense of his network's unabashedly exploitative programming.

Chao looked nervous as he took the podium and I could see his hands trembling as he read his prepared text. I tried to focus on his salient points so I could crush him in rebuttal (yeah, I'm a shamefully aggressive debater), but his speech rambled from one inane observation to another, with no discernable focus or connecting thread. The one point that emerged from the muddle involved the relativistic notion that different people make different value judgments in assessing mass media; some might object to foul language, others could resent graphic sex or nudity, still others might consider violence most offensive. Since clear-cut consensus seemed impossible, Chao rejected the whole idea of outsiders (like me) attempting to draw lines on acceptable or unacceptable media content, and insisted instead that such decisions must always reside with the artist himself.

As he approached his climax (and ran over his allotted time), he nodded toward a stranger in cowboy boots who suddenly emerged from backstage and sauntered out in front of the podium. While Chao continued to read his stream-of-consciousness address, the tall, well-muscled, pony-tailed interloper pulled off his boots, lifted his shirt over his head, and then, as the audience gasped and murmured, stepped out of his jeans. He paused for a moment, glowering at the crowd, before pulling down his underpants, dangling his fully displayed maleness just a few feet over the head of the startled secretary of defense in the front row. At this point, with an unknown hippie triumphantly exhibiting his total nudity before the crowd of startled newspaper, broadcast, and movie executives, the howls of protest and indignation drowned out the remainder of Chao's speech. Young children in the audience beat a hasty retreat on their parents' assumption that they didn't need exposure to a strange man's intimate equipment. The naked interloper gathered up his clothes and disappeared as soon as Chao stopped speaking, making clear to all that he had served the purpose of a highly unconventional visual aid.

We tried to finish the debate (and I expressed total disgust at Mr. Chao's pointless stunt), but the crowd found it difficult to settle down. As soon as the program ended, Rupert Murdoch rushed the stage. His deeply creased, weather-beaten, usually inscrutable face displayed visible rage behind the wire-rim glasses as he loomed over his employee Stephen Chao and demanded an apology. "That was a very stupid thing to do, Stephen. A very serious mistake. You need to apologize, Stephen. While the crowd is still here."

Chao tried to argue with him for a moment, as I witnessed the conversation with the same sense of excitement and dread one might bring to watching a developing car crash. Murdoch demanded a second time that his president of Fox Television Stations deliver an immediate apology; Chao said no. So the billionaire media titan made a snap decision. "Then you are sacked, Stephen. Effective immediately. Gather your things and go home."

Shortly after the conclusion of the conference, the media gave big play to the story of the "stripper" who made an unauthorized appearance at an off-the-record Murdoch function and thereby ruined the career of one of the whiz kids at Fox. Those of us in close proximity to this bizarre spasm of self-destruction tried to make sense of Chao's demented gesture, and one of his friends who remained for the conclusion of the meetings offered confidential explanations of the original intent. Since Stephen meant to stress the inevitable disagreements about whether sex or violence caused greater discomfort, the friend said, he planned a cleverly produced show-and-tell session to illustrate his point. According to this account (strictly unverified, to this day), Chao had originally planned to react to the nude guy in front of his podium in the spirit of an unhinged bluenose, drawing a realistic pistol from his pocket and pumping a few noisy blanks toward the naked victim, who would then explode a bag of stage blood under one armpit and fall over the edge of the stage. This gripping display might have provided an indelible illustration for his key question—what's worse in entertainment, nudity or violence? At the last moment, he purportedly changed his mind on the fake gunplay when he got a good look at the burly, formidable, we-mean-business bodyguards who never allowed the secretary of defense more than a few feet away from their protective care. If Stephen Chao had discharged a phony firearm a few feet away from the civilian chief of America's awesome military might, he might have paid for the display with his life instead of his job.

Despite his temporary disgrace, the imaginative Mr. Chao eventually resumed his triumphal career and went on to new jobs (including the leadership of the USA cable network), and Diane and I went on to a new baby: our little boy, Daniel Joshua, arrived on July 30, shortly after our return from the eventful conference in Colorado. To rejoice with our neighbors and pals, we hosted a bris (circumcision ceremony) for a hundred people, but despite the elaborate breakfast spread, the bracing taste of early morning Starbucks and schnapps, the songs, blessings, and brief speeches, the big event played out with an unexpectedly bittersweet undercurrent. While accepting congratulations and baby gifts, we couldn't escape the sad reality that many of the people who meant the most to us no longer lived nearby.

My father had moved to Israel a year and a half before Danny's birth, on the eve of his sixty-fifty birthday. After selling his high-tech company, MERET, he had decided to indulge his lifelong dream of planting himself in the miraculously reborn Jewish state. He had originally planned an Israeli retirement, but my indefatigable, perpetually youthful dad hardly felt prepared for a quiet life. Within less than two weeks of his arrival in the Middle East, he'd crossed paths with an exotic new love interest and used his resources from the sale of one company to launch an ambitious new enterprise called JOLT—Jerusalem Optical Link Technology. By the time of the bris, in fact, he had married his Jerusalem sweetheart—Yael Amishav, an elegant, blonde, charming, and outspoken Frenchwoman who had become a controversial fixture in Israeli right-wing politics. Even though he traveled halfway around the world to attend Danny's bris, his beaming presence only highlighted the painful fact that he now connected to our lives as a visitor rather than a neighbor.

My brother Jonathan, who used to live just four doors away with his witty, wonderful wife, Jane, and his own young children, had followed our father to a new home in Jerusalem, where he started his own new company as a high-tech venture capitalist. Even Harry moved out of our guesthouse (after eight years) to make room for Diane to shift her psychology office there; after the arrival of the third baby, we needed more space in the main house.

Fortunately, Harry relocated only six blocks away, but Rabbi Lapin stunned us (and the rest of the community) by moving his wife and seven children twelve hundred miles to the north. He had served Pacific Jewish Center for twelve years without payment of any kind while trying to build an independent mortgage and real estate business. When that enterprise faltered, he decided to take a one-year sabbatical on a suburban island near Seattle, enjoying a scenic part of the country he had always loved. Inevitably, he longed to apply his formidable energy and brilliance to larger challenges than sustaining our endearing but idiosyncratic synagogue on the beach. During the years that I discovered America's flourishing Christian counterculture, Rabbi Lapin had become even more absorbed with the dream of religious Jews making common cause with their Catholic and Evangelical fellow citizens in defense of the values and institutions that we shared. In Seattle, he began work on his book *America's Real War* (which became a major best-seller in Christian bookstores), about the ongoing struggle between people of faith and the intolerant secular fundamentalists who dominate academia and pop culture. He also organized Toward Tradition, a national think tank and activist organization devoted to applying timeless truth to timely issues and developing the alliance of serious Jews and committed Christians.

Meanwhile, I hadn't entirely given up on my own dreams of an alliance with former comrades in the Democratic Party, who might support my push for more wholesome alternatives in mass media. With these hopes in mind, I accepted a January 1993 invitation to attend an exclusive "reunion" associated with Bill Clinton's inauguration. Since the president-elect's service as Third District coordinator for the 1970 Duffey for Senate campaign represented his first significant political experience, Joe Duffey (now president of American University) and his wife, former campaign manager Anne Wexler, hosted a gathering of their one-time staff to celebrate the installation of one of our own in the nation's highest office. Despite the fact that I'd worked hard for the defeated President Bush, I made the trip to Washington, D.C., in part because Clinton himself had expressed positively Medvedian sentiments in an interview with *TV Guide* just a few weeks before his inauguration. "The cumulative impact of the banalization of sex and violence in the popular culture is a net negative for America," opined the president-elect. "I think the question is, what can Hollywood do, not just to entertain, but to raise the human spirit." He also endorsed the idea of the new administration initiating a "broad national discussion" of media responsibility.

Of course, a gala cocktail party on the eve of his swearing-in hardly represented the ideal venue for such a discussion, but I still felt somewhat surprised by the hostile reaction of most of my former colleagues to my current work. Though I enjoyed renewing my friendship with Lanny Davis (whom I saw for the first time in twenty years) and talking about the challenges of Jewish observance with the always-affable Senator Lieberman, the other former Duffey devotees treated me like a vulnerable lost soul with a fragile grip on reality—as if I'd just enlisted in a demanding, esoteric cult, or else recently won my discharge after an extended psychiatric hospitalization. "Oh, yeah, Michael—you wrote that *Republican* book on media, didn't you?" more than one of my former comrades inquired. "I understand you're part of the far, far right." I'd traveled so far to the right, in fact, that I chose to leave town early and to skip the inaugural gala featuring the song stylings of another old friend, Barbra Streisand.

Without question, the advent of the Clinton administration coincided with a new spirit of partisanship, a taste for bruising political combat, and an emphasis on choosing sides. In part, this ideological aggression stemmed from the famous rise of the New Media, with conservative talk radio leading the way. In the late '80s, Rush Limbaugh single-handedly revived the fading medium of AM talk and showed that if a host deployed enough humor, insight, and showboating flair, he could draw a huge audience without the slightest pretense of objectivity or unpredictability. Unlike the left-leaning anchors on TV, who made an effort to veil their biases behind a pompous pretense of disinterest, Rush never apologized for partisanship. His listeners (and detractors) knew exactly what to expect, but tuned in every day to hear the conservative case presented with peerless energy, ingenuity, and impudence. Meanwhile, the fledgling Internet developed political Web sites that provided the infrastructure for the conservative movement to emerge as a community and not just a cause. At the same time, the explosion of new alternatives on cable TV solidified other niche audiences—from MTV to American Movie Classics to Oxygen to Trinity Broadcasting Network—helping opinionated Americans escape into a media universe populated entirely by people who thought just like them.

In the spring of 1993, I got the chance to play my own role in this process when Rupert Murdoch persuaded the FCC to vary its ownership rules in order to allow him to reacquire Gotham's perpetually troubled daily, the *New York Post*, which had been on the verge of collapse. The deep-pocketed, last-minute rescuer planned to turn the tabloid into a much-needed conservative alternative for New York. Within days of establishing himself in his new office at the *Post*, editor Ken Chandler called me during a *Sneak Previews* shoot in Chicago to offer me the job of principal film critic. He understood that if the paper sought to appeal to New York's substantial but underserved conservative minority, it made no sense to have the dominant voice on movies be a reviewer (Jami Bernard) who prominently identified with leftist, feminist, and gay rights causes. After receiving assurances that the *Post*'s offer implied no obligation to move to New York, I eagerly accepted the job—in part because it meant writing reviews of the same movies I covered anyway for *Sneak*, and in part because I felt drawn to the exhilaration and adventure of Murdoch's unapologetically conservative gamble in New York City. At first, I functioned in an uncomfortable tandem with Jami Bernard, but after several weeks, she escaped to our liberal crosstown rival, the *New York Daily News*. This left me in sole possession of the august title chief film critic of the *New York Post*, with responsibility for churning out an average of three pithy, provocative, reasonably entertaining reviews every week.

In terms of winning even minimal acceptance in the New York movie community, I faced two gigantic obstacles: first, and most importantly, my well-earned reputation as a cantankerous conservative, and second, my insistence on maintaining my California residence. Despite my regular visits to the *Post*'s ramshackle (and seriously rat-infested) headquarters near South Street Seaport and my regular appearance on a national TV show that aired every week in New York, my colleagues persisted in identifying me as one of the "hicks from the sticks" who couldn't possibly play a constructive part in the cultural conversation in the world's most sophisticated metropolis. My out-of-towner status became a particularly sensitive issue when I gave some of Woody Allen's least impressive efforts (*Manhattan Murder Mystery, Mighty Aphrodite, Deconstructing Harry*) the mediocre reviews they deserved, in contrast to other critics in town who offered knee-jerk hosannas to any piece of scarcely digested celluloid belched forth by their hyperproductive homeboy. My refusal to worship at Allen's altar (though I did like his oddball musical *Everybody Says I Love You*) led the members of the august body known as the New York Film Critics Circle to congratulate themselves, publicly, on their good judgment for refusing to include "the out-of-towner, Medved" during all five years I served as principal reviewer for the *Post*.

In my reviews, I made a conscious effort to avoid political preaching or pronouncements, addressing ideological issues only when the movie itself put them on the table. For the clumsy, soporific John Travolta courtroom drama *A Civil Action*, for instance, the one-sidedly sympathetic view of the ambulance-chasing plaintiffs' bar and the crude cartoons of corporate corruption undoubtedly play a role in the movie's failure. For the most part, however, I tried to answer a single question in evaluating any movie: did it succeed in doing what it set out to do? Jackie Chan's *Rumble in the Bronx* (which I liked) pursued far more modest artistic ambitions than *The English Patient* (which I didn't like), so it made no sense to judge the two films by the same standards.

Despite this flexible approach to my work I managed to generate more than my share of controversy in a brief commentary about the leading critical awards of 1994. On a weekday afternoon, my editor called me at home in California to ask me to write a column explaining why both the New York Film Critics Circle and the LA Film Critics (another group I never had been invited to join) had produced an odd and uncommon split between their top two awards, selecting *Schindler's List* as Best Picture while honoring Jane Campion (of *The Piano*) as Best Director. In explaining the obvious "snub" of Steven Spielberg for his decisive, masterful role in crafting one of the finest films of recent years, I cited three factors: First was the lingering resentment of Spielberg for his populist past and record-breaking success. Second, it seemed to me obvious beyond argument that the critical establishment desperately wanted to encourage female directors (many critics said so openly, in fact), and by anointing Jane Campion (despite the intrusive, ham-handed direction of *The Piano*), they managed to make an affirmative-action-oriented, pro-feminist statement. Finally, I suggested, some "sympathy votes" might have been cast on Campion's behalf because of worldwide publicity involving her series of painful miscarriages and the recent death of an infant son.

The reaction to my analysis from my fellow critics and indignant letter-writers ranged all the way from mild disgust to burning outrage. The critical organizations on both coasts issued strong statements condemning me for my alleged sexism; one reviewer said that my "hate-spewing screed" somehow suggested barring women from all future directorial assignments. A critic in Orange County, California, blamed me for causing "immeasurable pain" to Campion and her family by "outing her very private grief." I knew something about the grief associated with miscarriages, but I also knew that if your loss provides a major focus for an interview in the *New York Times Magazine* (as in Campion's case, a few months before my column), then your suffering can no longer count as "very private." In any event, in the midst of all the withering attacks, I felt grateful for the consistent support I received from my editors at the *Post*, who worked hard to create a feisty, politically incorrect voice in the midst of "enlightened" New York, and offered a welcome contrast to my controversy-averse bosses at WTTW and PBS.

The *Post*'s strategy of identifying the paper as openly, unequivocally conservative, with no charade of moderation or balance, worked slowly but effectively to build public awareness and mass circulation, culminating with particularly strong numbers in the past few years. In the political arena, Newt Gingrich followed a similar scheme with his "Contract with America"—promising red meat to true conservatives rather than attempting to appeal to undecided voters with a meringue of messages from the mushy middle. I had corresponded with Gingrich about his ideas after he wrote to commend me for a piece I wrote for the *Wall Street Journal* in 1986 (in which I argued that the antiwar demonstrations of the Vietnam era for which the Baby Boomers congratulated themselves actually arose more from self-interest than idealism), and I strongly endorsed his revolutionary fervor as he took over the congressional Republican leadership and replaced the timid "Democrats lite" approach with a sweeping, ambitious, unashamedly conservative agenda. Sure enough, that agenda swept the GOP into power, as the Republicans gained control of both houses of Congress for the first time in forty years.

Just weeks before Gingrich took the gavel as Speaker of the House, I traveled to Washington to address the Gingrich-affiliated fund-raising operation GOPAC (the GOP Political Action Committee). After the formal program concluded, he invited me to join about a dozen people in a hotel room for beers and private conversation until the small hours of the morning. With Newt, "private conversation" means that an intimate group, rather than a huge crowd, sits there and listens to him—the man counts as an intellectual dynamo, spinning out significant insights, observations, plans, schemes, overarching strategies, and visions of the glorious future like a broken soda machine unstoppably disgorging Coke bottles.

Whatever the disappointments over the Contract with America or Newt's leadership, his 1994 Revolution receives too little credit for its permanent rearrangement of conventional wisdom on American politics. B.G. (before Gingrich), smart politicos counseled caution and conciliation, urging candidates to "rush to the middle" in the hopes of picking up undecided moderates and perhaps even peeling off some of the opposition's support. Gingrich understood, however, that in an era of New Media and polarization, of the proliferation (on both sides) of nonintersecting, hermetically sealed, ideologically committed communities, the numbers of wavering or persuadable constituents had dramatically dwindled. It made far more sense to rally your core supporters for a high rate of participation on Election Day than to appeal to notoriously fickle swing voters. After all, a candidate who drew support from only 40 percent of the general public but generated enough enthusiasm for an 80 percent turnout would beat a rival with much broader, 60 percent backing from a more tepid cadre that provoked only 50 percent turnout. Simply put, success in politics required more partisanship, not less. Surveys may suggest that the public at large prefers candidates who seem to be middle-of-the-road and above the fray, but the recent record suggests that it's true believers and activists who provide the energy and dedication to win, both in primaries and general elections.

I saw a similar phenomenon at work in my religious involvement, where the denominations and congregations that took firm positions and made unambiguous demands enjoyed far stronger growth than the all-things-to-all people compromisers. In the Christian world, the so-called mainline churches, with their timid leadership and wavering perspective, faced a steady drain in membership, while fervent Evangelicals, traditionalist Catholics, and highly disciplined Mormons saw explosive growth. On the Jewish side of the divide, those elements of our community that stress the unconditional sanctity of traditional teaching and the obligatory nature of God's commandments represent the greatest new centers of energy and influence, especially among young people. Youthful personalities respond poorly to uncertainty, double-talk, and equivocation, in both religion and politics.

That is why I ignored all warnings from well-meaning friends and jumped at the opportunity to associate myself with the most polarizing conservative of them all, Rush Limbaugh. In 1993, after five years of phenomenally successful broadcasting, he launched his *Limbaugh Letter* to provide subscribers with more of his thoughts, commentary, witticism, and news from the manifold fronts of political battle. He also included a transcribed interview (a conversation, really) with one conservative newsmaker featured in each issue, and when he called to interview me (we never met face to face), I thoroughly enjoyed our wide-ranging conversation about Hollywood's irrational obsessions and left-wing tilt. Readers applauded this interchange after it appeared in the newsletter, and I got the chance to meet Rush shortly thereafter through an unforgettable Manhattan dinner party put together by the glamorous conservative intellectual Heather Higgins. The other guests included the great novelist and social commentator Tom Wolfe (and yes, he wore an immaculate white linen suit), the UCLA and Harvard sociologist and philosopher James Q. Wilson, and legal scholar Clint Bolick. Rush, savoring fine cigars provided by our hostess, looked vastly thinner and younger than the "big fat idiot" often portrayed in the media, and bore almost no resemblance to the braggadocious blowhard he often played on the radio. He possessed the effortlessly elegant manners that an earlier age associated with refinement and good breeding, listening far more than he talked, and making a point to forge solidarity within the conservative cause.

Several months later, I received a phone call from Rush's long-time producer, James Golden (known on the air as "Bo Snerdly"). Reaching me at home, Golden discussed his boss's plans to take time off during the upcoming holiday season, and said Rush would like me to guest-host his radio program during the week between Christmas and New Year. I made a show of carefully checking my calendar, but in truth I would have gladly chucked any other commitment for the chance to host a talk radio show for the first time, let alone America's highest-rated talk show. I had appeared as a guest on countless radio programs and felt no doubt at all that I could handle the job of host, thinking of dozens and dozens of topics I might enjoy discussing with the more than twenty million Americans who tuned in to Limbaugh's show every week.

As the Christmas season unfolded and the date for my debut approach, my *Sneak Previews* partner Jeffrey Lyons (who proudly described himself as an "unreconstructed Mario Cuomo liberal") warned me repeatedly and sternly against associating myself with Rush by guest-hosting his show. "You're going to ruin your career, you're going to ruin *Sneak Previews*. Please don't do it," he pleaded. "Isn't it hard enough that you're already swimming upstream—a conservative in a liberal industry? But at least you're a decent conservative, and you don't shout and call names, so Hollywood people can respect you if they get to know you. But Limbaugh is a demagogue. He's the devil. He's a fascist, a hate-monger. Once you're associated with that, you can't go back. You're tainted forever. Why would you want to do that?"

I explained to Jeffrey that most Hollywood liberals already viewed me as irredeemably tainted, and by guesting for Rush I'd introduce myself to millions of new people who liked, or even shared, that particular taint. I tried to explain my whole theory of the new era of partisanship, arguing that it made no sense anymore for people in the media to feign impartiality. The public looked more askance at those who simulated detachment than at commentators who honestly, proudly proclaimed their own points of ideological departure, whether from the right or the left.

I arrived in New York City shortly after Christmas, with Manhattan gleaming and glittering with holiday cheer. I met with James Golden on the evening before my first show and tried to imbibe every detail of his coaching and counsel. An imposing African-American (6'3", with a commanding, resonant voice), Golden had worked with Rush since Limbaugh began his national show in New York and he understood more about talk radio than any other producer in the business. He felt especially pleased to introduce me to the medium because he had read and enjoyed my book *The Shadow Presidents* long before he ever saw my work as a movie critic. In fact, James suggested that we spend some time talking about the White House staff during my first show since that topic could give the audience some concept of the depth and diversity of my background. He also passed on the most important advice from the vacationing Rush: I should make no effort to imitate or echo the legend I'd been assigned to briefly replace, but rather must try to be myself in every aspect of my conversation with the audience. The listeners could easily forgive some minor disagreement—even a disagreement with Rush himself—but they would never accept phoniness.

Before the first minutes of that first broadcast, I gulped five or six cups of black coffee, paced like a caged beast in the legendary studio, and tried to find the right balance between the overpreparation that would destroy all spontaneity and the let's-wing-it improvisation that could embarrass me on the air. The producers had recorded a special introduction with the booming voice of the Limbaugh show, Johnny Donovan, declaiming, "And now . . . sitting in for the vacationing Rush Limbaugh. . . . He's a nationally televised film critic, and the best-selling author of *Hollywood vs. America* and *The Shadow Presidents*. . . . Heeere's . . . Michael Medved!" Strangely enough, when I began speaking into the microphone (there really is a "Golden EIB Microphone" in Rush's studio) and hearing my own voice coming back through the headphones, my nerves settled almost instantly.

Before the first break and the deluge of callers, I'd developed an overwhelming sense of comfort, even pleasure, with the entire process. After completing the first hour of the first show as guest host for Rush, I felt hopelessly hooked, in fact—ready to drop my literary projects and my film critic's work and all other elements of the career I had built over twenty years in order to find more work in talk radio. It's the connection with the listeners—the immediacy, the intimacy—that becomes fatally addictive. Actors all claim that they prefer working on the stage to working in film because in the theater you can feel the audience responding to you. Talk radio offers that same advantage over TV. On television, you may know that hundreds of thousands of viewers will ultimately watch what you do, but you can't feel them, you can't talk to them, while you're doing it. I remember appearing on Larry King's old late-night radio show during the promotional tour for *The Shadow Presidents*; he kept the studio almost completely dark, for the atmosphere, and when the calls began to come in, Larry pointed with enormous satisfaction to two banks of brightly flashing lights, since those lines connected with people in every corner of the country. That sort of connection felt like enchantment to me, and that first afternoon on the Rush Limbaugh show I felt even more directly wired to the noble heart of the country.

The callers, bright and eager to test a new voice on the airwaves, helped the afternoon spark and sizzle with their borrowed electricity, taking me in unexpected and satisfying directions as I responded to their questions and challenges. I reveled not only in the personal connection I could forge with so many Americans but also in the sheer array of topics we could cover. That first day I talked about Hollywood bias, the challenges for a conservative film critic, about the White House staff, and some of the latest depredations of the Clinton administration. The next day, December 31, I discussed the best and worst movies of the year, assayed a series of year-end oddities selected by James Golden, talked about my hitchhiking days as a college student, traveling across the country on the kindness of strangers, and surveyed the history of the ubiquitous, achingly nostalgic Robert Burns drinking song "Auld Lang Syne," which everyone sings on New Year's Eve but almost no one understands:

> *Should auld acquaintance be forgot,*
> *And never brought to min'?*
> *Should auld acquaintance be forgot,*
> *And days o' auld lang syne?*

This isn't a suggestion; it's a question, which the poet answers decisively in the negative. Rather than forgetting about the "auld lang syne" (the old days long past), we're supposed to "tak a cup o'kindness yet / For auld lang syne." At the very conclusion of the broadcast, with a boozy instrumental version of the song playing in the background, I proposed to "tak a cup o'kindness" in honor of James Golden, the rest of the Limbaugh staff, and Rush himself, who had done so much to enrich the national dialogue with his passion and partisanship and to make my year-end visit to New York memorable and moving.

After finishing the broadcast, I grabbed a cab and went directly to the airport so I could make it home in time to join Diane for the strike of midnight (blessed by the time difference operating in my favor). We faced a new year and new beginnings, as I explained to her my determination to do everything in my power to launch a new career.

Talk Radio Is a Source of Hope
Rather Than Hatred

None of my acquaintances or colleagues in the entertainment industry could ever understand my fascination with conservative talk radio. Despite the fact that this combative format represents one of the most dynamic segments of the overall media marketplace (with more than 1,300 all-talk stations compared to just 75 in 1980), liberal doubters display a thorough misunderstanding of the essence of the medium and its sturdy appeal. My friend Jeffrey Lyons, for example, now the respected movie and theater critic for WNBC in New York, still assumes that the majority of people who listen to political talk on the AM dial sport missing teeth and permanent brain damage, along with gun racks and Confederate flag decals attached to their mud-splattered pickup trucks. In the esteemed pages of the *New Yorker*, Hendrik Hertzberg expressed similar sentiments in August 2003, asserting that "right-wing radio is niche entertainment for the spiritually unattractive. It succeeds because a substantial segment of the right-wing rank and file enjoys listening, hour after hour, as smug, angry, disdainful middle-aged men spew raw contempt at reified enemies, named and un-named. . . . To the chronically resentful, they offer the sadistic consolation of an endless sneer. . . . For the radiocon audience, political hate talk *is* comedy and drama. To their ears, it's music."

In Minneapolis, a letter to the editor took the caricature to its inevitable extreme: "I was troubled when I saw that the *Star Tribune* featured a commentary by Rush Limbaugh, a notorious racist hatemonger," wrote one Cathy Grisham in the summer of 2003. "I will not hesitate to discontinue my subscription should more of his work appear in so prominent a position again. It is embarrassing to have such a paper delivered to the door of my otherwise enlightened and tolerant home and community. . . . He is nothing but a right-wing demagogue and haranguer of the intolerant and undereducated."

As a matter of fact, every available market survey of the massive talk radio audience proves that the listeners to conservative shows possess more, not less, education than the general public. In a survey in *American Enterprise* magazine, those who said they listened to "a political talk radio show today or yesterday" proved far more likely to hold a college degree than Americans at large (38 percent to 21 percent) and to earn a family income above $60,000 (30 percent to 20 percent). The results of the 2004 Talk Radio Research Project from *Talkers* magazine provides further surprises about the audience—which is more black than the nation at large (20 percent to 12 percent), as well as far more moderate and independent than detractors like to suggest. Only 37 percent of listeners describe themselves as "ultra conservative" or "conservative," while 23 percent identify as "moderate" and a surprising 11 percent as "liberal" or "ultra liberal." It's true that Republicans strongly outnumber Democrats (24 percent to 13 percent), but a startling 54 percent of the members of the audience consider themselves "independents"—a much higher number than the nation at large. Most significant of all, 73 percent of talk radio junkies took the trouble to vote in the absurdly close election of the year 2000, while close to 50 percent of the general public chose to stay home. In a study by the Pew Research Center in January 2004, 17 percent of the public said they "regularly" got their news about the presidential race from "talk radio shows," while another 29 percent reported that they "sometimes" used that source for their campaign information. In other words, close to half of all Americans—a staggering 46 percent—at least occasionally connected with political developments through the profoundly powerful medium of talk radio.

Even before I became aware of such statistics I felt satisfied and elated by my ability to communicate with millions of my fellow citizens as guest host for the *Rush Limbaugh Show*, and relished the dialogue with the callers. After my first two appearances, James Golden invited me for other stints behind the Golden EIB Microphone and I became a regular fill-in—the most popular fill-in, in fact—serving (along with Tony Snow and Walter Williams) whenever Rush couldn't handle a live broadcast. Before beginning my own national show, I substituted for Rush nearly thirty times, learning the mechanics of talk radio and developing a reputation with a huge national audience. Contrary to the fears of my associates at *Sneak Previews*, my politicized, nakedly partisan sessions on the Limbaugh show did nothing to undermine our PBS credibility and actually helped substantially in publicizing our movie review show. I did lose a few lectures in the Jewish community from organizations that no longer welcomed me because of my association with "that anti-Semite," Limbaugh. Ironically, Rush qualified as one of Israel's most stalwart supporters in American media, he enjoyed a warm personal friendship with Prime Minister Benjamin Netanyahu, and he had never given the slightest hint of anti-Jewish bigotry, but some leaders of our community couldn't (or wouldn't) escape from the ancient, irrational assumption that outspoken conservatism somehow equated to anti-Semitism.

Though I spoke less frequently at Jewish venues, the exposure on the Limbaugh show (on some six hundred radio stations across the country) led to more invitations from Christian and conservative organizations than I could possibly handle. In the spring of '96, I agreed to travel to Seattle with my entire family for a joint appearance with Diane sponsored by the Washington Family Council, an activist operation loosely affiliated with Dr. Dobson's national Focus on the Family organization. We agreed to make the trip not only because we supported the cause but also because a visit to Seattle (which had always been one of our favorite cities in the country) meant a reunion with our close friends the Lapins.

To promote our appearance, Diane and I did a number of press interviews, including a drive-time hour on Seattle's conservative talk station, KVI. The host was John Carlson, who had already established a reputation as one of the nation's most promising young conservative voices for his wry, sophisticated commentary combined with an earthy boy-next-door personality. Later, he became the Republican nominee for governor of Washington (he earned a "silver medal," as he put it, losing to an entrenched Democratic incumbent), but when we first met he seemed content—delighted, in fact—with his position as one of the local kings of radio talk. The hour went so well that as we were leaving the radio station, the acting program director stopped me in the hallway and asked if I would be able to come back the next day, Friday, to guest-host for three hours on their local station.

That night, I discussed the opportunity with Rabbi Lapin, who hosted his own Sunday night show on KVI. He believed that the bosses' request for me to substitute on Friday indicated that they wanted to make me an offer. Just a few days before, they had fired their popular but perpetually embattled midday host, Mike Siegel. In the midst of his live show, Mike had made the mistake of allowing (though not initiating) extensive discussion of an unsubstantiated rumor about Seattle's liberal (and purportedly happily married) mayor suffering a gunshot wound when surprised during a homosexual tryst. In the midst of his struggling campaign for governor, the mayor naturally called an indignant press conference and demanded an apology, but Mike—a rabble-rousing populist and fearless scourge of the local establishment—delayed his response long enough to cost him his job. His departure left a gaping hole in the lineup, from noon to three every day—the crucial segment of the schedule that connected the "ratings Godzilla" Rush Limbaugh with the solid drive-time performer John Carlson. After Siegel's highly publicized problems (the Seattle media had piled on for weeks), management promised to replace him with a "major conservative voice" and used various part-timers and local activists to fill in until they could find one.

When I went to the studio the next day, then, I understood that my time on the air amounted to an audition. I arrived early to work with Siegel's producer, a sharp, personable, kinky-haired twenty-six-year-old kid named Dan Sytman. For the first hour of the program, we agreed to stage a confrontation—challenging the *Seattle Times* reporter who had written up our Washington Family Council lecture from the night before with an abundance of snide remarks about "the Christian right" and weird, insulting distortions of the substance of our speeches. Most conservatives feel annoyed by the persistence of smug, reflexive liberalism in supposedly objective media, but with the power of a radio microphone I had the chance to strike back—and eventually forced the poor, unprepared reporter to apologize on the air and to acknowledge his mistakes. In order to make clear my lack of personal animosity, I extended an invitation to the guy to join us later that same night for a Sabbath meal at the Lapins: he surprised me by accepting, and we enjoyed an unexpectedly friendly evening with him.

At the end of my three hours on the air, Dan Sytman told me he'd never had so much fun in radio, and the station's general manager, Shannon Sweate, came into the studio to ask for a few minutes of my time. In his office, Shannon and the program director told me they wanted to hire me for the choice noon-to-three slot. My first instinct was to accept their challenge without even discussing details, but fear of financial consequences led me to restrain myself. Putting my plum gigs as cohost of *Sneak Previews* and chief film critic for the *New York Post* at risk for the sake of a strictly local radio show sounded like a giant step backward for my career. But I was floored by their financial offer, which easily doubled my expectations: like most Americans from outside the talk radio industry, I hadn't fully grasped the booming, prodigiously prosperous position of leading talk stations. I asked for the chance to think about my decision over the Sabbath and promised to get back to them by Sunday.

Walking out of the radio station into the brilliant sunlight (no, it doesn't rain in Seattle every day), I felt dazed, lightheaded, with my feet barely touching the ground, as if I were floating through a strange but pleasant dream. Diane met me downtown and we used the hours before Shabbat to walk around Pioneer Square, the handsomely restored historic district, and to talk about the thrilling new possibilities we faced. Part of my inclination to take the job stemmed from my long-time infatuation with the Northwest. My parents brought me up to Seattle for the World's Fair in 1962 and since then I'd visited the city, both by hitchhiking and by plane, more than twenty-five times. I loved the landscape of mountains and water, the sleek, functional downtown, and most of all the abundance of towering fir trees that seemed to thrive in even the most unexpected places. I had taken my family on vacations to Washington's glorious national parks (Mount Rainier, Olympic, and North Cascades), and the Lapin family's visibly happy adjustment to their new home in the Northwest encouraged us to believe that we could also handle the move.

A few years before, our commitment to our close friends and fellow congregants at Pacific Jewish Center would have ruled out any possibility of relocation, but recent developments had transformed our communal responsibilities from a source of spiritual nourishment to an increasingly painful burden. After the departure of Rabbi Lapin, the congregation had gone through a five-year patch of turbulence and identity crisis, much of it centered on his brooding, profoundly polarizing successor. The new leader of the community (who drew a generous salary, in contrast to Lapin's many years of volunteer work) determined to take Pacific Jewish Center in a more rigorously observant, "black hat" direction. Instead of seeing our institution as a unique, independent outpost by the beach that provided a welcoming portal for those taking their first baby steps to traditional commitment, he wanted to build a more "normal," strictly governed Orthodox community that offered a refuge for those families who had already arrived. For instance, the flourishing, world-class day school that I had started with Rabbi Lapin and had long been known as the Emanuel Streisand School now got a name change to *Yeshivat Ohr Eliyahu*—erasing any suspect Hollywood associations, and appealing more directly to fervently religious Jews. The new rabbi drew support from many members of the congregation for such changes, but the disagreements soon devolved into all-consuming disputes. In the end, we spent weeks in a huge legal battle before a Jewish religious court (*Bet Din*) over proper division of communal assets. Our side prevailed in that nightmarish fight, but those months of travail made the notion of moving to Seattle feel more like deliverance than desertion.

We talked about these issues with the Lapins over the Shabbat we spent with them, going on a long walk after Saturday's lunch through forest preserves, lakefront parks, and leafy suburban lanes. On one side street overlooking the glittering blue of Lake Washington I saw a "For Sale" sign on an inviting two-story home sheltered by towering Douglas firs. We paused for a moment to consider the exterior of the available property and I told my wavering wife, "You see, Di, if we decided to move up here, we could buy *that* house!"

As it turned out, we *did* buy that house: we decided to risk everything on our Northwest adventure, and the new home we chose was the one we first spotted on our Shabbat walk that balmy summer afternoon. Although the relocation involved a major life change for our family, it made it easier knowing that my children were young enough (Sarah was nine; Shayna, seven; Danny, four) that they wouldn't experience the dread, wrenching change my parents had imposed on me when they moved us from San Diego to LA after my sophomore year in high school.

The first broadcast of *The Michael Medved Show* beamed out to the Great Northwest on July 29, 1996. I insisted on choosing my own theme music rather than relying on the generic rock or country sounds preferred by every other host in the country. Given my national profile as a film critic, it made sense to use movie music and I wanted something lush, orchestral, distinctly heroic, and inescapably American. I finally settled on Bruce Broughton's stirring main theme from *Silverado*, whose unforgettable score outshines the only so-so movie (starring Kevin Kline and Danny Glover). Like all of the best movie music, the *Silverado* theme instantly grabs your full attention, seizes you by the throat, in fact, announcing with blaring brass and soaring strings that something important, something dramatic is about to happen—and I try to deliver on that promise of significance and drama every day on the radio.

In addition to the distinctive theme music, I wanted to devise a catchy phrase or slogan to brand my show—in much the same way that Rush identified himself with saucy declarations such as "Talent on Loan from God" or "America's Truth Detector and Doctor of Democracy." After kicking around ideas with Diane, I came up with the thought of beginning each show by intoning, "And . . . another great day in the greatest city on God's green earth!" In part, this announcement meant to signal the local Seattle audience that this newcomer from California yielded to no one when it came to hometown pride. The reference to "God's green earth" also seemed particularly pertinent to Seattle, which claimed the mantle of "Emerald City" because of the luxuriant greenery our damp climate provides. More significantly, I wanted to mention the word "God" at the beginning of each broadcast because I hoped to differentiate my program from other secular news-talk shows in part through my willingness to discuss religious issues.

In this, I hoped to follow the example of my good friend Dennis Prager. I first got to know Dennis when he served as the precocious, boy-genius head of a major Jewish retreat center and invited me to participate as a scholar-in-residence for discussion of my book *What Really Happened to the Class of '65?* We immediately discovered shared passions for politics, classical music, and irresponsibly expensive audio equipment, in addition to the odd confluence of our religious perspectives. Dennis, raised in an Orthodox home in Brooklyn, moved to the left (or the center, really) as he studied and wrote about Judaism, while I, raised in a nonobservant, officially Conservative home, moved decisively to the right. As a result, we still disagree on many issues of theology and observance, but I've been significantly inspired by Prager's ability to raise such questions in a stimulating way to both Jewish and general audiences. On the air he speaks about the most significant questions in relationships, faith, culture, and politics without ever talking down in any way to his listeners. His example encouraged me to believe I could engage in similarly substantive conversation.

My show enjoyed strong ratings and significant success from the very beginning, despite unanticipated protests against the slogan with which I began each broadcast. Station management showed me several angry letters protesting my invocation of "the greatest *city* on God's green earth" as showing disrespect to the majority of our listeners who lived in the suburban and rural communities outside the Seattle city limits. Responding to their indignant concern, I modified the catchphrase to reference "the greatest *region* on God's green earth" but hoped that I'd soon be able to adopt the far more felicitous "greatest *nation* on God's green earth" by taking the show into national syndication.

That welcome development occurred earlier and more easily than I had expected, following my participation in a controversial conference at Georgetown University on "Homosexuality and American Public Life" in June 1997. On that occasion, I joined a number of other cultural commentators (Richard John Neuhaus, Robert P. George, Robert Knight) in braving a cordon of angry, sign-waving demonstrators to deliver presentations in response to the powerful movement for so-called gay rights. I spoke on "Homosexuality and the Entertainment Media," suggesting that the emphasis on gay themes and characters in so many movies and TV shows had nothing to do with market demand (in fact, most of these ventures failed with a skeptical public) but rather reflected a conscious strategy explicitly outlined in homosexual publications as early as 1984. As part of that strategy, gay activists announced their intention (in an authoritative article by leaders of the National Gay Task Force in the magazine *Christopher Street*) to demonize any opponents as "ranting homophobes whose secondary traits and beliefs disgust middle America. These images might include: the Ku Klux Klan demanding that gays be burnt alive or castrated; bigoted southern ministers drooling with hysterical hatred to a degree that looks both comical and deranged." Defenders of traditional morality could counteract such images, I argued, only by avoiding at all costs playing into the hands of the radicals with any appearance of intolerant homophobia. "We must not define ourselves as anti-gay, but as pro-marriage," I stressed. "The main threats to the family in America do not come from the gay community. They come from infidelity, they come from divorce, they come from all of the temptations that heterosexuals fear and feel in a hedonistic culture. Our response should not be targeted specifically at homosexuals or homosexual issues. It should be targeted on the need to uplift and sanctify and defend the family and the institution of marriage."

The cable TV network C-SPAN sent a camera crew to cover the conference and broadcast a tape of my entire speech on numerous occasions. The letters and e-mails and phone calls I received in supportive response to this talk convinced me that C-SPAN drew a larger—or at least more attentive—audience than anyone assumed. One of those calls came from a significant radio executive who immediately got my attention by declaring his interest in arranging national syndication for my show. Greg Anderson worked for Salem Communications, the world's largest broadcaster of Christian programming and an ambitious company that had recently entered the fiercely competitive field of secular, conservative talk with prominent personalities like Oliver North and Alan Keyes. Both of those two shows relied on celebrities with no radio experience, and neither program fared well in the marketplace—the unfailingly furious, constant candidate for office Alan Keyes became a particularly acute disappointment. Salem planned to drop the contracts of both their stars and hoped to build a more successful business with radio professionals. Greg said that he thought the reasoned, persuasive tone of my Georgetown speech struck just the right chord, and he'd been impressed when he looked up our dominant ratings during my first eight months on the radio in Seattle.

Within days, he flew to the Northwest with the president of the company, Ed Atsinger, who had begun his radio empire nearly forty years earlier, when, as an English professor and debate coach at Los Angeles City College, he used his life savings and modest investments to rescue a struggling country music radio station. From that modest beginning, Atsinger and his brother-in-law, Stu Epperson, bought and sold new stations, patiently accumulating assets until they had built one of the six largest radio companies in the country. The most impressive facet of these people involved the combination of business acumen and visionary idealism: Ed and Stu meant to influence the culture for goodness and righteousness, and they had become increasingly convinced that they needed to operate in the secular world to do so. Christian preaching-and-teaching stations played an important role, but by their very nature they preached, quite literally, to the converted. Limbaugh, the ultimate model of radio success, had demonstrated the ability to reach a much larger, far more diverse audience through the medium of conservative talk, and Salem meant to follow that model for the sake of profits, and the Prophets. In this endeavor, Atsinger and Anderson assured me over dinner that my Jewish commitment represented a positive factor for our potential partnership: no one could accuse them of representing and serving only a narrow band of right-wing Christian fanatics if their premier radio host happened to be a conspicuous spokesman for Jewish traditionalism.

Salem graciously accommodated my preexisting relationship with my Seattle station: I'd continue to originate the show from its downtown studios and to occupy the same position in the daily schedule, but now with a national rather than a local focus. We kicked off the new coast-to-coast hook-up in March 1998, with 30 stations; we've built the syndication steadily since that time to more than 140 affiliates in nearly all the nation's major markets.

Meanwhile, my colleagues at Salem have built on the popularity of our show to assemble a genuine network, hiring some of the most accomplished talkers in the country. Much to my delight, they heeded my recommendation and lured Dennis Prager from KABC to take his show national, and they secured another respected Los Angeles broadcaster and personal friend of mine, Hugh Hewitt (who's also a law professor and Republican activist). The personable "Everyman" Mike Gallagher produces his entertaining show in Dallas, and most recently we've added an early-morning program with former secretary of education (and author of *The Book of Virtues*) Bill Bennett.

One of the most common mistaken assumptions about my show is that I rely on a huge staff of dozens of dutiful drones to research the issues, arrange guests, produce comical segments, answer mail, schedule trips, and so forth. It might be satisfying to supervise such resources (applying some of the administrative lessons from *The Shadow Presidents*), but the Medved show has always managed with just two employees to support the host. I've been especially fortunate to keep the same two remarkable associates who first launched the local show with me in 1996—Dan Sytman and Jeremy Steiner. Dan (also known as "Darth" due to his altogether unhealthy obsession with the *Star Wars* saga) had worked as a producer before my arrival and I happily inherited him when I took over Mike Siegel's slot. He's considered the black sheep in a family full of ridiculously overachieving surgeons—but this black sheep has established himself as one of the top radio producers in the country and hosts his own popular talk show on weekends for our Seattle station. On the Medved show, Dan takes the calls, forcing those who hope to make it on the air to vault over the "Sytman wall" by proving that they're coherent and passionate enough to make for good conversation.

The other member of "Team Medved," Jeremy Steiner, continues my close, productive relationship with Hillsdale College—when he started working on my show (at the very beginning) he'd recently graduated from that fine, conservative Michigan institution (where he served as student body president, no less) and hence he bears the on-air designation of "Jeremy Steiner, Pride of Hillsdale College." Charismatic, athletic, instantly likable, and wickedly funny, Jeremy is responsible for the little sound bites of political and pop culture figures that give the show its texture; selecting and programming the musical bumps that take us into and out of breaks; producing the comical bits and ironic promos that listeners love (including our "Call of the Week," honoring the most inane and reality-challenged caller of the seven days just passed); and generally controlling the elaborate system of buttons and levers that keep the show on the air and sounding professional. Before the show, Jeremy surfs the Internet to find stories or backgrounds for the broadcast, as does Dan: I get two invaluable newsletters every morning, "Dan's News Tidbits" and "Jeremy's Daily News and Gossip," that help me sound smart and informed on the air.

Every day when I come into work I'm consciously aware that working with Jeremy and Dan amounts to a significant blessing and that we enjoy a stable, long-term, productive three-way partnership that is extraordinarily rare in radio. I'm proud to consider Dan and Jeremy two more kid brothers; to me, they're family members, not just business associates. That is why I've felt so pleased to see the two of them build their own families: both Dan and Jeremy started with me as single guys; both got married to wonderful women and bought their own homes during the time we've worked together; and both welcomed adorable babies into those homes in the course of 2004.

In January of 2003 Dan and Jeremy moved with me to a brand-new flagship station, Talk 770 KTTH ("The Truth"), a 50,000-watt powerhouse specifically designed around the *Michael Medved Show*, which, within one year, became the dominant talk radio station in the Northwest. Despite these changes, my two longtime producers continue to play a major role in shaping the distinctive identity of our show as "Radio's Foremost Forum for Substantive and Civilized Debate." We've always tried to avoid the "amen corner" aspect to talk radio, and to invite, encourage, and privilege disagreeing phone calls. Arguing with antagonists—even very hostile antagonists—strikes me as the best way to change minds and to arm those on our side of the political divide with arguments they can use to change more minds. Our emphasis on the clash of ideas also determines our attitude toward guests. For the most part, national shows either avoid guests altogether, as Rush Limbaugh does (he'll use maybe a half dozen guests in the course of a year), or else they'll rely heavily on big-name guests, as Sean Hannity does, featuring three or four (or more) each day. We've tried to steer a middle course—usually devoting three of our fifteen hours each week to authors, politicians, movie people, or others who might contribute a unique perspective to the show. For the most part we confine to guests with whom I passionately disagree, and we'll fight it out on the air (with callers on both sides generally joining the fray). I've battled Noam Chomsky,

Michael Moore, Oliver Stone, Howard Zinn, Ralph Nader, Alan Dershowitz, Warren Beatty, Al Franken, Madeleine Albright, Molly Ivins, Robert Reich, Jim Hightower, Al Gore, Richard Dreyfuss, Bill Press, and, frequently, my old friend Lanny Davis.

We've also developed a special focus on the weird excesses of the left with special updates from the Berkeley City Council (to flood me with nostalgia for my four years in Berserk-ley). On one memorable occasion, council member Donna Spring explained the city's new ban on "space weapons," denying the government the right to deploy any of these dread devices anywhere above Berkeley city limits within five miles of earth. Under questioning, Ms. Spring suggested that the Berkeley Police Department might someday develop the equipment they needed to shoot down U.S. government space weapons in the portion of the stratosphere claimed by the city. Needless to say, we also discussed the important debates in the city councils of both Berkeley and Santa Cruz concerning successful resolutions demanding the immediate impeachment of President George W. Bush.

Republican and conservative guests face a much tougher time getting on our show because agreement and mutual admiration can quickly become boring. Nevertheless, with significant national figures we make exceptions, so I have talked on the air with George W. Bush, Laura Bush, Dick Cheney, Lynne Cheney, Colin Powell, Tom Ridge, John Ashcroft, Bil Frist, Arnold Schwarzenegger, Charlton Heston, and other important leaders of the conservative coalition. At times, our friendly guests seem shocked when Dan puts through challenging or hostile callers, but we believe that the best talk radio is about the battle of ideologies, not one-sided cheerleading.

Every day, I feel stimulated and energized by what I do, engaging in spontaneous conversation with the unfolding history of our time. I get up at five in the morning and begin reading newspapers as the strong coffee brews; before the show starts at noon, I'll cover the *Wall Street Journal*, the *New York Times*, *USA Today*, the *Seattle Times*, the material that Dan and Jeremy feed me, plus the *Hotline*—a dauntingly thorough, massive digest (nearly fifty pages, single spaced) of political news from across the country. We select three discrete topics from this wealth of material, one for each hour; unlike other shows, we don't do stream-of-consciousness riffs on all the big stories of the day, or carry over subjects from one hour to the next, because new listeners tune in at all points in the show and it's useful for them to get a clear idea of the issue at hand. Many Americans feel frustrated at moments of national crisis and drama at their inability to respond, but on talk radio we never face that problem. On 9/11, I ended up broadcasting the three hours of my national show and then did six more live hours of local programming, helping the listeners cope with the magnitude of the event and the changes it would bring in its train. Whatever the news of the day, talk radio allows me to consider a vastly broader range of topics (anything I feel like talking about, in fact) and accommodates far more emotion and meaning than, say, my tightly focused, two-minute *Sneak Previews* arguments with Jeffrey about whether or not movie fans should shell out money to see Sylvester Stallone in *Judge Dredd*.

I flew to Chicago to complete my last tapings for *Sneak Previews* a few weeks after we'd launched the local Seattle show. After twelve years with the program, it felt strange to walk away, and in explaining to my friends and colleagues why I preferred to do conservative talk radio, I emphasized the fact that in my new gig I'd at least face no need to worry about grooming, makeup, haircuts, or dummy glasses. For me, one of the joys of radio involves the ability to wear faded jeans and flannel shirts almost every day: a standard (if unhip) Seattle uniform. I continued to review movies for the *New York Post* during our first year in the Northwest but I believe the paper felt increasingly uncomfortable with my provincial home base. A New York readership might accept the idea of a movie critic operating out of Hollywood, but why should they rely on someone who left the beaten path for the land of fir trees, Sasquatch, and strong coffee? The same week in 1998 that I began my national radio show, I wrote a farewell column to my readers with the *Post,* after exactly five years and a staggering total of seven hundred movie reviews. Even then, however, I continued to review movies on the radio, devoting part of each Friday's show to a discussion of the new releases and also producing a one-minute "Eye on Entertainment" syndicated radio segment that covered new feature film and DVD releases.

In the spring of 2003, a new Hollywood controversy emerged that made me grateful that I had kept my critical credentials up to date. At times, it seemed that my entire career had served as specific preparation for my role in the raging national debate over Mel Gibson's movie *The Pas-*

sion of the Christ: for nearly twenty years, I'd been writing and talking about the intersection of Hollywood and religion, and my commitment as an observant Jew (and former synagogue president) gave me some standing to address the poisonous charges of anti-Semitic intent.

From the beginning, those allegations struck me as ridiculous. Before Gibson had even completed filming, the *New York Times Magazine* ran an article attacking the project based on an interview with Mel's eighty-five-year-old father (who had no role in the production) in which he expressed bizarre anti-Jewish beliefs. On June 24, 2003, the Anti-Defamation League, the nation's most powerful Jewish defense organization, issued a press release reporting the results of an analysis by five scholars, Jewish and Catholic, who had examined a stolen script (which the Gibson camp insisted had been superseded anyway) and found it "replete with objectionable elements that would promote anti-Semitism." Despite the fact that none of these critics had watched any version of the film, the ADL expressed very public concerns that *The Passion of the Christ* would "portray Jews as bloodthirsty, sadistic, and money-hungry enemies of Jesus."

The angry tone of the press release left me distraught at the prospect that important leaders of the Jewish community would mishandle their response to one of the most important religious projects in Hollywood history. I'd spoken on behalf of the ADL on several occasions in the past and hoped that they would address my concerns when I called their offices in New York. Most of all, I wanted to offer my services as a sort of intermediary, since I already enjoyed a friendly relationship with Steve McEveety—Mel Gibson's soft-spoken business partner and the producer of the new film—and I knew that he felt genuine concern over the first signs of Jewish hurt and hostility toward *The Passion*. It seemed obvious that off-the-record, behind-the-scenes consultation would work far better than ADL's shrill public denunciation of a still unfinished project—the sort of frontal assault that threatened to eliminate any possibility that Gibson might work with the Jewish establishment in fine-tuning his film. The intense and combative Gibson never would allow the public to believe that he had surrendered to threats from pressure groups, since doing so would mean abandoning the uncompromising independence and integrity that he cherished, and for which he had invested $30 million of his own money rather than working on the project with a major studio. Moreover, my close and regular contact with serious Christians showed phenomenally high awareness of the film and a great eagerness to see it. I concluded that if the ADL staged a confrontation with Gibson, they would only demonstrate the impotence of the Jewish community, because the moviemaker wouldn't back down and hordes of eager believers would embrace the film anyway. I expressed these concerns privately to ADL officials. I also invited the organization's director, Abe Foxman, to discuss the issues with me either on my radio show or in private, but over the next several months Mr. Foxman, through his underlings, repeatedly declined.

During this early stage of a gigantic international controversy I also spoke extensively to Steve McEveety about responding to the worries of the Jewish community, and Steve put me on the phone directly with his partner, Mel, to discuss the situation. Of all the bitter, irresponsible charges against Mel Gibson and his associates regarding *The Passion of the Christ*, perhaps the silliest (put forward aggressively by Frank Rich of the *New York Times*, and others) suggests that the filmmaker deliberately provoked the wrath of the Jewish community as a marketing ploy—hoping for priceless publicity while mobilizing latent anti-Semitism in support of the film. My personal conversations with Gibson (which ran to many hours during the prerelease maneuvering) showed the absurdity of this suggestion: he expressed frequent anguish over the persistent misunderstanding of his motives and the charges of bigotry against him, and invested considerable time and money in efforts to defuse them. As Gibson said repeatedly—and sometimes plaintively—in interviews, he had made the movie in the hopes of uniting people, not dividing them.

In July, I received a personal invitation from the director to watch a rough cut of the still-unfinished project at the offices of Icon Productions near my former home in Santa Monica. I flew down to California for the occasion, and got approval from the Gibson camp to bring my movie-savvy brother Harry along for the screening. We joined a group of twenty in the company conference room, finding seats alongside a few skeptical Protestant ministers, three priests, part of the team that had worked on the movie (including the scholar at Loyola Marymount University who had translated the script into Aramaic), and a half-dozen teenaged students from a local Catholic high school. Gibson came into the room, incongruously dressed in a loose-fitting Hawaiian shirt, baggy pants, and clogs. He patiently explained the project's status as a work in progress, and assured us that he planned to greatly enhance the finished product with color adjustments, sound improvements, and some discreet, subtle special effects.

Despite this disclaimer, the movie that I saw that summer night overwhelmed me with its lyrical sweep and devastating immediacy. Unlike most biblical films, with their cheesy miracles and their stilted dialogue ("Oh, Moses! Moses! You stubborn, splendid, adorable fool!" says Anne Baxter to Charlton Heston in *The Ten Commandments*), *The Passion of the Christ* offered heartfelt performances on a human scale and a convincing, richly imagined re-creation of first-century Judea. The dialogue in Aramaic and Latin added an unexpected sense of authenticity, emphasizing the distance between that world and our own and, incidentally, allowing the filmmaker some flexibility in adjusting the subtitles to turn away some objections from the Jewish community.

After the film concluded and Gibson spent a half hour answering questions from the little crowd, the others went home and he asked to meet in a private office with me, my brother Harry, and Steve McEveety. We spoke for more than three hours as I tried to explain some of the complicated religious and political strains in the Jewish community that would determine the reaction to his film. I made it clear that despite my admiration for what he had accomplished, the movie remained a difficult experience for any committed Jew. Mel insisted that his film meant to make everyone uncomfortable, not just Jews. For us, however, there's a special squirm factor, knowing that the Gospel account of the persecution of Jesus by the Judean power elite of the time (an account dutifully dramatized by Gibson) has provided an excuse for horrendous anti-Jewish persecution for nearly two thousand years. In the course of our conversation and in follow-up memos, Harry and I made a dozen specific suggestions for minor changes that could make a major difference in the underlying message moviegoers took away from the film. For instance, Simon of Cyrene, the heroic bystander who feels spontaneous compassion for Jesus and helps him carry the cross, could be much more clearly identified as Jewish, undermining the charge that all of the movie's Judean characters (with the essential, obvious exception of Jesus and his followers) are negatively portrayed. In response to this concern, Gibson altered the soundtrack to include a curse by a sadistic Roman guard who insults Simon by spitting out the word "Jew!"—an identification appropriately noted in the subtitles. In another instance, the earlier version of the film included one Roman official complaining to another about their assignment to "this stinking Temple." Harry made the important point that such dialogue only underscored a negative attitude toward a long-destroyed structure that religious Jews still mourn and revere as a holy gift from God. The new subtitles refer, much less offensively, to a "stinking outpost."

As Mel continued to show his work-in-progress to selected audiences (mostly including Evangelical Protestants and his fellow Catholics, with a sprinkling of Jewish conservatives), I repeatedly expressed the hope that he would invite representatives of the most prominent Jewish organizations, assuming that the film itself would allay many of their fears. Gibson, however, felt understandably uneasy about exposing his labor of love to officious leaders who had preemptively attacked the film, its director, the director's father, and their traditionalist Catholic faith. Nevertheless, at my urging the Gibson camp began planning an ambitious "Jewish Initiative" to show the film at synagogues and other community venues, while preparing study guides and other educational materials for wide distribution that featured contributions from leading rabbis describing a Jewish perspective on the Crucifixion.

As a crucial first step in this process, Gibson and his associates traveled to Houston on August 8 for a special screening of the still-unfinished motion picture. More than thirty leaders of the local and national Jewish communities accepted invitations to the showing, along with fifty prominent Christians. Rabbi Eugene Korn, director of interfaith affairs for the ADL, signed a confidentiality agreement, as did all other members of the audience, promising not to discuss what he had seen prior to the film's release. This pledge did not prevent the rabbi from telling the *Jewish Week* within hours of the screening that the movie "portrays Jews in the worst way as the sinister enemies of God."

"Jews Horrified by Gibson's Jesus Film" proclaimed the headline of *Jewish Week*'s article, while the Internet Movie Database announced its story with the line "Jews Slam Gibson Movie After First Screening." Korn reportedly engaged in an acrimonious exchange with Gibson after the showing and told the press that the star "seems to be callous to the fear and concerns of his critics." Not surprisingly, Gibson, McEveety, and their colleagues quickly dropped their plans for a Jewish Initiative, rightly (and sadly) concluding that any such effort would only exacerbate the mounting hysteria within our community.

At this point, I aggressively entered the public debate to try to urge a more sane, more practical perspective. I used my radio show for frequent discussions of the film and the issues it raised, concentrating on responding to anxious or angry Jewish callers, or debating some of the scholars who had condemned the movie before its release. I also wrote about the subject in my column for *USA Today* (where I served as a member of that newspaper's Board of Contributors) as well as providing more lengthy pieces for the *London Telegraph, American Enterprise Magazine, Christianity Today, American Legion Magazine,* and other journalistic outlets. In more than thirty appearances on network and cable TV, I tried to convey the important idea that some religious Jews rejected the apparent willingness of community spokesmen to go to war with Gibson and his fervent Christian supporters over the release of the movie. In this effort, my most prominent allies turned out to be two close friends and neighbors from the Seattle area—Rabbi Daniel Lapin, of course, with his nationwide Toward Tradition organization, and David Klinghoffer, former literary editor of *National Review* and author of two highly praised books on Jewish religiosity.

Tragically, the leaders of the Jewish community who fired the most vitriolic assaults on Gibson did far more than the film itself to associate insidious images of the first-century Temple establishment with the Jewish people of today. In the past, Passion plays aroused anti-Semitic rage by portraying the Judean officials who persecuted Christ as indistinguishable from contemporary Orthodox Jews with their skullcaps and prayer shawls; Martin Scorsese's loathsome *The Last Temptation of Christ* even depicts one of those oppressive priests wearing the same tefillin (phylacteries) with which I pray every morning. Gibson, on the other hand, emphasizes the Jewishness of Christ and his disciples more than he identifies the priests in the Temple with current Jewish images. The subtitles employ the words "Jew" or "Jewish" only a half-dozen times, and on each of these occasions the reference counts as positive—as when the noble Simon is identified as a "Jew," or the sadistic Romans refer to Jesus himself as "King of the Jews." Gibson pointedly omitted any of the Gospel passages when Jesus personally decries the officials of his time as "a synagogue of Satan" or suggests "the Devil is your father."

Given the fact that most Jewish historians share a dim view of the priestly hierarchy of that time as corrupt Roman collaborators, it made no sense that we should demand that Gibson portray them positively. Why would Jewish viewers of a contemporary film identify with the pompous and cruel religious functionaries rather than the other Jewish figures who turn up throughout the picture asking for more fair, compassionate treatment of Jesus? Unlike Abe Foxman and his associates, I couldn't understand why the Jewish community found it necessary to force a retroactive rehabilitation or exoneration of the long-dead, unlamented figure of Caiphas, as an essential element in our present security.

The timing of the entire *Passion* debate proved especially unfortunate. With anti-Semitism on the rise in France, Russia, Latin America, and around the world, with hundreds of millions of Muslim fanatics threatening bloody attacks on all Israelis and all Jews, it made little sense to select this particular moment to debate the reliability of the Gospel accounts of who killed Christ. I remain convinced that left-leaning organizations and individuals within the Jewish community overreacted so foolishly to *The Passion of the Christ* at least in part because of their general fear of the burgeoning alliance between conservative Christians and committed Jews in defense of Israel and in support of the Republican Party. Tina Brown, former editor of the *New Yorker*, acknowledged as much in a *Washington Post* commentary in which she explained, "The Gibson phenomenon makes Hollywood denizens nervous because it brings home the scary power of what they fear most: Bush country. It's not the supposed anti-Semitism of the movie they're worried about now. . . . No, it's Mad Mel's vaunted alliance with the alien armies of the right that are determined to return their mortal foe George W. Bush to the White House this November."

In February 2004, just before *The Passion*'s Ash Wednesday release, I received disquieting reports of an unexpectedly destructive development. I had already heard that in a very early version of the film, Gibson had included a needlessly explosive line from the Gospel of Matthew (27:25) in which the Judean mob, demanding the death of Jesus, eagerly welcomes the idea of perpetual Jewish blood guilt: "Then answered all the people, and said, His blood be on us, and on our children." By the time I saw the film, Gibson had excised the poisonous line, but now I heard from reliable sources that it had inexplicably reappeared.

I spent a sleepless night over this new revelation, and after the conclusion of the Sabbath I sat down to write an emotional, emergency e-mail directly to Mel and Steve McEveety, knowing that they had less than seventy-two hours to "lock" the film in its final form before sending it out for duplication and distribution. I wrote: "The big problem with all of this is the one line from Matthew 27 that has reportedly reappeared in the movie. I do hope to speak with you to plead with you with all my heart, brother to brother, to remove that line from the subtitles. . . . If one of your sequences (which wasn't in the cut I saw!) includes a curse that applies to my three children, then I will feel, frankly, betrayed. Worst of all, that one line will make your movie utterly indefensible in the Jewish community—and this is no exaggeration." I went on to write about my oldest daughter, Sarah, who planned to study at a religious seminary in Israel after her upcoming graduation from high school: "I feel personally wounded by the suggestion that my sweet, innocent, wonderful God-loving daughter who is making her way to Jerusalem, bears personal and specific guilt for the blood of Jesus Christ. I know that you might say that we all bear that guilt, as representatives of fallen humanity, but if the Judean mob in the movies says 'OUR children' then it sends a different message that would seem to exclude gentiles."

Steve McEveety responded almost immediately to say that Mel would digest and consider my plea, and two nights later I arrived home to find my eleven-year-old son, Danny, excited at a phone message he had taken. "Somebody called who said he was Mel Gibson," my boy reported. "It sounded like Mel Gibson, too. I told him I liked his voice in *Chicken Run*. He said he would call back." He did call back, and promised me that he had reached a last-minute decision to make the change I requested, striking the painful line from the subtitles. He acknowledged that he had made no attempt to include every detail or every pertinent verse from the four different Gospel accounts, so the sentence from Matthew would hardly be missed and "the movie didn't really need it." He also explained that traditional Catholic teaching suggested that when the crowd in the Gospels said "let his blood be upon us" they spoke for the entire human race in taking responsibility for the death of Christ, but he recognized the impossibility of communicating that subtle idea with a fleeting reference in a film. We talked for a while in emotional terms about our children (he has seven) and our respective faiths, and he made a special point of clarifying the basis for his decision on the line from Matthew. "It's not because of the Foxmans and the threats and the hysteria and the rage. It's because of what you said. And it's the right thing to do." I put down the phone feeling grateful that my unique position in the prerelease frenzy over the film gave me a chance to make a small but significant difference in one of the most important movies ever made.

The phenomenal box office returns after the movie's release confirmed that importance: even before the DVD release, *The Passion of the Christ* became the top R-rated moneymaker of all time, with nearly $400 million in domestic box office gross. In conversations with Gibson, I had predicted that he would take in more than $100 million, but he disagreed and said "we'll be happy if we do fifty." The unprecedented success of the movie (in Aramaic and Latin, with subtitles!) did nothing to temper the alarmist voices in the Jewish community. Professor Paula Fredriksen of Boston University wrote a piece in the *New Republic* (under the title "Mad Mel") flatly predicting a violent, bloody reaction (to a movie she still hadn't seen). One Orthodox rabbi decried the project as "religious pornography" and suggested that it might actually result in shifting the world center of Jew hatred away from Islamic fanatics and "back to the Christian sphere." Dr. Yehuda Shabatay, a professor of Jewish studies in San Diego, urged Jewish activism to somehow "stop" the film: "Let us contact our friends among Christian clergy and among government officials and ask for their active support." One group—the New Jersey–based Messiah Truth Project— seemed to follow the absurd suggestion of calling for official censorship, demanding that the Justice Department launch an immediate investigation of Mel Gibson for a film that supposedly "violates state and federal hate crime statutes for the purposeful encouragement of anti-Semitic violence." Attorney General John Ashcroft wisely decided to concentrate on confronting al-Qaeda as a more immediate threat to the Jewish community (and all Americans) than al-Gibson.

Predictably, I sustained a certain amount of collateral damage in all of the heavy-caliber bombardment of Gibson's project. In a nationally broadcast debate on MSNBC, Rabbi Shmuley Boteach attacked me as "the Jane

Fonda of the Jewish people"—for giving aid and comfort to the enemy in a time of maximum peril. Then in April, the *Jewish News Weekly of Northern California* described me as "the most prominent Jewish apologist for Mel Gibson" and anointed me "the clear winner" of "the Noam Chomsky Award for the Jewish Celeb most unpopular in the mainstream Jewish Community." Considering Professor Chomsky's record as a rabid anti-Zionist and an opponent of the very existence of Israel (who has also dabbled in Holocaust denial), I hardly felt I deserved the prestigious prize named in his honor.

Meanwhile, I set off for Israel, where *The Passion of the Christ* was inspiring panic in every segment of the ideological spectrum. I felt gratified to broadcast my radio show from Jerusalem, where I addressed the controversy over Gibson's film, interviewed top Israeli officials (including three cabinet members, to persuade them to resist the pressure to make *The Passion* a political issue in the always embattled Jewish state), and reported to my listeners from one of the major battlefields of the ongoing War Against Terror. On a more personal note, the trip to Israel allowed me to visit my father at an important moment. Unbeknownst to any members of the family (except his wife), he had been diagnosed with lymphoma some ten years before but had, after treatment, appeared to make a full recovery. He kept the entire experience a secret until a recurrence of the condition necessitated a punishing new course of chemotherapy for this vigorous, courageous, previously tireless, seventy-eight-year-old physical fitness fanatic. When I visited with him, my father appeared suddenly enfeebled but unfailingly optimistic.

As the furor surrounding *The Passion of the Christ* gradually died down, I welcomed the opportunity to use my daily radio forum to make the most important, most obvious point about the entire affair: none of the dire predictions of Gibson's film inspiring outbreaks of anti-Semitic violence ever came true, in the United States or around the world. One Norwegian neo-Nazi told the local press he had been stirred by the movie—and promptly confessed to and asked forgiveness for an unsolved five-year-old crime in which he had tried to torch a synagogue. In the United States, more than a half dozen criminals (including a wife-murderer) turned themselves in to authorities after seeing the film, hoping to connect with the spirit of sacrifice and innocence so movingly portrayed on the screen. An early poll on the impact of the movie appeared with the headline "*Passion* Having Unexpected Impact: Film and Surrounding Debate Might Be Lessening Hostility Toward Jews." The Institute for Jewish and Community Research (IJCR) conducted a nationwide survey of 1,003 randomly selected adults; by a margin of more than two-to-one, respondents said that viewing the movie made them "less likely to hold today's Jews responsible for the death of Jesus." The lack of negative repercussions for the Jewish community became so conspicuous that even the left-leaning *Los Angeles Times* offered an article in July called "The Furor, The Fizzle," with a subhead stating that "*The Passion* spurred predictions of wrath, violence. Didn't happen." Roy Rivenburg reported that "critics warned that Mel Gibson's blood-drenched epic *The Passion of the Christ* would lead to firebombed synagogues and other anti-Jewish violence. . . . Yet, five months after the film's debut, the prophecies have yet to materialize."

Of course, the incontestable facts surrounding the film's reception did nothing to shake Hollywood's irrational consensus that the movie represented some marginal, hate-filled, dangerous assault on secular enlightenment and religious minorities. Sharon Waxman in the *New York Times* reported that "Jeffrey Katzenberg and David Geffen, the principals of DreamWorks, have privately expressed anger over the film, said an executive close to the two men. The chairmen of two other major studios said they would avoid working with Mr. Gibson because of *The Passion of the Christ*." Four months later (June 24, 2004), the *Times* ran another piece quoting another executive of another major studio "saying he would strenuously resist casting Mr. Gibson in one of his films. . . . Significantly, in the movie industry, which tends to be liberal and secular in outlook, as well as disproportionately Jewish, few people interviewed about *The Passion* said they had actually seen the movie."

This last sentence may stand as the most startling single declaration in all of the millions upon millions of words generated by the controversy. The idea that leaders of an industry supposedly dedicated to connecting with the public would avoid even seeing the most successful religious movie in history, and one of the top motion-picture moneymakers of all time, definitively rebuts the idea that Hollywood honchos care only about their bottom line. The fact that they would pledge to avoid working with Mel Gibson (declared by the December 2003 Harris Poll "America's Favorite Movie Star") should serve as definitive proof that the pop culture power elite upholds other agendas beyond the pursuit of profit.

Despite the incontrovertible evidence that the doomsayers misjudged everything about the impact of *The Passion of the Christ,* I received no apologies or retractions or reevaluations from those who had branded me a dangerous traitor for my defense of Gibson. The intense, fleeting nature of contemporary confrontations over pop culture or politics precludes neat, definitive resolutions, or conclusive victories or defeats. In newspaper commentaries, on TV, or on the radio, advocates on both sides take their best shots every day, following the shifting battlefields and moving on quickly to the next skirmish.

LESSON

35

Do-It-Yourself Conservatism
Provides the Best Cure for the
Do-Something Disease

Every father inevitably embarrasses his teenaged children from time to time. My long-suffering kids, on the other hand, complain that I humiliate them almost every day by publicly indulging an appalling idiosyncrasy. On the way home from work each afternoon, I make it a habit to invest a few minutes in stopping the car by the side of the road to clean up accumulations of litter. For me, this represents far more than a commitment to communal cleanliness: it is a demonstration of a viable, comprehensive strategy for improving the world.

As I point out to my children and my neighbors, we are lucky enough to live in a pleasant Seattle suburb—a self-contained island, in fact—so it makes no sense that cigarette boxes and beer cans and fast food wrappers should accumulate so rapidly on these otherwise manicured residential thoroughfares. It makes even less sense that most of the privileged people who live here seem oblivious to the mess. They dress in the most stylish jogging suits, and run regularly right past the trash, or else walk their tidy, pedigreed dogs without pausing for even a moment to pick up the water bottles or Starbucks cups that lie on the middle of the sidewalks in their path.

One day, having parked my car on a side street to gather an especially unsightly accumulation of filth, I took special note of some paperwork that accompanied the usual potato chip bags and candy wrappers. Someone had tossed aside an opened piece of correspondence, complete with name and address, from the well-known conservation group the Sierra Club. The form letter began: "Dear Mr. Lang: We know from your record of generosity you are concerned with the environment . . ." and went on to solicit funds in the battle to protect 6 percent of the vast and remote Arctic National Wildlife Reserve from prospective exploitation by oil companies.

I gasped at the startling contrast between the substance of the letter and the message of its thoughtless and casual deposit on the shoulder of a woodsy suburban street. On the one hand, the recipient of the letter is "notably concerned about the environment," and on the other, he thinks nothing of trashing that environment in his very own neighborhood. He presumably feels more concerned over the discomfort of caribou in Alaska that might be disturbed by oil drilling in desolate tundra he will never visit than about preserving and respecting the surroundings he will see every day.

Similar madness turned up at our local middle school (attended over the years by each of my three children), which boasts the highest test scores in the state of Washington, but also displays a veritable mountain of litter on the tree-lined avenue leading to its main entrance. Among the sticky wrappers and Pepsi cans I have gathered from this depressing site, I've also found discarded curriculum materials—including freshly copied pages about the importance of young people involving themselves in the worldwide struggle for ecological sanity. This award-winning school, in other words, proudly teaches its students about the importance of fighting global warming or stopping the plunder of the Amazonian rain forest, but fails to instill in them the much more attainable goal of depositing used worksheets in a trash receptacle rather than tossing them on the ground at a bus stop across from campus.

This annoying carelessness highlights one of the most depressing, dysfunctional aspects of contemporary culture: the focus on faraway problems over which we have no control rather than achievable aims in our immediate surroundings. Television (which absorbs more of a child's weekly time than all his classroom work combined) encourages the idea of a menacing world in which environmental degradation, abject poverty, decaying family life, rampant warmongering, outrageous injustice, and brutal, incurable racism require sweeping, visionary, global solutions. Since the world's economic, political, and cultural establishments offer scant chance for overnight change, there's a natural tendency toward cynicism and despair. What difference does it make if you throw a Tootsie Roll wrapper in a city park, one might ask, if the whole world will inevitably choke to death on greenhouse gases?

Television enhances ratings, and journalists win admiring attention, by grossly exaggerating the dire nature of every threat and the vast scope of every fresh disaster. Broadcasters love to cover the most destructive hurricanes, the most devastating fires, the most ruinous floods, the most jarring earthquakes, the bloodiest murder sprees, the biggest, costliest economic collapses. If a plane lands safely and on time, it never makes the news, but if it crashes and burns and, best of all, kills hundreds, we can count on hearing all about it. This built-in bias for bad news comes with a serious social and political cost: the more dramatic the danger, the more sweeping and utopian the necessary response—and the more powerless the position of each individual in the grip of purportedly implacable forces.

Media addiction thereby encourages a dread epidemic I frequently discuss in my radio broadcasts: the "Do-Something Disease." This aggressive infection assaults a defenseless America, dominating our discourse and distorting public policy. Liberals, with their inherent affection for uncovering some crippling new crisis that demands a new burst of ambitious activism, prove especially vulnerable to this dread affliction, but in one way or another the malady manages to penetrate every corner of our culture.

The Do-Something Disease is the dysfunctional instinct to respond to every problem, private or public, with some sweeping society-wide solution, usually involving an aggressive governmental initiative. Under the influence of the illness, it doesn't matter if that effort serves a practical purpose; taking collective action—doing something, anything—will salve the restless conscience of the infected populace. In the grip of the Do-Something Disease, you don't worry about solving problems; you concentrate instead on feeling better about them. You focus not on the sufferers and victims and their long-term welfare, but on your own emotions—and the soothing assumption that you've somehow made a difference.

Do you worry about the pitiable homeless in our streets? Then ask the government to provide generous feeding programs that do absolutely nothing to address their underlying problems.

Do you obsess over the glaring failures of public education? Then demand the imposition of standardized federal tests that altogether ignore the troubled home environments that cripple the majority of underachieving students.

Do you lose sleep over the threat of Islamic terrorists launching another deadly strike like 9/11? Then call upon our leaders to fix airport security instantly by transforming the same workers into federal employees and giving them new uniforms with the magical initials "TSA."

Do you fret that the poor and the downtrodden can do nothing to improve their status in our harshly competitive economy? Then demand more spending on antipoverty programs and organized compassion, even if those services only make the poor more dependent and helpless than ever before.

The ultimate cure to the Do-Something Disease involves a radical but righteous readjustment I call "Do-It-Yourself Conservatism." This approach begins from a simple premise: no matter what the Congress decides to do about the delicate disposition of the caribou in the Arctic National Wildlife Reserve, nothing on earth should prevent you from picking up the litter in your own neighborhood.

Early visitors to America like Alexis de Tocqueville marveled in admiration at our can-do spirit: our restless character as builders and fixers who never waited for outside help or formal permission before toiling to improve themselves while uplifting their communities. In his history of the founding of the United States, *Freedom Just Around the Corner*, Professor Walter A. McDougall of the University of Pennsylvania defines "the American people's penchant for hustling. . . . Americans have enjoyed more opportunity to pursue their ambitions, by foul means or fair, than any other people in history." This openness to both honest and dishonest effort has spawned a nation of "builders, doers, go-getters, dreamers, hard workers, inventors, organizers, engineers, and a people supremely generous." Ralph

Waldo Emerson, impassioned advocate of self-reliance, captured this perpetually youthful confidence in lines I have cherished since adolescence:

> *So nigh is grandeur to our dust,*
> *So near is God to man,*
> *When Duty whispers low,* Thou must,
> *The youth replies,* I can.

For every problem we encounter, in politics or pop culture, private or public life, the Do-It-Yourself Conservative sees solutions ready to hand. No one need wait for the reform of government, the restructuring of the economy, or the moral regeneration of his neighbors before tackling dilemmas on his own. For instance:

➤ If you worry about the national shortcomings of public education, then consider the possibility of home schooling—an alternative explored with conspicuous success by more than two million American families. Before we accepted the solid quality of our local public schools (and the outstanding religious Jewish high school that both daughters have attended), Diane supervised the home schooling of our children during the first two years after we arrived in Seattle. For those unable or unwilling to make a commitment on that level, there's still the opportunity to supplement a child's class work, or to become more directly involved with the school, the teachers, and their assignments.

➤ If you're concerned about congestion and worsening commuter traffic, you don't have to wait for a multibillion-dollar mass transit boondoggle: you can try the bus, or organize a carpool, or even get your daily exercise by riding a bicycle to work.

➤ If you lament the disappearance of forests and open space, then contribute as much as you can to land conservancies in your region that buy scenic properties to preserve them in perpetuity. It's also hugely satisfying to plant as many trees as possible: we've planted more than forty of them since we moved to Seattle, mostly cedars and Douglas firs, both on our own property and as gifts for friends. As Ludwig van Beethoven appropriately observed in an 1807 letter, "It seems as if in the country every tree said to me 'Holy! Holy!' Who can give complete expression to the ecstasy of the woods?"

➤ If you feel undermined by a culture that's increasingly disrespectful of traditional ideals of marriage, then select friends who share your approach, join a community of like-minded families, and commit more time for communication with your spouse.

The same sort of do-it-yourself approach can apply to every conceivable challenge. If you feel insecure about Social Security, then use the magic of compound interest and plan for your own retirement; if you're troubled by rampant materialism, make sure you spend less than you earn; if you're the victim of discrimination of some sort, then make the extra effort to transcend and ignore it, as have so many other Americans of every ethnic or interest group. The most essential affirmation to facilitate success is the frequent, fervent declaration: "I am not a victim."

Whatever the menace that threatens your well-being, it's counterproductive to depend on top-down change; on any issue, you can take the first step on your own. Perhaps the best example of all involves the frustration so many decent people feel over the destructive messages from movies, television, and other forms of entertainment—the focus of so much of my work over the past quarter century. To counteract these influences, literally millions of our fellow citizens will sign petitions, participate in boycotts, write to congressmen or studio heads, and join various watchdog organizations.

The bad news is that such efforts, however impassioned or well intentioned, won't redeem the soul of Hollywood or uplift the standards of broadcast TV. The good news is that you don't have to wait for NBC or Fox to change its lineup, because without delay you can change the schedule of what you watch. Making more discerning choices in the popular culture we consume, and generally disentangling ourselves from TV addiction, can also help to overcome the notion that all our difficulties count as vast, remote, impervious to change—thereby playing a part in rolling back the depredations of the dreaded Do-Something Disease. Diane and I have always lived in a TV-free household—though we do maintain a DVD player to allow the kids some access to carefully selected products of the popular culture. This policy not only provides vastly greater control of the content of what the children see, but also facilitates more responsible scheduling.

Rather than arranging their lives according to the whims of network pro-grammers, the kids arrange their media consumption according to their other responsibilities, including chores and homework. To skeptics, this policy may sound oppressive, authoritarian, and restrictive, but it's worked well in our home and helped protect our children from the jaded, brittle, pseudo-sophistication of their media-saturated peers who grow up before their time.

Diane's special sensitivity to the fleeting nature of childhood made us especially protective of the three children and stubbornly resistant to ma-lign influences in the culture. Shortly after we arrived in Seattle, our sec-ond daughter, Shayna, celebrated her eighth birthday as our guests donned party hats and serenaded her over cake, while our glamour-girl-in-training triumphantly beamed. Toward the end of the Sunday afternoon in April, as the visitors departed, she came over to me, sat down in my lap, looked into my eyes, and affectionately put her two little arms around my shoul-ders. "Baba," she began, sweetly and solemnly, "it's time to say goodbye."

"Why?" I asked with some surprise and alarm.

"Because," Shayna explained, "after today, you're never going to see a seven-year-old daughter again."

And my incomparably adorable middle child was exactly right, of course, contributing some of the insight that informed our next book proj-ect, *Saving Childhood: Protecting Our Children from the National Assault on Inno-cence.* I got the contract (from HarperCollins, again) to do the book before we moved to Seattle, but after I began the daily talk radio show I found it almost impossible to make progress. With the approval of the publisher, Diane joined me as coauthor (marking our first formal collaboration, other than the kids). She had already served as the coauthor on the best-seller *The American Family: Discovering the Values That Make Us Strong,* working with former vice president Dan Quayle. Diane conducted and edited all of the interviews and wrote the first draft of that book; unlike most other political heavyweights like Hillary Clinton, Quayle (who bore no resem-blance to the dim-witted buffoon so often caricatured in the press) gave my wife full credit for her contributions. Now she did almost all of the writing on *Saving Childhood,* based on my opening chapter and detailed outline of the rest of the book. After delineating the nature of the assault on childhood—from media, from schools, from peers, and from parents themselves—we applied a Do-It-Yourself approach to dealing with the situation, recommending accessible, practical, private tactics for defending the essential elements of innocence.

In a sense, I viewed the radio show as one more means to apply the gradualist Do-It-Yourself approach by winning one argument at a time, changing a few minds every day, and building support bit by bit to advance the causes I cared about. Our continued involvement in religious and congregational life provided similar power, since we never lost sight of the ability of a single Shabbat meal, or holiday celebration, or Torah class to touch strangers or newcomers in unexpected ways. In 2004 we received an important reminder of that potential from an interview on a Jewish Web site with David Weiss, the Emmy-nominated screenwriter for *Rugrats* and other kids' programs, who had just scripted the record-breaking movie hit *Shrek 2*. Weiss had wandered a long way from his assimilated Jewish upbringing before making a midlife turn to Orthodox observance. Asked what brought about the transformation, he answered, "I met Michael Medved, the film critic. I thought he was Christian from his writings, because I'd see him quoted in Christian magazines. I met him at a film festival, and he was wearing a yarmulke. He invited me to his house for Shabbat lunch. It was just gorgeous, with the shul and the families and the children. I met my wife during this time, and we began taking introductory Judaism classes. . . . Now, thank God, we have two beautiful Jewish children attending Jewish day school, we keep Shabbat and have a kosher kitchen."

The Pacific Jewish Center community that I founded with Rabbi Lapin in 1978 exerted similar influence on hundreds of other individuals, and continues to thrive with my brother Harry as one of its stalwarts and leaders. We don't play a similar leadership role in our fledgling congregation in the Great Northwest, but I do enjoy walking more than two miles to services every Saturday morning through parks and forests, and watching our homey community adding several new families each year.

The flinty, tough-minded Judeo-Christian tradition that built this country comports comfortably and completely with Do-It-Yourself Conservatism. Our ancestors didn't depend on some sweeping system to change the world but took their own bold steps to change themselves—and their circumstances. The Massachusetts Puritans never hesitated about crossing a forbidding ocean to build their own uncompromising little communities, rather than waiting at home with their cousins for a revolution to alter all of England. Pioneers carved out their private utopias on the frontier and immigrants pursued their personal dreams in crowded cities, transforming the world through their individual efforts rather than counting on world changes to redeem individuals.

In his fascinating book *Good to Great,* Jim Collins and his team investigated companies that outperformed the overall stock market from the 1970s through 1990s by anywhere from 300 to 1,800 percent. "Throughout our research," Collins reported, "we were struck by the continual use of words like 'disciplined,' 'rigorous,' 'dogged,' 'determined,' 'diligent,' 'precise,' 'fastidious,' 'systematic,' 'methodical,' 'workmanlike,' 'demanding,' 'consistent,' 'focused,' 'accountable,' 'and responsible.'" David Brooks observed in a *New York Times Magazine* article called "A Nation of Grinders" that "these are the classic, staid but unexciting bourgeois virtues. . . . This work ethic is different from what you might call the creativity ethic or the lifestyle ethic. It emphasizes neatness, regularity and order." As a product of that ethic, "Americans do move upward as we age. Only 5 percent of the individuals who were in the bottom income quintile in 1975 were still there in 1991. But an individual's mobility is likely to be measured in decades, not years. We rise as we age and as we get gradual promotions, not because we strike it rich."

In other words, even in the daunting arena of economic advancement, the steady application of properly regulated habits—"the classic, staid but unexciting bourgeois virtues"—can guarantee progress. Despite the alarming pronouncements of big government demagogues who want us to feel powerless and paralyzed without their grandiose new programs, we can make the private choices that determine destiny. Sometimes it seems that chance plays a potent role: looking back at my own life, I wonder about the different turns I might have taken had I visited the beach on a different day in 1983 and never met Diane, or if I'd appeared on the *Tonight Show* on some other night and never attracted attention from producers of *Sneak Previews,* or if a harried dean on commencement day in Boston had remembered to mention my name, thereby avoiding the plagiarism scandal that fatefully publicized my work. My experience indicates that we can benefit from random collisions and apparent coincidence, but only if we trace the patterns and messages such happenstance suggests, and put those patterns to work in our behalf.

Even with the most conscious planning or the most patient implementation of do-it-yourself principles, we can't control the brute facts of time and change and age, as demonstrated by my mother's sad condition at the end of the last millennium. Since completing her own childbearing years with Harry's birth in 1961, she had dreamed openly and incessantly about grandchildren, while her four recalcitrant sons dawdled in their delivery of a new generation. After Sarah finally arrived to fulfill my mother's fondest wish, she could enjoy the gift for only six months before a stroke at age sixty-two crippled her forever. The damage left her mind undimmed but paralyzed the right side of her body and confined her to a wheelchair. Watching her expanding, far-flung family from the sidelines, she gamely battled an aggressive, seemingly endless array of ailments—heart attack, diabetes, amputation, and, ultimately, leukemia. Her pain ended in the spring of 2000, with Harry and Ben already at her side while I flew down to LA from Seattle and arrived just a half hour too late to see her alive. Jonathan also flew in from Israel to join us for the traditional seven days of mourning after the simple funeral, with all four brothers confined in the cluttered hillside house our pack-rat mother left behind. During that week of mutual captivity, we renewed our acquaintance—bumping against one another at virtually every moment, crying together, laughing, arguing (sometimes bitterly), and, most of all, eating our way through the lovingly made foodstuffs that our friends brought to the house of the mourners. The occasion provided a rare chance to interact with Ben, too often tagged "the missing Medved" because he never came to share the right-leaning religious and political values the other three embraced. He worked as a marriage and family counselor near Silicon Valley, taught part time at California State University Hayward, married a bubbly kindred spirit, and attended a very liberal Reform—not Orthodox—Jewish congregation.

Six months after our mother's death, the four boys gathered again for another reunion in LA, this time to celebrate the long-awaited wedding of our baby brother, Harry. He began his own family just weeks before his fortieth birthday, after an exhausting, risky, selfless, but unflinching effort to date every vaguely available Jewish woman in Southern California. The conclusion of this punishing process yielded the ultimate prize—our new sister-in-law Michele, an instructional designer and immigrant from South Africa who possessed a charming Capetown accent, along with exactly those "classic bourgeois virtues," that organizational and self-disciplined ability, that dreamy Harry needed most. My mother had met Michele just weeks before she died, and heartily approved of Harry's choice. At the wedding, under the traditional canopy, my brother stomped on the wine-glass with such exaggerated force that a shard cut through the thin sole of his rented patent leather shoe and tore open his foot, providing a trail of blood reminiscent of Valley Forge as he and his new bride retreated down the aisle of the beachside synagogue.

Despite the inauspicious if full-blooded beginning, Harry's marriage yielded two new children for the Medved clan. Meanwhile, in 2004, the oldest of the new generation—my darling superstar Sarah—prepared to leave home for a destination halfway around the world. I understood the theory that says I should feel perfectly proud of her, but it was hard to see any upside in the sudden disappearance from our house of the angel who for seventeen years had illuminated all our lives with her gentle light and shy laughter. With a kind heart, lovely face, and an obvious gift for loyal, intimate friendships, she managed to graduate as valedictorian of her high school class—achieving, the principal announced, the highest grade point average in the thirty-year history of the school. She not only starred in the school play, but scored a perfect 800 on the verbal half of her SAT test and qualified as her school's only National Merit Scholarship finalist. Natu-rally, every university on the planet made an effort to recruit her—includ-ing Oxford and Cambridge, Princeton and Yale—but Sarah turned aside all offers of scholarships and special programs and refused even to apply because she felt her fervent religiosity wouldn't fit at one of the secular, leftist campuses. For her first year following graduation from her yeshiva high school, she insisted (despite the pained reluctance of her mother) on studying in an intensive and exclusive women's seminary in Jerusalem. After that, she planned to enroll at Stern College in New York City, the women's branch of the Orthodox flagship school, Yeshiva University.

In writing her valedictory speech, she refused her father's offers of help and found a voice inescapably her own: "The most important thing that I learned in my four years at this school is the courage to be different. . . . Abraham, the first Jew, had the courage to recognize that his society was incorrect, and to follow what he knew to be right, despite the great risk it posed to himself. Our mission as well is to live our lives differently, and to be willing to stand alone. The idea of conformity—of going along with the crowd and following the path of least resistance—is the opposite of the eternal mission of the Jewish people. We are expected to be separate . . . to disregard what others may think of us, and to take a stand for what is right." By the time she finished, with her soft face shining beneath the bright blue mortarboard, she had reduced her normally strong, self-confident mother to a blubbering mess, while her father struggled for control.

Following the graduation ceremony we comforted ourselves to think that we could enjoy one more full, precious summer of Sarah's golden company, but the weeks disappeared in a rush due in no small part to my preoccupation with finishing this book. In the middle of August, my father arrived after the completion of his course of chemotherapy and his lymphoma once again in apparent remission. He had lost thirty pounds (which he couldn't afford to lose from his fit, trim frame) but his hair had begun to grow back and he could hike with us joyously, if deliberately, in the Cascade Mountains. One Friday night during his visit, we sat down together at dusk for our Shabbat meal and just before chanting the sanctification prayer over the wine, we turned to the traditional blessing of the children. In the manner of all Jewish fathers for many centuries, I place my hands every week on the head of each child (in birth order) and pray, according to the formulation in the Book of Numbers: "May the Lord bless you and safeguard you. May the Lord illuminate His face for you and be gracious to you. May he turn his face to you and establish peace for you." After completing the recitation and kissing the top of Sarah's head, I sighed and took note of the fact that this would be the last time I had a chance to bless her before she left home for the other side of the world. At the mere mention of that painfully obvious reality, our firstborn showed a look of sudden fright, then covered her face with her hands, began to sob, and desperately hugged her mother. I embraced my dad, thankful for his gradually returning health. We tried to get through the meal without further break-downs, but we couldn't escape the reality that our little family would never be the same.

What, we wondered, were we supposed to do with Sarah's room? She keeps several shelves stocked with Beanie Babies, Barbie dolls, porcelain princesses, and other sweet reminders of childhood. Would we maintain this chamber unchanged as other empty nesters do, keeping her space in-violate as a permanent monument to our vanished older child?

On the August day she departed for Israel (with her mother accompa-nying her to get Sarah established in Jerusalem), I devoted a full hour to collecting litter in our neighborhood. In the hot sun, I climbed embank-ments, reaching for bottles and plastic bags and paper cups with the flex-ible "grabber" Diane had given me for my birthday. Nothing could dull the pain of that suddenly empty room upstairs, but filling a plastic bag with rubbish made me feel better. Even with all the distracting emotions of this transitional day, I could assure myself that I'd done my bit to clean up the island where I live, to provide some tangible improvement to this tiny cor-ner of the world because I happened to pass by today. At the end of his impossibly eventful youth, Voltaire's Candide learns to "cultivate his gar-den." I learned the importance of leaving my garden litter-free.

As I worked in the warmth of the summer afternoon, I could imagine my Sarah scoffing—as she always did—at my rubbish-clearing obsession. "Why do you do it, Baba?" she would demand to know. "In a couple of days you'll pass by again and it's going to be just as dirty as it was before. You never get it to stay clean. So what's the point?"

In answer to that query—to that challenge to the Sisyphean nature of the whole idea of Do-It-Yourself Conservatism—I would tell my daughter a famous story about the watchman of Chelm. This fictional town in the lost world of Eastern European Jewry became famous—and beloved—as a village of fools. Once, a rumor spread through the region that the Messiah might appear at any moment, so the wise men of Chelm, appropriately fearing that the long-awaited deliverer might bypass their town, appointed a watchman to stand by the bridge at the edge of the settlement to welcome the Messiah.

After months of faithful performance of his job, the watchman went to the town elders to ask for an increase of his pitiful salary of ten gulden a month. To his chagrin they turned him down. The rabbi who headed the council admitted that the payment didn't amount to much, but pointed to the job's important advantages.

"Advantages? What advantages? I stand there day and night, heat and cold, watching, waiting, for someone to come."

"That's all true," Chelm's rabbi replied. "But you've got to admit—it's steady work."

ACKNOWLEDGMENTS

With a highly personal project of this nature, the author faces a powerful temptation to acknowledge everyone who ever helped or encouraged him over the years. I've resisted that inclination in order to confine my appreciation here to those who participated directly in assisting me with this manuscript.

First, I feel profoundly grateful to my gifted editor, Jed Donahue. *Right Turns* amounts to my tenth book and I've never before received stronger support or assistance from an editor. Jed's care and commitment to every aspect of this project resulted in a stronger, tighter book and he participated in a crucial, creative way in carving out the final version from a much longer first draft.

I'm also appreciative of Doug Pepper, who initially persuaded me to work with him at Crown Forum—and I forgive him for his Canadian origins. My friend Ann Coulter convinced me that this ambitious publishing venture represented the right home for this project. My agent, Richard Pine, also deserves thanks for continuing a business relationship that has now flourished for thirty-five years, and two generations.

My radio producers, Dan Sytman and Jeremy Steiner, provided invaluable encouragement and helped take up the slack during the most demanding stages of this project. Laura Steiner, Jeremy's wife (who represented the *Michael Medved Show* in affiliate relations before the birth of her beautiful daughter, Madison), also delivered welcome support.

My personal assistant, Jennifer Tripp, helped with research, organization of background materials, and fact-checking—while enriching our entire family (she worked from our home) with her brilliance and sunny charisma for the six years she gave to us. Jen is irreplaceable, but my friend

Joan Sammon served as a heroic stand-in at a crucial moment. Brian Crouch, from the Medved Fan Blog and interim executive director of our little company, also deployed his formidable Internet skills to find information I needed. Judd and Denise Maglinick—our neighbors and best friends in Santa Monica—gave sage advice and reliably savvy guidance: I'm proud that Judd is now the president of Pacific Jewish Center, which is frequently referenced in these pages.

The support I've received from my syndicator, Greg Anderson, and the leaders of Salem Communications, Ed Atsinger and Stu Epperson, has been extraordinary, reflecting their characteristic commitment to doing good while doing well. Ken Berry, the general manager (and founder) of our flagship radio station, the ratings powerhouse, Talk 770 KTTH in Seattle, is one of the finest media professionals I've ever encountered, and his confidence in me and in this literary project helped to make it possible.

My neighbor and teacher, Rabbi Daniel Lapin, has advised me on elements of this book (and most other facets of my life) over more than a quarter century of collaboration and teaching.

My father, Dave Medved, has worked with me even longer than that—and gave me all of the gifts that matter most. He continues to inspire me every day, and his enthusiasm for these pages (as I sent them off to Israel for his comment and correction) helped ensure that I could actually finish this ambitious scheme. Two of my brothers, Harry and Jonathan Medved, also helped with family recollections and suggestions.

Most of all, my wife, Dr. Diane Medved, deserves part of whatever credit accrues from this project (but no blame for its shortcomings). She not only helped steer each lesson to its final form, but played an important role in shaping the initial concept. She remains the most facile, eloquent, naturally gifted writer I have ever encountered, and she placed her own book projects on hold to help with this one—while continuing to administer a complex household with joy, aplomb, and incomparable sweetness. She nourishes each member of her family every day and we, in turn, unanimously adore her.

INDEX

About the Author

MICHAEL MEDVED is the host of a daily three-hour radio program, *The Michael Medved Show,* which reaches more than two million listeners coast to coast. He is the author of nine other books, including the bestsellers *Hollywood vs. America* and *What Really Happened to the Class of '65?,* and a member of *USA Today*'s board of contributors. For more than a decade he served as cohost of *Sneak Previews,* PBS's weekly movie review show. An honors graduate of Yale, Medved lives in the Seattle area with his family.